New Critical Legal Thinking

New Critical Legal Thinking articulates the emergence of a stream of critical legal theory which is directly concerned with the relation between law and the political. The early critical legal studies claim that all law is politics is displaced with a different and more nuanced theoretical arsenal. Combining grand theory with a concern for grounded political interventions, the various contributors to this book draw on political theorists and continental philosophers in order to engage with current legal problematics, such as the recent global economic crisis, the Arab Spring and the emergence of biopolitics. The contributions instantiate the fact that a new and radical political legal scholarship has come into being: one which critically interrogates and intervenes in the contemporary relationship between law and power.

Matthew Stone is a Lecturer in Law at the University of Essex. His research addresses questions of law's relation with ethics and subjectivity, with particular focus on continental theory. He holds a PhD from Birkbeck College, University of London.

Illan rua Wall is a Senior Lecturer in Law at Oxford Brookes University. He holds a PhD in legal theory from Birkbeck College, University of London, and is the author of *Human Rights and Constituent Power* (Routledge, 2012).

Costas Douzinas is a Professor of Law at Birkbeck College and the Director of the Birkbeck Institute for the Humanities. His recent books include *Resistance and Philosophy of the Crisis* (Athens, 2011), *The Idea of Communism*, edited with Slavoj Zizek (Verso, 2010) and *Human Rights and Empire: The Political Philosophy of Cosmopolitanism* (Routledge-Cavendish, 2007).

New Critical Legal Thinking

Law and the Political

Edited by Matthew Stone,
Illan rua Wall and
Costas Douzinas

Birkbeck
LAW PRESS

First published 2012
by Routledge
2 Park Square, Milton Park, Abingdon, Oxon OX14 4RN

Simultaneously published in the USA and Canada
by Routledge
711 Third Avenue, New York, NY 10017

A Birkbeck Law Press title

Birkbeck Law Press is an imprint of the Taylor & Francis Group, an informa business

First issued in paperback 2014

British Library Cataloguing in Publication Data
A catalogue record for this book is available from the British Library

Library of Congress Cataloging in Publication Data
New critical legal thinking : law and the political / edited by Matthew Stone, Illan Rua Wall and Costas Douzinas.
pages cm
Includes bibliographical references.
ISBN 978-0-415-61957-8 (hbk.)
1. Law—Political aspects. 2. Critical legal studies. I. Stone, Matthew, 1981- editor of compilation. II. Wall, Illan Rua, editor of compilation. III. Douzinas, Costas, 1951- editor of compilation. IV. Whyte, Jessica (Jessica Stephanie). Human rights.
K487.P65N49 2012
340'.11—dc23
2011049716

ISBN 978-0-415-61957-8 (hbk)
ISBN 978-0-415-53305-8 (pbk)
ISBN 978-0-203-11446-9 (ebk)

Typeset in Baskerville
by RefineCatch Limited, Bungay, Suffolk

Contents

Notes on contributors

Jason A. Beckett is a Lecturer in Law at the University of Leicester, and a Visiting Professor at the American University in Cairo. He holds a PhD from the University of Glasgow. His current research focuses on the use of normative and epistemic structures to shield citizens of the developed world from their implication in, and subsidisation by, the perpetuation of extreme global poverty.

Brenna Bhandar is a Lecturer at the School of Law, Queen Mary, University of London. Her research focuses on the relationship between practices of ownership and dispossession in colonial settler contexts and, more generally, the relationship between property and ontology. She has published articles on the themes of indigenous rights, critical race theory, secularism and multiculturalism, and the politics of recognition.

Costas Douzinas is a Professor of Law at Birkbeck College and the Director of the Birkbeck Institute for the Humanities. His recent books include *Resistance and Philosophy of the Crisis* (Athens, 2011), *The Idea of Communism*, edited with Slavoj Zizek (Verso, 2010) and *Human Rights and Empire: The Political Philosophy of Cosmopolitanism* (Routledge-Cavendish, 2007).

Ben Golder is a Senior Lecturer in Law at the University of New South Wales, Australia. He is author of *Foucault's Law* (Routledge, 2009) and his current research proposes a critical re-reading of contemporary human rights discourse via Foucault.

Oscar Guardiola-Rivera is the author of the award winning book *What If Latin America Ruled the World?* (Bloomsbury, 2010). He teaches at the Birkbeck School of Law and collaborates with the Birkbeck Institute of the Humanities, the BBC World Service and Monocle 24.

Vincent Keter held a PhD from Birkbeck College, University of London.

Tarik Kochi is a Senior Lecturer in Law at the University of Sussex. He is the author of *The Other's War* (Birkbeck Law Press, 2009).

Gilbert Leung holds a PhD from Birkbeck, University of London. He is currently working on a monograph entitled *Jean-Luc Nancy: The First Question of Law.*

Elena Loizidou is a Senior Lecturer at the School of Law, Birkbeck College. She is the author of *Judith Butler: Ethics, Law, Politics* (Routledge-Glasshouse, 2007). She is currently working on a book, *Anarchism: an art of living* and an edited collection on *Disobedience: concept/practice* (2012).

Connal Parsley teaches legal theory and legal ethics at the University of Melbourne, where he is currently completing doctoral studies on the relation between law, the image and juridical personhood in the work of Giorgio Agamben.

Matthew Stone is a Lecturer in Law at the University of Essex. His research addresses questions of law's relation with ethics and subjectivity, with particular focus on continental theory.

Illan rua Wall is a Senior Lecturer in Law at Oxford Brookes University. He is author of *Human Rights and Constituent Power* (Routledge, 2012) and works on questions of human rights, political theory and continental philosophy.

Jessica Whyte is a Lecturer in Cultural and Social Analysis at the University of Western Sydney, Australia. Her current research is on the politics of human rights, and explores the emergence and political implications of the idea of the 'right to intervene'. She wrote a PhD on the political thought of Giorgio Agamben and has published widely on his work.

Preface

Whilst the critique of law now has an insistent presence within the wider academic landscape, what is common among critical scholars is considerably more complex than before. Today it would be factually negligent, as well as politically misguided, to make a claim of a homogenous 'movement'. Interdisciplinary critique exists as a language or method of thinking of law, transcending the body of people, publications and conferences that operate as its transient embodiment. The idea for this collection arose from the hope that a (fractious and fractured) statement of critical legal position would be useful. We intend that the statement in these pages resists reductive or disciplinary self-identification, but still suggests a series of directions around which these current discourses can be orientated.

This book is an articulation and a continuation of a conversation amongst legal academics who share a concern to think about law upon terms that breach the boundaries of traditional legal education. It is intended as a snapshot, a moment of dialogue, and an affirmation of the centrality of law to the irrepressible exigencies of acute political and economic crisis. Indeed, if there is an overarching argument to the book, it is an argument for the renewal of our understanding of legality's complicity with politics and power.

In periods of crisis, the taken for granted 'natural' or 'objective' premises of the dominant discourse and practice come to the surface and are seen for what they are: artificial, provisional, ideologically charged. But ideology is not just false consciousness. It creates subjects with specific desires, hopes and expectations and stitches the social fabric together by offering imaginary idols and ideal projections of a happy society at peace with itself. Dominant ideology must support in part the interests of working people, the poor and disenfranchised. The rule of law and human rights are such ideological constructions that seek to turn legality into legitimacy. They give limited protection to vital interests and promote formal conceptions of equality and social justice. This way they attract the approval and even devotion of ordinary people. At the same time, the rule of law and rights both formally and in substance promote a socio-economic system radically opposed to the interest in emancipation.

But the law is not just ideological. It is also a site of social conflict and political contest. Historically, property was the first right and all rights are modelled on property. But the struggles of working people and minorities have introduced into law ideas and protections antithetical to its core socio-economic and ideological role. As a political field, law is always contested, its meaning never closed, its force questioned and confronted. Critical lawyers are both in and out of the law, deepening its limited conception of justice and importing another justice from beyond the confines of legality.

This volume is evidence of such double commitment to the many and multiform trajectories of critical scholarship and theory, and to the politics of emancipation. Nobody represented better this combination of critical theory and radical practice than our friend, colleague and comrade Vincent Keter. Vincent was a man of great talents and, like all greats, of great modesty. Erudite in many fields of scholarship, accomplished musician and brilliant artist, fervently committed to people and causes, politically active and passionate. He was part of this project and of the group of friends that animated it from the beginning. He brought to us both the radicalism and experience of the struggles in his native southern Africa and his amazing knowledge and understanding of so many cognitive fields. His untimely death brought together old and new friends and created a community in his name. This book, blessed to include Vincent's last writing before his passing away, is dedicated to his memory.

Introduction

Law, politics and the political

Matthew Stone, Illan rua Wall, Costas Douzinas

In the early days, critical legal studies (CLS) cohered around the demand that law is a form of politics. While legal reasoning perpetually mystified its own operation, law itself was directly and immediately political. Legal decisions were choices which formed part of the 'ideological struggles in society'.[1] This generation of 'Crits' looked at 'the undeniably numerous ways in which the legal system functions to screw poor people', but also 'at all the ways in which the system seems at first glance basically uncontroversial, neutral, acceptable'.[2] However, these early forays into CLS – largely associated with the major US law schools – took a narrow approach to the relation between law and politics. Typically, theorists depended on broad post-Marxist political commitments, which too often failed in their radical aspirations or petered out after the limited nature of the law school site became apparent.[3] Gathering a number of 'young' Crits, this collection revisits the relation between law and the political. However, we want to suggest that there is something distinctive about this return: it is far from a simple rehashing of the themes and tools of early CLS. It is not adequate, we suggest, to treat law as a mere instrument of political power, to reduce our outlook to the claim that law is politics by other means. Nor is it enough to claim that the mythic formality and neutrality of the law functions as an ideological mask for the machinations of politics. Times are different. That law is politics would be welcomed by many states who preside over the evacuation of any antagonistic sense of politics. Nowadays, not only does law increasingly resemble politics, but politics increasingly resembles law. In an indistinct fuzzy middle zone, what emerges are techniques of management,

1 A. Hutchinson and P. Monahan, "Law, Politics and Critical Legal Scholars: The Unfolding Drama of American Legal Thought' (1984) 36(2) *Stanford Law Review* 199, 206.

2 R. Gordon, 'New Developments in Legal Theory' in D. Kairys (ed) *The Politics of Law: A Progressive Critique* (Pantheon Books, New York, 1990) 286.

3 This was noted from within the critical community itself. Peter Goodrich explained this problem precisely in the final chapter of *Law in the Courts of Love: Literature and Other Minor Jurisprudences* (London: Routledge, 1996). See particularly 'Sleeping with the Enemy' ch 8 at 185.

security, strategy and policy. The real 'field of pain and death',[4] upon which legality is predicated, is no longer merely the courtroom, but also the planning office, the social security department, the job centre.

The contemporary situation is marked by the increasing role played by law in the political, social and economic spheres. Everywhere we see a tendency to render law at the heart of things, subjecting ever-growing domains of life to a knowledge structured by legal concepts, practices and methods. The diagnosis of juridification as an imperial process of colonising other disciplinary structures and spheres with specifically legal modes of thought has been widely noted in legal and political theory.[5] The increasing prevalence of law can be seen as a manner of inserting the state into everyday life, intertwining sovereignty, regulation and normativity with our everyday being-together. However, as with all colonial logics, the order seeking dominance is not untouched by those that it infects. What we witness is not, therefore, the sheer dominance of law, but the dissipating of the legal form in ways that allows power to assert a more pervasive grip on life. Through these new processes of juridification, law's sense of *Nomos*, *Jus* or even simply 'Law' is obscured. Law understood and appreciated as a social bond or a command to justice is increasingly lost, eclipsed by new techniques of control which have appropriated and corrupted the legal mode, emptying it of any remaining sense of right. At the same time, those increasingly juridified discourses are closed with the authority and legitimated violence of law. This phenomenon is thus profoundly different from a simple proliferation of extra laws. Rather, this is a deep juridification which intertwines life with power, and which some will term bio-politics.

Bio-politics refers to the ongoing tendency of governance to operate with reference to a normalised understanding of how humans and populations are expected to live. Power thus becomes entwined with all sorts of scientific and social knowledge. Law in a bio-political setting, far from being a supreme and singular arbiter of command, is merely one – albeit highly significant – site in a much wider matrix of power relations. Without specific deference to either the Foucauldian, Negrian or Agambenian theories, the effect of bio-politics can be understood as a practice of power in a setting where norm is blurred with fact, ought is reduced to is, and the brutality of dominance over human beings is achieved in the name of a bastardised and apolitical rationality. There are arguably few simpler examples

4 R. Cover, 'Violence and the Word' (1986) 95 *Yale Law Journal* 1601 at 1601.

5 In very different ways, each of these authors grapple with precisely this question. See G. Agamben et al *Democracy – In What State?* (New York: Colombia University Press, 2011); G. Agamben, *Homo Sacer: Sovereign Power and Bare Life* (Stanford: Stamford University Press, 1998), G. Agamben, *State of Exception* (Chicago: University of Chicago Press, 2005); W. Brown, *States of Injury: Power and Freedom in Late Modernity* (New Jersey: Princeton University Press, 1995); C. Douzinas, *Human Rights and Empire* (London: Routledge, 2007); C. Douzinas, *The End of Human Rights* (Oxford: Hart, 2000); C. Douzinas and A. Gearey, *Critical Jurisprudence: The Political Philosophy of Justice* (Oxford: Hart, 2005); G. Teubner, *Juridification of Social Spheres* (New York: de Gruyter, 1987); I. R. Wall, *Human Rights and Constituent Power* (Abingdon: Routledge, 2012).

of this than the multifarious juridical techniques of repressing otherness at jurisdictional borders. 'Antiterrorism' has become a new horizon by which people can be excluded, detained and stripped of their rights in the name of security, demonstrating how law's bio-political instrumentalisation has further accelerated in the last decade. These developments necessitate a renewed thinking of 'the political' that transcends the reductive assumptions of the post-1989 politics of consensus. At the heart of this collection, this question of the political is posed in its inescapable relation with law.

In the early 1980s, Jean-Luc Nancy and Philippe Lacoue-Labarthe suggested that the demand that everything is political in fact obscured that which was most political about politics. They claimed that 'the question of the political, that is the question as to its exact nature or essence, retires or withdraws into a kind of self-givenness, in which that which is political in politics is taken for granted or accorded a kind of obviousness which is universally accepted'.[6] This reduction to mere 'politics' is identifiable in the conflation of political discourse with the routine political debates of the day, and around the machinations of parties, ministers and lobbyists. This is the politics of 'political science' which turned social and economic conflict into a matter of accountancy, and ideology into calculated party manifestos. A shallow consumerism of policy was embodied in a façade that would cover over real political divisions. Nancy and Lacoue-Labarthe sought to withdraw from this clatter of 'politics', regressing back to the adjectival term 'the political' to nominate a renewed contestation of the very terms and structures of political discourse and action.

The differentiation between politics and the political is something already shared by many continental thinkers, whether or not they explicitly share its terminology. For Chantal Mouffe, for example, in a reinvigorated reading of Carl Schmitt, the political is born out of a critique of the prevailing modes of liberal politics which are predicated on an entirely false belief in the possibility of rational consensus.[7] The political transcends any adopted mode of politics, and denotes a fundamental social dissensus. Similarly, within Jacques Rancière's version of the political it is argued that authentic political action occurs not in the everyday politics of Westminster or Washington, but in those rare moments of radical democratic action that rupture the everyday view of the world.[8] For Jacques Derrida, the political holds a character of productive aporia in the radical potentiality of a Nietzchean perhaps,[9] or in the path of deferral marked by a democracy 'to come'.[10]

6 I. James, 'On Interrupted Myth' (2005) 9(4) *Journal for Cultural Research* 331, 336.
7 C. Mouffe, *On the Political* (Abingdon: Routledge, 2005) 11.
8 He renders the difference between politics and the political as 'the police' and 'politics', but the reasoning behind this terminological difference need not be investigated at this stage. J. Rancière, *Disagreement: Politics and Philosophy* (Minneapolis: University of Minnesota Press, 1999).
9 J. Derrida, *Politics of Friendship* (London; Verso, 2005).
10 J. Derrida, *Specters of Marx* (London: Routledge, 1994) 87.

Clearly, important differences exist between these thinkers, but what one can see is a recurrent concern in continental thought to engage in a political thinking that questions the very basis of politics. Thinking the political is an emphatically critical project through which it is hoped one can identify and resist the power structures whose presence have become veiled by a dubious appearance of neutrality and necessity. Therefore, it should come as no surprise that the chapters in this collection engage repeatedly, although not exclusively, with major continental thinkers such as Hegel, Marx, Arendt, Levinas, Derrida, Dussel, Foucault, Butler, Agamben and Esposito. If, for instance, the exemplary problematic of law is its relation with bio-politics, it becomes clear that traditional doctrinal legal theory is impotent owing to its incapacity to provide any meaningful thinking of resistance and critique. It is a central tenet of this collection that critical legal thinking must, by necessity, involve a thinking of the political: this is the ineluctable terrain upon which thought takes flight, laid down by the blurring of law and politics into regimes of coercive regulation. The chapters we bring together therefore signal an emergent awareness of the complicity of legality with politics, the capacity of legal structures to obfuscate political thinking, and hence the necessity of a critical interrogation of law to the critical work of the political.

In the years since the critical legal studies collections of the late 1980s and early 1990s,[11] there have been few, if any, collections on contemporary critical legal studies. The death of the movement has been announced repeatedly. Again and again, with conspicuous reduplication, CLS has been declared finished, dead, irrelevant. For instance, Brian Bix, in his jurisprudence textbook, discusses it in the past tense,[12] and Brian Tamanaha pointedly suggests that it is a 'dead horse'.[13] Many such legal theory texts include cynical passages on why CLS failed to change the landscape of legal education and practice. Yet with each official death certificate, duly registered with a major Anglo-American law journal or jurisprudence tome, the uncanny body of critique has re-emerged. In the British context, there were fewer of these definitive declarations, but nonetheless there was a sense in which the historical survival of critical legal theory was perpetually threatened. Perhaps what has confounded these opponents, to a large extent, is the refusal of critical legal theory to stick to a core set of principles. Most textbooks, monographs and review articles will emphasise outdated ideas that are closely associated with the first North American wave of critique: indeterminacy, trashing, alienation and the political nature of adjudication are apparently the acme of

11 A. Hunt and P. Fitzpatrick (eds) *Critical Legal Studies* (Oxford: Blackwell, 1987); A. Hutchinson (ed) *Critical Legal Studies* (New Jersey: Rowman & Littlefield, 1987); J. Boyle (ed) *Critical Legal Studies*, (New York: NYU Press, 1994); I. Grigg-Spall and P. Ireland (eds) *Critical Lawyers' Handbook* (London: Pluto Press, 1992); P. Ireland and P. Laleng, *Critical Lawyers' Handbook II* (London: Pluto Press, 1997).

12 B. Bix, *Jurisprudence: Theory and Context* (London: Sweet & Maxwell, 2009) 231–35.

13 B. Tamanaha, 'Conceptual Analysis, Continental Social Theory, and CLS' (2000) 32 *Rutgers Law Journal* 271, 305.

critical legal theory. This is perhaps an understandable misconception, given the early movement's predilection for catchy slogans and roughly similar arguments, which allowed mainstream scholars to regard it as a delimited and contained school in an ironic ignorance of its core values.

Admittedly, European critical legal studies developed in a relationship of both tension and alliance with American CLS, with the early years of the movement following wider cultural trends. Yet by the 1980s and early 1990s the more delimited mode of critique was already being surpassed by the so-called 'Brit-Crits,' who introduced semiotics, hermeneutics and deconstruction to the study of law, insisting on the textual organisation and aesthetic reception of legal texts.[14] They held that the injuries of law, whether racism, sexism or homophobia, should be shown on the body of its text. Opening the text of law to the law of the text thus revived the repressed link between jurisprudence and the humanities. The deconstruction of logonomocentrism was the European answer to the American CLS's 'trashing'. The return to rhetoric, semiotics and hermeneutics can be seen as a retort to and completion of the American focus upon law's 'fundamental contradiction'. Shifting away from its initial concerns, critical legal thought in the 1990s turned to emphasise the ethical dimension of legal operations.[15] Abandoning the neutrality of orthodox jurisprudence, critical scholars argued that its many moral failings were deeply related to the facile and inaccurate claim that law does not promote any particular morality or ideology. For these critics, the law promoted a self-satisfied and complacent version of sameness while marginalising and excluding the other. The many miscarriages of justice and the persistent failure of law to deliver even on its most anodynous promises of non-discrimination and equality turned critical legal thinking towards the ethics of otherness and the suffering face.

The new millennium has seen the consolidation of the earlier aesthetic and ethical directions, and their cross-fertilisation with a strengthened political strategy.

14 For notable examples see B. Jackson, *Law, Fact and Narrative Coherence* (Roby: Deborah Charles, 1988); B. Jackson, *Making Sense in Law: Linguistic, Psychological and Semiotic Perspectives* (Liverpool: Deborah Charles, 1995); P. Goodrich, *Languages of Law: From Logics of Memory to Nomadic Masks* (London: Weidenfeld & Nicolson, 1990); C. Douzinas, R. Warrington and S. McVeigh, *Postmodern Jurisprudence: The Law of Text in the Texts of Law* (London: Routledge, 1991); Peter Fitzpatrick (ed) *Dangerous Supplements: Resistance and Renewal in Jurisprudence* (London: Pluto, 1991); Drucilla Cornell et al (eds) *Deconstruction and the Possibility of Justice* (London: Routledge, 1992). The 'Brit Crits' were so-called because of their loose basis in institutions in the UK, rather than any national or nationalist association. In fact the 'Brit Crits' were overwhelmingly from other areas of Europe and, indeed, the world and there were a number of academics in American law schools who pursued similar themes in distinction to early CLS directions.

15 eg C. Douzinas and R. Warrington, *Justice Miscarried: Ethics and Aesthetics in Law* (London: Harvester Wheatsheaf, 1994) 115; C. Douzinas, P. Goodrich and Y. Hachamovitch (eds) *Politics, Postmodernity and Critical Legal Studies: The Legality of the Contingent* (London: Routledge, 1994). M. Diamantides, 'Ethics in Law: Death Marks on a "Still Life", A Vision of Judgement as Vegetating' (1995) 6(2) *Law and Critique* 6 209.

The rise and decline of the 'new world order' after the collapse of communism, the 'war on terror', the global penetration of neo-liberal capitalism and the return to brutal oppression and exclusion have led to the revival of a politics of resistance. At the same time, 'grand' theory, somewhat prematurely pronounced dead by a certain playful post-modernism, returned like the repressed. It is precisely this current wave of thought which responds to the exigent return of the political to the popular landscape, marking an emphatic restatement of the central role of critique in legal scholarship and education.

In this collection, we aim to gather a number of new critical legal scholars who, in this vein, attempt to return to theory with political effects. Whilst making no claim to represent critical legal thought exhaustively and in all its diversity, this collection offers a fractured and fractious statement of the position today. We have structured the collection in three parts, suggesting that each set of chapters engages with a particular constellation of concerns. However, there is often more in common between the sections than within them. Thus, they should not be seen as mutually exclusive or programmatic. In the first part, entitled 'Resistance, dissensus and the subject', the chapters focus on the possibilities of dissensus, the effect of law in the constitution of different modes of subjectivity, and the place of the human within the contemporary configuration of law's politics. Running through this section is a concern to refigure, rework or even think beyond the subject. This operates as a mode of critique of, resistance against, or as escape from, the law. This continues a radical challenge to traditional legal subjectivity, questioning its embodiment of rationality and rights, instead theorising a subject that is determined by its constitutive opposition to, or exclusion from, the legal order. The urgency of such questions in the light of contemporary uprisings and revolutions is tackled directly. Jess Whyte begins the section by tracing Foucault's late involvement with human rights. She draws out a possible Foucauldian 'right to intervention', while keeping an eye on the militarised humanitarianism that would later emerge. Costas Douzinas analyses the varieties of resistance against economically-driven governance, with a detailed analysis of the significance of the recent protest movement in Greece. Illan rua Wall engages with the recent events in Tunisia, developing the question of constituent power in the context of Ben Ali's bio-political regime. He puts the recent revolt in Tunisia in a productive tension with Giorgio Agamben's dismissal of the possibilities of the constituent moment. Working on Agamben with a little more fidelity, Connal Parsley looks at the 'Tranny Cops' political parody of police and sovereign power. He investigates the possibilities of a politics of a 'means without end'.

The second part, 'The state, violence and biopolitics', collects pieces that diagnose the contemporary strata of power and sovereign force. The chapters consider the shifting function of the state as a source of law and as an element within wider patterns of bio-politics, empire and the international normative order. The prevailing assumptions of liberal theory and its capacity to regulate conflict and violence are critiqued from philosophical standpoints, whilst also offering practical instantiations recognisable to us all. Ben Golder looks to the uses of Foucault's notion of bio-politics for a critical engagement with contemporary criminal law. Through an analysis of the 'homosexual advance defence' he suggests that criminal law plays a complex role in the differential exposure of some (others) to violence and death through the opening of a biological *caesura* within the population to be governed. Brenna Bhandar, in contrast, utilises post-colonial theory and bio-ethics jurisprudence to think about the relation between property, the legal subject and discourses of racialisation. Drawing upon the work of Hegel, Tarik Kochi questions the relation of social antagonisms to the production of ethical norms and systems of law. Jason Beckett considers the failure and future of the international legal system, and the role and effect of critique within theories of public international law. Finally, Vincent Keter presents a critique of the dominant economic ideology of Western jurisdictions, which has recently led the world into financial crisis.

In the final part, we gather a number of contributions on the politics of law's relation to critique itself. These chapters are speculative and productively incongruent in their investigation of possible approaches to the theorisation and critique of law today. Elena Loizidou grapples with the matter of life in its relation to legality, offering an analysis of three evocative literary narratives of encounters at law's borderline. Matthew Stone draws attention to a perceived return to central questions of law's origin, arguing for a critical method that instead allows us to think of life outside or against the law. Oscar Guardiola Rivera's chapter challenges us to imagine a future history. He attempts to displace the hegemony of the question of the Leviathan – the state – in critical legal theory, with a meditation on the production of material scarcity. Finally, Gilbert Leung closes the collection with a reading of the possibility of a radical cosmopolitanism, in which conventional notions of international jurisprudence are displaced in favour of a global *polis* to come.

This collection thus instantiates the manner in which the question of law and the political has come to the fore in recent critical legal studies. It was once noted that there appeared to be more review articles about the core tenets of the first wave of American CLS than there were primary texts actually undertaking that analysis. This collection will not provide an easy yardstick against which to judge whether a text 'belongs' to a 'critical school'. It will not identify, categorise and worship a canon. It does not offer a programme for future research. Rather, we hope that it acts as a challenge to *think* critical legal theory, to think again about the relation between law and the political, and to think radically about a politics of transformation.

Part I

Resistance, dissensus and the subject

Chapter 1

Human rights: confronting governments?

Michel Foucault and the right to intervene

Jessica Whyte[1]

> The accumulated anguish of individuals who fear for their lives brings about a new power.
>
> — Carl Schmitt, *The Leviathan in the State Theory of Thomas Hobbes*

In 1981, Michel Foucault delivered a speech entitled 'Confronting Governments: Human Rights' at the UN in Geneva to coincide with the creation of an International Committee Against Piracy.[2] Addressing 'all members of the community of the governed', he argued that the 'suffering of men', too often ignored by governments, 'grounds an absolute right to stand up and speak to those who hold power'.[3] The specific suffering that had sparked Foucault's intervention was that of the Vietnamese asylum-seekers who had left their country after the fall of Saigon. Under the leadership of Bernard Kouchner of *Médecins du Monde* (Doctors of the World), the committee sought to protect the asylum-seekers from pirates who were viciously attacking boats in the South China Sea. Foucault's short

1 An earlier draft of this chapter was presented at a symposium on 'Democracy and Violence', organised by Justin Clemens. I thank Justin for inviting me to speak, and all the participants in the symposium for questions and discussions that enabled me to hone my ideas. My thanks also to Ben Golder, Peter Chambers and Jon Roffe, all of whom read a draft of the chapter and provided incisive criticism and suggestions, to Paul Patton for valuable feedback about the larger project and to Nick Heron for stimulating discussions about Foucault and government.

2 M. Foucault, 'Confronting Governments: Human Rights' in J. D. Faubion (ed) *Essential Works of Foucault 1954–1984 Vol 3: Power* (London: Penguin, 1994). The collection which includes this text notes: '[t]he occasion for this statement, published in *Libération* in June 1984, was the announcement in Geneva of the creation of an International Committee against Piracy'. It does not note, however, that this statement was given as a speech three years earlier, in 1981, when the committee was founded amidst the height of the boat departures from Vietnam. See D. Macey, *The Lives of Michel Foucault* (London: Random House, 1993) 436; M. Guigni and F. Passy (eds) *Political Altruism? Solidarity Movements in International Perspective* (Maryland: Rowman & Littlefield Publishers, 2001) 219; and W. Connolly, 'Beyond Good and Evil: The Ethical Sensibility of Michel Foucault' (1993) 21(3) *Political Theory* 380.

3 Foucault, 'Confronting Governments: Human Rights' 475.

speech, in which he evoked an 'international citizenship that has its rights and its duties, and that obliges one to speak out against every abuse of power, whoever its author, whoever its victims' is both powerful and passionate.[4] Nonetheless, it leaves us with many questions, not least about the nature of this new right advocated by the thinker whose prior view of rights had been most starkly encapsulated in a phrase from a 1976 lecture: 'Right in the West is the King's right'.[5] In that, now justly famous, lecture, Foucault suggests that the function of the theory of right, since medieval times, has been to erase the problem of domination by framing power as a question of legitimacy – to secure both the legitimate power of the sovereign and the legal obligation to obey. In contrast, he describes his own 'general project over the past few years' – that is, in the period in which he was writing *Discipline and Punish* and *The History of Sexuality: An Introduction* – as an attempt to reverse the mode of analysis of the discourse of right in order to show that right is itself an instrument of domination. In language that is both stark and seemingly unambiguous, he writes: 'The system of right, the domain of the law, are permanent agents of these relations of domination, these polymorphous techniques of subjugation'.[6]

Foucault's approach in his Geneva intervention is starkly different; no longer is right the prerogative of kings and no longer is it bound to the problem of legitimacy. Rather, those who would exercise such a right have 'no other grounds for speaking, or for speaking together, than a certain shared difficulty in enduring what is taking place'.[7] Somewhat surprisingly, given his previous distrust of attempts to oppose the individual to power, Foucault uses the phrase 'private individuals' to describe the bearers of this new form of right.[8] He also gestures, however, to the organisations

4 ibid 474. I thank Paul Patton for drawing Foucault's relationship with Kouchner to my attention.

5 M. Foucault, 'Two Lectures' in C. Gordon (ed) Power Knowledge (New York: Pantheon Books, 1980) 94. 'Two Lectures' is a slightly abridged version of the first two lectures of Foucault's 1975–76 lecture course at the Collège de France 'Society Must Be Defended'; M. Foucault, 'Society Must be Defended': Lectures at the Collège de France 1975–76 (trans. D. Macey) (London: Allen Lane, 2003). 'Two Lectures' was available in English long before the publication of the lecture series.

6 Foucault, 'Two Lectures' 96.

7 Foucault, 'Confronting Governments: Human Rights' 474.

8 ibid 474–75. I suggest this is surprising, due to Foucault's argument that 'the problem is *not* to try to liberate the *individual* from the state and from the state's institutions *but* to liberate us both from the state and from the type of *individualisation* which is linked to the state'. See M. Foucault, 'The Subject and Power' in K. Nash, *Readings in Contemporary Political Sociology* (Massachusetts: Wiley-Blackwell, 2000) 16. The individual, Foucault makes clear in *Society Must be Defended,* is not 'power's opposite number; the individual is one of power's first effects'. See Foucault, *Society Must be Defended* 29–30.

As Duncan Ivison notes, however, the point of Foucault's critique of the individual was to promote 'new forms of subjectivity by refusing the model of the individual that has been imposed on us for centuries'. See D. Ivison, *The Self at Liberty: Political Argument and the Arts of Government* (Ithaca and London: Cornell University Press, 1997) 43. It may be that Foucault saw the 'private individual' who would bear the right to intervene as

to whom he attributes the responsibility for bestowing rights upon those with no official capacity in which to exercise them: 'Amnesty International, *Terre des Hommes*, and *Médecins du Monde*', he writes, 'are initiatives that have created this new right – that of private individuals to effectively intervene in the sphere of international policy and strategy'.[9] In this short speech, right no longer appears as an instrument or mask of domination but, rather, as that which enables 'the will of individuals' to wrench from governments the monopolisation of the power to effectively intervene.[10]

For some later thinkers, Foucault's advocacy of such a right is evidence of a late reconsideration of humanism and reappraisal of the idea of a pre-discursive subject, after which, in Eric Paras's words, he 'embraced the ideas that he had laboured to undermine: liberty, individualism, 'human rights' and even the thinking subject'.[11] There are moments in Foucault's later works, and particularly in those texts he drafted as specific political interventions that, on the surface, would seem to support such a contention. It is no doubt difficult to reconcile his declaration that the discourse of right is a mask for domination, with his argument, in the wake of the Iranian revolution, that '[a]gainst power one must always set inviolable laws and unrestricted rights'.[12] If we were to accept Paras's position, however, Foucault's new right would simply be the old right – the right of sovereignty, the right of the 'rights of man'. My contention, in contrast, is that we would be mistaken to assimilate this new form of right to the sovereign right he had previously criticised in such detail.[13] During the 1970s and early 1980s, the period in which he had regular recourse to the discourse of right in his political interventions, Foucault was working on what he termed *governmentality* – that is, that ensemble of institutions, practices and tactics that allows for a form of power that 'has the population as its target, political economy as its major form of knowledge,

precisely such a new form of subjectivity, insofar as its interventions did not rely on a legitimacy bestowed by the state.

9 Foucault, 'Confronting Governments: Human Rights' 475.

10 ibid.

11 E. Paras, *Foucault 2.0: Beyond Power and Knowledge* (New York: Other Press, 2006) 4. In a similar vein, Richard Wolin argues: 'Considerable evidence suggests that, later in life, Foucault himself became frustrated with the antihumanist credo. He underwent what one might describe as a learning process. He came to realize that much of what French structuralism had during the 1960s rejected as humanist pap retained considerable ethical and political value'. See R. Wolin, 'Foucault the Neohumanist?' *The Chronicle Review* (1 September 2006) available at http://chronicle.com/article/Foucault-the-Neohumanist-/23118/ (accessed 19 January 2012). For an insightful critique of Paras's reading of Foucault, and the 'narratives of return, revelation and recantation', which position his late works as evidence of an embrace of humanism and an essentialised subject, see B. Golder, 'Foucault and the Unfinished Human of Human Rights' (2010) 6(3) *Law, Culture and the Humanities* 327. I thank Golder for sharing with me his forthcoming work on Foucault and human rights.

12 Foucault, 'Useless to Revolt?' 453.

13 I discuss this critique of rights at length below.

and apparatuses of security as its essential technical instrument'.[14] The new form of right he advocates during this period, I suggest, should be situated in relation to a phenomenon Foucault suggests arose along with government – that is, 'the art of not being governed, or the art of not being governed like that and at this price'.[15] Through appeals to a new form of right the late Foucault, I suggest, believed it was possible to develop this art of not being governed, and thus to undo relations of coercion from within the strategic field in which they are engendered.[16]

Nonetheless, there remain real questions about whether rights discourses can be wrenched away from the role of bestowing legitimacy upon domination, and about whether they can effectively renounce their humanist presuppositions. The risks inherent in utilising rights claims in opposition to government will become clearer if we trace the genealogy of what Foucault defines as the 'right to intervene' in the practices of those organisations to whom he grants the credit of making it a reality – most importantly, *Médecins Sans Frontières (MSF)* and *Médecins du Monde*, which pioneered a form of interventionist humanitarianism that challenged the prerogatives of sovereign power.[17] No name is more closely associated with the attempt to develop such a new form of right than that of Bernard Kouchner, who worked closely with Foucault while he was president of *Médecins du Monde* and who was, until recently, Foreign Secretary in France's Sarkozy Government. In what follows, I trace Kouchner's crusade to have the right to intervene accepted into international law, and his mobilisation of Foucault's legacy for that purpose. In a context in which many have become suspicious that the moral language of humanitarian intervention is simply another justification for the domination of less powerful states by stronger ones, I ask what we can make of Foucault's attempt to formulate a new right to intervene in violation of the Westphalian principles of sovereignty.

Foucault's critique of rights

In an influential article on human rights and liberalism, Rhoda E. Howard and Jack Donnelly write: 'If human rights are the rights one has simply as a human being, as they are usually are thought to be, then they are held "universally" by all human beings'.[18] Few thinkers have done as much to call into question the belief

14 M. Foucault, *Security, Territory, Population: Lectures at the Collège de France 1977–78* (trans. Graham Burchell) (Basingstoke: Palgrave Macmillan, 2007) 108.

15 M. Foucault, 'What is Critique?' in James Schmidt (ed) *What is Enlightenment? Eighteenth Century Answers and Twentieth Century Questions* (Berkeley and Los Angeles: University of California Press, 1996) 384.

16 ibid.

17 While Foucault does not specifically mention *MSF* in his Confronting Governments intervention, it was this organisation that was central to the development of this new right of intervention, as I discuss below. At the time of Foucault's speech, Kouchner had recently split from *MSF* in order to found *Médecins du Monde.*

18 R. Howard and J. Donnelly, 'Liberalism and Human Rights: A Necessary Connection' in M. Ishay, *The Human Rights Reader: Major Political Essays, Speeches and Documents From the Bible to the Present* (New York: Routledge, 1997) 268.

in what the Universal Declaration of Human Rights terms the 'equal and inalienable rights of all members of the human family'[19] as did Foucault, whose critique of humanism undermined the idea of an ahistorical human subject that serves as the ground for the 'rights of man'. As Alain Badiou writes, in the 1960s Foucault 'outraged his readers with the declaration that Man, in the sense of constituent subject, was a constructed historical concept peculiar to a certain order of discourse, and not a timelessly self-evident principle capable of founding human rights or a universal ethics'.[20] Even more scandalous than the argument that 'man' was 'an invention of recent date',[21] was Foucault's suggestion that this invention may be nearing its end. With a change of arrangements akin to that which led to the crumbling of the ground of classical thought in the late 18th century, he infamously argued at the conclusion of *The Order of Things* that 'man would be erased, like a face drawn in sand at the edge of the sea'.[22]

The key danger with humanism, Foucault suggested in a late interview, is that it 'presents a certain form of our ethics as a universal model for any kind of freedom'.[23] Any attempt to found a vision of society or a universal ethics on a conception of human nature must therefore naturalise a historically specific conception of humanity – that is, in Nietzsche's words, it must 'take the recent form of man, as it developed under the imprint of certain religions or even certain political events, as the fixed form from which one must proceed'.[24] While Foucault saw the idea of natural rights as normalising, in that it presupposed an ideal and natural human subject as the bearer of rights, in this interview, as in many of his later political interventions, he does not dismiss the reliance on human rights altogether. If we recognise that what we call humanism is historically specific and capable of being wielded for a diverse range of political projects, he suggests, 'this does not mean that we have to get rid of what we call human rights or freedom, but that we can't say that freedom or human rights has to be limited at certain frontiers'.[25] Recently, a number of thinkers have argued that Foucault's challenge to the ahistorical human subject presupposed by human rights discourses is not inconsistent with a different conception of human rights as, in Ben Golder and Peter Fitzpatrick's words, 'the carrier of future inventions and different ways of being'.[26] Similarly, Paul Patton argues that 'the manner in which Foucault

19 United Nations Universal Declaration of Human Rights in Ishay, *The Human Rights Reader* 407.
20 A. Badiou, *Ethics: An Essay in the Understanding of Evil* (trans. Peter Hallward) (London: Verso, 2001) 5.
21 M. Foucault, *The Order of Things: An Archaeology of the Human Sciences* (London: Routledge, 2002) 422.
22 ibid.
23 Michel Foucault cited in B. Golder and P. Fitzpatrick, *Foucault's Law* (London: Routledge-Cavendish, 2009) 124.
24 F. Nietzsche, *Human, All Too Human* (Nebraska, University of Nebraska Press, 1986) 14.
25 Foucault cited in Golder and Fitzpatrick, *Foucault's Law* 124.
26 Golder and Fitzpatrick, *Foucault's Law* 124.

historicises and therefore particularises discourses of right is . . . consistent with appealing to rights in particular contexts'.[27] A Foucauldian account of rights, he suggests, would not treat them as natural or inalienable aspects of the human condition but, rather, as the codification of ever-shifting power relations.[28]

Foucault's argument in his earlier writings was not merely that rights reflect existing power relations, however, but that the discourse of right serves to *mask* social relations of domination. His infamous statement: 'we need to cut off the king's head; in political theory that has yet to be done', has often been taken to suggest that he abandoned the problems of sovereignty and right altogether, in exchange for an analysis of power relations, discipline and bio-politics and, later, what he termed government.[29] The account he offers of the relation between these forms of power, however, is more nuanced than this criticism would suggest.[30] Certainly, he traces the development in the 17th and 18th centuries of what he terms 'disciplinary power', stressing that the discourse of right is inadequate for understanding a form of power that operates through a range of non-juridical techniques that are 'absolutely incompatible with the relations of sovereignty'.[31] In contrast to the concern with right, contract and legitimacy that typified juridical thought, he proposed a methodology that focused attention on power in its capillary forms, on *how* power operated, rather than on its representation and legitimation.[32] In short, he argued that we should direct our researches on the nature of power 'not towards the juridical edifice of sovereignty, the state apparatuses and the

27 P. Patton, 'Foucault, Critique and Rights' (2005) 6(1) *Critical Horizons* 270.
28 ibid 272.
29 M. Foucault, *Power/Knowledge: Selected Interviews and Other Writings 1972–1977* in Colin Gordon (ed) *Power Knowledge* (New York: Pantheon, 1980) 121.
30 Nonetheless, there is a tension in Foucault's work concerning the precise relation of biopolitics to sovereign power. For instance, his articulation of the relation between these two forms in *The History of Sexuality: An Introduction* is not entirely consistent with his account in the 1975–76 lecture course *Society Must be Defended*. In the former, he suggests that biopower came to replace sovereign power, noting that the 'old power of death that symbolised sovereign power was now carefully supplanted by the administration of bodies and the calculated management of life (139–40). In the latter, however, he suggests that while 'the power of sovereignty is increasingly on the retreat', racism enables the reintegration of the old sovereign power to kill into a political system supposedly committed to fostering life (Foucault, *Society Must be Defended* 254.) As Mariana Valverde suggests, however, there is a risk in turning Foucault's terms into 'sociological concepts' that they become simplifying mechanisms that treat society itself as static. Foucault's thought, Valverde argues, is 'driven by the practices being studied and not by existing concepts, and . . . therefore thoroughly revises the conceptual apparatus as the problem to be analyzed demands'. See M. Valverde, 'Beyond Discipline and Punish: Foucault's Challenge to Criminology' in B. Harcourt, *Discipline, Security and Beyond: The Carceral Notebooks Vol 4* available at http://www.thecarceral.org/cn4_valverde.pdf (2008) 213 (accessed 10 February 2012). I thank Ben Golder for bringing this text to my attention.
31 Foucault, 'Two Lectures' 104.
32 ibid 97–102.

ideologies which accompany them, but towards domination and the material operators of power, towards forms of subjections and the inflections and utilisations of their localised systems, and towards strategic apparatuses'.[33] Rather than tracing the disappearance of the theory of right, however, he argues that it persists in a disciplinary society, and for two reasons: first, the theory of right operates as a 'permanent instrument of criticism of the monarchy' that is useful for overcoming obstacles to the development of disciplinary power.[34] Secondly, and more importantly, its persistence 'allowed a system of right to be superimposed upon the mechanisms of discipline in such a way as to conceal its actual procedures, the element of domination inherent in its technologies.'[35] Rather than being simply opposed to each other, the discourse of right and the norms of the disciplines remain irreducible but nonetheless operate together, as the former proves particularly suited to disguising the domination inherent in the latter.

This complementary relation between right and discipline, as Foucault was particularly aware, posed a problem for every attempt to contest domination. What do we do today, he asks, when we wish to object to the disciplines? We appeal, he answers, 'to this canon of right, this famous formal right, that is said to be bourgeois, and which in reality is the right of sovereignty'.[36] And yet, this leads us into a blind alley, as the tight bond between right and discipline in the general social mechanism of power means that discourse of right cannot be wielded to oppose disciplinary power. Instead, he provides a suggestion that remains unelaborated in this lecture, but which seems to have informed many of his subsequent political interventions:

> If one wants to look for a non-disciplinary form of power, or rather, to struggle against disciplines and disciplinary power, it is not toward the ancient right of sovereignty that one should turn, but towards the possibility of a new form of right, one which must indeed be anti-disciplinary, but at the same time liberated from the principle of sovereignty.[37]

This suggestion makes it clear that Foucault was not proposing any simple return to the old sovereign right of the 'rights of man'. In the following section, I examine the right to intervene developed by organisations such as *MSF*, in which the late Foucault seemed to have seen the possibility of a form of right that was both explicitly wielded in opposition to the prerogatives of sovereignty, and which attempted to neutralise the question of legitimacy by recasting the right to intervene as a right of private individuals. An examination of the development of this new right, however, suggests that it was unable to avoid the problems Foucault

33 ibid 102.
34 ibid 105.
35 ibid.
36 ibid 108.
37 ibid.

had so astutely analysed in relation to the old one: that is, it could not resist its transformation into one more, particularly successful, mask for domination.

A boat for Vietnam

As Foucault delivered his 1981 speech 'Confronting Governments: Human Rights' the corridors of the United Nations 'were decked with giant photographs of the boat people staggering ashore from their crippled vessels'.[38] Three years earlier, Foucault had been part of the committee '*Un Bateau pour le Vietnam*',[39] which resulted in Kouchner and a team of doctors anchoring a boat, a 'floating hospital',[40] off the Malaysian island of Poulo Bidong, which was then being used as a refugee camp for the Vietnamese asylum-seekers. Paul Berman writes: 'Kouchner's mission in East Asia was meant to save lives, and yet the mission could easily be interpreted as an intervention into the affairs of a sovereign state, the People's Republic of Vietnam'.[41] As Foucault's remarks about the role of organisations such as *Médecins du Monde* in creating a new right to intervene suggest, this was not the first time (and nor would it be the last) that Kouchner had sought to intervene in the name of human rights in matters that could be considered internal to the sovereignty of a state. *Médecins Sans Frontières* pioneered a new form of interventionist humanitarianism that negates state borders, and combines humanitarian relief with a duty to speak out against human rights violations – a form that has since then largely eclipsed the old style of neutral humanitarianism of the Red Cross.[42]

The origins of this new humanitarianism can be traced back to 1968, when Kouchner was a young doctor who left the barricades of Paris to volunteer as a medic with the Red Cross in Nigeria, where the Ibo Christian minority had declared an Independent Republic of Biafra. Patrick Aeberhard, a founding member of *MSF*, describes Biafra as the period of 'initiation' of the new generation of humanitarianism:

> A few physicians, united around Bernard Kouchner, found in action the answer to their political dissatisfaction or even their religious engagement.

38 Macey, *The Lives of Michel Foucault* 437.

39 D. Eribon, *Michel Foucault* (trans. B. Wing) (Cambridge: Harvard University Press, 1991) 279.

40 B. Taithe, 'Reinventing (French) Universalism: Religion, Humanitarianism and the "French Doctors"'(2004) 12(2) *Modern and Contemporary France* 150.

41 P. Berman, *Power and the Idealists: The Passion of Joschka Fischer and its Aftermath* (New York, Soft Skull Press, 2005) 237.

42 D. Chandler, 'The Road to Military Humanitarianism: How the Humanitarian NGOs Shaped a New Humanitarian Agenda' (2001) 23(3) *Human Rights Quarterly* 678–700. See also D. Rieff, *A Bed for the Night: Humanitarianism in Crisis* (London: Vintage, 2002); C. Foley, *The Thin Blue Line* (Verso, London, 2008); A. Orford, *Reading Humanitarian Intervention: Human Rights and the Use of Force in International Law* (Cambridge University Press, Cambridge, 2003).

> They violated the pledge they had given to the International Red Cross, to 'abstain from all communications and comments on its mission . . .' they bore witness to what they found intolerable.[43]

Upon returning to Paris, Kouchner left the Red Cross, which he believed took neutrality to the point of complicity, and circulated a statement about the Biafra conflict that was also signed by Jean-Paul Sartre and Simone de Beauvoir. In the background of this decision to speak out was the memory of the Red Cross's failure to do so when it learned of the Nazi gas chambers in 1942.[44] Kouchner reflected afterwards: 'By keeping silent we doctors were accomplices in the systematic massacre of a population'.[45] In breaking the Red Cross vow and founding *MSF*, Kouchner hoped that never again would humanitarians stand by silently and allow a genocide to take place; that never again should the prerogatives of sovereignty provide justifications for states to dispose of their populations as they saw fit. This rhetorical stance was undeniably compelling and helped to garner support for the new interventionist humanitarianism. The facts, however, were murkier; today, few are prepared to argue there was a genocide in Biafra. The actions of the humanitarians are widely considered to have prolonged the conflict and the crucial role played by the public relations company hired by the Ibo leadership in garnering support for their cause is acknowledged even by those who were most committed to this cause at the time.[46]

For some, however, the lesson was learned that media attention was central to compelling action. The Boat for Vietnam stands out as a key event in the history of this new media-savvy interventionist humanitarianism. The question of the boat provoked a split within *Médecins Sans Frontières* and led to the resignation of Kouchner, who failed to convince the organisation he had founded that the boat was anything more than a publicity stunt, and he left to found *Médecins du Monde*.[47]

43 P. Aeberhard, 'A Historical Survey of Humanitarian Action' (1996) 2(1) *Health and Human Rights* 38.
44 Rieff, *A Bed for the Night* 76.
45 ibid 83.
46 Oxfam, for instance, in its official history, 'describes itself as having fallen "hook, line and sinker" for the propaganda'. See Foley, *The Thin Blue Line* 18. Bernard Taithe notes that this 'origin narrative' contains 'many of the contradictions and ideological issues which have marred the humanitarian movement since', and stresses that the conflict was far more complex than the humanitarians understood. See B. Taithe, 'Reinventing (French) Universalism: Religion, Humanitarianism and the French Doctors' (2004) 12(2) *Modern and Contemporary France* 148. David Rieff writes: 'aid workers such as Bernard Kouchner mistakenly believed that the goal of the Nigerian army was to destroy the Biafran civilian population. It now appears clear that, for all the horrors of that conflict, there was no genocide in Biafra' See Rieff, *A Bed for the Night* 256.
47 In his insightful genealogy of the militarisation of humanitarianism, *A Bed for the Night*, David Rieff frames the split as the product of 'a conflict of visions about whether humanitarianism should ally itself with the state or try to be independent', and positions Kouchner in the pro-state position. Rieff, *A Bed for the Night* 310.

Central to Kouchner's vision was the idea of humanitarianism as a new *politics* of human rights, capable of superseding the political divisions of the Cold War period. The *Île de Lumière* served as an important marker of this changing political landscape; at a 1979 press conference in support of the original boat, with Foucault in the audience, André Glucksmann welcomed to the podium two Cold War foes, Sartre and Raymond Aron. For some this signalled that the old divisions of the Cold War had been overcome by a new commitment to human rights that transcended the border between left and right, and Glucksmann himself described the event as the 'end of the Cold War in our heads'.[48] Yet, this did not stop many from conceiving of the asylum-seekers as political trophies in a bipolar world; as a 1980 article in *The Rotarian* framed it, the 'boat people' were 'voluntary exiles who feel that risking death on the open seas is preferable to life under a communist regime'.[49] For those still aligned with the French Communist Party, and those who had rallied to the cause of the North in the Vietnam War, such a message was not welcome.

The changing Cold War climate played an important role in the genesis of the new humanitarianism. 'MSF comes to prominence' as David Rieff notes 'at almost the exact moment that Solzhenitsyn's *The Gulag Archipelago* transforms the political debate in France'.[50] Solzhenitsyn's account of the Gulags, which he traced directly to Marx's writings, led to profound tumult amongst the French left, and to the reconsideration of revolution and of its relation to human rights. In his account of the impact of the Russian dissidents on French political life, Robert Horvath argues that they played a key role in discrediting revolutionary Marxism, which had, until then, acted as a barrier to the widespread acceptance of human rights as a radical cause.[51] Their revelations about the USSR led to a reconsideration not only of the Russian Revolution but also of the French Revolution, which sought to detach the Universal Declaration of Human Rights from the Terror.[52] The rise of humanitarian intervention thus coincided with the demise of the form of utopian thinking embodied in Marxian Communism, and a moralising reorientation of

48 J. Traub, 'A Statesman Without Borders' *The New York Times* (3 February 2008) available at http://www.nytimes.com/2008/02/03/magazine/03kouchner-t.html?_r=1&pagewanted=1 (accessed 19 January 2012).

49 A. Hagan, 'New Home in Illinois: A "Boat Family" Finds Sanctuary in the U.S.A.' *The Rotarian* (July 1980) 29.

50 Rieff, *A Bed for the Night* 106.

51 R. Horvath, '"The Solzhenitsyn Effect": East European Dissidents and the Demise of the Revolutionary Privilege' (2007) 29 *Human Rights Quarterly* 879.

52 ibid 880. Francois Furet's *Penser la Révolution français*, published in 1978, turned the criticisms of Bolshevism against France's own Revolution, in an attempt to abolish what Furet termed the 'exorbitant privilege assigned to the idea of revolution' in French thought. See S. Khilani, *Arguing Revolution: The Intellectual Left in Postwar France* (Newhaven and London, Yale University Press, 1993) 157; and M. S. Christofferson, 'An Antitotalitarian History of the French Revolution: François Furet's *Penser la Révolution francais* in the Intellectual Politics of the late 1970s' (1999) 22(4) *French Historical Studies* 557–611.

politics towards the suffering of the victims of political struggles. It arose in the context of what Glucksmann would term a 'humanism of bad news',[53] which aimed to ameliorate the status quo while recasting the promise of emancipatory social transformation as inherently totalitarian. This shift was most starkly articulated by Bernard-Henri Lévy in his *Barbarism with a Human Face*: 'Like everyone else, I believed in a new, joyful "liberation": now, without hope, I live with the shadows of my past hopes'.[54] Those shadows were conceived as the victims of barbarism, and politics, for Lévy and those around him, would henceforth be limited to bearing witness to 'radical evil and the tragic dimension of history'.[55] We no longer have a politics, a language or a recourse, Lévy writes towards the end of his book, but only an ethics and a moral duty.[56] 'Humanitarianism', in David Rieff's words, 'is a hope for disenchanted times.'[57]

Not everyone would share in this new orientation of politics towards suffering. 'What I find really disgusting', Gilles Deleuze wrote of the so-called *Nouveaux Philosophes*, 'is that they are writing martyrology: the Gulag and the victims of history. They live off corpses'.[58] In contrast, for Foucault, who had long been disenchanted with Marxism and the Communist project,[59] this new determination to stand up for the victims of political rationalities seemed to offer an answer to the question of how it was possible to formulate a new right detached from the principle of sovereignty. Indeed, given that the right to intervene was explicitly grounded in opposition to the prerogatives of Westphalian sovereignty, we can understand why it seemed to offer an ideal solution to the problem of such a right.

53 Berman, *Power and the Idealists* 235.
54 B.-H. Lévy, *Barbarism with a Human Face* (trans. George Holoch) (New York, Harper and Row, 1979) x.
55 ibid 78. By 'those around him', I refer to the so-called *Nouveaux Philosophes.* In this work, Lévy explicitly credits Solzhenitsyn, who he terms 'the Dante of our time', with transforming the ideological landscape by stressing an internal connection between Marxism and the Gulags, and thus making clear that 'the sin is Marx' (154). 'I owe more to Solzhenitsyn than to most of the sociologists, historians, and philosophers who have been contemplating the fate of the West for the last thirty years' (153).
56 ibid 190.
57 Rieff, *A Bed for the Night* 92.
58 G. Deleuze 'On the New Philosophers (Plus a More General Problem) in *Two Regimes of Madness* (New York, Semiotext(e), 2006) 144.
59 Specifically, Foucault's disenchantment was with the Stalinised French Communist Party (PCF), which, as he wrote in 1979, 'laid down the law to everything that claimed to be of the left' in the post-war period, 'either subjecting it to its own law or outlawing it'. See M. Foucault, 'For an Ethic of Discomfort' in Faubion (ed) *Essential Works of Foucault 1954–1984 Vol 3: Power* 445. The relation of Foucault's thought to Marx's is a far more complex problem and one that is often overshadowed by the particular Stalinised brand of Marxism that permeated Foucault's intellectual milieu. For instance, Wendy Brown has convincingly argued that Foucault's critique of conceiving power as a commodity relies on a reading of Marx that dramatically underestimates the complexity of the latter's understanding of the commodity form. See W. Brown, *Politics Out of History* (Princeton, Princeton University Press, 2001) 75–76.

In language that parallels that used by Kouchner, Foucault had provided an argument in favour of such intervention in a 1979 letter to the Iranian Prime Minister Mehdi Bazargan in the aftermath of the Iranian revolution: 'It is good when a person, no matter who, even someone at the other end of the world, can speak up because he or she cannot bear to see another person tortured or condemned. It does not constitute an interference with a state's internal affairs'.[60] Rather, he suggests that those who, under the Shah, protested the torture of one person were 'interfering in the most universal thing there is'.[61] In a similar vein, in the same year that he delivered his 'Confronting Governments' speech, he drafted a petition with Pierre Bourdieu about the recent suppression of Poland's *Solidarnosc* movement, which warned the French Government that 'it must not let it be believed that the establishment of a military dictatorship in Poland is an internal matter'.[62] In language that prefigures that of much of the contemporary support for military intervention on humanitarian grounds, the petition reminds the government 'that it promised that the obligations of international morality would prevail over Realpolitik'.[63]

In today's context, in which the mobilisation of an international morality often serves to legitimise the brutal state interests of Realpolitik – providing a 'moral warrant for warfare' in places such as Afghanistan, Iraq and Libya[64] – the faith in such a distinction seems a naïve one. Despite his support for the right to intervene, however, Foucault was not entirely naïve about its dangers: we 'must guard', he warned late in life, 'against reintroducing a hegemonic thought on the pretext of presenting a human rights theory or policy'.[65] Subsequent events, however, call

60 Foucault, 'Open Letter to Mehdi Bazargan' 441.

61 ibid.

62 Macey, *The Lives of Michel Foucault* 440. In 1982, Foucault travelled to Warsaw as a member of a humanitarian convoy, delivering medical supplies, books and printing equipment, accompanied by the actress Simone Signoret, two doctors from *Médecins du Monde* and, once again, Bernard Kouchner – then that organisation's president. In a subsequent interview, he praised the ability of the *Solidarnosc* movement to struggle for basic rights by exercising those rights. 'If governments make human rights the structure and the very framework of their political action, that is well and good' he told his interviewers. 'But human rights are, above all, that which one confronts governments with. They are the limits one places on all possible government.' See M. Foucault and G. Anquetil, 'The Moral and Social Experience of the Poles Can No Longer Be Obliterated' in Faubion (ed) *Essential Works of Foucault 1954–1984 Vol 3: Power* 471.

63 Macey, *The Lives of Michel Foucault* 440.

64 Rieff, *A Bed for the Night* 209. Rieff notes (at 241) that: 'the humanitarian rhetoric of the US and British governments about Afghanistan descended almost directly from Bernard Kouchner's rhetoric about Kosovo'.

65 Foucault and Anquetil, 'The Moral and Social Experience of the Poles Can No Longer Be Obliterated' 472. As Costas Douzinas points out, human rights have certainly achieved such hegemonic status today. Douzinas's book, *The End of Human Rights*, begins with the following evocative passage: 'A new ideal has triumphed on the world stage: human rights. It unites left and right, the pulpit and the state, the minister and the rebel,

into question the possibility of his rearticulated right to resist being transformed into such a hegemonic thought. Indeed, the recent trajectory of the right to intervene is prefigured, as it were, by events in the years leading up to his death. In 1984, Foucault asked Kouchner to 'entrust him with a mission' and the two men discussed a number of possibilities.[66] 'Finally, the physician suggested that he organise and be responsible for the new "boat for Vietnam". Foucault accepted. He intended to leave as soon as he had finished *Histoire de la Sexualité*.'[67] His death would prevent this. By that time, a different model of humanitarian intervention was already in preparation. Indeed, in the previous five years, the main force responsible for the rescue of asylum-seekers from the South China Sea had not been *Médecins du Monde* but the US navy, which had seized on the human rights rhetoric under President Carter.[68] As the idea of international solidarity was detached from any broader emancipatory perspective and became focused not on collective struggle but on the rescue of victims, the right to intervene began its trajectory from a prerogative of private individuals to one of states.

The right of the governed

Before returning to examine this trajectory further it is necessary to examine Foucault's appeal, in his 'Confronting Governments' speech, to a 'mutual solidarity' premised on a shared belonging to the 'community of the governed'.[69] In the preceding years, he had devoted his courses at the *Collège de France* to 'governmentality', that is, the range of techniques and practices that are utilised to influence the conduct of individuals. In his 1977–78 course *Security, Territory, Population,* he traces the emergence of a community of the governed to the practices of the Christian pastorate, which sought to guide its members towards salvation. This role required an 'art of government' that was individualising, as the pastor's ability to guide his pastorate to salvation was premised on 'a never ending knowledge of the behaviour and conduct of the members of the flock he supervises'.[70] When this pastoral power gave rise to a governmental power, dedicated not to salvation in the next world but to material salvation in this one, this power would remain an individualising one but it would also bring about a new object of intervention – *the population*. Distinct from a juridical set of subjects who relinquish a right to the sovereign, the population is conceived naturalistically as a set of processes motivated by desire.

the developing world and the liberals of Hampstead and Manhattan'. See C. Douzinas, *The End of Human Rights* (Oxford, Hart Publishing, 2000) 1.

66 Eribon, *Michel Foucault* 308.

67 ibid.

68 See Berman, *Power and the Idealists* 240–41.

69 Foucault, 'Confronting Governments: Human Rights' 474.

70 Foucault, *Security, Territory, Population* 181.

It is in the context of this new figure of the population that Foucault would place the figure of man. With: 'the emergence of mankind as a species, within a field of the definition of all living species, we can say that man appears in the first form of his integration within biology'.[71] It is *man,* this new naturalistic figure, which replaces the old juridical subject; thus: 'man is to population what the subject of right was to the sovereign'.[72] This shift from subjects of right to population brings with it a shift in the techniques of power, as the population cannot be subjected to 'injunctions, imperatives and interdictions';[73] rather, the role of government will be one of *laisser faire,* which aims to allow natural processes to work and to ensure that interventions do not steer these processes away from a course which is assumed to lead to the general good. The population cannot be managed through the artificial paradigm of the social contract but requires techniques of government and management that seek to effect its natural processes by analysing, calculating and acting upon variables such as sanitation, exports and currency flows. This shift from the juridical model of subjects of right to the naturalistic model of the population profoundly transformed the very idea of nature. No longer would nature be the outside power, that state of nature prior to the social contract, or those natural rights that form an external limit to power. Rather, governmentality internalises nature, it discovers 'a certain naturalness specific to the practice of government' itself.[74] Subsequently, to govern properly would be to know and to respect the nature of the objects of government. The governmental state takes on a 'new function of responsibility for the population in its naturalness' and with it a new responsibility to protect the lives of those who comprise it.[75]

Foucault had already discussed the rise of the population as an object of political intervention in his 1975–76 *Collège de France* course, where he described it as a new element 'of which both the theory of right and disciplinary practice knew nothing'.[76] In the final lecture of that course, he focused on those new techniques of power that he termed 'bio-political', which sought to regulate the population as a natural phenomenon. In his later courses on government, in contrast, he turns his attention to the way in which the need to respect the natural processes of the population makes *freedom* indispensable for government. Like nature, freedom is no longer conceived as being outside of government, as that which escapes its grasp or which exists prior to it and may be alienated in exchange for the protection of a sovereign. Rather, freedom appears as an *internal* limit on governmental power, such that '[f]ailing to respect freedom is not only an abuse of rights with regard to

71 ibid 75.
72 ibid 79.
73 ibid 352.
74 M. Foucault, *Birth of Biopolitics: Lectures at the Collège de France 1978–79* (trans. Graham Burchell) (Basingstoke: Palgrave Macmillan, 2008) 15.
75 Foucault, *Security, Territory, Population* 353.
76 ibid 245.

the law, it is above all ignorance of how to govern properly'.[77] In the new governmental rationality, respecting the freedom of natural processes becomes a central aspect of governing well.

It is on this basis, Foucault suggests, that governmental power can also be challenged. As he wrote in his 1979 open letter to Mehdi Bazargan, the right that a government 'exercises to defend the people itself burdens it with very heavy responsibilities'.[78] In the 1978 lecture 'What is Critique?', he notes that along with the problem of government comes the question of how not to be governed or 'not to be governed like that'.[79] The first definition of critique, he suggests, would be 'the art of not being governed quite so much'.[80] Similarly, in *Security, Territory, Population*, he proposes that the techniques of government have become 'the only political stake and the only real space of political struggle and contestation' as both the survival of the state and the question of its limits can only be understood on the basis of the tactics of governmentality.[81] The freedom that provides an internal limit to power is not a universal that we would find more or less of at a particular point in time. 'Freedom is never anything other—but this is already a great deal—than an actual relation between governors and governed, a relation in which the measure of the "too little" is given by the "even more" freedom demanded.'[82] Foucault stresses the correlation between the development of the art of government, and the development of specific counter-conducts, which sought to open spaces of independence for the governed. Just as the counter conducts that opposed the Christian pastorate, of which the Reformation was the most profound, did not occur outside Christianity but on its borders – relying on a set of elements that included eschatological expectations, the formation of communities and a return to scripture to challenge the power of the Church – the counter-conducts that contest governmentality rely on the same elements as this governmentality itself, that is on '[s]ociety, economy, populations, security, and freedom'.[83] Government, as the conduct of conduct, and counter-conducts both find their support in 'the absolute value of the population as a natural and living reality', and thus operate together, through a series of mutual exchanges and correspondences.[84]

It is in the context of these counter-conducts that aim to establish a degree of independence of the governed that Foucault's new form of right should be placed. The shift from an external limitation to an internal limitation of power, he suggests,

77 ibid 353.
78 Foucault, 'Open Letter to Mehdi Bazargan' 441.
79 Foucault, 'What is Critique?' 193.
80 ibid.
81 Foucault, *Security, Territory, Population* 109.
82 Foucault, *The Birth of Biopolitics* 63. For Foucault, as Duncan Ivison stresses: 'No a priori theory can promise us freedom, which we achieve only in relation to particular practices and struggles'. See Ivison, *The Self at Liberty: Political Argument and the Arts of Government* 45.
83 Foucault, *Security, Territory, Population* 354.
84 ibid 355.

does not avoid the problem of the appropriate juridical form through which to limit the power of governmental authorities. This receives two starkly different responses: a revolutionary one, epitomised by Rousseau, which Foucault depicts as broadly continuous with the previous natural law tradition, and a radical-utilitarian one, which finds its support in the new governmental rationality. While the former retained a juridical account of freedom as that original portion of the will that is not ceded, the latter conceives it in terms of a transaction that marks out a sphere of independence for individuals. These two conceptions of freedom, one of them premised on the rights of man and the other on the independence of the governed, are, Foucault stresses, 'absolutely heterogenous'.[85] Of them, it is the utilitarian, radical response that 'has been strong and has held fast', yet this does not mean that the revolutionary, natural rights, conception of freedom has disappeared. Rather, he writes:

> With regard to the problem of what are currently called human rights, we would only need to look at where, in what countries, how, and in what form these rights are claimed to see that at times the question is actually the juridical question of rights, and at other it is a question of this assertion or claim of the independence of the governed vis-à-vis governmentality.[86]

Given Foucault's profound challenge to the juridical model of freedom, and the presupposition of natural rights that it entails, it seems clear that it is on the basis of this second form of right that he believed it would be possible to develop a new form of right that would be liberated from the principle of sovereignty. In moving away from the natural rights approach, however, this new form of right nonetheless finds its support in a naturalistic conception of the population.

The view that the natural life of the population can provide the basis for resisting power had already been foreshadowed in *The History of Sexuality: An Introduction*, where Foucault writes that in the face of the new bio-political power of the 19th century, 'the forces that resisted relied for support on the very things it invested, that is, on life, and man as a living being'.[87] Dismissing the question of whether or not these struggles were utopian, he stresses that 'life as a political object was in a sense taken at face value and turned back against the system that was bent on controlling it'.[88] At first sight, it would seem that such a process of struggle would eschew the language of rights. Foucault notes, however, that while these new

85 Foucault, *The Birth of Biopolitics* 42. Although Foucault does not mention him here, John Stuart Mill provides a succinct statement of this heterogeneity in *On Liberty*, where he stresses that he will forego 'any advantage which could be derived to my argument from the idea of abstract right, as a thing independent of utility'. See J. S. Mill, 'On Liberty' in *On Liberty, and Other Essays* (Oxford: Oxford University Press, 2008) 15.

86 Foucault, *The Birth of Biopolitics* 42.

87 Foucault, *History of Sexuality: An Introduction* 145.

88 ibid.

struggles were concerned primarily with life rather than law, they were nonetheless articulated in the language of right.[89] This new concern with 'life as a political object', he suggests, led to the formulation of a right 'which the classical juridical system was utterly incapable of comprehending' and which 'did not derive, either, from the traditional right of sovereignty' – a '"right" to life, to one's body, to health, to happiness, to the satisfaction of needs, and beyond all the oppressions or "alienations", the "right" to rediscover what one is and all that one can be'.[90] At the point at which the state declares itself responsible for the biological life of its population, Foucault suggests, this life itself becomes the locus of rights claims.

Paul Patton has suggested, in relation to Foucault's advocacy of a right to intervene in his Geneva speech, that this 'new right arises party because governments of all persuasions believe and would have others believe that they are concerned for the welfare of their citizens'.[91] The right of governments to act is constituted, he argues, by the fact that the governed accept that 'their welfare falls within the sphere of governmental power', and this acceptance makes governments accountable for their actions.[92] This acceptance, however, serves also further to enmesh life in the realm of the state, and to make biological life the key stake of political projects. In *Homo Sacer*, Giorgio Agamben argues, in response to Foucault, that the human as a living being, the body, and life itself – when conceived as a natural property – are always-already entangled in the realm of sovereign power, and can provide no basis for resistance; '[T]he 'body", he writes, 'is always a biopolitical body and bare life, and nothing in it . . . seems to allow us to find solid ground on which to oppose the demands of sovereign power.'[93] It is with this suggestion in mind, that I would now like to turn to the afterlife of the right to intervene of the activist NGOs, in which Foucault saw the possibility of a new, non-sovereign right.

Masking domination: the afterlife of the right to intervene

In 1987, Kouchner and *Médecins du Monde* organised an international conference in Paris under the patronage of Lech Walesa, leader of Poland's *Solidarnosc* movement, and Desmond Tutu. The conference 'insisted on the right and indeed the duty to interfere in other countries in the name of human rights'.[94] Its published proceedings were prefaced by Foucault's Geneva speech. Two years later, in a book chapter entitled 'Morals of Urgent Need', Kouchner, begins by saying: 'I would

89 ibid.
90 ibid.
91 P. Patton, 'Foucault, Critique and Rights' (2005) 6(1) *Critical Horizons* 279.
92 ibid.
93 G. Agamben, *Homo Sacer: Sovereign Power and Bare Life* (trans. Daniel Heller-Roazen) (Stanford: Stanford University Press, 1998) 186.
94 Macey, *The Lives of Michel Foucault* 438.

like to start by quoting my friend Michel Foucault. His words express the ideas that I would like to set forth today'.[95] After quoting from 'Confronting Governments: Human Rights', he writes of his attempt to 'impose this new right, that of intervening on behalf of despairing populations all over the world'.[96] Although the essay mirrors Foucault's statement in referring to a right of intervention that would be available to private individuals, as Richard Seymour notes, in the course of the development of the doctrine of humanitarian intervention, 'to the argument that victims had a right to humanitarian assistance was added the stipulation that the state had an obligation to help provide it'.[97] Indeed, at the time of the essay's publication, its author was already serving as France's Minister of State for Humanitarian Action and, within just over a decade, was to become the Chief UN Administrator in Kosovo, during a war that was justified explicitly through the doctrine of humanitarian intervention.[98] More recently, Kouchner served as Foreign Secretary in France's Sarkozy Government, and stands out as one of the very few French politicians to have provided moral support to the United States' war on Iraq. In March of 2003, as the US engaged in desperate lobbying aimed at securing UN support for the war on Iraq, Kouchner told an audience at Harvard University: 'I would like to address the suffering of the Iraqi people: Shiites, Kurds, Sunnis, Assyrians, Turkmens, they are calling us. They want to be rescued and liberated'.[99] Kouchner was introduced as someone whose 'ongoing campaign has been to introduce the "right to intervene" into international law and UN practice'.[100]

The story of the subsequent history of the right to intervene, however, is much bigger than Bernard Kouchner.[101] The decades following the end of the Cold War have seen the strong presumption in favour of the inviolability of national

95 B. Kouchner, 'Morals of Urgent Need' in Fritz Kalshoven (ed) *Assisting the Victims of Armed Conflict and Other Disasters* (Dordrecht: Martinus Nijhoff Publishers, 1989) 55.

96 ibid.

97 R. Seymour, *The Liberal Defence of Murder* (London: Verso, 2009) 172.

98 See D. Chandler, 'War Without End(s): Grounding the Discourse of Global War' (2009) 40(3) *Security Dialogue* 243–62. David Rieff suggests that it was in Kosovo that 'the political instrumentalisation of humanitarianism' was almost completed. See Rieff, *A Bed for the Night* 197.

99 Bernard Kouchner, Jonathan Mann Lecture, Harvard University (6 March 2003) available at http://ww.harvardfxbcenter.org/resources/. . ./FXBC_WP15—Kouchner.pdf (accessed 19 January 2012).

100 ibid. In a 2004 *Time Magazine* article written in praise of Kouchner, Glucksmann writes: 'In the name of human rights, he approved the U.S. intervention in Iraq: "The No. 1 weapon of mass destruction is Saddam Hussein," he said'. André Glucksmann, 'Bernard Kouchner' *Time Magazine* (26 April 26 2004).

101 It is worth noting that the legal concept of a 'right of intervention' was itself developed by the French academic Mario Bettati but, as David Chandler notes, Kouchner is generally viewed as the figure responsible for 'popularising' the concept. See D. Chandler, 'The Road to Military Humanitarianism: How the Human Rights NGOs Shaped a New Humanitarian Agenda' (2001) 23(3) *Human Rights Quarterly* 685.

sovereignty that typifies the Westphalian state system, challenged by an emerging consensus that large-scale human rights violations generate an imperative to intervene across state borders to protect the vulnerable.[102] For its supporters, the right to intervene on humanitarian grounds is a great development that will stem the global tide of suffering. Fernando Tesón, for instance, argues that 'the goal of saving lives and restoring human rights and justice is compelling enough to authorise humanitarian intervention even at the cost of innocent lives'.[103] There are many reasons to be suspicious, however, that this new fervour for saving lives, and restoring human rights and justice is generated by what is at best a new instantiation of the 'white man's burden' and, at worst, the brutal, geopolitical and economic self-interest of the more powerful states.

Today, the doctrine of humanitarian intervention is a key legitimating discourse for state militarism. One need not be a pacifist to be concerned by this development. It may be that there are situations when military action may lead to a more just outcome but determining those situations is a necessarily political question, which requires thought, historical sense and an examination of the complexities of each conflict. Humanitarian interventions, in contrast, thrive on a mediatised sense of horror, a temporality of urgency and a moralising language that generates the belief that it is necessary to 'do something' – and do it now! This mobilisation of the rhetoric of emergency, combined with a 'fable of warlords and innocent victims' and a moral discourse that is often little more sophisticated than that of good versus evil, serves to generate public support for military expeditions that may have far more complex, and less benign, motivations.[104] The discourse of humanitarian intervention, as Anne Orford notes, makes 'high violence' responses to conflict situations 'marketable to citizens of the USA and other democracies, in ways rendered unimaginable in the immediate aftermath of Vietnam',[105] In this rhetoric of rescue, the idea that those who are subject to human rights abuses may have the capacity to act on their own behalf is rarely considered, as the range of available options in conflict situations tends to be reduced to two – outside military intervention, or genocide.[106]

None of this is to suggest that Foucault should be held responsible for the subsequent development of the doctrine of humanitarian intervention, or to assume that he intended such a development. As he suggested, we should study power not at the level of intentions but at the level of effects. Although we can

102 For an analysis of Foucault's account of the treaty of Westphalia, see Jessica Whyte, '"Is Revolution Desirable?" Michel Foucault on Revolution, Neoliberalism and Rights' in Ben Golder (ed.) *Foucaultian Legalities*, Routledge, Forthcoming 2012.

103 F. Tesón, 'The Liberal Case for Humanitarian Intervention' in J. L. Holzgrefe and R. O. Keohane *Humanitarian Intervention: Ethical, Legal, and Political Dilemmas* (Cambridge: Cambridge University Press, 2003) 117.

104 Rieff, *A Bed for the Night* 172.

105 Orford, *Reading Humanitarian Intervention* 12.

106 See Orford, *Reading Humanitarian Intervention* for an insightful account of this narrowing of possibilities.

never know what he would make of what the right to intervene has become, it is worth noting that the one occasion on which he broke with Kouchner during the period in which they worked together closely was in 1983 when the latter drafted a petition with Glucksmann calling on the French Government to take action against Gaddafi. Foucault refused to sign on the basis that he did not wish to appear to be calling for war.[107] In the context of a new war against Gaddafi, carried out ostensibly to protect civilians and prevent 'crimes against humanity',[108] Foucault's position highlights the transformation of what he saw as a right available to 'private individuals'. The important question today is thus not that of Foucault's intentions, but that of what becomes of his desire to formulate a new form of right in the wake of Kosovo, Somalia, Iraq or Libya. Can we still believe today that the suffering of men grounds an absolute right to intervene?

The subsequent development of the doctrine of humanitarian intervention should give us pause to question the effects of mobilising the natural life of a population as a political object and to reconsider the idea of a right grounded in suffering. The step from inscribing suffering at the heart of politics to reconceptualising politics as a rescue mission, in which the rescue and the victim roles are pre-assigned, has proven to be a small one. Foucault's right of intervention was envisaged as a non-sovereign right, available to private individuals whose only authority stemmed from their inability to bear the suffering of others. As the Boat for Vietnam demonstrates, however, the state is ultimately better equipped for such rescue (or humanitarian protection) missions than private individuals. And as Wendy Brown has convincingly argued, albeit in another context, the conception of vulnerability that underlies such demands for protection is not without its costs. The 'heavy price of institutionalised protection', she writes, 'is always a measure of dependence and agreement to abide by the protector's rules'.[109] In the context of humanitarian interventions, the protection of the so-called 'international community' brings with it the need to obey the rules of the new world order, with its 'democracy promotion' schemes and structural adjustment programmes. The new politics of humanitarianism is premised on the abandonment of any real challenge to this world order and its structural inequalities.

Foucault, it would seem, saw in the right to intervene a form of right capable of renouncing the humanist presupposition of a natural and idealised bearer of rights. In its place, however, this new right ultimately placed a figure of the human reduced to its biological existence, a pure figure of suffering. Badiou has noted that today, 'it is never really a question of man except in the form of the tortured, the

107 Eribon, *Michel Foucault* 267.

108 United Nations Resolution 1973, 2011 available at http://www.un.org/News/Press/docs/2011/sc10200.doc.htm#Resolution (accessed 19 January 2012).

109 ibid 169. That those rules are, crucially, the rules of the free market is made clear by the assertion by USAID Administrator Andrew Natsios that 'foreign assistance helps nations prepare for participation in the global trading systems and become better markets for US exports'. See Rieff, *A Bed for the Night* 239.

massacred, the famished, the genocided'.[110] Today's humanism, he suggests, is an 'animal humanism' in which man exists only as worthy of pity.[111] 'But pity', he continues, 'when it is not the subjective instance of propaganda for "humanitarian" interventions, is nothing but the confirmation of the naturalism, the deep animality, to which man is reduced by contemporary humanism.'[112] These words find their confirmation in Kouchner's suggestion that intervention is the protection of 'the essential species: man the potential victim'.[113] Such a vision of the human ultimately treats man as a species amongst others, which can hope for nothing more than a survival that must be managed by the state. In attempting to avoid a humanist understanding of rights, Foucault, however inadvertently, lent support to one premised on what Giorgio Agamben has termed 'bare life', that is a life that enters into the calculations of power on the basis of that which is natural in it, the politicisation of biological life itself: 'humanitarian organisations can only grasp human life in the figure of bare or sacred life', Agamben writes, 'and therefore, despite themselves, maintain a secret solidarity with the very powers they ought to fight'.[114] As humanitarianism and militarism become increasingly indistinct, we would do well to question their shared investment in this mute, suffering life.

The attempt to ground a new right in biological life and to turn government's investment in the life of its population into the grounds for a political claim, has ultimately served to re-enforce the role of the state as protector of an animalised humanity. The militarisation of the right to intervene demonstrates the extent to which the old sovereign power to kill can co-exist with, and gain support from, this newer bio-political 'protection' role. In the course of this decade, the language of humanitarian intervention has given way to that of the 'responsibility to protect', which relies on the belief that rather than being opposed to sovereignty, the right to intervene can be reconciled with sovereign power if the latter is reconceptualised as responsibility for 'protecting the safety and lives of citizens and promotion of their welfare' – a responsibility which falls to the 'community of states' if a given state is unwilling or unable to accept it.[115] The attempt to mobilise the natural life of the population against government and to ground a new form of right in suffering has proved unable to offer a real challenge to the power of the state and has, in fact, created a new basis for the legitimacy of state militarism, as well as a new foundation for sovereign power. In such a context, Foucault's willingness to look for the domination masked by discourses of right and his warning that we should beware of introducing a new hegemonic thought under the guise of human rights seem more important than ever.

110 A. Badiou: *The Century* (trans. Alberto Toscano) (Cambridge: Polity, 2008) 175.
111 ibid.
112 ibid.
113 In Rieff, *A Bed for the Night* 216.
114 Agamben, *Homo Sacer* 133.
115 International Commission on Intervention and State Sovereignty, *The Responsibility to Protect* (December 2001) 13.

Chapter 2

Stasis Syntagma

The names and types of resistance

Costas Douzinas

The urban space has always expressed the inequality of social relations and offered a site of conflict. Urban legality comprises planning, architectural and traffic regulations, public entertainment, protest and expression rules, licit and illicit ways of being in public. It imposes a grid of regularity and legibility, ascribing places to legitimate activities while banning others, structuring the movement of people and vehicles across space, ordering encounters between strangers.

Yet from the regular urban riots of early modernity to the Bastille, the Paris Commune, the British reform movement and the suffragettes, the American civil rights movement, May 1968, the Athens Polytechnic, Prague, Bucharest, Tehran and Cairo uprisings, to name a few iconic cases, the 'street' has confronted and unsettled urban legality. Urban space offers ample opportunity for political action, which has changed social systems, laws and institutions across epochs and places. The vote, the vote for women, basic laws to protect labour and stop discrimination and many other entitlements, today taken for granted, were the result of street protests, violence and riots. The abstract denunciation of protests for violence combines the defence of the status quo with historical ignorance.

This chapter uses instances of resistance against the injustice of recent policies in Greece to explore the contemporary politics of social conflict. The austerity imposed by the three neo-colonial administrators of Greece (the infamous 'troika' of the International Monetary Fund, the European Commission and the European Central Bank) is leading the country to abject poverty. According to the September 2011 figures, the country has a –6 per cent growth in 2011, the fourth year of a deep depression, a 30 per cent cut of the public sector, 50 per cent salary and pension cuts for all civil servants and up to 200,000 losing their jobs over four years, abolition of collective bargaining and a huge reduction of minimum wage. Austerity has led unemployment to 21 per cent and youth unemployment to 50 per cent. A whole generation is destroyed; Greece is going through what can only be called a 'genocide'. The austerity cure is much worse than the disease.

The most common types of resistance can be presented under three toponymies, the first for a building (*Ypatia*), the second for a village (*Keratea*) and the third for a public square (*Syntagma*). *Ypatia* is the name of the neo-classical building in central Athens used as refuge by 300 *sans papiers* immigrants during their 40-day-long hunger strike in early 2011. These were people who had lived and worked in the country for up to 10 years, doing the jobs the Greeks did not want to do during the boom years and being kicked out during the bust. The *Ypatia* hunger strikers rebelled unto death against their dehumanisation. They asserted their minimum humanity, what is same in all despite the differences. To do so they had to come to the threshold of death and become martyrs and *homines sacri*, witnesses and sacrificial victims. They reminded Greeks of the sovereign's theologico-political essence, telling the story of a sovereignty already hurt, abandoned and transferred to foreign powers.

The *Keratea* and the 'can't pay, won't pay' movements are perhaps easier to identify. They are typical cases of civil disobedience against policies which attack a group's or locality's interests, asking people to sacrifice the integrity of their lives and their legitimate expectations. The proposed introduction of the landfill in *Keratea*, a village outside Athens, which had been decided without proper consultation and without an examination of alternatives, would degrade the environment and have adverse effects on property values. The largely conservative inhabitants blockaded the main road in the area for weeks and obstructed the contractors building the landfill. Large riot police units were stationed in the area and regularly fought the locals. Eventually the plan was abandoned in June 2011. The 'won't pay' movement was a reaction to the huge increase in road tolls and public transport fares in 2010. Members of the group raise the bars in the toll stations and let drivers pass without payment or block the validation machines in Metro stations and buses, allowing the public free travel. In late 2011, this movement expanded to the non-payment of new special income taxes and a poll tax on property, which will be collected through electricity bills, resulting in many families having their electricity cut off. These regressive taxes impose further unjust burdens on poor and lower middle class families who have already lost a large part of their income through salary cuts and indirect tax increases.

Unlike the hunger strikers, the protesters in these cases promote particular issues and concerns. Their citizenship right to participate in the decision-making process of a policy with devastating effects on them has been violated. If *Ypatia* shows the humanist deficit of Greece, the *Keratea* resistance indicates its democratic deficiency and the authoritarianism of power. *Keratea* and 'can't pay, won't pay' are the most common type of disobedience. For the ordinary person, disobedience is the deeply moral decision to break the law. It is the strongest mark that the morality of citizens has not atrophied like that of politicians. It happens when someone reaches the point at which he says to himself: 'enough is enough – I can't take it any more' and is prepared to risk punishment. This decision may be an immediate and violent reaction, an acting out, following an extreme injustice. The decision to disobey the law is a difficult decision, simultaneously inevitable and traumatic.

One could argue, therefore, that civil disobedience is a 'dangerous freedom'; it represents morality at its highest. In normal circumstances, morality and legality represent two different types of overlapping but not identical duty: the external duty to obey the law (in formal terms a heteronomous duty) and the internal moral responsibility that binds the self to a conception of the good (autonomy). In cases of disobedience these two duties come into conflict. In these rare instances, in choosing difficult freedom and justice against unconstitutional or unprincipled legality or simple evil we become temporarily autonomous. This kind of autonomy does not exist for those who believe that morality and legality is the simple obedience to an external code. The obligation to obey the law is absolute when it is accompanied by the judgment that the law is morally right and democratically legitimate. In disobedience autonomy and existential freedom temporarily coincide.

Finally, there are the *aganaktismenoi* (indignant) occupations in Syntagma Square, other Athenian suburb squares as well as in Thessaloniki and some 60 provincial Greek cities. The daily assemblies and rallies of the *aganaktismenoi*, sometimes involving more than 250,000 people, have been peaceful, with the police observing from a distance. The outraged have attacked the impoverishment of working Greeks, the loss of sovereignty that has turned the country into a neocolonial fiefdom of bankers in Germany, and the turning of dynastic parliamentary democracy into a corruption, tax evasion by the rich, cleptocracy and clientelism. Syntagma developed two sets of demands. The first is encapsulated in the slogan 'we don't owe, we don't sell, we don't pay', a masterful combination of the particular and the universal. Specific claims about the debt (we don't owe) and economic deprivation (we can't pay) become linked, with the common good (we don't sell) acquiring universal significance. The 'troika' have demanded that Greece sells off its publicly held assets. These range from its airports, electricity and water companies to its land and sea, with regular references to the sale or lease of a number of its islands.

The demand for direct or real democracy, the second *Syntagma* call, acts as a performative. A performative statement does what is says; it uses language to change the world. When the priest says 'I pronounce you man and wife' the status of the couple changes significantly and irreversibly. Similarly, the *Syntagma* popular assembly puts into operation direct democracy. It manifests practically what it asks for and shows what a wider adoption of the practice might involve. *Syntagma* operates a type of non-representative democracy and asks that it be universalised.

In doing so, *Syntagma* both adopts and sublates the positions of human and citizen active in *Ypatia* and *Keratea*. The *Syntagma* person represents the essence of humanity and citizenship. She has the dignity and respect of the human, as she stands upright in *Syntagma* facing *Vouli* (Parliament), like the Real that is prohibited by the symbolic but always returns. The upright gait of *stasis*, of the physical turning upwards to the stars, Kant's sublime, is precisely what characterises *anthropos*, the *ano throskon* animal, according to one etymology. In this sense, she is the representative human. But the *Syntagma stasiastis* (rebel) standing statically opposite Parliament expresses with her stance the distance from power and the demos of democracy. As she stands against her putative representatives opposite, she is also someone who *epana-statei* (revolves her stance or rebels; *epanastasis* means revolution). The *Syntagma* person is the *arche-polites*, the essence of citizenship.

If we add to these the Athens December 2008 uprising, we have a panorama of resistance.[1] Are these different types of resistance related?

On naming

Omen est Nomen. The name is destiny, a blessing or a curse that conditions a life's or project's trajectory. For medieval theology a good name was half the way to paradise. And there is nowhere that this applies more than in politics. Naming is the business of politics. Names are marks for identification (Marxism–Leninism), symbolic reminders (Tiananmen Square) and signs of identity (PASOK, New Labour). Nomination brings together and makes actual what is only potential; it constructs a political subject (the working class, the middle classes etc.). Nomination is therefore an imaginative political act indicating more than specific policies and projects: what the group, party or organisation stands for, its identity. Nomination chooses the name that will hopefully unite the greatest number of people, causes and interests.

In this sense, giving a name is a hegemonic practice. It takes a determinate particularity and turns it into universality. The name of the universal is posited discursively, taking into account the common sense of a society and using it in order to construct the widest possible alliance of forces. The name EAM (National Patriotic Front, the resistance organisation during the German occupation of Greece) for example, was one such hegemonic operation, bringing together the nation and emancipation under the banner of a popular front. Similarly, PASOK (Panhellenic Socialist Movement), by calling itself a movement instead of a party was able in its early days to co-opt and combine the attractiveness of the decolonisation movements as well as of the social movements of the Western world.

The politics of resistance, like all politics, operates through the giving of names. A gathering, a protest or an organisation survives its transient happening and acquires identity and effectiveness only by being nominated. December, the name given to the 2008 insurrection, is a temporal identification. In the recent struggles the names are toponymies: *Ypatia, Keratea, Syntagma.* Why? According to Michel de Certeau, urban resistance takes strategic and tactical forms: 'A strategy assumes a place that can be circumscribed as proper (*propre*) . . . The "proper" is a victory of space over time. On the contrary, because it does not have a place, a tactic depends on time – it is always on the watch for opportunities that must be seized "on the wing" '.[2] Strategy establishes a new place against already existing static places of authority or against structures of power. This spatial base facilitates resistance

1 C. Douzinas, 'Athens Revolting: Three Meditations on Sovereignty and One on its (Possible) Dismantlement' (2010) 21(3) *Law and Critique* 261; A. Kalyvas, 'An Anomaly? Some Reflections on the Greek December 2008' (2010) 17(2) *Constellations* 351.

2 M. de Certeau, *The Practice of Everyday Life* (Berkeley: University of California Press, 1988) 91–131.

against temporal synchronicity and cyclical legality. Tactics, on the other hand, utilise temporality, the *kairos* or the timely; through an acceleration or disjuncture of time; the propriety of place or structure is unsettled.

In these terms, December, *Ypatia* and *Keratea* were a recognisable form of 'street' resistance. December's temporal nomination is apt. Its tactics used time and movement. The opportunities offered by school, university or pre-Christmas time (the burning of the Christmas tree, the disruption of shopping districts, the occupation of schools and universities) unsettled the propriety of official cyclical temporality. *Ypatia* and *Keratea*, on the other hand, used the stability of place, turned into a defensive base.

I have called the direct democracy exercised in the squares *Stasis* (Station) *Syntagma*. *Stasis* is a strange word. It means, first, the upright posture, standing tall and serene, holding your stance. This first meaning is associated with the meaning of the English word stasis as stillness or immobility. But the Greek *stasis*, in one of those tricks of the cunning of language, means also sedition, revolt or insurrection, the opposite of stillness. *Syntagma*, on the other hand, is the Constitution. *Stasis Syntagma* (literally the bus and metro station in the Square) is a symbolic nomination. It reminds us that the *aganaktismenoi* insurrection, which performs a novel constitutional imaginary, is associated with particular places and stations. It brings together place (the square and the public transport station) and demand (to stand up together opposite and against the Parliament building in a constitutional assembly). The **sta* in the word *stasis* or con-sti-tution is the most metaphysical etymological root. **Sta* is the root of stance, sub-stance, con-sti-tution and in-sti-tution. **Sta* is the foundation on which self and collective stand together and take a stance of protest and insurrection. *Stasi Syntagma* philosophically, politically, topographically, is the name of hope.

Ypatia

As the world has followed the North African revolutions with bated breath, a less public North African revolt and tragedy took place in Athens and Thessaloniki, when 300 non-documented immigrants mostly from the Maghreb went on hunger strike in January 2011. The strike lasted for some 40 days. Many were taken to hospital in pre-comatose condition and were reaching the state of non-reversible organ failure and death just before they ended their strike when the government, after many refusals, decided to negotiate and accept the bulk of their demands.

The strikers had lived and worked in Greece for up to 10 years. They picked olives and oranges, they looked after the old and the sick and they worked on building sites and orchards for a fraction of minimum wage. After years of exploitation and humiliation they were told that they were no longer wanted because of the crisis and they must go back or be deported. They were the double victims of boom and bust. During the period of fake growth, their underpaid, uninsured work did the necessary tasks the locals would not do. EU and IMF austerity measures welcomed by the government led to prolonged depression and they became surplus to requirement, to be disposed of like refuse.

But what did the hunger strikers demand? The wanted to make Greeks notice their meagre, insignificant existence and to ask for basic labour protections and minimum living conditions. They asked the minimum recognition that they live and work in Greece but have worse treatment than convicts on chain gangs. They were just saying: '[w]e the invisible, uncounted and undocumented are next to you, worked for pennies and are part of who you are and what your government is doing to you'. They are people punished not for what they have done (criminality or illegality) but for who they are, not for their evil but for their abject innocence. They are *homines sacri*, persons who are legally non-existent and therefore non-persons who can be treated in the most cruel way by the state, employers, landlords and the xenophobic minority.

The Greek Government claims that it fully respects human rights. According to standard liberal philosophy, human rights belong to humans precisely because they are humans rather than members of narrower groups such as nation, state or group. Nation and state give political and civil rights to their citizens according to their law and constitution. Human rights, on the other hand, are the extra and international legal recognition offered to people who do not have the protection of a state and its law.

This is a comforting thought. The treatments of the *sans papiers* shows these claims to be ideological half-truths. In theory, human rights are given to all humans but, in practice, only to citizens. This is further confirmed by the treatment of asylum-seekers. As recently as January 2011, the European Court of Human Rights held that sending refugees back to Greece amounted to torture, inhuman and degrading treatment, because of the living and detention conditions in immigration camps.[3] Furthermore, Greece virtually never gives political asylum to refugees. Belgium, which was also condemned for taking Greece as a humane place and sending back an Afghan refugee, and other European states including Britain, will no longer return asylum-seekers to Greece. The Greek Government has been condemned as a violator of the basic dignity of the wretched of the earth. This is a sad conclusion for a country last condemned for systemic torture in the 1960s during the Colonels' dictatorship. Many of the governing party members including Mr Papandreou, the then prime minister, found refuge during that dark period in foreign countries.

The hunger strikers were humanity reduced to degree zero. They are martyrs in a double sense, both as witnesses and as sacrificial victims. As witnesses, they stated that there are higher truths than life, that life is worth living for values that are worth dying for. In this sense, the strikers are exercising what philosophers from Rousseau to Derrida consider the essence of freedom: acting against biological and social determinations in the name of a higher truth.

3 *M.S.S. v Belgium and Greece* Judgment of Grand Chamber 21 January 2011 (Application no. 30696/09).

In modernity, it is the prerogative of the sovereign to demand martyrdom from his subjects and to sacrifice his enemies. After God, the sovereign has administered and channelled the human 'desire to violate the limit insofar as it exposes finitude'.[4] Modern sovereignty performs its theologico-political role by maintaining a separation between the holy and the secular through the political function of the sacred. Sacrifice is an offering to a higher cause and gives access to truth. The sovereign negotiates the link between secular and holy by making sacred (*sacer facere*); war, the death penalty, rituals of sacrifice and consecration are ways through which the transcendent absolute is both acknowledged and kept at a distance. The mediation, exemplified by the king's two bodies and his power to take life and offer mercy, introduces the divine into the secular in a symbolic form and places limits on its action, both necessary for the conduct of social life.

Sacrifice – making the ordinary sacred – bridges everyday life with what transcends it. The truth the hunger strikers defended at the personal level is dignity – what makes each unique in our human similarity. Identity is built through the reciprocal recognition others give to self and self to others. I feel good, clever or beautiful to the extent that intimate and remote friends consider me such. The absence of all basic rights of work and life for the *sans papiers*, on the other hand, leads to absence of all recognition, making them less than human. At the collective level, their sacrifice brought the Greek state and law before an infinite justice and hospitality, preconditions of law and policy. But what is justice? We are surrounded by injustice but we do not often know where justice lies. In Greece, justice has miscarried in the austerity measures and the Athens ghettos, in the unemployed and the salary cuts for the low-paid and pensioners, in the treatment of the refugees and the wall built to keep the poor out and the Greeks in. But this unknown justice, which is always still to come, defines the struggles here and now.

Protesting against the worst abuses, asking to be seen, heard and acknowledged in a minimum way, even if they need to go to death for that, was the greatest service the *sans papiers* offered to Greece. They fought to be acknowledged as living by going to death. By resisting their dehumanisation, they became free and fought for the honour of Greeks against the iniquities of their government. They reminded that the theologico-political order, based on the ability to take life and let live, can be disrupted by removing the power of life and death from the sovereign. In Hegel's master and slave dialectic, the master achieves his position by going all the way in his struggle for recognition – prepared even to die – at which point the slave, fearing for his life, capitulates and accepts his servitude.

The strikers reversed the dialectic. Servants and almost slaves legally, without any formal recognition, they faced death in order to remove from the master the power to kill. In doing so collectively, they traced the promise of a new type of power not based on sacrifice, whether imposed or voluntary, but a type of power

4 J.-L. Nancy, 'State, Church, Resistance' (on file with author).

that goes to the edge of finitude and touches it but does not pierce or transcend it, as Jean-Luc Nancy puts it, because it does not need a bridge to an absolute outside or transcendent other. Their gift to the immigrants all over Europe was to tell them that they can take their lives in their hands against the iniquities and humiliations of governments, authorities and human rights fanatics. Their gift to the Greeks, in those hard days of February and March 2011, was to become the only truly free people of Athens. Their victory, at the end, was the victory of all and everyone.

Stasis syntagma

The Greek resistance to the catastrophic economic measures was expected. Throughout modern history the Greeks have resisted foreign occupation and domestic dictatorship with determination and sacrifice. In April 2010, I concluded an article in the *Guardian* that 'commentators fear that the Greek malaise is part of a wider attack on the euro'. Now that the measures are proving worse than the disease, their imposition may mark the return of radical politics. The defence of the common good and democracy, a proud Hellenic tradition, shows the political way out not just for Greece but for the whole of Europe. As the Icelandic volcano reminded us, the eruption of life-changing events is still an historical possibility.[5]

I was right. The Greek resistance against the austerity measures that have descended on Europe like the medieval plague has been more dynamic and successful than anywhere else. The austerity measures have led to 24 one- and two-day general strikes, numerous regional and sectional strikes and various imaginative acts of resistance and solidarity. Domestic and foreign media avidly reported, however, only the confrontations between youths and the riot police that followed demonstrations, leaving a thick cloud of teargas over-hanging Athens. Led by the parties of the left and the unions, these protests outshone the anti-austerity demonstrations in the rest of Europe. However, the politics of fear and guilt, peddled by government and mainstream media, extensive police provocation and the exaggerated reporting of the limited violence that followed the demonstrations had curtailed and contained the protests. The Greeks have been told that they had enjoyed life too much in the previous period, they had 'sinned' and overspent. Their punishment is therefore not undeserved. Yet the majority of the population, the low-paid and precariously employed, the pensioners, the unemployed, the young and the immigrants had not participated in the excessive consumption of the 1990s but are now asked to pay instead of the rich, the tax-evading professionals and the elites who prospered through state and political patronage and then siphoned their gains into Swiss bank accounts. No penalty is

5 C. Douzinas, 'Greece can fight back against neoliberals' *Guardian* (27 April 2010) available at http://www.guardian.co.uk/commentisfree/2010/apr/27/greece-imf-eu-welfare-state (accessed 26 November 2011).

visited, however, on those who actually enriched themselves through state borrowing and largess.

But suddenly something totally unexpected, almost miraculous, happened. On 25 May 2011, a motley multitude of indignant men and women of all ideologies, ages, races and occupations, including the many unemployed, began occupying Syntagma Square – the central square of Athens opposite Parliament; the area around White Tower in Thessaloniki; and public spaces in other major cities. Calling themselves *aganaktismenoi*, the 'outraged', the people have attacked the unjust impoverishment of working Greeks, the loss of sovereignty that has turned the country into a neocolonial fiefdom of bankers, and the turn of representative democracy into corruption, cleptocracy and clientellism. They have two demands: first the debt is not ours and we should not pay a penny; but this first demand opens to a wider call for direct democracy. The false democracy and the corrupt political elites who have ruled the country for some 40 years should go. Political parties and banners of all colours are discouraged.

Thousands of people came together daily in the *Syntagma* popular assembly to discuss the next steps. The parallels with the classical Athenian demos, which met a few hundred metres away, are striking. Aspiring speakers are given a number and called to the platform if that number is drawn, a reminder that the majority office-holders in classical Athens were selected by lots. The speakers stick to strict two-minute slots to allow as many as possible to contribute. The assembly is efficiently run without the usual heckling of public speaking. The topics range from politics and ideology to new types of resistance and international solidarity, to alternatives to the catastrophically unjust measures and to organisational matters. The topics for discussion are approved at the start by vote after a short presentation by the proposer and no issue is beyond proposal and disputation. In well organised weekly debates on specified topics of wide interest, invited economists, lawyers, political philosophers and activists present alternatives for tackling the economic crisis and discuss them with the people, again under strict time limits. Both panel topics and panellists are chosen through nominations and votes.

Syntagma's highly articulate debates have discredited the banal mantra that most issues of public policy are too technical for ordinary people and must be left to experts. The realisation that the demos has more collective nous than any leader, a constitutive belief of the classical *agora*, is now returning to Athens. The outraged have shown that parliamentary democracy must be supplemented with its more direct version. It is a timely reminder as the belief in political representation is coming under pressure throughout Europe.

The mainstream media have blamed the protests and the limited violence that followed them in set-piece confrontations between youths and the police on the divided left. This tactic cannot work with the outraged. They come from all parties and none but, more importantly, the *Syntagma* multitude has repeatedly declared its non-violent character. This repudiation of violence was much in evidence during the unprecedented events of late June 2011. The popular assembly decided to launch a determined campaign to stop Parliament enacting the law implementing a new tranche of austerity measures, the government had agreed with the bankers and Germany's Chancellor Merkel. To paraphrase Mae West, 'you cannot get enough of a bad thing'.

On 28 and 29 June, the *aganaktismenoi* tried to encircle Parliament and put pressure on the MPs voting on the legal measures implementing the *troika* demands. Trade unions and parties had also called for a two-day general strike and a march on Parliament. When the marchers reached Syntagma Square, the usual skirmishes started. The *aganaktismenoi* tried to stop the youths from hurling missiles and defended the square. After the initial exchanges, *Stasis Syntagma* experienced the most brutal recent police attack, with indiscriminate physical violence and the use of three tons of tear gas and other chemicals against the protesters. In times of war, as the Greek Medical Association and the Athens Bar stated, such extensive use of chemical weapons amounts to a war crime. The government adopted a different response to the multitude from that of a routine march and rally. The multitude stands opposite Parliament and challenges the political system; therefore, it must be attacked as the enemy, as a global and fundamental threat, not just as a case of protest and dissent. Police repressions have thus been gradually morphing into an undeclared war.

The peaceful spirit of the square carried the day. Despite attacks on the health and media centres, and on masses of people gathered in the metro station, the *aganaktismenoi* quickly returned, after the police withdrew, cleared the debris and held a mass assembly to discuss their next steps. The 28–29 June campaign formally failed to stop the passing of the policies into law. The government was able to collect the necessary 154 votes by pressurising its own MPs. After the June attacks, the riot police surrounded Syntagma Square and eventually violently removed the encampment in late July. In early September, smaller numbers started assembling again but brutal police repression showed that the government was determined not to allow the permanent occupation of the symbolic square again. The government is proposing a large increase of police measures and surveillance. George Papandreou, the Greek prime minister (until he was forced to resign in November 2011, partly as a result of popular resistance), has repeatedly stated that Greece is at war. It is becoming clear that the enemy is its own people.

The sequence December-*Syntagma*

The *Syntagma* events should be compared and contrasted with the December 2008 insurrection in Athens following the unprovoked killing by the police of 15-year-old schoolboy Alexis Grigoropoulos. Although totally different, even opposite at face view, the two events are nonetheless part of sequence that included the Paris riots in 2005 and 2007, Tunis, Tahrir Square and Puerta del Sol, as well as London 2011. They are different instantiations of the politics of resistance and the multitude. Most were reactions to specific events, the death of two boys in a Paris suburb in 2005, the killing of Alexis Grigoropoulos in Athens 2008, the self-immolation of Mohammed Bouazizi in Sidi Bouzid Tunisia in 2010, a rally of solidarity to the Spanish *indignados* in Athens 2011 and, finally, the killing of Mark Duggan in London in 2011. They all escalated into something much more general – some into widespread riots and insurrection; others into a confrontation with the political system. December 2008 and London 2011 did not articulate a central demand and this was perhaps their dominant characteristic.

Stasi Syntagma is the continuation and transcendence of December 2008. December was a condensation of causes, strategies and actions. As events developed, the insurrection took on an impetus of its own, drawing in ever larger numbers in a snowballing effect that kept unsettling every attempt at explanation or pacification. The listing of possible causes could not help to explain the effects. The before and the after became indistinguishable; causes, effects and actions were intertwined into a knot that could not be unravelled. In the same way that the coming of the insurrection could not have been predicted, its happening could not be controlled and its long terms effects are only now becoming clearer. This was a type of political action that could not simply be explained from what predated it or reduced to the sum of factors that made it possible.

It was precisely the rejection of routine politics that turned the insurrection into an *event*, in the technical sense of philosopher Alain Badiou. Every social and political situation has an infinite series of elements, classes, groups and people with different interests and ideologies, customs and habits. But in the midst of this infinity of differences there is an empty place, a void which, while invisible for the dominant forces, supports the stability of the totality. This void lies close to the most anonymous and vulnerable. An event is precisely a type of political action, which does not belong to the standard matrix of the situation from which it emerges. The December insurrection disrupted this settled state of recognised differences: what was invisible, unspoken and unspeakable (under the pre-existing rules) came to the fore. This made the insurrection difficult to comprehend. It turned these events from a common protest by students or workers into something new, which both retained the characteristics of urban resistance and politics and yet overtook them, radically changing the situation.

The antagonism that became visible in Athens resulted from the tension between the structured social body with its political representatives and, on the other side, groups, causes and interests radically excluded from the political order. Huge numbers of people cannot formulate their most essential demands in the language of a political problem. In this sense, the insurrection was an expression of political agency at its degree zero. The protesters do not say 'I want this or that' but simply, 'here we are, we stand against'. They do not say 'we claim this or that right'; instead they say 'we claim the right to have rights'. They seem to be saying that 'We, the nobodies, the schoolkids, the suffering students, the unemployed, the generation that must survive on a salary of €600, are everything'.

Before the event, political change is a matter of policing and consensus. After the event, politics returns to a certain normality; its terrain will have changed, however, through the appearance of newly politicised subjects and the rearrangement of the rules of political participation. The event is evanescent; its very purpose is to disappear. But its effect was immediate and drastic. A name was given, the 'December events'. Over the following year, political visibility and the meaning of politics was redefined. The right wing government was defeated in early elections, the PASOK government was elected on a false manifesto and, after it solicited the austerity measures, the new types of resistance began.

Let us compare the two events in the sequence: December was characterised by time, *Syntagma* by place, December by transience, *Syntagma* by permanence, December by violence, *Syntagma* by repudiation of violence, December by mobility, *Syntagma* by static presence. The mark or *Syntagma* is *stasis*. The upright posture as well as insurrection, the re-evolving or revolution of *stasis*. *Syntagma*'s relationship to space and time differed from December. Public spaces, squares in particular, are given to leisure, commercial activities and mild erotic encounters. *Syntagma* turns the square into a public space where different singularities exist in common, discuss, decide and act together. The square becomes *plethos*, a counter-hegemonic power with its distinct spatial and temporal aspects, something that the occupations of university buildings cannot offer.

The square allows the coming together of the multitude, in a material co-existence of bodies with a common political desire. It is doubly counter-hegemonic. Its strongest characteristic is the lack of a common ideological or political line, the absence of organised parties and political groupings, the banning of party banners, the wide nature of the slogans and the wide ranging nature of the popular assembly debates. People come to *Syntagma* as singular unique persons with their views and beliefs and not as representatives of political positions or ideologies. To be sure, many of the participants are party members and have strong ideological positions. But when they address the multitude, they are encouraged to speak for themselves and leave the party badges behind. This is of course impossible and perhaps undesirable. But the insistence that people join as individual members instead of representatives of absent views or causes is a major difference from standard party, union or university assemblies. This also means that people from all political views and none can join except for racists and extreme right-wingers. The *Syntagma* person is singular, unique even, bringing to the assembly her views and beliefs and respecting those of others, even if she strongly disagrees.

But *Stasis Syntagma* also mirrors, reverses and annuls the organisation of the state. A number of groups organise and offer the main public services: there is a medical group with a clinic in a tent, media, artistic and cultural groups, the cool group (the security), the food and water group, the cleaning group, the open democracy group etc. They are run democratically and more efficiently than any state department. The media group was so well organised and professional that I commented that if these unemployed PhD holders were transferred into the Inland Revenue as a group that tax evasion would be seriously restricted. But, unlike state organs, the groups and the daily popular assembly discuss every proposal directly, decide and act.

As far as time is concerned, December was characterised by spontaneity and unpredictability in response to the killing. It organised its temporality around institutional time, university and school term time and the Christmas period. *Syntagma* started equally in spontaneous fashion, the catalyst here being a rally of solidarity to the Spanish *indignados*. Here, however, the organisation of time follows the regularities of work. The thematic groups and popular assemblies meet every evening at 6.30pm after work. The major rallies take place on Sundays with the first three Sundays bringing out close to 1 million people; indeed, 47 per cent of the population visited the squares and 83 per cent approved their actions. *Syntagma* time is organised in strictly equal segments and is allocated according to a strict axiom of equality. The random choice of speakers is a reminder that many office holders in classical Athens were selected by lot. The views of the unemployed and the university professor are given equal time, discussed with equal vigour and put to the vote prior to adoption. Once a thematic assembly is decided, expert speakers are nominated and votes taken. When I was invited to speak on direct democracy, the panel had four speakers, 13 minutes were allocated to each speaker, 1 minute to the audience for questions and 3 minutes for the answers. These time limits were kept strictly.

But if there are so many differences between December and *Syntagma*, why insist that they should be seen as part of the same sequence? The persistent series of insurrections of the last decade, which include the Paris *banlieus*, Tehran, Tunisia, Egypt and Syria, as well as Puerta del Sol and London 2011 amongst many others, cannot be explained exclusively by technological innovation (the Facebook revolutions) nor is it a mere coincidence. Neither standard political science obsessed with the machinations of leaders, parties and state machinery nor orthodox Marxist class analysis can fully understand the new phenomenon that has changed the role of the street as a terrain of political action and conflict.

Biopolitical neoliberalism and the post-Fordist economy of services do not produce just commodities for subjects; instead, they create subjects. Material, social, affective, ethical and cognitive strategies are involved in this process. On the material side, working people have been integrated into late capitalist service economy with its emphasis on financialisation through private and public debt and consumption. People are treated as desiring and consuming machines and debt for consumption becomes the main motor of the economy. However, this has weakened intermediate institutions such as parties, unions, even the churches. It has also weakened the principle of representation both at the general political and at local and work levels.

The indebted white collar worker has an increased interest in the success of financial capitalism and has accepted that freedom of choice and personal responsibility are criteria of success. But this achievement is also the Achilles heel of late capitalism. The worker can withdraw abruptly and even violently if the main parameters of his integration become frustrated. If one of the links in the integration chain breaks (sudden loss of job or deterioration in conditions of life or expectations, persistent humiliation, attacks on personal or national dignity, frustration of desires or promises), the overall psychological and political architecture collapses. The violent disengagement from dominant behavioural patterns or the frustration of cultivated expectations leads either to acting out (violent attacks and public disorder) or innovative political resistance of which *Stasis Syntagma* is the best example. This is what unites all these events and turns them into a sequence of resistance that will dominate the world political landscape in the future. Both types are political: December politics at degree zero, *Stasis Syntagma* the emerging essence of new democratic politics.

Biopower creates subjectivities through the control of conduct and emotions while being relatively indifferent towards ideas. This means that traditional theories of ideology or hegemony have lost some of their purchase, as affect, bodily discipline, control and comportment become more important for system integration than ideological alignments. If hegemony operates as control of conduct, counter-hegemony attacks the channelling or the conduct of conduct and tries to undermine dominant behavioural patterns. Democratic and civil disobedience, massive peaceful and democratic counter-power challenge post-political governance and place power's operation on the agenda. The biopolitical project to control individual bodies and minds and turn the people into a pliant body politic fails. This de- and re-subjectification of people is what power fears most.

Extensive civil disobedience, spontaneous insurrections, multitudes without leaders but with strong political desire for radical change and hegemonic confrontation of the ruling elites have become the mark of politics in the 21st century. *Stasis Syntagma* has come closer to Cairo's Tahrir Square than to Madrid's Puerta del Sol. The collective withdrawal of legitimacy and the individual experience of standing daily and confronting the Parliament opposite have changed the politics of Greece for good and made the elites worried for the first time. The square was named after the 19th century demonstrations, which demanded a constitution (*syntagma*) from the king. This is what the *aganaktismenoi* repeat today: they are standing upright, demanding a new political arrangement to free them from neo-liberal domination, political corruption and post-democratic malaise. As I write, Syntagma Square is kept empty by the riot police. Whether it fills again or not, as the Greek tragedy reaches its endgame, the *stasis* had radically changed politics by creating new political subjects. Massive disobedience today is the antechamber for radical political change, perhaps the only one we have.

Chapter 3

A different constituent power

Agamben and Tunisia

Illan rua Wall[1]

Introduction

Constituent power is fundamentally the potentiality of radical political change. Revolt, rebellion and revolution are usually imagined when we talk about this power, but we might also include radical dissent, dissensus, subversion and even treason (understood collectively). It remains crucial to current legal and political relations. Even aside from the political unrest and anger currently unfolding around the globe,[2] constituent power is at the heart of our understanding of the legal and political constitution of the modern state. It pervades questions of power, authority and right. Therefore it is perhaps a little surprising to hear Giorgio Agamben suggest that 'concepts of sovereignty and constituent power which are at the core of our political traditions have to be abandoned or, at least, to be thought all over again . . . and those who continue to use these concepts uncritically literally do not know that they are talking about'.[3] For Agamben, constituent power is too overburdened with biopolitical sovereignty. Constituent power, as traditionally portrayed, presents a paradigm for political and legal modernity. The people *wills* the legal order – they conceive (of) a constituted order which is imprinted with the stamp of their authority. The law's legitimacy is thus guaranteed by the originary

1 I would like to thank: Tom Frost, who invited me to present an early draft of this at the *Symposium on Agamben and the Future of Law*, at the University of Newcastle; Carolina Olarte Olarte (Birkbeck College), Stacy Douglas (University of Kent), Matthew Stone (University of Essex) and Bríd Spillane have constantly and productively interrogated these ideas. I would also like to express my thanks to Hager Westlati (Kingston University, London), Elena Loizidou (Birkbeck College), Daniel McLoughlin (University of Adelaide) and Daniel Matthews (Birkbeck College), who have all read and commented on earlier versions of this text. Any and all mistakes, misreadings or oversights are entirely my own.

2 As I finish this work in 2011, the Arab Spring is continuing, the Spanish *indignados* seem to have waned, the Chilean student protests continue, the Occupy movement remains encamped in Wall Street, St. Paul's Cathedral and a massive variety of economic and political targets, the Greek crisis is deepening and spreading, apparently 'infecting' the Eurozone itself. Crisis is on everyone's lips.

3 G. Agamben, *Means Without End: Notes on Politics* (Minneapolis: University of Minnesota Press, 2000) 112.

will of the people. The metaphysics of this schema is not difficult to spot – the manner in which the people is constituted as a unity or the authority guaranteed by this unity are direct transpositions of theologically constituted sovereignty. In the wake of the 'death of God' the problem for continental philosophy, and Agamben in particular, is how to interrupt sovereignty in a manner which does not simply repeat metaphysical structures.

I want to develop Agamben's suggestion of a different possibility of 'constituent power' (although he disposes of the term), through a reading of certain aspects of the events in Tunisia from December 2010 to March 2011. The Ben Ali regime presented an intensive regime where disciplinary techniques of surveillance and governmentality were mixed with sovereign logics of exceptionality and decisionism. Whilst to a large extent these apparatuses of sovereign power can be seen around the world in both 'democratic' and 'authoritarian' states,[4] it remains worthwhile to examine their particular constellation in Tunisia. My argument is ultimately that by understanding the techniques of power utilised by Ben Ali, we may begin to see commonalities with various strategies of resistance to biopolitical regimes around the world. However, I must clarify from the outset that by putting these strategies of resistance in Tunisia together with Agamben's thoughts on constituent power, I intend to make use of a certain tension or friction. I will neither attempt to make the Tunisian events fit with Agamben's theoretical paradigm, nor will I seek to reduce the multiplicity of the Tunisian events to one aspect. Nevertheless, I do suggest that there are certain points of consonance, certain parallels between 'the coming community' and the overthrow of Ben Ali.

Ben Ali: biopolitics and sovereignty

Ben Ali came to power in 1987 after a 'medical coup', where the attending doctors declared President Habib Bourguiba no longer medically fit to remain in office. Ben Ali proposed gradually to introduce representative democracy, liberalise markets and ensure European security. He was hailed by the IMF as a 'good pupil'

4 The bifurcation of 'authoritarian' and 'democratic' states is distinctly unhelpful. The current Western projection of authoritarian and democratic is a historically constructed constellation, whose borders are constantly in flux depending upon global political tensions and alliances. An extension of this is that the demand that certain states be deemed 'democratic' and therefore are granted an unquestionable legitimacy is deeply problematic. The mechanisms of power described in this chapter are often exercised in different fashions in western 'liberal-democracies'. The recent attempt at 'total policing' in London around student protests demonstrates this. There has been intensive surveillance, letters explaining activists' precariousness if they attend protests, open 'kettling' and a variety of other deeply chilling approaches to statements of discontent. This should be read, as Nancy suggested in the early 1980s, not in opposition to 'totalitarianism' but as new and ever changing instances of 'soft totalitarianism'. See J.-L. Nancy and P. Lacoue-Labarthe, *Retreating the Political* (ed S. Sparks London: Routledge, 1997).

for undertaking privatisation, increasing foreign investment and emphasising tourism.[5] However, as has been widely reported, he generated conditions of deep insecurity for the majority of the population and facilitated the development of a cleptocracy for his inner circle. The question presented by Tunisia is how Ben Ali maintained his power for over 20 years. Salvatore tells of a joke often repeated during the overthrow of Mubarak in Egypt: a protestor demands, 'Mr President, isn't it time to prepare a farewell speech to the people?' to which the Mubarak replies 'Why, where are the people going?'[6] At the base of this joke is the dissonance between the projection of popular sovereignty and the naturalness of Mubarak's rule. It is more conceivable that the people would leave the country than that 'their' leader would step down. In Tunisia, this apparently 'natural' quality to the regime was called the 'pact of obedience'[7] or the 'security pact'.[8]

In a work of extraordinary depth and precision, Beatrix Hibou explains that this pact should not be understood as a traditional social contract where the people grant some sort of natural liberty in order to gain security and governance. This is not a Hobbesean or Lockean paradigm.[9] Rather, the pact 'expresses the permanent and ubiquitous solicitude of the state, the way it claims to present itself and legitimise itself in the eyes of its population. A security pact is a relation within which the state attempts to forestall all uncertainty, risk and danger'.[10] The pact is a narrative of governance, whereby a social contract style of agreement is *projected*, in order to legitimate the government. It was constantly reperformed in periodic (rigged) elections and public rituals of obedience. It made use of various economic and political fictions (security, employment and growth being three central tenets); however, these were not the real purpose of the pact. Rather, it was a political projection designed to ensure *obedience* through physical and psychological force.

5 A. Honwana, 'Youth and the Tunisian Revolution' *SSRC Conflict Prevention Forum* available at http://webarchive.ssrc.org/pdfs/Alcinda_Honwana,_Youth_and_the_Tunisian_Revolution,_September_2011-CPPF_policy%20paper.pdf (accessed 29 November 2011) at 12.

6 A. Salvatore, 'The Elusive Subject of Revolution' available at http://blogs.ssrc.org/tif/2011/02/16/the-elusive-subject-of-revolution/ (accessed 11 November 2011).

7 N. Marzouki, 'From People to Citizens in Tunisia' *Middle East Research and Information Project No 259* available at http://www.merip.org/mer/mer259/people-citizens-tunisia#_3_ (accessed 30 November 2011).

8 See B. Hibou, *The Force of Obedience: The Political Economy of Repression in Tunisia* (London: Polity Press, 2011) 181–207.

9 This is precisely the mistake that Arieff makes in the US Congression Report on Tunisia. He suggests that: 'During the presidency of Ben Ali, many analysts contended that there was an implicit social contract between the government and its citizens, which promoted economic stability and middle-class standards of living at the expense of political freedom'. However, as Hibou demonstrates, this is precisely *not* what the security pact is about. A. Arieff, 'Political Transition in Tunisia' *Congressional Research Service 2011* available at http://fpc.state.gov/documents/organization/161570.pdf (accessed 11 November 2011) at 15.

10 Hibou, *The Force of Obedience* 181–82.

The security pact had nothing to do with exchange of natural liberty for security between the people and the sovereign, but rather framed the *necessity* of habitual obedience by establishing the naturalness of Ben Ali's rule.

At the heart of this pact was a layering of inclusion and exclusion. The narrative of the state emphasised that the regime could promise eternal growth of around 5 per cent, foster real development, generate inward investment, be business friendly, support home and car ownership etc. The correlation of this was that all Tunisians would be *included* in this economic miracle – guaranteed by the genius of the regime. However, whilst this narrative of public benefit remained universal in its projection, it was premised on a fine delineation of 'loyalty'. Fidelity to the regime was measured by one's relation to the RCD party. The party became the nervous system of the country, with access to and control over vast resources, both public and private. The party used the threat of being cut off from any possibility of social progress as a manner of generating a certain biopolitical fealty. The potential gain of loyalty to the party was being 'cut-in' on the corruption and cronyism embodied by the Ben Ali clan. However, for most of the population inclusion meant periodic ritualised expressions of support generating a spectacle of loyalty in the public sphere. Hibou gives the example of the presentation of images of Ben Ali in people's houses and places of work, arguing that the images

> . . . did not express any belief in the benefits of the President's 'solicitude', they did not praise his 'progressiveness', they did not declare the 'faith' of the citizen in a protective regime. They were merely a way of participating in a formalized ritual, thereby showing that people knew the system and that they recognized its mechanisms: such behaviour showed that they knew (full well) how to behave in a ritualized context so as to maintain or even improve their social status without thereby rejecting or accepting the rules of the political game.[11]

Thus the regime generated two possibilities: proactive support or habitual obedience. Either would be supported or tolerated because they did not allow any space for the expression of alienation from the regime.

Biopolitics operates to deny any space for alienation from sovereign power. In *Democracy and the Foreigner*, Honig suggests that Rousseau's foreign law-giver and Freud's portrayal of Moses demonstrate two symbolic expressions of alienation from law.[12] Both figures come from beyond the *demos* and impose a law. She suggests that both Rousseau and Freud are tapping into a crucial experience of sovereignty as foreign, suggesting that this alienation is fundamental to any resistance against unjust laws. Biopolitics, when used in conjunction with sovereignty, attempts to

11 ibid xvii.
12 B. Honig, *Democracy and the Foreigner* (Princeton: University of Princeton Press, 2001).

close the space opened up by this alienation. It weaves the authority and power of the sovereign through every aspect of life itself, generating the projection of a fundamental inclusion where its subjects identify their prosperity and survival with sovereign power. In Tunisia, there were many mechanisms managing this delineation of loyalty. Hibou suggests that credit and taxation, for instance, were used to facilitate micro-surveillance.[13] Tax avoidance might be tolerated by local party officials, but such implicit tolerance would come with the knowledge that any hint of dissent would lead to the full enforcement of the law. The power and authority of the government was tied both to the everyday desire of its subjects and to exceptional instances of the power of life and death – as Foucault suggested in a different context.[14] With this, bio-power and sovereign power were thus intertwined with the very life of subjects.

I should make it clear that 'inclusion' is not simply a liberal understanding of 'toleration of difference'. Rather, it is a much more violent process whereby the terms of one's inclusion are generated on the excision of any directly political opposition. The Ben Ali regime sought to regulate dissent tightly. However, it did not simply crush all opposition. Quite the opposite. Ben Ali allowed minor disagreement from what was called the 'loyal opposition'. Despite the lack of any major showing in elections, he granted this 'loyal opposition' a fifth of the seats in the Parliament.[15] This meant that the oppositions' place in political life was dependent upon Ben Ali's decision and their privileged position was entirely dependent upon their loyalty. Thus, any dissent that they might express was limited. The condition of their continued existence in Parliament was that they should not succeed in gathering any real support among the population. Their opposition was premised on *not* presenting any real challenge to Ben Ali. Thus, again we can see the structuring around a trope of inclusion/exclusion. Certain opposition was included but limited and controlled, while at the same time real opposition was excluded.

Let me turn to the exclusion. The sovereign decision of friend or enemy was operationalised in the Ben Ali state apparatus by rendering it as an everyday occurrence, distributed to every level of the regime's apparatus. When it came to macro-level opposition or disobedience on a micro-level, the regime could exclude any subject from its 'protection'. This might entail the exercise of the regime's full violence: torture, disappearance or exile were not uncommon for those involved in the radical left or Islamic politics. However, perhaps a more subtle exercise of disciplinary power was the use of a 'social death'. This included the confiscation of all paperwork associated with accessing any healthcare, public services or the labour market. One subject of this 'social death' explained:

13 Hibou, *The Force of Obedience* chs 1, 2 and 5.

14 M. Foucault, *Society Must Be Defended* (Picador: London, 2003) ch 11.

15 B. Powel and L. Sadiki, *Europe and Tunisia: Democratization via Association* (London: Routledge, 2010) 129. See also Arieff, 'Political Transition in Tunisia' 15.

> There's a constant attack on private life. When the police come into a house, when they seize your passports, ID, diplomas and medical cards. And at any moment, even if you've done your time in gaol, even if your case is theoretically closed, you can be summonsed, questioned, detained, re-sentenced.[16]

The constant harassment at once punishes the dissident, but occurs in the most public of senses. 'Social death' occurs *in* a society; it does not come from isolation. Rather, it forces the socially excluded dissident to live among others who continue as normal. Thus, these others act as an example to the dissident, and the dissident acts as an example for the rest of society. If the dissident's family were to rally around their excluded member, they too would become *persona non grata*.[17]

At the juncture of inclusion and exclusion, there was the intense operation of the state apparatus. Surveillance and other disciplinary mechanisms were the *sine qua non* for this biopolitical sovereign structure. We hear echoes of various police states in the plentiful descriptions of Tunisians' perceptions that everyone around them was a potential spy.[18] The police ran a network of informers. It was not uncommon for people to be picked up by police after making loose political remarks in a café. Taxis were a famous place for the exercise of governmental power, to the extent that the word 'taxi' became synonymous with 'nosy cops'.[19] These mechanisms of surveillance instantiate the theory of the panopticon, where the watchful gaze of the state is internalised. However, it also opens onto another reading. Let me suggest that the power of the police to pick up subjects and beat up or detain them for some time is what Benjamin called the 'real state of exception'.[20] This does away with the juridical question of whether a *de jure* emergency has been declared, and instead insists that the oppressed of any society are always subject to an indistinction between force and violence.[21] In other words,

16 Hibou, *The Force of Obedience* 5.
17 An instance of this comes from radical philosopher Mehdi Belhaj Kacem, who was working in France in the years of Ben Ali's regime. He wrote of his fear of speaking out against events in Tunisia, for fear that his family would become targets of the regime. See 'A Tunisian Renaissance: Interview with Mehdi Belhaj Kacem' available at http://www.lacan.com/thesymptom/?page_id=1046 (accessed 11 November 2011).
18 Kacem describes this: 'In Tunisia, you couldn't find a single café that wasn't watched by the police; if you made a joke about Ben Ali on the phone, within an hour you'd be missing a few teeth' ibid.
19 Hibou, *The Force of Obedience* 83.
20 In his eighth thesis on the concept of history, he writes that the: 'tradition of the oppressed teaches us that the "state of exception" in which we live is the rule. We must attain to a concept of history that accords with this fact. Then we will clearly see that it is our task to bring about the real [*wirklich*] state of exception, and this will improve our position in the struggle against fascism'. See W. Benjamin, 'These on the Concept of History' in G. Agamben, *State of Exception* (Chicago: University of Chicago Press, 2005) 57.
21 See G. Sorel, *Reflections on Violence* (London: George Allen & Unwin, 1916) or Benjamin 'A Critique of Violence' in W. Benjamin, *Reflections* (New York: Schoken Books, 1978) for further elaboration of this distinction.

in the real state of exception every 'fiction of a nexus between violence and law disappears here: there is nothing but a zone of anomie, in which a violence without any juridical form acts'.[22] In this zone of anomie the state may act without restraint. This would be a sovereign logic of decision and exception, except in Ben Ali's regime the decision of inclusion/exclusion was rendered everyday by its distribution throughout the polity. In a sense, anyone might exercise the decision by informing.[23] The apparatuses of power developed in Ben Ali's regime demonstrate the precariousness of life under a real state of exception. But when the revolt began, the zone of anomie which he had created became crucial to the very nature of the rupture.[24]

Let me pull out two aspects of the revolt that have been largely overlooked, and which I suggest are crucial: refusal and suspension. Over the initial three months 'the people' on the streets cried '*dégage*' (go away, clear off, get out). This was first and foremost a simple statement of refusal, but it was a refusal of the situation as a whole. First it was levelled at Ben Ali, but later at the RCD, the secret police and the succession of those who would reperform the old order.[25] However, a rejection of the situation as a whole is at once too broad to be a 'political demand' and too indeterminate to be a clear critique. As such, there was no immediate content to this refusal. At various stages the protestors placed many different demands in this refusal. If you like, the refusal became a vehicle for multiple determinate material demands. Crucially, however, the refusal did not entail a positive representational position from the protestors. This meant that at no point could Ben Ali or his successors gain purchase. There was no party or ideology that preconstituted this refusal. It was not planned or willed by a central committee.

22 Agamben, *State of Exception* 59.

23 In *Society Must be Defended* (at 259) Foucault described the manner in which biopower and sovereign power was brought together in Fascism by spreading the power over life and death through-out society, by giving anyone the power 'over his or her neighbours, if only because of the practice of informing, which effectively meant doing away with people next door, or having them done away with'.

24 G. Agamben, *Homo Sacer: Sovereign Power and Bare Life* (Stanford: Stanford University Press, 1998).

25 Usher suggests that there were two revolutions in Tunisia: The first everyone knows about, starting from the self-immolation of Mohamed Bouazizi and ending with the flight from power of Ben Ali on 14 January 2011. The second, however, is often overlooked. 'From January 14 . . . to March 3 a grassroots national/popular coalition of trade unions, leftists, lawyers associations, human rights organisations and Islamists mainly but not only from Nahda laid siege to Casbah Square and other sites in the capital to protest any and all attempts by the ancien régime to steal back the revolution . . . Rolling campaigns of civil disobedience swept away two cabinets, forcing the resignation of Ben Ali-appointed governors in the provinces; the dissolution of his ruling Constitutional Democratic Party (RCD); and the disbanding of the state security apparatus.' See G. Usher, 'That Other Tunisia' *The Nation* (12 September 2011) 32.

There was no revolutionary organisation that could be said to 'author' the events.[26] All that was held in common in this constituent moment was an anger at the state of the situation, the negative imprint of the regime's everyday injustice.

The regime could not perform the usual inclusion/exclusion, precisely because they were faced with a *refusal*. They could not triangulate with the protestors because they made no 'policy' proposal.[27] Until he was deposed in mid-January 2011, Ben Ali clearly hoped to be able to 'include' the protestors. This is evidenced by his visit to the death-bed of Bouazizi, his constant attempts to talk down the significance of the protests and his denial of 'military' violence. The regime demanded that the force/violence[28] mobilised against the protestors was merely a 'police' rather than a 'military' force/violence. The evidence of assassination and massacre calls this directly into question, but on a symbolic level such a material rebuttal is less signficant. Ben Ali sought (violently) to 'include' the protestors. He relied upon his experience of quashing the Gafsa revolt in 2008.[29] If this was

26 Kacem suggests in 'A Tunisian Renaissance' that: 'It's a revolution that has more in common with the Situationists or Rancière, that is, a revolution carried out directly by the people, than with the Leninist or Maoist "Revolution", in which an armed avant-garde takes over power and replaces one dictatorship with another without ever passing through "democracy"'.

27 This did not stop Ben Ali trying. At various stages he offered to 'invest $5 billion in development projects and to employ 50,000 university graduates in the next few months . . . to create 300,000 jobs over the next two years'. He also offered to release everyone arrested in the unrest, and actually sacked Rafik Haj Kacem, the Minister of the Interior. See Honwana, 'Youth and the Tunisian Revolt' 3–4. Honwana describes Ben Ali's last grasp at inclusion: 'On January 13, a curfew was declared for Greater Tunis, which includes Tunis, Ariana, Ben Arous, and La Manouba, from 8 p.m. until 5:30 a.m. Ben Ali addressed the nation and promised to respond positively to the unrest if violence ended right away. He declared that he would not seek reelection in 2014. Ben Ali said: "I have understood you all . . . I'm speaking to you because the situation needs radical change; yes, a radical change . . . I understand the unemployed, the needy, the politicians, all those demanding more freedom. I have understood everyone. But what is happening today is not the way Tunisians do things". Ben Ali announced that he had ordered his security forces not to use firearms against the protestors. For the first time in his twenty-three year presidency, he used colloquial Tunisian rather than Modern Standard Arabic (MSA) in parts of his speech. According to El Mustapha Lahlali, an Arabic scholar, "by switching to dialect, Ben Ali may have been trying to appeal to a wider section of Tunisian society, especially those less educated people who could not easily follow his speech in MSA. He may also have wanted to remind his own people that he is a Tunisian and try to bridge the social gap between himself and the wider Tunisian public. The use of dialect could also be interpreted as an attempt to bypass the middle-class people taking part in the protests"' (at 5).

28 I use this awkward construction here to allude to Sorel and Benjamin's deconstruction of the authorisation of violence. See Sorel, *Reflections of Violence* and Benjamin, 'Critique of Violence'.

29 I should just make clear that the 'inclusionary' violence is no less violent. There is murder, torture and rape going on, but it lies behind the mirage of the neo-liberal state. The Gafsa protest was managed by hiding it from the international media, by confining it to the interior of the country and then by crushing it with mass detention and violence.

merely 'unrest' then it could be dealt with through everyday police operations. The other possibility open to him was to mobilise a full and unrestrained 'military' force/violence, as we have since seen in Libya, Syria, Bahrain and Yemen. The symbolic significance of this would be to eschew any claim to the (violent) 'inclusion' and instead manifest the exclusionary power of the state in all its violence.

The refusal entailed in the Tunisian *dégage* is the first aspect which is shared by many of the recent revolts in Africa, Europe and Latin America: a resistance which refuses originary manifesto or demand. Rather, it is gathered by the refusal of the particular situation. We see this from Puerto del Sol to the Occupy movement. An indeterminate and empty signifier is used to generate points of consonance between multiple political trajectories. In Tunisia, as elsewhere, these bodies of protest were held together by anger. Nancy writes:

> Anger is the political sentiment par excellence. It brings out the qualities of the inadmissible, the intolerable. It is a refusal and a resistance that with one step goes beyond all that can be accomplished reasonably in order to open possible paths for a new negotiation of the reasonable but also paths of an uncompromising vigilance. Without anger, politics is accommodation and trade in influence; writing without anger traffics in the seductions of writing.[30]

This anger traced the contours of the biopolitical regime. Without wishing to render the self-immolation of Mohammed Bouazizi an originary moment, I suggest that what made Bouazizi's intimate act of desperation and futility so resonant was that it communicated this in common. It was a gesture that marked and traced the everyday injustice shared by all in the situation, but about which all had to remain silent. Bouazizi sparked the initial anger, but the real story is how he then fades from the picture. Rather than fetishising him as Western media has done, in Tunisia he is seen in the context of a wider struggle against Ben Ali; nevertheless, the self-immolation remains the spark that lit the tinderbox of tensions.[31] Chomiak explains that 'an unintended consequence of regime strategies to obliterate oppositional political spaces is that such strategies indeed produce the various forms of opposition and resistance that they attempt to silence'.[32] In this sense, the biopolitical fealty demanded by Ben Ali was productive of biopolitical resistance. Bouazizi's gesture was a withdrawal from the situation, but marked in flame. It summed up the hopelessness and utter fury towards a regime that cannot allow expression of alienation. It marked this withdrawal through the site of such

30 J.-L. Nancy, 'The Compearance: From the Existence of Communism to the Community of Existence' (1992) 20(3) *Political Theory* 371.

31 See Honwana, 'Youth and the Tunisian Revolution' 8, for a further analysis of the contrast between Western fetishisation and Tunisian contextualisation.

32 L. Chomiak, 'The Making of a Revolution in Tunisia' (2011) 3 *Middle East Law and Governance* 68, 76.

regulation – the body. As such it was, perhaps, the most radical of refusals, manifesting the negativity of death in the public square as rejection of the entire situation. My argument is that we should read both this self-immolation and the revolt that follows it as a reappropriation of the negativity at the heart of the regime.

The question of suspension is perhaps more straightforward. Ben Ali's regime operated in an advanced state of sovereign power where the *real* state of exception was manifested on ordinary people, while it could appear to foreign observers and tourists that everything was 'normal'. The precariousness of the population generated by the apparatuses of the security pact ensured obedience by atomising risk. This individuation ensured the subjective experience of being alone in one's inclusion/exclusion, excluded precisely from any solidarity that might generate an outside to the pact of obedience. In this, the sovereign decision became entwined with the everyday relationships of the population. One's 'inclusion' in the sovereign order became premised upon certain modes of being-together. However, what was demonstrated in the months after Bouazizi's self-immolation is the manner in which the structure of the sovereign state of exception could be displaced. Just as Ben Ali ran the country in a perpetual real state of exception, the protests took hold of the exception and suspended the sovereign decision at its heart by refusing the everyday sovereignty (of police, RCD and the Ministry of the Interior).

The real state of exception that the protestors grasped sought to suspend the violence of the state apparatus – the everyday regime of biopolitical sovereignty. In both Tunisia and Egypt there was a huge effort to disrupt the ordinary running of the state. In both countries people grappled with the civil service, police and army in order to convince them to refuse. One of the most powerful acts of the Tunisian protests occurred on 14 January 2011 – the day that Ben Ali sacked his cabinet and resigned. The country came out in a general strike, and thousands of people surrounded the Ministry of the Interior.[33] They restrained and blocked the civil service from undertaking the ordinary workings of the state bureaucracy. Workers were not allowed into the building and no one could gain any form of permit or document. This was an act followed later in Egypt when protesters stood before the doors of the *Mugamma* building in which the bureaucracy was based. In Tunisia it had a particular resonance. Writing during Ben Ali's regime, Hibou suggested that:

33 'Tunisia: President Zine al-Abidine Ben Ali Forced Out' (15 January 2011) available at http://www.bbc.co.uk/news/world-africa-12195025 (accessed on 30 November 2011). In 'A Tunisian Renaissance' Kacem describes this focus: 'Young proletarians, thousands of them, set out on foot from one of the cities where the revolt started, a city that's been severely hit by unemployment and poverty, Sidi Bou Zid. They arrived in front of the interior ministry then set up at the Kasbah in Tunis. They slept on the ground. At first they were offered a thousand dinars each (and even, it seems, hashish!) to return to their homes. They adamantly refused: "We didn't come here for your money, we came here for *our* freedom!" "Power to the people!" – all day in front of the interior ministry'. See also Honwana, 'Youth and the Tunisian Revolution' 4–5.

> The ubiquity of the Ministry of the Interior is not merely physical. It is also moral, administrative and political. Moral first and foremost, in the sense that all public policies or economic projects have taken on board [their] watchwords of stability, security and public order. All the other administrations depend in some way on the Ministry of the Interior.[34]

Ben Ali had realised, very early on, that it was the country's *interiority* that was crucial. Between the Ministry and the RCD party, he had sought to create a powerful nervous system that would be omnipresent and could control social, economic and political wellbeing.

The pact of obedience operated through an everyday sovereignty – the monotony of regulation and discipline. Thus, there could be nothing more powerful than sealing off the site of regulation. Crucially, the suspension of the state's bureaucratic operation did not somehow immediately defeat the state. This was no taking of the Winter Palace. However, as can be seen over and over again, there is no site that is so invested with power that its occupation would effect an immediate overthrow. Rather, in biopolitical regimes a suspension of the ordinary and everyday operation of the state has a different goal. In this case, the police and bureaucracy were the two faces of the regime – the façade where the common people touched constituted power. The suspension of the state's everyday authority and force does little to the state; however, it generates a different space. The point is precisely that in Boulevard Habib Bourguiba or Tahrir Square: life continued without the police and without the civil service. The constituted order was suspended and instead spaces of alegality were generated.[35]

Ben Ali's regime manifested an intensive form of biopolitics. The resistance engendered by the revolt sought to suspend the everyday decision on inclusion/exclusion and suspend the force of obedience. It came together around the negative imprint of the regime itself. However, most Western readings have focused upon the substance of demands generated through political representation. They have been guided by a liberal understanding of constituent power, which sees the significance of the rupture in the law which it institutes afterwards. The underlying reading was that a people were rising up against their tyrant. The events were portrayed as a democratic upwelling of the will to freedom. However, this will to freedom was also a will to constitution. Thus, once the political revolution had been 'achieved' – when Ben Ali was removed – the Western narrative shifted. Increasingly there were demands of stability from the West, thereby stopping the unrest and determining what was achievable in the revolt. Demands for economic justice, employment and the end of cleptocracy were eschewed in this mantra of security. Increasingly, commentators talked of their fears for a state that 'lacked a

34 Hibou, *Force of Obedience* 82.

35 See H. Lindahl, 'The Opening: Alegality and Political Agonism' in *Law and Political Agonism* (ed A. Schaap Aldershot: Ashgate, 2009).

democratic tradition'.[36] The ideal progression of a liberal revolt is thus perfectly captured. Just as in Locke, Kant or Sieyès, the emphasis of the democratic will to freedom was on law. The problem, I would suggest with such a narrative, is that it fundamentally misunderstands the manner in which biopolitics and sovereignty have become entwined. It places the legal as the end point of the constituent moment. Agamben's critique of constituent power is thus a useful rejoinder. Let me turn to it, in order to draw out some of the points of consonance and dissonance.

Constituent power and the problem of biopolitics

In *Homo Sacer* Agamben suggests that constituent power does not provide any sort of counter-power to the sovereign's order. Rather, it is tied to and subsumed by its relation to the constituted order. The problem of constituent power for Agamben demonstrates the operation of biopolitics entwinement with sovereignty, and the difficulty of escaping this problem. He turns to the French revolutionary theorist Sieyès to explain this position. Sieyès argues that the third estate (the common people, as distinct from the aristocracy and clergy) is the entire nation, and therefore is authorised to overthrow the existing monarchic system. The nation, he explains, can be understood in *substance* and *form*. The substance of the nation is its economic and social existence, and the form of nationhood is 'a common law and a common representation'. The substantive preconditions of nationhood are divided into two, what Foucault renames 'functions and apparatuses'. The functions are agriculture, handicrafts, industry, trade and the liberal arts; and the apparatuses are the army, justice, the church and the administration. Sieyès tells us that the third estate in pre-revolutionary France already has the substance of a nation, but not the form.

36 An instance of this was the BBC Radio 4 programme, 'The Moral Maze' (2 February 2011) available at http://www.bbc.co.uk/iplayer/episode/b00y2snp/Moral_Maze_02_02_2011/ (accessed 29 November 2011). Michael Buerk, the host, began the programme with the question: 'What should we do when the autocracies we support, not always selfishly, are overthrown by their peoples, and if that's the question why do we think democracy is the answer? Is democracy really the unqualified good its made out to be? Or in societies that are poor, ill-educated, ethnically divided, lacking the rule of law or an indpendent judiciary or a passingly free media, can it make things worse? So two questions. Is it wrong to support regimes we don't like because we think we'll like the alternative even less? Or if this plan A comes unstuck, is democracy, the will of the people, however imperfectly it is derived, the only morally acceptable alternative?' Throughout, Buerk hints that Egyptians, Tunisians and others are 'a people' not quite enlightened enough to take up the burden of democracy. This is developed by his insistence that the West does not always *selfishly* support these autocrats. He is hinting, quite clearly, that in certain instances, the West must take up the 'white man's burden' and prop up autocracies for the good of the unenlightened people. The questions from 'the panel' circle around whether 'we' – the West – should intervene. Over and over, there is a refusal to see any true sense of agency in the North African countries.

The formal (juridical) precondition of the nation then is the nexus between common law and the agency to create law (legislature). Thus, Sieyès argues that for a nation to be a nation it must take this form of common law legislature. For the nation to crystallise, the third estate must realise itself as the nation. The third estate has been nothing, should be everything, but only wants to become something. But if the third estate is the nation, then it is authorised to grasp *its own* power – the constituent power. Such a move is made *natural* in Sieyès. The nation is the power and the authority to give itself the form of state. However, this form of state is already determined by his formal definition of the nation as a common law and common representation. Thus, the exercise of the third estate's constituent power is intimately bound with a higher order of sovereignty, given in the form and content of the third estate. The exercise of this power is pre-authorised by pre-figuring both the manner in which the new emerges and in the form of the state that must emerge. With this the possibility of the constituent moment is reduced to the realisation of nationhood.

However, Agamben is interested in the manner in which Sieyès conceives of the relation between the constitution and the nation's constituent power. He quotes Sieyès: 'The constitution first of all presupposes a constituent power'.[37] Agamben argues that this is not a simple truism, but that 'the constitution presupposes itself as a constituent power'.[38] Here Sieyès is not suggesting that constituent power can be superseded by the constitution; in fact, precisely the opposite. Sieyès explicitly says: 'The nation exists prior to everything; it is the origin of everything. Its will is always legal. It is the law itself'.[39] Thus, Agamben's reading can be clarified as saying that Sieyès makes constituent power into the very constitution itself. The nation *wills* the law; this is why its form is given in a legal manner. As such the exercise of constituent power *is* the constitution. What Sieyès is trying to do here is to authorise the exercise of constituent power by setting a transcendent set of conditions and effects in place. However, Agamben's point is slightly different. From Sieyès, he can argue that 'the sovereign power divides itself into [constituent] power and constituted power and maintains itself in relation to both, positioning itself at their point of indistinction'.[40] Sovereign power in Sieyès is not the constituted order of laws and legislature, nor the constituent power of the nation, but rather the point of indistinction between the two. Constituent power is other to constituted power, but the sovereign power stands above these and subsumes them in their difference.

We see this more clearly in *State of Exception*, where Agamben returns to this question through the debate between Schmitt and Benjamin. He argues that a conversation occurs between those authors, starting with the publication of *The*

37 Agamben, *Homo Sacer* 40.
38 ibid.
39 E. J. Sieyès, *Political Writings* (ed M. Sonenscher Indianapolis: Hackett Publishing Co, 2003) 136.
40 Agamben, *Homo Sacer* 41.

Dictator. There Schmitt posits constituent and constituted power as constitutive of the sovereign dictator. Against this, Benjamin suggests that these are both forms of authorised violence – one is law-making and the other law-preserving.[41] Law-preserving violence is the violence exercised by constituted order to protect and preserve the order. Law-making violence, on the other hand, is the violence exercised in the revolutionary foundation of the state.[42] Where Schmitt saw constituent power as other to law, Benjamin claims that it is part of the sovereign order. As law-making power, constituent power is continually manifested within the constituted order, as the constitution of authority.[43] For Agamben, this demonstrates precisely the crisis of constituent power, which never truly escapes the legal, and remains ultimately determined by its relation to the constitution.

Recent constitutional theory performs precisely this crisis of constituent power. Martin Loughlin's massive attempt to reconceive a 'pure' public law, published in *The Idea of Public Law* and *The Foundations of Public Law,* proposes that constituent power should be seen as constituting the law's authority. It helps us, he says, to 'locate the source of modern political authority, and . . . identify the base upon which the structure of the legal authority rests'.[44] For Loughlin, constituent power is other to the constituted order; it 'cannot be absorbed into some basic norm'.[45] He rejects this 'normativist' position. But he also rejects Negri's 'materialist' position, where constituent power would be reduced to 'the [factual] existence of strength or force',[46] which, as we will see in a moment, would be without unifying representation. With these rejections flanking him, Loughlin can proclaim that '[c]onstituent power is the power that gives constitutions their open, provisional, and dynamic qualities, keeping them responsive to social change and reminding us that the norm rests ultimately on the exception'.[47] The norm rests upon the exception – constituted power is founded by the constituent moment. It provides a ground for the authority of the constituted order, precisely by ensuring 'the need for agencies of the state to work actively to maintain the allegiance of their citizens'.[48]

41 Law-making is *recthsetzende – setzung* also means 'settle' or 'posit'. Law-preserving on the other hand, is *rechtserhaltende – erhaltung* means maintenance, conservation or preservation.
42 There have been many varied accounts of the *Critique of Violence*, which remains one of the most important critical legal texts. I do not have space here to discuss it or its literature in greater depth. In the broadest of terms, see J. Butler, 'Benjamin's Critique of Violence' in *Political Theologies* (ed L. Sullivan and H. de Vries New York: Fordham University Press, 2006) 211; W. Hamacher, 'Affirmative, Strike, Benjamin's "Critique of Violence"' in *Destruction and Experience* (ed A Benjamin and P. Osborne Manchester: Clinamen Press, 2000) 108; Agamben, *State of Exception*; I. R. Wall, *Human Rights and Constituent Power* (Abingdon: Routledge, 2012) 63–69; J. Derrida, 'Force of Law: The "Mystical Foundation of Authority"' in J. Derrida, *Acts of Religion* (London: Routledge, 2002) 230.
43 See Wall, *Human Rights and Constituent Power* 45–59.
44 M. Loughlin, *The Idea of Public Law* (Oxford: Oxford University Press, 2004) 99.
45 ibid 113.
46 ibid.
47 ibid.
48 ibid.

This idea of constituent power falls victim to Agamben's critique. The constituent power is included into the constituted order *as exception*; it is the negative imprint which sets the entire system off and which insures the continued fidelity to the democratic principle. Constituted power, along with its apparent negation in the constituent moment, are held in the 'ban structure' in sovereign power. Whyte summarises:

> Agamben uses the term 'ban', borrowed from Jean-Luc Nancy, to signify the exposure through which life is at once excluded from the political community and captured in the realm of sovereign power . . . Nancy highlights the double meaning of the term 'ban' – the one who is banned is both abandoned, or banished, and held in a ban. The one who is banned is 'therefore not simply set outside the law and made indifferent to it but is rather abandoned by it, that is, exposed and threatened on the threshold in which life and law, outside and inside become indistinguishable'. This ability to hold life in a ban by abandoning it is, for Agamben, the originary political relation. Agamben uses the term 'inclusive exclusion' to define this limit relation, in which people are included in the political community purely by virtue of their exclusion – an exclusion which leaves them utterly exposed to sovereign violence.[49]

The problem with constituent power for Agamben is that through this ban structure (the inclusive exclusion) constituent power becomes a juridical form. 'Politics has suffered a lasting eclipse because it has been contaminated by law, seeing itself, at best, as constituent power (that is, violence that makes law), when it is not reduced to merely the power to negotiate with the law'.[50] Constituent power, as the exceptional aspect of sovereign power, is ultimately constituted by its relation to law, and with this the political disappears.

Elsewhere Loughlin expounds on his conception of the relation between constituent and constituted power. He demands that there is a dialectical relation at work between the *Staatsvolk* (the people as an active political agency) and *Staatsgewalt* (the institutional apparatus of governmental authority), that is, between the people as a constituent power and the 'office of government' as a constituted power.[51] This dialectic generates power, whose essence 'inheres in the way it is generated, and it is generated by the drawing together of a people in ties of allegiance to a particular constitution of the state'.[52] Loughlin's dialectical relation replays, with little nuance, the law-making and law-preserving violence critiqued

49 J. Whyte, 'Particular Rights and Absolute Wrongs: Giorgio Agamben on Life and Politics' (2009) 20 *Law and Critique* 147, 152.
50 Agamben, *State of Exception* 88.
51 M. Loughlin, *Foundations of Public Law* (Oxford: Oxford University Press, 2010) 228.
52 ibid 229.

in Benjamin and Agamben.[53] Sovereignty is neither constituent power nor constituted order, but a dynamic collection of these: it excludes the constituent moment from legal rationality, but includes it as a source of authority; it includes constituent power by way of an exclusion or suspension.

Alongside this duality, Benjamin describes a sense of 'pure' or 'divine' violence. There is much debate about what this would entail, but Agamben argues that it interrupts the relation between the two types of legal violence with the ruptural quality of 'pure means'. Benjamin sees that the dialectical version of constituent/constituted power provides no critical purchase to think beyond liberal political forms. Constituent power, as negation of a corrupt constituted order remains merely the means to the end of a more just polity. Benjamin's conception of 'divine violence' as a pure means is radical. He references Sorel's general strike as an instance of a violence that interrupts the means-end logic with an action of rupture. By introducing this discussion Agamben poses a different sense of constituent power, one which no longer even uses the term. This different politics of a 'pure means' is not connected to the juridical, but neither is it purified of a relation to the legal in a substantive sense. It is not some sort of formalist notion of a politics.[54] Rather, Agamben suggests that this divine violence is violent precisely in the sense that it deposes the legal. As such, it is not a substantive matter of purification. It is not that this violence should become utterly cleansed of the legal – this would be an impossibility. Rather, it removes the question of ends, and the *necessity* of posing the constitutional question in advance of the event. It is deposing in the precise sense that it does not govern or execute but rather purely acts or manifests something other than juridically constituted life.

Let me go back to Negri, in order to put this problem in a different context. In *Homo Sacer* Agamben singles out Negri, suggesting that his conception of constituent power lacks any condition that would isolate it from sovereign power. He quotes quite a long passage from *Insurgencies*. This opens with an assertion which Agamben accepts, that constituent power should not be derived from nor limited to instituting the constituted order. Negri says:

> it is the act of choice, the punctual determination that opens a horizon, the radical enacting of something that did not exist before and whose conditions of existence stipulate that the creative act cannot lose its

53 For a different critique see Wall, *Human Rights and Constituent Power* (London: Routledge, 2011) chs 4–6.

54 Agamben clarifies Benjamin's term, a 'pure violence'. It is a mistake, he explains, 'to postulate anywhere a purity that exists in itself . . . The purity of a being is never unconditional . . . it is always subject to a condition. This . . . condition varies according to the being whose purity is at issue.' See W. Benjamin, 'Critique of Violence' in Agamben, *State of Exception* 61. Also see J. R. Martel, *Divine Violence: Walter Benjamin and the Eschatology of Sovereignty* (Abingdon: Routledge, 2012).

> characteristics in creating. When [constituent] power sets the [constituent] process in motion, every determination is free and remains free. Sovereignty, on the other hand, arises as the establishment – and therefore as the end – of [constituent] power, as the consumption of the freedom brought by [constituent] power.[55]

However, Agamben argues that this 'still says nothing as to [constituent] power's alterity with respect to sovereign power'.[56] In other words, constituent power and the constituted order remain within sovereign power, through his conception of the ban structure. Negri cannot find any criterion by which he could isolate the constituent from sovereign power, he claims.

In a response to this critique Negri accepts Agamben's argument, but suggests that it misses the point about constituent power. Of course constituent power is captured within the sovereign logic, but it also exceeds it. Constituent power does not rely upon the constituted order or sovereign power for its existence; rather, the strength (*qua potenza*) of the multitude is of a different order to sovereign power. Nevertheless, he suggests that Agamben's argument remains external to his, as his thought 'does not allow for any constitution of the political whatsoever'.[57] While Negri's response is helpful to some extent, the argument that Agamben's thought lacks a constitution of the political should be approached carefully. As I have already said, Agamben suggests that politics has been contaminated by law. This juridification must be coupled with the economic-managerial administration of life. These apparatuses of power operate through the maintenance of an indistinction between 'bare life' and 'political life'. For Agamben, this cannot be solved by a reconstitution of the political around the *potenza* of the multitude – their eternally creative political power.[58] Even these expressions of 'strength' are

55 Negri in Agamben, *Homo Sacer* 43.

56 Agamben, *Homo Sacer* 43.

57 A. Negri in C. Casarino, *In Praise of the Common: A Conversation on Philosophy and Politics* (Minneapolis: University of Minnesota Press, 2008) 158.

58 The distinction between *potenza* and *potestas* is crucial for Negri. In *Insurgencies*, his translator writes: 'I have translated the two Italian words *potere* and *potenza* as *power* and *strength*. Both Italian words would commonly be translated into English as *power*, but Negri's discussion rests heavily on the distinction between them. *Power*, for Negri, is always constituted power and it often refers to the power shaped by and into existing State and political institutions. Strength, instead, is a radically democratic force that resides in the desire of the multitude and is aimed at revolutionising the status quo through social and political change. Strength is at the core of the concept of constituent power itself as the force that produces (but cannot be contained within) power and its institutions; constituent power is fuelled by strength. Negri stresses more than once here that strength, as well as constituent power, enables but is not realised in constitutionality'. See M. Boscagli (translator) in A. Negri, *Insurgencies* (Minneapolis: University of Minnesota Press, 1999) ch1 at 337. See also S. Douglas, 'Between Constitutional Mo(nu)ments: Memorialising Past, Present and Future at the District Six Museum and Constitution Hill' (2011) 22 *Law and Critique* 171.

caught in the folds of biopolitical sovereignty, or at least their representation and theorisation as constituent power allows for this capture. He suggests that we must think otherwise if we are to re-treat the retreat of the political.[59]

Thus the problem, for Agamben, with constituent power is that, while seeming to offer an other to the legal order, it is in fact a fundamental part of legal authority by way of an inclusive exclusion. This inclusive exclusion allows biopolitical sovereignty to demand that it is the culmination of any expression of constituent power, and therefore the necessary point through which all expressions of politics must travel. There does remain a possibility for a challenge to this totality; however, it comes in the guise of a disordered and entirely inconsistent politics. I have pointed to two aspects of the Tunisian events that would seem to underline the possible power of this politics. Agamben suggests that the novelty of this coming politics is 'that it will no longer be a struggle for the conquest or control of the State, but a struggle between the State and the non-State (humanity)'.[60] This would be in direct opposition to the conventional Western European reading of the Tunisian events. They would project 'the people' coming together in order to will a new order – a version of Loughlin's constituent power. In this conception the revolution is dependent upon the unity of the people generating a constituted order capable of holding authority and of maintaining consent. This reading sees a liberal-capitalist political system as the necessary conclusion of the events. Ultimately, this is why so many commentators wonder, in a barely concealed racial tone, whether Tunisians (or sometimes 'Arabs') 'are ready for democracy'. Agamben's coming politics would displace the question of whether a new sovereign order is imposed after a revolt, and instead ask as to the everyday suspension of the state's authority. The problem for liberal readings of this politics is that, in many instances, it lacks the condition of unity – it lacks a representational apparatus.[61]

However, there is also a fairly major friction at play here between Agamben's framing of the coming community and constituent power, and the narrative presented of the events in Tunisia. This is even setting aside the directly post-colonial question.[62] Agamben suggests that the coming politics is marked precisely

59 Nancy and Lacoue-Labarthes, *Retreating the Political.*

60 G. Agamben, *The Coming Community* (Minneapolis: University of Minnesota Press, 1993) 85. For further elaboration of the sense in which I am using the idea of an 'anti-humanist humanity' see B. Golder, 'Foucault and the Unfinished Human of Rights' (2010) 6(3) *Law, Culture and the Humanities* 354 or B. Golder, 'What is an Anti-Humanist Human Right?' (2010) 16(5) *Social Identities* 651.

61 See Loughlin's dismissal that this is possible in *The Idea of Public Law* 112.

62 This would be a critique both of Agamben, (see D. Vukovich, 'China in Theory: The Orientalist Production of Knowledge in the Global Economy' (2010) 76 *Cultural Critique* 76 148) and of the exercise that I am undertaking here – of putting these events in the context of a 'European' constitutionalist discussion. I am in no position to answer the critique of Agamben; however, as I have said above I am not attempting to impose Agamben, or an Agambenian analysis on the Tunisian events, but rather to draw out

by a lack of any condition of belonging together. Thus there is not any closed community of nation, production or race. In the most radical reading of this there can be no claim to old 'operative' communities,[63] such as the 'patriotism of nation'. Rather, this is a new (coming) community whose being-together is marked by no condition other than their subjection to biopolitical sovereignty.[64] However, while we can clearly say that the Tunisian events lacked a representative mechanism, this radical reading of 'lacking any condition' does not match. There were a number of direct assertions of 'nation' and 'people' on the streets of Tunis and beyond. Equally, the national flag was important in the squares and boulevards. However, perhaps I might suggest a less radical reading of Agamben. In the attempts to suspend the everyday sovereign practices of Ben Ali's biopolitical apparatuses, in many instances, there was no *condition* of belonging together in the protest. By contrast, in Libya, the Benghazi based military resistance very quickly racialised the movement, detaining, murdering and expelling those with 'darker skin' as mercenaries. Very clearly then this was a sovereign expression of a *condition* of belonging-together. In Tunisia, where the revolt did not take on a militarised-sovereign structure, there was no *condition* of belonging together. Instead there was the insistence upon an open conception of the people. Without being too reductive, this would seem more in line with a Negrean subjectivisation in multitude than an Agambenian desubjectivisation in bare life.

This tension between the multiplicity of the Tunisian events and the purity of the Agambenian schema can be seen equally when it comes to the question of the lack of determinate demand, instantiated by the *dégage*. Certainly this was an utter refusal of the situation. There was no 'taking of the state' and reordering it along predetermined lines. Instead, the *dégage* attempts to suspend the operation of the sovereign inclusion/exclusion. However, this is not the end of the story, because there were many determinate demands with which the *dégage* is filled – multiple points of representation. Yet with each of these moments of representation, the closure implicit within representation is always reopened. The indeterminacy of the *dégage* is filled and refilled, and in doing so the purity of representation and the purity[65] of Agamben's refusal of it is unworked. These tensions are also present in

points of dissonance and consonance. Thus, I hope that the tools of critique can be of use to defetishising constitutionalism as the ultimate expression of all political movements.

63 See J.-L. Nancy, *The Inoperative Community* (Minneapolis: University of Minnesota Press, 1991).

64 Perhaps, the term inoperative is useful here. See Nancy, ibid. See also G. Rose, 'Performing Inoperative Community: The Space and the Resistance of Some Community Arts Projects' in *Geographies of Resistance* (ed S. Pile and M. Keith London: Routledge, 1997) 184, 185. There Rose says 'that it is the ways in which [an operative sense of] "community" constructs the distinction between its members and non-members that are intolerable for a radical politics'.

65 This is certainly not the substantive purity that modern representative regimes claim, but the demand that he makes for this Benjamanian purity (Agamben, *State of Exception* 61).

both the possible new mechanisms of constitutionalism and in the question of life beyond surveillance, regulation and control. Again here we do not find a purified, theoretically clean, desubjectivised politics. Thus, I will hazard the minor position that while Agamben's political theory is certainly useful and carries much positive political valence, its method and set of concerns will often become problematic when taken in the absolute sense that his tone seems to imply. However, this should not blind us to the critical utility of some of his work.

Conclusion

It is always a dangerous move to write an academic paper about continuing events, especially when those events will, without doubt, alter in tone and significance in the period between writing and publication. Hindsight, the acme of academic debate, must be eschewed and instead we are left only with possibilities. In the late 1970s Foucault made his 'Iranian mistake'; he committed himself to the Iranian revolution against the Shah and to the demand for Khomeini's return. In *media res* he argued: 'I cannot write the history of the future, and I am also rather clumsy at fore-seeing the past. However, I would like to grasp *what is happening right now*, because these days nothing is finished, and the dice are still being rolled'.[66] Subsequently, when the repression began in Iran, Foucault remained silent. He was condemned for this 'folly' – just another philosopher who failed to read the patently obvious effects of a revolution. This fallacy is expressed by his biographer David Macey, who says that Foucault was so impressed by the events of 1978 that he failed to recognise 'the probable future developments he was witnessing'.[67] What is missed, in a very precise sense, in this diagnosis is the position of Foucault within the events themselves. We are told that the Iranian refusal of the Shah, as people stood before his machine guns, already contained within it the seeds of the repression that was to follow. But lacking from these accounts is any sense of the contingency and potentiality of the constituent moment. Macey projects a steady and necessary progression from revolt to repression. Writing after the fact it is always possible to pick out the signs, to see the moments of significance for what is to come. However, in this the sense of the to-come, as an open and creative possibility, is lost. This chapter has sought to write of the contingency and potentiality of constituent power in that moment when nothing is finished.

When the Tunisian events are discussed in Britain as I write this – in November 2011 – they are placed in a teleological narrative where success or failure is measured by the presence of a constitution which creates stability and security. With this, the people that does not present a unified face is merely imperfect. The story is totalising in that it conditions our horizon of meaning concerning

66 M. Foucault, 'The Mythical Leader of the Iranian Revolt' in *Foucault and the Iranian Revolution* (ed J. Afary and K. Anderson Chicago: University of Chicago Press, 2005) 220.

67 D. Macey, *The Lives of Michel Foucault* (New York: Vintage Books, 1995).

constituent power and revolution: that of a people willing their new liberal-capitalist constitution. Thus, Agamben's critique of constituent power is crucial. There is nothing necessarily within that discourse which interrupts the inter-twinement of biopolitics and sovereignty. Instead, he suggests that a different desubjectified politics is emerging, where the question is precisely not of re-subjectification in another discourse of substantive community, but rather of being-together without the sovereign gesture of a condition of belonging together. Seen in this context, the Tunisian events present us with a whole set of interesting problems and ideas. This chapter has sought to underline aspects which are usually covered over in the traditional constitutionalist narrative: the disordered disruption of biopolitical regulation; the refusal of a clear representational strategy. Yet, revolts are too multiple to begin to present a simple narrative, even a critical one. There are tensions and frictions between Agamben's framework of a coming community and the narrative of the events in Tunisia. In closing, I would like to suggest that this should not distract us from the question at hand, which is, as Foucault said above, the attempt 'to grasp *what is happening right now* . . . [while] the dice are still being rolled'. Critical legal theory must resist the liberal-legal attempt at its inclusion and pacification. Instead, without any transcendent warranties and historical certainties, it must constantly attempt to interrogate the new political and legal faces of power relations. Constituent power presents precisely this possibility.

Chapter 4

Para-protest

Reading a parody of police gesture as political protest with Giorgio Agamben

Connal Parsley

Introduction

In 2009 Juliet Rogers published an article concerning the problem of formulating credible dissent to the apparently inexorable drift of modern politics.[1] Her article gave an example which addresses the difficulty of being able coherently to *say anything* of any *political* consequence against a piece of legislation passed by the Commonwealth of Australia under then prime minister John Howard. Rogers describes Green Party leader, Senator Bob Brown, speaking against the Anti-Terrorism Act 2005 (Cth) at a demonstration in Melbourne. Senator Brown's complaint was that the legislation infringed on civil liberties, would 'take away our freedoms' and 'that we needed to maintain, in this country, respect for individual rights'.[2] Howard, for his part, stated the rationale for the Act as being 'a necessary defence of our freedoms as a people, and that it protected our rights as citizens to be free from terror'.[3] Rogers's point is that Senator Brown's remarks, in resorting to the same powerful language of rights and freedoms as did Howard, were unable to address what is really politically objectionable about the legislation. Instead, she suggests, it 'reified Howard's political philosophy and arguably even reinforced his position'.[4]

As unsurprising as this situation is – given the fortune of liberal political theory and its determination of political space – this example is elegant because it highlights the problem of how to speak dissent. As Rogers puts it in a phrase to which I will return shortly: '[t]his kind of parroting, or mirroring the gestures and language of the sovereign, ensures that the language of the sovereign and that of

1 J. Rogers, 'Beyond the Script of Law' (2009) 18(2) *Griffith Law Review* 269.
2 Senator Bob Brown, speaking at Demonstration for Civil Liberties, Parliament House, Melbourne (22 October 2005) as cited in Rogers, 'Beyond the Script of Law' 270.
3 Prime Minister John Howard and Commonwealth Attorney-General Philip Ruddock, 'New Counter-Terrorism Laws' speech delivered at press conference in Parliament House, Canberra (8 September 2005) available at www.pm.gov.au/news/interviews/Interview1553.html (accessed 21 January 2012), as cited in Rogers, 'Beyond the Script of Law' 270.
4 Rogers, 'Beyond the Script of Law' 270.

the critique are the same'.[5] Again, there is nothing surprising in this idea that non-violent protest would speak – would *need* to speak – the language of the sovereign in order to gain traction. After all, we are by now accustomed to the idea that even something as apparently radical as revolution, despite all its power – or in fact *precisely because of its resort to power, force* – does not succeed in exiting the stage of the historico-political forum that produced it. It suffices to recall Hannah Arendt's famous remark that: '[i]t is well known that the most radical revolutionary will become a conservative on the day after the revolution'.[6] In fact, from this point of view, a common thread seems to unite revolution with the spectrum of other attempts to resist the power of a politico-legal regime. A claim or assertion of right;[7] a complaint directed at those in power, howsoever couched and howsoever founded;[8] a protest (violent or non-violent) which aims either to increase the political visibility, representation and *recognition* of a given cause or identity or to effect a symbolic destruction in its name;[9] or indeed a revolution, violent or non-violent: each of these strategies could be said to remain within a certain 'scene' of sovereign power.[10]

This frequently addressed problem has been considered in many ways and through innumerable categories. Remaining for a moment with the paradigm of revolution, for example, Giorgio Agamben has described revolution as 'the complex of actions directed at changing a determinate situation *within* historical time'.[11] This feature of revolution appears sharply to circumscribe its possibilities, in Agamben's account,[12] to a corresponding metaphysical (that is, negative)

5 ibid.
6 H. Arendt, *Crises of the Republic* (Harmondsworth: Penguin, 1972) 78.
7 See the discussion in J. Halberstam, 'Imagined Violence/Queer Violence: Representation, Rage, and Resistance' (1993) 37 *Social Text* 187.
8 See K. Epstein and K. Iveson, 'Locking Down the City (Well, Not Quite): APEC 2007 and Urban Citizenship in Sydney' (2009) 40(3) *Australian Geographer* 271, especially at 280–83.
9 On protest's becoming a question of political representation see Halberstam, 'Imagined Violence/Queer Violence' 190.
10 I am borrowing this term from Rogers too (who borrows it from Dylan Evans), although I am expanding her claim somewhat here.
11 G. Agamben, 'Il Talismano di Furio Jesi' (introduction to *Furio Jesi, Lettura del 'Bateau Ivre' di Rimbaud* (Quodlibet, 1996)) 6 (my translation).
12 In fact, Agamben is uncharacteristically indecisive on the question of revolution, which seems to stem not only from the constitutive problem of distinguishing constituting from constituted power in sovereign forms (see G. Agamben, *Homo Sacer: Il Potere Sovrano e la Nuda Vita* (Giulio Einaudi, 1995) 41–42) but also the specific approach taken in Furio Jesi's reading of Rimbaud. In this text, what is crucial is the unclear distinction between revolution and revolt: as Agamben has it in his introduction to the volume, 'the entire text proceeds along an unresolved opposition between revolt, which is always the experience of a suspension of historical time, and revolution, which is instead defined as the complex of actions directed at changing a determinate situation *within* historical time' (at 6). Despite being clearly stated here, this indistinction is not fully evaluated in Agamben's own consideration of it in a somewhat different context, that of Karl Marx's

conceptualisation of the subject and history and an intertwined political tradition inheriting from Aristotle; a fact which, Agamben claims, has polluted politics with the question of sovereignty.[13] As is well known, Agamben characterises this conception of politics by the sacralising function of the caesura between natural and political life, which results in the production of 'bare life:' life which is produced by political relations only so it can be 'abandoned' to politico-legal power. In his more recent works, Agamben continues to affirm and deepen the significance of his claim that the politico-legal ban-structure as originally characterised by Nancy corresponds precisely to the structure of language as it has been thought – and experienced – in philosophy.[14] The consequence of this position is that the political subject, which is always the subject of language, is not 'locked into' a political apparatus from which 'it' could be discretely conceived and from which it could therefore be considered more or less free. Rather, as Roberto Esposito has elegantly put it, 'it is power that produces the subject: including the subject of anti-power'.[15] The subject is thus always already both the power-subject (unable to 'do' anything, *perform* any *willed action* for or against power that is not itself characterised by power), and the subject-to-power (unable therefore unable to do anything *in its status as a subject* to escape subjection by the law of power and the power of law). And according to Agamben, this ensures that the subject – which constitutively finds itself in the ban relation of law and language – has, in dissent, an extraordinarily difficult task. Particularly, the voluntary assumption of a task for the subject potentially already reconsigns that subject to the scene of power and relation.[16] Thus, the ban relation, which for Agamben is not exclusively a juridical

relation to St Paul, in G. Agamben, *The Time That Remains: A Commentary on the Letter to the Romans* (Stanford: Stanford University Press, 2005) 30–34. It is also the case that for Agamben, like Benjamin, messianism is a paradigm of historical time, yielding the possibility that revolution, as internal to 'historical' time, is not necessarily circumscriptive in the sense intended here. However, two exit-trajectories from this question may render it less important than it first appears. First, Agamben's relation of this problem to Heideggerian facticity and the failure of either the will or external circumstance to account fully for the revocation of 'class' in messianic time itself bears an important connection to his critique of power and the subject. And, secondly, Jesi's certainty that the 'machine that produces mythologies' overbears on both revolution and revolt, rendering them conceptually indistinguishable (along with Agamben's suggestion that this machine is in fact none other than language) seems to bring Agamben's own use of the phrase 'anthropological machine' (in relation to the economy of power, glory and politics, in *The Open* (Stanford: Stanford University Press, 2004) and *Il Regno e la Gloria* (Nerri Pozza Editore, 2007) back to the centre of the frame in question here.

13 See G. Agamben, *State of Exception* (Chicago: University of Chicago Press, 2005) 1–2.

14 See Agamben, *Homo Sacer* especially 7–8, 21; G. Agamben, 'K' in *Nudities* (Stanford: Stanford University Press, 2010).

15 R. Esposito, *Categorie dell'Impolitico* (Il Mulino, 1999) 179.

16 Agamben generally makes the question of the tasklessness of man increasingly central to his considerations of government and the state in the present historical situation, for example in *The Open* and in *Il Regno e la Gloria*. Meanwhile, the potentiality offered

or political concept, is 'so ambiguous that nothing could be harder than breaking from it'.[17] Indeed, it would not be inaccurate to cast Agamben's *oeuvre* in its very many facets as an attempt to reckon with this ambiguity and thereby overcome it, which means, amongst other things, overcoming *relation itself* as the basis of politics.[18]

Rogers's Lacanian consideration of dissent and protest leads her to articulate the predicament which unites disparate strategies of protest, dissent or resistance in a similar way. In her account, the Lacanian subject of language may participate in the world, in my loose paraphrase, only through the acceptance of language and the symbolic order, which belong to the other – this is the 'law of the father'. The subject must therefore begin from a compromise, in the acceptance of the law as the prohibition of its own need. In this way, 'language begins along with law'.[19] A relatively easy if superficial link may thus be drawn between the fundamental syncretism of law and language in both accounts, but also between the Lacanian subject's constitutive inclusion and prohibition, exclusion from law and language, and the *point of departure* for Agamben's interventions into the plight of the subject of law, language and semiosis.[20] Rogers thus points to the difficulty of finding a language, which is always the law's language, to dissent against the law in order to protest the very loss that marks the subject's entry into political life: the difficulty of 'speak[ing] beyond the language of the sovereign'.[21]

Claiming that '[w]hat is at stake here is the capacity to initiate speech acts, as gestures of protest, which perform critique beyond the determined presence of the sovereign's rhetoric',[22] Rogers seeks the possibility of an act *not in relation* to the sovereign as a form of protest, and finds one in a consideration of the Australian

through an effacing interpretation of acts usually thought of as volitional is a recurring theme in Agamben's writing. See the discussion in 'Bartleby, or on Contingency' in *Potentialities* (Stanford: Stanford University Press, 1999) 243–71; in the context of the nullification of the subject in messianic vocation in *The Time that Remains* (St Paul's affirmation of not seizing but being seized at 33; Agamben's remarks on destruction of the subject at 41), and regarding Agamben's conception of scholarship in *The Idea of Prose* (Albany: State University of New York Press, 1995) 'The Idea of Study'.

17 Agamben, *Homo Sacer* 109.

18 See *Homo Sacer* especially at 28–29 and A. G. Düttmann, 'Never Before, Always Already: Notes on Agamben and the Category of Relation' (2006) 6 *Angelaki: A Journal of the Theoretical Humanities* 3, 3–6.

19 J. Lacan, *Ecrits: A Selection* (trans. Bruce Fink) (New York: W.W. Norton, 2002) 225.

20 See the brief sketch of this question by K. J. Seshadri, 'Other/Alterity: Lacan and Agamben on Ethics, the Subject and Desubjectification' (2009) 14 *Psychoanalysis, Culture & Society* 1, 65–73; and on a specific Freud/Agamben nexus and apposite remarks on the importance of psychoanalysis to Agamben generally see Justin Clemens's recent article: 'The Abandonment of Sex: Giorgio Agamben, Psychoanalysis and Melancholia' (2010) 13 *Theory & Event* 1.

21 Rogers, 'Beyond the Script of Law' 272.

22 ibid 271.

'street theatrical protest group' called the Tranny Cops. I see no reason to stop quoting Rogers now:

> The Tranny Cops . . . initially began their theatrical activist work dressing and performing as Transport Police in Sydney . . . they have now transited to performing as riot police. In this role, the Tranny Cops are replete with blue overalls and anarchist badges – which have been described as resembling police badges – and they brandish drawn moustaches, sideburns and (possibly) hefty dildos. They march in rows, they dance and direct traffic – indeed, in 2007 two of them were arrested for impersonating police offers in performing this function. By way of describing their parodying capacity, a police witness testifying in the case stated that one of them 'had her thumbs in her belt and rocked back and forth on her toes'. At the G20 in Melbourne . . . [t]hey marched through the crowds towards police barricades and when they arrived they performed a kind of 'line dance' in time with their own acoustic accompaniment. . . .[23]

For Rogers, what is parodied in the Tranny Cops' theatre is 'the imagined (im)potency of the state' (in the swapping of truncheons for dildos), but also the 'current impotency of a liberal democratic subject before the sovereign'.[24] In this Lacanian reading, in making themselves an 'impossible object', and at the same time both sovereign police and subjects themselves, the Tranny Cops perform a sovereignty that is not sovereign, a relation that cannot be consummated and an 'impossible symbol', thus presenting the possibility of an act that is a non-relation.[25] Whereas Rogers's discussion predominantly handles the role of dildos in the Tranny Cops' scene in terms of the melancholic psycho-subjective relation with the sovereign, the current chapter attempts to explore the central paradox entailed in Rogers's premise that an act 'not in relation' to the sovereign and its law might be found in precisely one of the clearest and most straightforward examples of 'parroting, or mirroring the gestures and language of the sovereign'. The rather modest aim of this chapter is to see whether Giorgio Agamben's writing on parody, which is itself framed in terms of a paradox, might offer an ulterior understanding of the Tranny Cops as *political protest*.[26] Importantly, many possibilities for this reading will not be pursued here, principally because of their number and complexity. For example, the potentially melancholic-or-mourning relation to the sovereign which is at play in Rogers's analysis might be extended with Agamben's reflections on that theme.[27] Or equally, through a direct confrontation with – which

23 ibid 276 (references omitted).
24 ibid 276–77.
25 ibid 278.
26 This work arises out of a series of conversations with Rogers about this prospect, which have influenced the aims of this chapter.
27 See the reference to mourning and parody in G. Agamben, *Profanations* (New York: Zone Books, 2007) 50 and some directions traced by Clemens, 'The Abandonment of Sex'.

is to say exegesis of – Agamben's writing on subject of language as desubjectification, or the remnant as political subject.

In attempting to address the paradox of parody which Agamben presents, my reading will also distinguish Agamben's understanding of parody from some other recent discussions of parody in a political protest context. Those other readings tend either to reinscribe parodic protest within the power relations of other kinds of protest described above, thus perhaps missing an opportunity to recognise parody's specific heterogeneity; or else they react differently to the essential *ambivalence* of political parody than might Agamben. This ambivalence, I argue, is not trivial and reflects something constitutive of parody in general (and, if after reading Agamben's account of parody, one would still be happy making the distinction, political parody in particular). The task of an Agambenian reading of parody would therefore be to show another possibility for this ambivalence.

Understanding the 'Tranny Cops' as (Agambenian) parody

In an essay on parodic literature found in the essay collection *Profanations*, Agamben supplies a definition of parody that suggests an immediate relevance to the Tranny Cops' actions. Relying on the centuries-old definition refined by Giulio Cesare Scaligero late in the 16th century, Agamben establishes parody's two canonical traits: 'the dependence on a pre-existent model that is subsequently transformed from something serious into something comic and the preservation of formal elements into which new and incongruous contents are introduced'.[28] The Tranny Cops, with their borrowing of Victoria police's colours, symbols and gestures, often stick fairly closely (in a low-budget sort of way) to the scripted repertoire established for them by the clichés of police comportment. And as can be seen in a YouTube video,[29] the Tranny Cops occasionally feign the utmost seriousness as they imitate the manner in which police behave in relation to crowds of (peaceful?) protesters. But even then, an unmistakeable exaggeration, a kind of camp 'too much' is insinuated into the display. The *faux* facial hair, the brusque self-satisfaction of the vocal delivery, the stage-managed (but seemingly improvised) conversation between Tranny Cops, all seem to supply the parodists' imagination about the *real* police's attitude to the business of policing a protest. Whether here, or in the throes of a sudden interjectory burst of the song 'Who let the dogs out?', accompanied by a gyrating dance routine,[30] the Tranny Cops seem the very paragon of this definition of parody. Corroborating the gesture Agamben identifies in the 'parodic countertexts of the Middle Ages' (the scatology of an Old French

28 Agamben, *Profanations* 39.

29 'Tranny Cops Give it to Police' YouTube available at http://www.youtube.com/watch?v=SkqACm8TRws (accessed 30 November 2011).

30 See another Tranny Cops video on YouTube: 'More Tranny Cops at G20' available at http://www.youtube.com/watch?v=xplxcVtxC58 (accessed 20 November 2011).

poem, and more generally for Agamben, chivalric literature and courtly love poetry), the Tranny Cops attempt the confusion of 'the prestigious sphere of the sacred' – the community's office of the police, grounded in the edifice of executive government – with the 'profane site of the dunghill'[31] – the crudeness, and baseness, of wielding a dildo in 'uniform'.

As Agamben remarks, it is only a short step from Scaligero's account of parody to the kind of modern dictionary definition of the term encountered by the central character in Morante's novel *Arturo's Island.* There, the supplied definition reads: '[the] imitation of someone else's verse in which what is serious in the other is made to be ridiculous, comic or grotesque'.[32] Leaving aside for a moment the possibility of a 'serious parody', it is worth noting first of all that parody seems to entail an imitation of someone else's *verse.* But parody is not restricted to a purely disciplinary question about written forms, circumscribed in some *simple* way as a riff which is exchanged between droll and droller dramatists. In order to attribute to parody the full importance which it assumes for Agamben, it is worth noting that the Italian term *verso,* which is correctly translated as 'verse', nevertheless has additional meanings in Italian; most importantly 'manner', or literally 'way', as in the various expressions '*non c'è verso di fare*' [there is no way to do it], '*andare nello verso giusto'* [to go in the right way] and, appropriately enough, '*rifare il verso di qualcuno*' [literally, 'to redo someone's manner', that is, to send someone up or parody them].

What is the implication for parody of this ascription to *verso* (verse) of a status as a manner, a form or a way of doing? What can be said, on the basis of this ascription, to be parodied by the Tranny Cops; if what they parody are the instantly recognisable gestures of policing generally, and the slightly less-well-famed comportment of police in protest situations more particularly? This question, at its foundation, inquires about and then displaces the status of an apparently 'representative' or 'signifying' structure (literature). Parody exposes the textuality of its object, thus also exposing its 'way' (or, the very fact of its *having* a way; its having *this* manner, rather than another). Parody, that is, opens a space for things to be other than the way they are; and an effect of the Tranny Cops' display is potentially, paradoxically, the holding open of this potential for a different political relation. This operation is paradoxical since it is precisely only because parody mimics or parrots its object that it can be parody, and its reliance on the thing that it parodies means that it does not offer an *alternative.* To put it another way, there is no apparent claim, plea for representation or coherent agenda to the Tranny Cops' acts. As such, the space of possibility that their parody opens is a necessarily *empty* or unfulfilled space.

Although elliptical, this point is absolutely essential for grasping Agamben's understanding of parody and we will reconsider it later. What must be noted

31 Agamben, *Profanations* 43.
32 ibid 37 (translation modified).

immediately are its two main, intertwined consequences for thinking the textual mediality of the gestures of the police as exposed by the Tranny Cops' parodic doubling of those gestures: a non-representational relation between gesture and life, as well as the unattainability of the object of parody, which together mean that parody introduces a 'dual tension' into being. I will now briefly address each of these points in sequence.

A non-representationalism

Reading the Tranny Cops as parody begins with the disruption of a semiotic/representative conception of both political life and language, because it disrupts the notion that this manner or way, this 'verse', is a 'representation' of some *definite thing* that would be articulable *without* gesture. It does suppose that the 'life' that is represented by literature (or the political, civic life represented by police behaviour) somehow exists *apart* from the forms in which it is instantiated. Yet its accusation is not that this literature or that way of policing is 'bad' because it is an unfaithful *representation* of that life. It uses a different logic of relation, which after Agamben we might call 'mysterious' rather than representative.[33] In order to grasp this logic and its mystery, it is important to recall that for Agamben, parody as a literary form is of peerless importance in the characterisation of Italian literature. By his reckoning, all of this tradition stands under the sign of parody: the Italian poets, taking up parodic strategies and introducing 'more or less comic content into a serious form' (the enraptured reflection on their object – 'the divine, love, the good, the city . . .')[34] were able to express a fundamental ambivalence: not necessarily just about those objects, but about the very practice and mode of 'representing' them.

An unattainable object

Thus, parody's object becomes not only whatever is represented, but 'the very structure of the linguistic medium' itself, which is a kind of indistinction of life from its representedness, or the *fact* of life's representation; its 'mediality'.[35] Parody is thereby elevated from a specific literary genre to being the very problem of language in its relation to its object.[36] This problematisation of the *means of representation* introduces a fundamental tension into them. Specifically, inbuilt

33 Agamben, *Profanations* 41–42. See also the notion of the mystery of economy in *Il Regno e la Gloria*.

34 Agamben, *Profanations* 45.

35 See G. Agamben, 'Notes on Gesture' in *Means Without End* (Minneapolis, University of Minnesota Press, 2000) 58, discussed in more detail below.

36 Agamben, *Profanations* 46. See also the much more extensive treatment of this theme in G. Agamben, *Stanzas: Word and Phantasm in Western Culture* (Minneapolis: University of Minnesota Press, 1993).

into parody is the presupposition of the unattainability of its object[37] and therefore a disabling of the efficacy – and in fact the presupposed function – of the representative relation. Parody is a strategy which operates through the renunciation of a direct representation of the object, insinuating and prioritising, instead, a focus on the employment of means – gesture, language – toward the conduct of life.

Cannot hold back a smile

In reading the Tranny Cops as parody, the gestures and 'ways' of policing are textualised. Specifically, they are endowed with a linguistic texture which lets us say that they, as the visible *object* of parodic protest, are in every way distinct from that protest's *aim* or *objective*. This objective is not merely unrepresented, but so invisble or unreconstructible that it might as well not exist. The protest's *objective* becomes utterly unretraceable; the Tranny Cops' *intentions* or *goals*, their *vision for political relations*, are entirely obscured. There is perhaps no more unique feature of parodic protest than the distance it opens up between object and objective. Faced with an excess or duplication of the object of protest, and correspondingly deprived of an invisible or intangible objective to be realised or argued for, we could say that the linguistic texture of the object-gestures becomes *exposed* and the protest satisfies itself with that exposure. The effect of parody is paradoxical, and in this case the paradoxical effect is that the police's relation to the mysterious object that is life – *political life* – may under an excess of attention open up and loosen before our very eyes, becoming textualised, de-naturalised. Those in doubt of this fact need only observe, in a video on YouTube, that the Tranny Cops somehow succeed in making the police's object unattainable even to the police themselves; their own gestures suddenly seeming ridiculous as a result of the mystical interval being introduced into the scene.[38] As Agamben remarks, 'in approaching a mystery, one can offer nothing but a parody; any other attempt to evoke it falls into bad taste and bombast'.[39] And in the video in question, as the Tranny Cops parody the dour police, working a parodic interval into the question of their comportment, it is suddenly the braced stances of the *police themselves*, their stern demeanour and their humourless facial expressions, which seem themselves to be the parody, suddenly seeming ridiculous (one officer himself [at 0:51] cannot hold back a smile).

37 Agamben, *Profanations* 46. Note also a preceding passage: 'There may be great seriousness in the reasons that drive the parodist to renounce a direct representation of his or her object . . . the object that she [Morante] must describe – the innocent life, that is, life outside history – is rigorously unnarratable' (at 40–41).

38 See http://www.youtube.com/watch?v=xplxcVtxC58 (accessed 21 January 2012).

39 Agamben, *Profanations* 41.

Fiction, parody and a dual tension in being

It is not that the police's gestures, along with those of the Tranny Cops, are reduced to the status of a 'fiction'. Rather, their reality is heightened. Agamben explains this operation by contrasting fiction and parody:

> Parody not only does not coincide with fiction, but constitutes its polar opposite. This is because, unlike fiction, parody does not call into question the reality of its object; indeed, this object is so intolerably real for parody that it becomes necessary to keep it at a distance. To fiction's 'as if', parody opposes its drastic 'this is too much'.[40]

What is therefore at stake here is a specific 'dual tension in being',[41] which is introduced by parody and its peculiar, mysterious relation to its object. The notion we summarised above as the opening of a necessarily unfulfilled space for things to be other than as they are comes into sharper view as a result of this relation. For Agamben, parody has a 'metaphysical vocation', which is, through the means just described, to effect a sort of duplication of being. Corresponding to a metaphysics which Agamben sees as a 'space alongside sensible experience (but a space that must remain rigorously empty)', parody too opens up such an aporetic space. Since the gestures of policing are no longer allowed to be unproblematically 'true', but now seem rather 'too true' (even to the police themselves), these gestures seem at once contingent, or not absolutely necessary, and at the same time inescapable.[42] The Tranny Cops' parody thus introduces a double relation to the object and to the gestures of policing.

This double relation is very easy to describe. On the one hand, the parody loosens the parodied gestures' tie with their object: life (or political life, a vision of instituted communal relations and the means and conditions for participating in them). In this regard, parody – and the Tranny Cops' parody – seems (to refer back to a possibility alluded to in Agamben's account) to be entirely serious, offering a *lament* about police and political life: a dolorous 'this is not it'.[43] And yet, on the other hand, since 'this is all there is'; (that is, since like all successful parodies the Tranny Cops also reaffirm the 'too true' nature of the police's gestures), a second relation to the object is visible: this policing is 'too much'. Parody, in being utterly parasitic on the forms it calls into question and in not offering anything like an alternative vision (to insist on this point once again), also reaffirms the being (or perhaps the 'being in force') of those forms, gestures, means and symbols with which we are in power relations, and which we both *may* use and *must* use, and be

40 ibid 48.
41 ibid 49.
42 ibid 49–50.
43 As Agamben writes, 'the space of parody – which is literature – is therefore necessarily and theologically marked by mourning and by the distorted grimace' (*Profanations* 50).

used by. Unlike those writers on parody who baulk at parody's reiterative function and its repetition or entrenchment of power relations and therefore doubt its 'effectiveness' as a strategy for protest,[44] Agamben's account dwells entirely in that function as one half of parody's paradox, without which it would not have the specific 'effect' that it does. The paradox of parody is that it only so radically opens a distance between means and object, *because* it attains an unbearable proximity to that object. Parody, which is also a 'para-ontology', expresses 'language's inability to reach the thing and the impossibility of the thing finding its own name'. But at the same time, for Agamben, 'in this way, parody attests to what seems to be the only possible truth of language'.[45] And wherever what is signified is mediality itself, Agamben suggests elsewhere, there will necessarily be an unresolvable ambiguity.[46]

A parodic protest

The immediately political significance of this linguistic para-ontology in Agamben's thought raises now the possibility of a politics of parodic protest,[47] which, I argue, whilst retaining its linguistic register, potentially reveals a 'truth' about policing that is worthy of the stakes which are really at play: the difficulty of imagining how political life might be. What is remarkable about the Tranny Cops' use of parody is that in working in this aporetic, 'impassable terrain',[48] it both laments and celebrates what we might call the absence of a *proper political form*. It is somehow legible as a protest, even though it does not conform to the familiar images, slogans and claims which attend most political protests. There are no invocations of the fundamentally exclusive logic of ownership or propriety (for example, reclaiming propriety over the streets). Although it is a repetition of policing's powerful speech, there is no attempt to grasp the powerful language of the state and *use* it either protectively or towards revolution. And equally, there is no proposed alternative vision conceived as independent of the existing political scene that pretends to overwrite or substitute for that scene. This parody's quality as protest – and even as *political* – emerges as a kind of *residual effect* of its parody: a parody, perhaps, of the very political claims and antagonisms which pass for engagement in public or collective life; antagonisms that both apparently require, and *are* policing.

To the extent that *every* parody laments the reduction of the political and communicative possibilities of public life, every parody – however humorous – is intrinsically a kind of protest. And in taking communicability as its subject, every such protest is above all a political protest. That is, I argue that here we do not identify the Tranny Cops as protesters necessarily because of their intentions, because of their announced aims or goals, because of a complaint levelled at an

44 Note the analysis of Judith Butler in *Gender Trouble* (London: Routledge, 1990).
45 Agamben, *Profanations* 50.
46 Agamben, *The Time That Remains* 43.
47 This unfortunate alliteration is unintentional but unavoidable.
48 Agamben, *Profanations* 50 (translation modified).

authority, or even because of their context as part of a general spectacle of protest. The object of the protest is not some determinate or propositional end or goal, some specific law or policy, and nor is this the simple exercise of power against the form of power *par excellence* (unlike in other non-parodic protests). The protest that arises out of parody is never 'propositional', 'assertive' or 'representative', but expositional: opening and suspending a space and for the possibility that things are only a 'way', and might be otherwise.

In acting to parody or double the sovereign gesture, and in so doing exposing the space alongside it (every gesture, being *this* gesture and not that, has this space alongside it, which is its pure gesturality, its pure 'way', which is to say its pure *means*), the Tranny Cops' parody acts partly in that space alongside – and not entirely in the space that belongs to those gestures as *those* gestures (their life, their politics). If those gestures' life and their politics is the politics of power and relation, subjection and sovereignty; this 'space alongside', in which parody acts, is not. But it is not a question of the *negation* of this life, since it leaves these gestures and their power intact (they remain 'too true'). As such, neither does it relate to *power* in the mode of a simple opposition or substitution – for example, passivity *instead of* action, parody *instead of* a rally, march, claim, critique, destruction or revolution. Nothing is substituted; nothing is destroyed. In fact, it is obvious that the moment of the Tranny Cops' parody could not exist without this power; borrowing its gestures, taking everything from them. What is crucial is that this act of parody itself barely qualifies as an 'act' at all; and certainly not an 'effective' act in the sense of achieving some 'real' political outcome – a redistribution of resources, say, or bending the ear of some politician to an undoubtedly worthy cause. This is why those who question the 'efficacy' of parodic protest – albeit in a different tone[49] – are quite right to do so: its strategy is in every way distinct from one which simply deploys means toward a determinate political end.

Two non-acts

The non-act of parody, together with the rigorous emptiness of the political possibility it exposes can be understood through a comparison with the account which Hannah Arendt gives of civil disobedience. This comparison will also elaborate the place of law and the political in Agamben's account. Arendt's reflection is framed as a response to a debate initiated by the American Bar Association, which raised the question of whether dissent by civil disobedience, which might secure desirable changes in the law, has a legitimate basis – with the additional, recuperative aim of reactivating citizens' 'moral relation to the law in a society of consent'.[50] Arendt probes the juridical reasoning at play in the debate and concludes that the idea of establishing a legal right through a personal act of

49 I am thinking again of Butler in *Gender Trouble*.
50 Arendt, *Crises of the Republic* 51.

disobedience amounts to 'a strange and . . . not altogether happy theoretical marriage of morality and legality, conscience and the law of the land'[51] Her remarks are perhaps best read as corrective of the thinking used by other participants to the debate, rather than propositional in itself, but important features of her reasoning, which ends up arguing strongly for the 'political legitimacy' of civil disobedience as a dissent strategy, are of direct relevance here.

Hannah Arendt and civil disobedience

As may be expected of a discussion on dissent framed through questions of legitimacy and moral relations, Arendt ultimately presents civil disobedience as a complex question of law and force. This is not just a question of the insight that civil disobedience tends to increase when law loses its force, enforceability, and therefore legitimacy (often in the period prior to a revolution).[52] Rather, for Arendt, civil disobedience can be carefully distinguished from revolution on the one hand (in being non-violent) and from a simple criminal transgression on the other (in being a public appeal made in the interests of a group, as opposed to a concealed act of mere self-interest).[53] The detail of these distinctions is important. First, it is significant that Arendt is able to agree that an essential feature of civil disobedience is the non-violence that distinguishes its practitioners from 'rebels'; but she does not for that reason accept the suggestion that the civil disobedient therefore necessarily endorses the existing authority and the 'general legitimacy of the system of laws'. On the contrary, she points out that:

> . . . the civil disobedient shares with the revolutionary the wish 'to change the world', and the changes he wishes to accomplish can be drastic indeed – as, for instance, in the case of Gandhi, who is always quoted as the great example . . . of nonviolence. (Did Gandhi accept the 'frame of established authority . . .'? Did he respect the 'general legitimacy of the system of laws' in the colony?)[54]

Civil disobedience is thus, paradoxically, a kind of non-violent act, the scope of whose political goals is on a par with those of revolution. This is just the beginning of a series of important inversions which now begins to manifest.[55] It is not only

51 ibid 52.
52 ibid 69–70.
53 ibid 75.
54 ibid 77.
55 The field of thought which attempts to think law's relation to force and the state's monopoly on violence is necessarily replete with such inversions, perhaps most emblematically signalled by Walter Benjamin's assertion in 'Critique of Violence' that the 'origin of every contract points towards violence' (in *Selected Writings Volume 1 1913–1926* (Cambridge, Mass.: Harvard University Press, 1996) 243). And through this attribution of violence to law, in the sphere of protest too, inversions begin to be noticed

that, as we indicated at the outset, the 'most radical revolutionary will become a conservative on the day after the revolution'[56] – a problem from which a civil disobedient such as Gandhi does not appear to suffer. Arendt also argues that despite being non-violent, civil disobedience – even *without* resorting to a purely legal-constitutional argument about disobeying law in order to 'test its validity' in court – is in fact invested with a kind of power to bring about change (a power that cannot therefore be described as simply legal power). It does so by influencing the Supreme Court in its choice of cases to be heard. Arendt's lucid insight about the nature of law in her time meant she herself was under no illusions about what legal change could achieve. Law, as a (necessary)[57] negative or restraining force can stabilise and legalise change, she cautions, but not create or enforce it – that is the function of the political. But where there is a rapid rate of politico-social change with the result that law lags far behind the social, legal change looks like real change. Arendt is thus able to attribute important legal innovations regarding the abolition of slavery to civil disobedience and not to law, whilst preserving for civil disobedience a compatibility with the law that is nonetheless not a complicity ('Not the law, but civil disobedience . . . forced upon the nation the recognition of the enormity of the crime . . . of slavery'[58]). This non-complicity is so important because of law's negative ambiguity: as the thing that protects the political from violence, but as itself always potentially violent in its function of impeding political change.[59]

What I wish to emphasise is the unusual character which civil disobedience takes on as a non-violent strategy for protest which maintains the political possibilities of a possibly violent law. What we have in civil disobedience, because of its being channelled through law (in *relation* to law) and not remaining wholly in the sphere of the political, is a *non-act* – and not simply a non-violent act (such as an active but peaceful protest) – that is legally an *act*. But nor is it a simple individual criminal transgression of the law by omission (which avoids the public eye and is undertaken to make the transgressor into an exception). This non-act is attributed with power to act as a catalyst for real – *political* – change, through a flirtation with or leverage of the sphere of law by which its very status as a (transgressive) act is generated. In this way, Arendt's civil disobedience could be seen as one answer to the problem of the political's relation to the 'latent violence of the law' as it is phrased by Roberto Esposito. As he wrote in 1988: 'In order to defeat the latent

everywhere, for example in Jack Halberstam's observation which regards non-violent law as violent and non-violence as 'dangerous': 'violent law demands violent resistance. Tactics of nonviolent resistance developed in the sixties and used nowadays seem to have become dangerously hegemonic rather than disruptive'. See Halberstam, 'Imagined Violence/Queer Violence' 189.

56 Arendt, *Crises of the Republic* 78.

57 Esposito, *Categorie dell'Impolitico* 132 interestingly insists on this point.

58 Arendt, *Crises of the Republic* 81.

59 Esposito, *Categorie dell'Impolitico* 132.

violence of the law, the political must have non-violent recourse to that origin which is always violence: it must combat the violence of a non-violent law with the non-violence of a violent origin'.[60]

How does Arendt's civil disobedience draw non-violently upon an origin which is always violence? From the very moment in which Arendt situates civil disobedience as a primarily American phenomenon and therefore seeks to find support for it in the '*spirit*' of American law, she suggests that finding for it a 'constitutional niche' would be as significant as the 'founding of the *constitutio libertatis*'.[61] As Esposito has noted, in Arendt there is always a favourable reproposition of political origins[62] and, in this case, we see her inscription of civil disobedience into a original political scene of 'voluntary association' that argues disobedients are legitimate and ought to have the same traction in daily government as do registered lobbyists.[63]

Arendt's homology between civil disobedience and voluntary association relies on a fundamental binding (and circumscription) of dissent to a more fundamental *consent.* After diagnosing American political life as founded on a social contract (which is 'horizontal' rather than 'vertical', and therefore based on the mutual but limited power of individuals bound together by promises), Arendt complicates the notion of 'original consent' upon birth which is implied in the Declaration of Independence's 'mutal pledge'. She does so by refining this fundamental legal fiction, interrogating the notion that birth into a pre-existing situation could be a relevant consent ('how could we will what is there anyhow?'). Arendt is nevertheless able to find that there is a relevant voluntarism in any society where 'dissent is also a legal and *defacto* possibility once . . . [one] has grown into a man'. Thus, 'dissent implies consent' – and not only because 'one who knows that he may dissent knows also that he somehow consents when he does not dissent'. Rather, consent becomes so important to political relations that it is *inherent in the human condition.*[64] For this reason, for Arendt, a much more general consent – which must now be distinguished from consent to individual rules or laws, to which we must be able to *dissent,* even at the scale of the 'system' or 'establishment'[65] – underpins political life. Despite noting contemporary scepticism of this idea of a Tocquevillian *consensus universalis,* Arendt's strategy is to reinscribe this fundamental consent into the mutual promise of the social contract, characterising its promises (like law) as an insulation against the radical change brought by the future, but working *against* the individualisation effected by law. Life thus becomes inscribed in the nation as political community, but with a definite split between politics and law: here we can clearly see that, as Esposito noted, for Arendt law is 'that which

60 ibid 132–33.
61 Arendt, *Crises of the Republic* 83–84.
62 Esposito, *Categorie dell'Impolitico* 132.
63 Arendt, *Crises of the Republic* 100–101.
64 ibid 88.
65 ibid 89.

distances us from the origin; that which blocks its transformative potential',[66] and civil disobedience as 'voluntary association' relies absolutely on this particular account of strictly *political* origins which begin as an intentional act of the will to promise. Importantly, for Arendt this means, first, that the origin is not simply chronologically located in the past but invoked in the moment of dissent and, secondly, that the origin as an intentional act of *accord* pre-empts and underpins the 'violence' of that *dissent*.

Agamben's gesture

Leaving aside a general discussion of Arendt's central importance to Agamben's framing of political problems (especially the nation and rights),[67] we may read the Tranny Cops' parody (through Agamben) as the precise inverse of Arendt's civil disobedience, and also an inverted reckoning with the problem given in Esposito's dense formula. For Arendt, civil disobedience is a non-act that is actually a politically powerful act of dissent – and a politically *legitmate* act, that reconducts transgressive political action to the legitimate original ground of politics as a voluntary mutual promise in every way distinct from law's negativity. On the other hand, an Agambenian protest-parody is an 'act' that is actually a non-act (an 'ineffective' act) that articulates and disarticulates the complete domination of life and the political sphere's origins by law and power, and the domination of every voluntary promise and duty by a juridical structure.[68] Heavily accenting the sacralising structure of every political origin conceived through a volitional act of the will (which inevitably results in a politics of the ban relation; that is, inclusive exclusion), Agamben's contention is that any politics which continues to adhere to a contractarian *representation* of political origin is constitutionally incapable of thinking 'a politics freed from the form of the State': the origin of the political must be assumed and confronted as the very ban structure itself.[69] In addition to the inversion already noted, Agamben reasons that these contractarian accounts of political origin (such as Arendt's, one may assume), 'condemn democracy to impotence' every time it must 'confront sovereign power'.[70] In this formulation, it is the exercise of power that is impotent, and it is the grounding of a non-act in the legitimacy of an original accord that occupies an illegitimate position (as an original accord distinct from law, it is also an impossibility in Agamben's thought). It is a short step from here to the conclusion that only a paradoxical means might

66 Esposito, *Categorie dell'Impolitico* 132.
67 Agamben finds a way not of negating Arendt's characterisation of the situation regarding rights and nationhood, but of totalising it towards new conclusions (see *Homo Sacer* 126–35).
68 This idea receives its most extended treatment in Giorgio Agamben *The Sacrament of Language* (Cambridge: Polity, 2011).
69 Agamben, *Homo Sacer* 109.
70 ibid.

confront the paradox of sovereignty's ban. Parodic protest draws attention to the tenacity of power's grasp over our every 'action' and, paradoxically, *in doing so*, loosens that grasp whilst still in that moment renouncing any *other* efficacy over power. This is why the idea of a non-action, an action that is not exhausted in its (political) potentiality by determining its 'end', is so important to Agamben's thought: it exposes *another* origin away from voluntarism and accord – a 'more originary' origin.[71]

The crucial difference between civil disobedience and parody is that, whereas the former seems to attribute power to a non-act's ends whilst referring its means to a 'legitimate' political origin (will/accord), parody, as we have said, in not exhibiting an end of any kind, displays the purity of means and thus offers these ambivalent means as the *only origin and the only goal of political protest.* Agamben's often discussed account of gesture supplies the notion of action that is necessary in understanding the Tranny Cops as political protest. This account emphasises a category of action which, he suggests, Varro added to Aristotle's *poeisis/praxis* distinction as a third possibility. In gesture, which is inscribed in the sphere of action but set apart from acting or making, 'nothing is being produced or acted, but rather something is being endured and supported'.[72] Whereas 'doing is a means in sight of an end and praxis is an end without means, gesture breaks the false alternative between means and ends'.[73] Importantly, in doing so, gesture 'opens the sphere of *ethos* as the most proper sphere of the human'.[74] It is this *ethos* (and not something that may be legitimately or illegitimately willed) that is the political 'origin' with which Agamben is concerned (although this *ethos* cannot truly function in the same way as an Arendtian political origin). Sometimes difficult to grasp, this proposition is lucid in the context of the Tranny Cops' parody. As Agamben continues, with a point that evidences his conviction that the originary human *ethos* is none other than our pure being-in-language: '*The gesture is the exhibition of a mediality: it is the process of making a means visible as such.* It allows the emergence of the being-in-a-medium of human beings and thus it opens the ethical dimension for them'.[75] Parody, which I have already suggested effects this same exposition, is therefore fundamentally linked to the gesture: parody is always the parody of a gesture, which is to say an exposure of mediality (whether of 'words' or 'acts'). And where a scene of parody has been framed, as witnessed by the police officer who could not hide his smile, every gesture, once exposed, risks itself entertaining a parodic relation to life.

71 See n 16 above. Note there are two main places in Agamben's recent work where the idea of origin is significantly complicated: in the notion of action's fundamentally ungrounded nature in relation to being in *Il regno e la Gloria* and in the elaboration of the notion of the idea of philosophical archaeology in *The Signature of All Things: On Method* (New York: Zone, 2009).

72 Agamben, *Means Without End* 57.

73 Agamben *Infancy and History* (London: Verso, 2007) 154 ('Notes on Gesture').

74 Agamben, *Means Without End* 57 (translation modified).

75 ibid 58.

Importantly, where an act like the Tranny Cops' parody is able to draw attention to gesture in this way, there is a moment in which the political scene that is governed by the assertion of the power/legitimacy of the will is temporarily given a reprieve. What takes place is the temporary destruction or occlusion of the *identity* and therefore also, as I have said above, the *political objective* or end of the participants in the protest. As Agamben remarks in the highly apposite context of the 'constructed situation':

> the destruction of the role's identity goes hand in hand with the destruction of the actor's identity. It is precisely this relationship between text and execution, between power and act, that is put into question . . . This happens because the mask insinuates itself between the text and execution, creating an indistinguishable mixture of power and act. And what takes place here – both onstage and within the constructed situation – is not the actuation of a power but the liberation of an ulterior power. *Gesture* is the name of this intersection between life and art, act and power . . . .

This quotation's two key elements are the destruction of the political role and the actor's identity, together with the ulteriority of the power that is 'liberated' in that event. First, this destruction is purely momentary, as we have said, and utterly dependent on the momentary doubling of the parodied gesture. It is only in drawing attention to the gesture of power and, in doing so, a more originary *ethos* alongside it, that the Tranny Cops do not act entirely within the sphere of political relations marked by volition, identity and political representation. That is to say, the Tranny Cops are not forever converted into identity-less non-subjects and nor is it in question that they acted volitionally in organising and undertaking their parody (or that they may have political intentions generally). But reading their act in the moment of parody means accepting as readers, as I think we must, the temporary invisibility of whatever articulated, volitional, political aims and goals they might otherwise hold in the scene of protest. Such political opinions and *intentions* for staging their parody (as individual, liberal, rational subjects of law) are occluded, or are only mysteriously relevant to the *ethos* that is exposed through an Agambenian reading. This *ethos* cannot be intended and it is exposed, regardless of any specific intention, because it takes place in the suspension of the politics of the will. Secondly, whereas for Arendt the power and efficacy of civil disobedience is inscribed in the legitimacy of an 'original' accord, the 'ulterior' power of parody in Agamben's claim, as something that cannot be willed, is not traceable to any predicable 'propriety' or 'legitimacy', being rather the very principle of the effacement of the powerful subject who nevertheless acts.[76]

76 Agamben, *The Signature of All Things* 84.

A summary, some consequences, some differences

This Agambenian reading of parody raises a complex constellation of categories and displacements that depart significantly from the habitual ways of conceptualising dissent and protest. It also differs slightly but significantly from other readings of parody in recent scholarship. It is perhaps useful to summarise the key features of this reading:

First, parody exposes the mediality of human gesture, which according to Agamben is the originary human *ethos* and the originary human capacity for politics (the sphere of 'pure means'[77]). In referring to the purity of means, this origin is neither 'prior to' action/power nor destructive or substitutive of it: it exists 'alongside'. It is therefore reliant upon it; borrowing from it and taking everything from it in order to give mediality back to the gesture itself.

Secondly, the exposition of this more originary *ethos* momentarily disables anything like a will or consent as the foundation of the political. The *ethos* is not intentional, but exists alongside intention, enabled by it. Parodic protest is therefore a momentary disabling of politics as framed by an origin/goal (which is always bound into the question of political membership and identity). The exposure of means does not seek a determinate end like the recognition of a cause, claim or political identity. As seen above, in gesture (and doubly so in the parody of political gesture), role and identity are effaced, thus disabling anything resembling a politics of representation. If there is an identity question posed by the Tranny Cops' gesture, it is the interrogation of the life to which these police belong: not 'recognise me and my claim'; but 'I do not recognise these police as my police: whose police are these? To what life do they belong?'

Thirdly, in acting alongside and not within the politics of power towards a determinate end, parody cannot be fully understood in terms of categories of its 'effectiveness' or 'power', and to do so reinscribes parody within that politics.[78] What is 'effected' by parody is only the exposition of human means. Complaining of parody's relative inutility (or conversely, prematurely attributing it with 'power' for change) only further exposes the domination of politics and critique by the modulations of power.

Fourthly, this means that as an operation of 'exposure', the doubling of gesture in parody cannot be thought of in Agamben as a 'performance' – a fact which

77 Agamben, *Means Without End* 60.

78 For example K. Kenny, '"The Performative Surprise": Parody, Documentary and Critique' (2009) 15(2) *Culture and Organization* 221, which asks whether a specific example of parody 'represents an effective critique, or is merely entertainment' (at 233). Such a dialectic would not make sense in Agamben's paradigm. Epstein and Iveson's article is an interesting one (Epstein and Iveson, 'Locking Down the City' 271–95) for its plurality of approaches. Whilst they seem to group parody in with 'complaint' and 'protest', the function they attribute to these strategies is one of 're-politicising'. which does not necessarily hurriedly supply parody with unearned power.

sharply distinguishes Agamben's approach to gesture from much other contemporary writing on parody.[79] According to the etymology of performance, the term begins in the juridical sphere, denoting the fulfilment of a legal duty (like an Arendtian civil disobedience) and only later comes to refer to acting generally, as in the acting of a play etc. Agamben's writing attempts to retrieve human action for itself and Agamben's gesture – parody – ought not be thought of as oriented toward the *carrying out* of an action: the accent is on *carrying* action (without an 'out'), undergoing and supporting it, thus remaining only itself without resulting in a particular form. Agamben's position is closer to Robert Hariman's, which suggests that the function of parody is to reveal the *prior* text 'an obviously contrived performance'.[80]

Fifthly, as the sphere of pure means, the political *ethos* exposed in parody is, for Agamben, resolutely 'empty'. That is, parody draws attention to the possibility of there being another politics, but does not rush to supply an imagination – a blueprint or model – for that politics. If it did, in supplying that end or goal (that vision of the political), this would amount to fixing the political to a determinate form and thus attributing to it a propriety. This form/propriety nexus is precisely what is avoided in parody through its paradoxical duplication of gesture: as we have seen, what parody does is both lament and celebrate the absence of a proper political form. As such, parody works not so much by the logic of representation, but one of exposition (of the structures of mediality and representation themselves). This important fact distinguishes Agamben's notion of parody from that of those writers who claim parody supplies an alternative political vision[81] (any reimagining of political life in parody would have to be an 'imagination without images'[82]), as well as from those who in reaching for terms to describe parody's efficacy, quickly refill the space it opens with a liberal juridical lexicon.[83]

79 The language of performance is so pervasive of literature on parody (and action in general) that references seem gratuitous. So much so that a technical-etymological reading almost seems misplaced, since it is far from clear exactly what is meant by 'performance' for many using the term. But in general see eg Judith Butler's *Gender Trouble* (although note Butler's emphasis on performance's 'vital instability'); Kenny, 'The Performative Surprise'; Epstein and Iveson, 'Locking Down the City' 289.

80 R. Hariman, 'Political Parody and Public Culture' (2008) 94(3) *Quarterly Journal of Speech* 247, 256. Hariman's accomplished article handles parody through a different literature, principally Bakhtin.

81 See Kenny, 'The Performative Surprise' 227, referring to du Gay.

82 G. Agamben, *Ninfe* (Torino: Bollati Boringhieri, 2007).

83 Epstein and Iveson's discussion ('Locking Down the City') centres on contested notions of citizenship, and they group complaint, protest and parody together as equivalent means of a 'citizenship claim' 'concerning the city' (at 273), even using the language of 'insurgent citizenship' (at 289). Epstein and Iveson's article concerns the almost complete domination of the city by the APEC conference in Sydney in 2007, and it is perhaps telling that their language of critique seems to replay the language of the sovereign in this case, although of course one ought not to rule out the reuse and repoliticising of terms such as citizenship in critique. In any case, Agamben's analysis takes its own cue

Sixthly, parodic protest – para-protest – is not exclusive of any other kind of protest and, because of its acceptance of parody's ambivalences, an Agambenian reading of parody is not necessarily exclusive of other readings of parody.

Finally, owing to all of the above, parody is *constitutively* ambivalent. In an Agambenian reading, the poles of this ambivalence ('subversion *or* incorporation') are not to be chosen between or weighed up to find a solution which, on balance, would tend to achieve or impede this or that political end.[84] Parody does not worry that it might take place 'within the terms of the law',[85] because it begins from doubling law's terms and not from an attempt simply to get outside of them (which would continue a sovereign topology). Nor does parody worry about the diachronic reincorporation of parodied gestures into the gestural vocabulary of power,[86] because what is important in each moment of parody is never this or that gesture in itself or in its power but the exposition of its mediality. Rather, according to Agamben's favoured account of the dialectic,[87] parody presents a simultaneous undecidability between the repetition of power's gestures and their weakening, and it this why it reveals a power which is 'ulterior': it is neither one nor the other.

Conclusion

The radical ambivalence of parody in Agamben's account, and the 'space alongside' political action that it opens, make it an oddity in the gestural vocabulary of protest and dissent. The 'only possible truth' about the 'being in force of language' that it attempts to expose is unlikely to be any political subject's intended goal *qua* political subject. This is because it cannot be a 'goal' of political action and it is only for this reason that it manages to expose a 'non-relation', to return to the language with which we established the intractable problem here. Parody may well be a protest strategy, but an Agambenian reading is not (primarily) intended as a model or manual for effective protest. Considering the distinction between Giorgio Agamben's account and that of other authors, it seems first and foremost to be a strategy of understanding; a specific mode of *vision*, a way of reading. This understanding shows itself here to be quite fragile, to the extent that the vision of mediality which it augurs always risks falling back *into* the medium. This is because every pure means is fragile or, as Agamben has said recently, *tenuous*, using a word

precisely from the co-extensivity of juridical thought with political space, which is what makes the emptiness of *ethos* important.

84 As seems to be suggested at times by Kenny, 'The Performative Surprise.'

85 See Butler, *Gender Trouble* 119 and discussion in Kenny, 'The Performative Surprise' 226.

86 Cf Butler, *Gender Trouble* 176. It should be noted that Butler's analysis, concerned with precisely the stability of this or that norm over time, has an evident explanatory and strategic power with respect to gender norms that Agamben's does not.

87 See Agamben, *The Signature of All Things* 19–20; Agamben, *Ninfe*.

that describes both his reading and its object.[88] But it is only in this fragility and its comportment with respect to ambivalence that it can exploit the conditions of the political spectacle towards a non-relation to power, residing in its ambivalence without prematurely foreclosing on it in order to claim efficacy, and the retotalisation of the space in which it acts.

88 S. Virgilio and G. Agamben, *La Natura Delle Cose* (Firenze: Maschietto Editore, 2008).

Part II

The state, violence and biopolitics

Chapter 5

The distribution of death

Notes towards a bio-political theory of criminal law

Ben Golder[1]

Introduction

In an article first published in 1991,[2] Duncan Kennedy interestingly compares Michel Foucault's poststructuralist genealogies of power to the work of the American legal realist Robert Hale. For Kennedy, whilst Hale's work on bargaining power is attentive to the ways in which legal 'ground rules' (primarily those of tort, contract and property) structure the field of possible economic action and thus asymmetrically distribute wealth, knowledge and power,[3] Foucault's work is blind to these aspects of law. Part of Foucault's problem is that in conceptualising law he is, according to Kennedy, here repeating Oliver Wendell Holmes's charge against John Austin, 'unmistakably a "criminalist" in his understanding of law' (that is, one who is 'obsessively focused on the fact that the sovereign orders or prohibits acts on pain of a sanction').[4] In Kennedy's account, Foucault's criminally synecdochic reading of law prevents him from appreciating law's 'distributive effects';[5] to wit, the ways in which pre-existing legal regimes constitute the matrix wherein power relations (here primarily conceived in terms of a bargaining process between capital and labour) take place – and thus (re)produce unjust socio-economic outcomes.

Although Kennedy's reading of Foucault on law is problematic for a number of reasons,[6] I am much less concerned with rewriting Kennedy (and rehabilitating

1 I would like to thank participants at the 2010 *Critical Criminology Conference* for their suggestions but, more especially, Elena Loizidou for her careful and encouraging reading of a previous draft of this chapter.
2 D. Kennedy, 'The Stakes of Law, Or Hale and Foucault!' (1991) 15(4) *Legal Studies Forum* 15 327 (reprinted with the same title in his *Sexy Dressing Etc.* (Cambridge, Mass.: Harvard University Press, 1993) 83–125.
3 ibid 329.
4 ibid 357.
5 ibid 327.
6 Kennedy does not purport to offer a full reading of Foucault's conception of law. As he puts it, '[t]he essay is more a rude appropriation of text-fragments of Hale and Foucault than a study of their thought', underaken in order to develop 'a method for analyzing the role of law in the reproduction of social injustice in late capitalist societies' (ibid

Foucault's legal theoretical credentials) than with using Kennedy's provocative reflections on Foucault and the criminal law as a starting point for my own purpose here; namely, to think about the uses of Foucault's notion of bio-politics for a critical engagement with contemporary criminal law. Kennedy's article raises a number of interrelated, prefatory questions to my own. Does Foucault think of law (or even just criminal law) in purely 'criminalist' terms? Indeed, what might it mean to maintain a distinction between a law that sanctions and a law which has distributive effect (or, conversely, are sanctions always already distributive)? Does this distinction (derived from Kennedy's reading of Hale) map onto Foucault's own distinctions between law and those extra-juridical technologies of power characteristic of modernity (discipline, bio-politics, governmentality) which he famously described in a number of works in the 1970s? And where exactly does the criminal law fit into this picture?

The answer I want to sketch in this chapter assumes not only that Foucault has a more expansive understanding of law that includes but goes beyond criminal law

327). Such an appropriation is of course entirely consonant with how Foucault encouraged people to use his work. Nevertheless, Kennedy's characterisation of Foucault's position on law is misleading in several respects. First, the attribution to him of a view of law as 'criminalist' fails to take into account some of Foucault's important discussions about civil forms of law. For just one example see M. Foucault, 'About the Concept of the "Dangerous Individual" in Nineteenth-Century Legal Psychiatry' in *Essential Works of Foucault 1954–1984 Vol 3: Power* (trans. by R. Hurley et al., ed J. D. Faubion) (New York: The New Press, 2000) 176, 196–200 (towards the end of which he discusses the important effect of civil law upon penal law). A second arguable element of Kennedy's reading is the contention that, for him, Foucault reified the notion of law and placed it in 'radical' opposition to disciplinary power – when in fact the better view (Kennedy's) is that '[t]he disciplinary is always already an element in legal power' (Kennedy, 'The Stakes of Law' 356, 364). A more generous reading of Foucault would allow that Kennedy's reading was in fact Foucault's as well. For such a reading see B. Golder and P. Fitzpatrick, *Foucault's Law* (Abingdon: Routledge, 2009) 26–29, 53–71. Thirdly, Kennedy argues that Foucault 'effaces legal institutions as loci of power/knowledge in their own right' (Kennedy, 'The Stakes of Law' 357). If by 'own right' Kennedy intends some kind of autonomous logic to law (in any of the four senses helpfully laid out by Roberto Unger – substantive, institutional, methodological or occupational) then the attribution is entirely apt but seemingly misses the force of Foucault's epistemological critique of modern law; but, if by 'own right' Kennedy simply means that Foucault fails to pay sufficient attention to how law, however dependently, does function as a system of power/knowledge, then the critique would not seem to pay sufficient attention to what Foucault is trying to achieve in texts such as *Discipline and Punish.* On the various meanings of autonomy see R. Unger, *Law in Modern Society* (New York: The Free Press, 1976) 48–58. Finally, Kennedy's assertion that 'Foucault's totalizing scheme brackets, along with the market, the whole area of legality' (Kennedy, 'The Stakes of Law' 357) could profitably be re-examined in the light of the recently translated series of lectures from 1978–1979 in which Foucault engages with questions of neo-liberalism and the interaction between the different forms of subjectivity required and produced by the market (*homo economicus*) and the law (*homo juridicus*). See M. Foucault, *The Birth of Biopolitics: Lectures at the Collège de France 1978–79* (trans. Graham Burchell) (Basingstoke: Palgrave Macmillan, 2008).

but that even his notion of criminal law itself cannot be reduced to the Austinian, 'criminalist' model adumbrated by Kennedy.[7] Indeed, this latter point is crucial both to grasping Foucault's critique of law and to situating my own arguments here. On a basic level, Foucault's critique is an attempt to problematise, indeed to confound, the traditional jurisprudential quarantining of 'law' from other forms of knowledge and power. As Foucault expresses in many places, but most exhaustively in *Discipline and Punish*, the apparatus of modern criminal law cannot be understood outside the terms of its investment by the strictly extra-juridical discourses of discipline and the human sciences.[8] In much of his work of the 1970s Foucault aims to show precisely how 'discourses born of discipline are invading right, and [how] normalizing procedures are increasingly colonizing the procedures of the law';[9] indeed, even how '[t]he penal machine can no longer function simply with a law . . . [but rather] needs something else, supplementary material'.[10] Thus, after Foucault, any simple distinction between the juridical and the extra-juridical dimensions of the apparatus we call 'criminal law' can only have an initial and attenuated heuristic value as the disciplinary supplement comes inevitably to challenge the putative integrity of law.

These are the starting, background assumptions I make here about the tenor and the texture of Foucault's engagement with the criminal law. Undoubtedly, Foucault's work of the 1970s (his specification of discipline, panopticism, normalisation, dangerousness, risk, and so forth) has been remarkably influential in expanding and reorienting criminological research agendas beyond the juridical frame.[11] As Mariana Valverde observes in a recent survey, Foucault's ideas breathed new life into critical criminology'[12] and this evidently continues to be the case. But,

7 This also raises the wider question of Foucault's position on law and what has been called his 'expulsion' of law from modernity. For the argument that Foucault expelled law from modernity see A. Hunt and G. Wickham, *Foucault and Law: Towards a Sociology of Law as Governance* (London: Pluto Press, 1994). I have addressed this question with Peter Fitzpatrick at greater length elsewhere and assume for present purposes that Foucault did not expel law from modernity but rather saw it as being integral and constitutive. See generally Golder and Fitzpatrick, *Foucault's Law*.

8 For example see M. Foucault, *Discipline and Punish: The Birth of the Prison* (trans. Alan Sheridan) (Harmondsworth: Penguin, 1991) 170, 221–24.

9 M. Foucault, *'Society Must Be Defended': Lectures at the Collège de France 1975–76* (trans. D. Macey) (London: Allen Lane, 2003) 38–39. See also Golder and Fitzpatrick, *Foucault's Law* 24.

10 Foucault, 'About the Concept of the "Dangerous Individual"' 177.

11 On dangerousness and risk in particular see the work of Mark Brown and John Pratt. See generally M. Brown and J. Pratt, *Dangerous Offenders: Punishment and Social Order* (London: Routledge, 2000); J. Pratt, *Governing the Dangerous* (Sydney: Federation Press, 1997).

12 M. Valverde, 'Beyond Discipline and Punish: Foucault's Challenge to Criminology' (2008) 4 *The Carceral Notebooks* 201. Of course, as Valverde goes on to state, the impact of Foucault's ideas upon what is called 'administrative criminology' (indeed, the impact of critical criminology as a whole upon the mainstream) has been markedly less effective (at 203). Valverde argues that there needs to be a wider reading of Foucault's work in critical criminology which engages with Foucault's notions of bio-politics, security and

bearing in mind the difficulty of the very distinction between the juridical and the extra-juridical in the wake of Foucault, what I want to do in this chapter is to make a return to the juridical criminal sanction and to examine its possible bio-political effects. That is, granted Foucault's more expansive appreciation of the penal apparatus as the interaction between a juridical law and various extra-juridical political technologies, is there nevertheless a bio-political function performed by the *mere* sanction? Can we limit the effect of a sanction to one of pure prohibition? Has the sanction's social ordering and redistributive dimensions been under-emphasised?[13] It might appear that an inquiry into the bio-political effects of the criminal sanction is necessarily forestalled by a Foucauldian frame of inquiry, insisting as it does upon the productive operations of power. But the present inquiry is intended to sketch some of the ways in which that very (supposedly negative and restraining) sanction is itself productive of a range of effects. Recalling Kennedy's earlier assertion that Foucault was a 'criminalist' in his understanding of law, the reading I propose here draws upon (and yet contests) the concepts employed by Kennedy of *sanction* and *distribution*. In my reading – one which implicates the semantic and juridical ambiguity of the *sanction* as that which both allows and disallows – Foucault's work on bio-politics can be used to rethink criminal law not as making provision for the protection of life but precisely as a mechanism for the distribution of death. That is, according to the reading pursued here, bio-politics and criminal law are not opposed but rather coincident (or at any rate convergent) modalities of power; criminal law in its juridical form can be seen to operate according to a bio-political logic, and that logic practises a distribution of death.

technologies of the self. For another positive assessment of the value of Foucault's work in the context of criminology (and one which does engage with some of this later work) see David Garland, '"Governmentality" and the Problem of Crime: Foucault, Criminology, Sociology' (1997) 1 *Theoretical Criminology* 173.

13 To clarify somewhat, and to situate my argument further, I take it as self-evident from Foucault's texts that the formal instruments of law intersect and interact with modalities of power such as discipline. However, much of the literature on the relations between law and power in Foucault's thought, following Hunt and Wickham (*Foucault and Law*), has stressed the dependence of law on these other forms of power, and suggests that this dependence is more in the nature of a subordination or an instrumentalisation of law. One of the things that I am trying to achieve in this chapter is to stress the ongoing relevance of juridical instruments in contemporary bio-political configurations. Another, related, aim is to stress not the repressive but rather the productive element of the criminal sanction. This productivity, or generativity, of the criminal sanction could be pursued via a critical genealogy of the objects and subjects of criminal regulation. On this possibility see the discussion of Judith Butler in n 21 below. Here I pursue another productive aspect of the criminal sanction – namely its redistributive effect and, more specifically, its capacity to structure the social field so as to distribute life and death. For an analysis of the criminal law in a different, psychoanalytic, register that contests the notion of criminal law as 'prohibitive' and focuses instead on its regulative dimension see E. Loizidou, 'Criminal Law and Punishment: Indexical Permission' (2004) 6(3) *Punishment and Society* 303.

What I hope to show in this chapter, then – focusing on the formal instruments of criminal law and not on extra-juridical technologies such as discipline – is that *even* at the level of its juridical instantiation criminal law operates in a bio-political register. The argument that I shall make – first through a reading of Foucault's texts on bio-politics and then through a critique of certain exemplary bio-political practices in liberal criminal law – is that from a bio-political perspective criminal law can be understood as an apparatus for the differential distribution of death within a population to be governed. Criminal law emerges from such a perspective not as some expressive, communal renunciation of transgression or immorality nor as a protection of interests (such as life, for example) but precisely as a mechanism for the rationing of life. As I hope to show, it is through the mechanism of the juridical *sanction* that the criminal law distributes death differentially. It does so – or can do so – along the axes of race, class and gender. Indeed, some of Foucault's explicit but scattered comments on the differential distribution of death (or, how bio-politics kills) are framed in terms of race. However, the perspective adopted here in order to excavate the bio-politics of contemporary liberal criminal law is that of *sexuality*. The examples I draw upon to illuminate this aspect of criminal law are the 'Homosexual Advance Defence' (HAD) and the criminalisation of gay sex. These are by no means the only examples, nor perhaps necessarily the most important historical or contemporary ones. Rather, the use made of them here as examples is to illuminate the productive logic of the criminal sanction. But let me begin in the next section by introducing Foucault's notion of bio-politics and extracting from it the question of the distribution of death. In so doing, my reading of Foucauldian bio-politics will aim to show how it is that death is not foreclosed by a politics of life but necessarily forms a part of it. Ranging over Foucault's examples of this persistence of death within the bio-political (examples of race war, of eugenic extermination, and so forth) I want next to focus upon the ways in which the contemporary liberal apparatus of criminal law itself distributes death through its sanctioning of homophobic violence and of gay sex.

Bio-politics and (the distribution of) death

According to Foucault's oft-cited formulation from the final part of *The History of Sexuality Vol 1* ('Right of Death and Power over Life'), power undergoes a 'very profound transformation' in the transition to modernity.[14] Once the 'threshold of

14 M. Foucault, *The Will to Knowledge: The History of Sexuality Vol 1* (trans. R. Hurley) (Harmondsworth: Penguin, 1979) 136. The present chapter focuses on Foucault's articulation of bio-politics and does not engage with more recent elaborations, the most notable of which is Giorgio Agamben's redeployment of the concept in his *Homo Sacer* project. The methodological differences between the two thinkers have been much observed (see for instance M. Ojakangas, 'Impossible Dialogue on Bio-power' (2005) 2 *Foucault Studies*; P. Patton, 'Agamben and Foucault on Biopower and Biopolitics' in *Giorgio Agamben: Sovereignty and Life* (ed M. Calarco and S. DeCaroli) (Stanford: Stanford

modernity' is crossed,[15] power ceases to operate predominantly according to a logic of *deduction* and increasingly becomes *generative*. Here is how Foucault explains the former logic:

> Perhaps this juridical form must be referred to a historical type of society in which power was exercised mainly as a means of deduction (*prélèvement*), a subtraction mechanism, a right to appropriate a portion of the wealth, a tax of products, goods and services, labor and blood, levied on the subjects. Power in this instance was essentially a right of seizure: of things, time, bodies, and ultimately life itself; it culminated in the privilege to seize hold of life in order to suppress it.[16]

In modernity, however, '"[d]eduction" has tended to be no longer the major form of power but merely one element among others, working to incite, reinforce, control, monitor, optimise, and organise the forces under it: a power bent on generating forces, making them grow, and ordering them, rather than one dedicated to impeding them, making them submit, or destroying them'.[17] If deduction represents a power to take life away (ultimately, a power of death) then the generative aspect of power represents a power over life itself. Updating his earlier theses on disciplinary power,[18] Foucault here argues that modern power is

University Press, 2007) 203–18; and Catherine Mills's chapter in the Calarco and DeCaroli volume 'Biopolitics, Liberal Eugenics, and Nihilism' 180–202)). Foucault's genealogical deployment of the concept as an analytic of power in situated, historical contexts is a more apt tool for the work I am trying to do in this chapter.

15 The notion of a threshold of modernity is a recurrent (yet changing) theme in Foucault's work. For example, we see in *The Order of Things* that 'the threshold that separates us from Classical thought and constitutes our modernity' is rendered by Foucault in epistemological terms, being of course the dissolution of the Classical *episteme* centered upon representation. See M. Foucault, *The Order of Things: An Archaeology of the Human Sciences* (New York: Vintage Books, 1970) xxiv. When genealogy replaces archaeology as Foucault's preferred methodology, we find a different explanation rendered this time in terms of technologies of power. Compare Foucault, *The History of Sexuality Vol 1* 143 ('But what might be called a society's "threshold of modernity" has been reached when the life of the species is wagered on its own political strategies'). Here the political replaces the epistemological as the index of the modern. When, finally, modernity is rendered neither as a temporal event nor as a set of features proper to an era (either political or epistemological), but rather as an 'attitude' that one takes towards the present, the thematic of the threshold and its relationship to modernity becomes reversed and thence reformulated as a question of how, if one is adopting a 'modern' attitude, one works critically upon one's limits (or thresholds) in order to go beyond them, to become otherwise than one is, and so forth. See M. Foucault, 'What is Enlightenment?' in *Essential Works of Foucault 1954–1984 Vol 1: Ethics, Subjectivity and Truth* (trans. Robert Hurley et al, ed P. Rabinow) (Harmondsworth: Allen Lane/Penguin, 1997) 303–19.

16 Foucault, *The History of Sexuality Vol 1* 136.

17 ibid 136.

18 Most fully developed in *Discipline and Punish*.

constituted by 'two poles of development linked together by a whole cluster of intermediary relations': on the one hand, there exists an '*anatamo-politics of the human body*' (namely, the disciplines) and now, on the other, a '*bio-politics of the population*'.[19] Modern power in its generative guise thus traverses the institutional subjection of the body and the regulatory intervention into the life of the population. In sum:

> The setting up, in the course of the classical age, of this great biopolar technology – anatomic and biological, individualizing and specifying, directed towards the performances of the body, with attention to the processes of life – characterized a power whose highest function was perhaps no longer to kill, but to invest life through and through.[20]

For Foucault, modern political technologies (discipline and bio-politics) are thus distinguished from premodern forms by a much greater attention to fostering life; that is, to constituting the conditions under which life emerges and to conducting the manner in which it is lived (both at the level of the individual body and at the level of the population). As Foucault pithily suggests: 'One might say that the ancient right to *take* life or *let* live was replaced by a power to *foster* life or *disallow* it to the point of death'.[21] Whereas the ancient sovereign acts only to take life, or to threaten to take life (and is only minimally interested in constituting the conditions of life), modern power seizes hold of life itself as a political object through a range of disciplinary and regulatory interventions (and is seemingly less interested in directly taking away the life of its subjects).

In places, Foucault tends to equate the deductive aspect of power with sovereignty and the generative aspect of power with technologies such as disciplinary power and bio-politics,[22] and to argue that the old forms of deductive

19 Foucault, *The History of Sexuality Vol 1* 139 (emphasis in original).
20 ibid 139.
21 ibid 138 (emphasis in original).
22 Judith Butler makes the point that a binary distinction between repressive power and productive power fails, and that repressive power merely disavows its own productivity (and that it is the role of a critical genealogy to unmask this disavowal). In places this reading is advanced as a critique of Foucault, and in others Foucault is credited with this very insight. For an example of the former see her 'Sexual Inversions' in *Foucault and the Critique of Institutions* (ed J. Caputo and M. Yount) (University Park, Penn.: Pennsylvania State University Press, 1993) 81–98. As she puts it there, the Foucauldian distinction between a repressive juridical law and a productive power is a false one and that in fact the juridical is '*already productive* power, forming the very object that will be suitable for control and then, in an act that effectively disavows that production, claiming to discover that [object] outside of power' (at 87, emphasis in original). See also her *Subjects of Desire: Hegelian Reflections in Twentieth-Century France* (New York: Columbia University Press, 1987) 228. But compare this critique of Foucault with the attribution to him in *Gender Trouble* of the very insight she has just developed: 'Foucault points out that juridical systems of power *produce* the subjects they subsequently come to represent' (Judith

power have been replaced (or supplanted) by these new forms of generative power. For example, we have already seen him state that the 'ancient right to *take* life or *let* live' is 'replace[d]' by the 'power to *foster* life' and he goes on to observe in *The History of Sexuality, Vol 1* that: 'The old power of death that symbolised sovereign power was now carefully supplanted by the administration of bodies and the calculated management of life'.[23] But then again in other places he is much more nuanced, insisting – as we have also seen above – that the logic of deduction does not entirely disappear but is rather de-emphasised, being 'no longer the major form of power but merely one element among others'.[24] As he puts it in the lecture series *'Society Must be Defended'*: 'I wouldn't say exactly that sovereignty's old right – to take life or let live – was replaced, but it came to be complemented by a new right which does not erase the old right but which does penetrate it, permeate it'.[25] According to this more refined view, then, sovereignty is not overcome but is rather supplemented and altered in modernity. Instead, as he memorably describes the co-existence of sovereignty, discipline and government in an earlier lecture series, *Security, Territory, Population*, technologies of power are not disposed of or usurped but rather taken up again, reactivated and made to function in different relations:

> So we should not see things as the replacement of a society of sovereignty by a society of discipline, and then of a society of discipline by a society, say, of government. In fact we have a triangle: sovereignty, discipline, and governmental management, which has population as its main target and apparatuses of security as its essential mechanism.[26]

It follows that Foucault is best understood not as offering a reductive historical argument about a given type of society and its definitive power structures being replaced in time (that is, some kind of caricatured Durkheimian thesis about

Butler, *Gender Trouble: Feminism and the Subversion of Identity* (London: Routledge, 1990) 2 (emphasis in original)). At any rate, Butler's/Foucault's insistence on the productivity of the juridical is indeed useful for theorising law. Law can accordingly be seen as both productive of *objects of control* (recall Foucault's description of discourses 'as practices that systematically form the objects of which they speak' in M. Foucault, *The Archaeology of Knowledge* (trans. A. M. Sheridan Smith) (London: Routledge, 1972) 49) and *subject positions*. Indeed, *The Archaeology of Knowledge* furnishes several examples of law (as discourse) constituting objects of control and subject positions (for example see the discussion of: 'objects that are differentiated in daily practice, in law, in religious casuistry, in medical diagnosis . . .' (at 33); 'law and penal law in particular' as discourses which alongside medicine 'delimited, designated, named, and established madness as an object' (at 42); and, finally, the way in which law 'statutorily define[s]' the medical expert (at 51)).

23 Foucault, *The History of Sexuality Vol 1* 138 (emphasis in original), 139–40.

24 ibid 136.

25 Foucault, *'Society Must be Defended'* 241.

26 M. Foucault, *Security, Territory, Population: Lectures at the Collège de France 1977–78* (trans. G. Burchell) (Basingstoke: Palgrave Macmillan, 2007) 107–8.

power)[27] but rather is trying to illustrate a more complex picture in which different technologies of power co-exist and interrelate at a given historical moment.[28] Deposed from its erstwhile position as organising principle and code of power relations,[29] sovereignty (as a given technology of power) nevertheless still persists in Foucault's account of modernity (if in altered form). But if a reading along these lines can be given of what at first glance looks like Foucault's simplistic historical periodisation (of a premodern sovereignty versus a modern and non-sovereign regime of discipline and bio-politics) then must the same be done with his founding and more important conceptual distinction – namely that between a (negative) power to deal death and a (positive) power over life itself (either in its disciplinary or bio-political manifestations)? Put another way, how does death figure in a bio-political economy? Can a power dedicated to the optimising of life nevertheless permit itself to kill?

An answer to this question – an answer made more explicit towards the end of the book – is initially suggested in Foucault's celebrated discussion of the 'repressive hypothesis' in the opening pages of *The History of Sexuality, Vol 1*. There, in terms now abundantly well known, Foucault attempts to debunk the notion that discussion of sex and sexuality in the modern West had been universally prohibited and repressed. Against this idea – or, more accurately, in an attempt to reformulate it critically – Foucault asserts that there has in fact not been a repression but a veritable explosion of sex talk. 'Rather than a massive censorship', he writes, 'beginning with the verbal proprieties imposed by the Age of Reason, what was involved was a regulated and polymorphous incitement to discourse'.[30] But if we have, according to Foucault, never talked with such garrulousness about our sex (and that of others) in the modern age, this does not result in a simple profusion of speech. There remain silences and gaps in the speech on sex. Silence does not disappear but rather is made to function differently in an overall economy of speech, or of the incitement to speech:

> Silence itself – the things one declines to say, or is forbidden to name, the discretion that is required between different speakers – is less the absolute limit of discourse, the other side from which it is separated by a strict boundary, than an element that functions alongside the things said, with them and in relation to over-all strategies. There is no binary division to be made between what one says and what one does not say; we must try to determine the different ways of not saying such things, how those who can and those who

27 Cf G. Rose, *Dialectic of Nihilism: Post-Structuralism and Law* (Oxford: Blackwell, 1984) 174–77.
28 G. Pavlich, *Governing Paradoxes of Restorative Justice* (London: GlassHouse Press, 2005) 9.
29 Foucault, *The History of Sexuality Vol 1* 89. See also M. Foucault, 'Truth and Power' in *Power/Knowledge: Selected Interviews and Other Writings 1972–1977* (trans. C. Gordon et al, ed C. Gordon) (Brighton: Harvester Press, 1980) 109–33, 121.
30 Foucault, *The History of Sexuality Vol 1* 34.

> cannot speak of them are distributed, which type of discourse is authorized, or which form of discretion is required in either case. There is not one but many silences, and they are an integral part of the strategies that underlie and permeate discourses.[31]

As Foucault insists here, the binary distinction between the plenitude of speech in sex-discourse and the absence of silence brought about through prohibition and repression cannot be maintained. Speech and silence are indissolubly bound up with each other, and for Foucault a whole range of more salient political questions is opened up here around the questions of the distribution of speech and the role which silence performs within a wider discursive strategy.

And just as in the midst of speech there is a necessary silence, so too in the midst of life there are necessary deaths. When Foucault comes at the end of the book to develop his theses about the bio-political nature of modernity he poses himself a question similar to the one which I formulated above: 'How could power exercise its highest prerogatives by putting people to death, when its main role was to ensure, sustain, and multiply life, to put this life in order?'[32] How to account for the ongoing fact of state killing and of explicit sovereign violence in an age where life had supposedly become the political object *par excellence*? Foucault is equivocal here but I want to insist (in part against him) that the answer he (ultimately) gives parallels the answer to the question of silence in sex-discourse. He writes that: 'Now it is over life, through its unfolding, that power establishes its dominion; death is power's limit, the moment that escapes it'.[33] Strangely, Foucault here maintains (and this is in conflict not only with the relation he sketches between speech and silence but also, more fundamentally, with the relation he describes between power and resistance)[34] that death is maintained in a relation of exteriority to life; that death somehow escapes or exists on a different plane from life. But the examples Foucault goes on to give in the text themselves contradict this purported relation between life and death and hint at a more nuanced and (for the purposes of contemporary critique) more useful answer. The examples he gives are war and the death penalty. In the case of the former, Foucault observes, 'wars were never as bloody as they have been since the nineteenth century, and all things being equal, never before did regimes visit such holocausts on their own populations'.[35] The seeming paradox of a bio-political war is accounted for thus: 'Wars are no longer waged in the name of a sovereign who must be defended; they are waged on behalf of the existence of everyone; entire populations are mobilised for the purpose of wholesale slaughter in the name of life necessity: massacres have

31 ibid 27.
32 ibid 138.
33 ibid 138.
34 ibid 95 ('this resistance is never in a position of exteriority in relation to power').
35 ibid 136–37.

become vital'.[36] If the example of modern warfare reveals the bio-political necessity of killing for the sake of life then the example of the death penalty – a putative 'limit', 'scandal' or 'contradiction' situated in regards to the politics of life[37] – reveals the disciplinary imperative to correct (and in default of this to delete) the aberrant individual. Foucault argues that 'capital punishment could not be maintained except by invoking less the enormity of the crime itself than the monstrosity of the criminal, his incorrigibility and the safeguard of society'.[38] In the sentence that follows this statement, Foucault raises the crucial spectre of race (to which we shall return shortly). He writes: 'One had the right to kill those who represented a kind of biological danger to others'.[39]

So, Foucault's two brief examples of war and the death penalty reveal the continued bio-political appetite for death. Death, furthermore, emerges through these examples not as posed in conceptual opposition to life but rather as immanent to, and co-implicated with, death. There is a field of life and death within which the bio-political actor operates and upon which it intervenes. Life and death are distributed within this field according to a principle of division and, famously, Foucault formulates this principle in the lecture series *'Society Must be Defended'* in terms of race and racism. Whilst race is evident in his discussion of bio-political killing in *The History of Sexuality, Vol 1*, it is very much foregrounded in the lecture series.[40] Racism emerges in the latter text as that which allows the bio-political to kill. 'When you have a normalizing society, you have a power which is, at least superficially, in the first instance, or in the first line a biopower, and racism is the indispensable condition that allows someone to be killed, that allows others to be killed', writes Foucault. 'Once the State functions in the biopower mode', he continues, 'racism alone can justify the murderous

36 ibid 137.
37 ibid 138.
38 ibid 138.
39 ibid.
40 Curiously, the thematic of race emerges in the lecture series *'Society Must be Defended'* but is then promptly discontinued in Foucault's written work and in his lectures. For example, in the lecture course for the year immediately following *'Society Must be Defended'* Foucault discusses similar themes to the racial sacrifice that opens up a biological *caesura* within the population, but he does so in somewhat different terms. Foucault's analysis is framed not in terms of race and the *caesura* that race opens up within the body politic (allowing 'others' to be killed so that some, 'we', may live), but rather in terms of a *caesura* between the 'pertinent' level of the population (which is the object of governmental management and control) and the merely 'instrumental' level of the individual who, accordingly, can be sacrificed (see Foucault, *Security, Territory, Population* 67). On the question of race in *'Society Must be Defended'* see A. Laura Stoler, *Race and the Education of Desire: Foucault's* History of Sexuality *and the Colonial Order of Things* (Durham: Duke University Press, 1995) 55–94. On the biological *caesura* in Foucault's thinking of bio-politics see G. Agamben, *Remnants of Auschwitz: The Witness and the Archive* (trans. D. Heller-Roazen) (New York: Zone Books, 2002) 82–86.

function of the state'.[41] How and why does race perform this role? Foucault explains:

> What in fact is racism? It is primarily a way of introducing a break into the domain of life that is under power's control: the break between what must live and what must die. The appearance within the biological continuum of the human race of races, the distinction among races, the hierarchy of races, the fact that certain races are described as good and that others, in contrast, are described as inferior: all this is a way of fragmenting the field of the biological that power controls. It is a way of separating out the groups that exist within a population. It is, in short, a way of establishing a biological-type caesura within a population that appears to be a biological domain. This will allow power to treat the population as a mixture of races, or to be more accurate, to treat the species, to subdivide the species it controls, into the subspecies known, precisely, as races. That is the first function of racism: to fragment, to create caesuras within the biological continuum addressed by biopower.[42]

Racism is thus the mechanism which allows a splitting of the bio-political field and a consequent division of lives into those to be lived and those to be killed. Or, as Colette Guillaumin puts it, 'race is a technical means, a machine, for committing murder'.[43] This is in fact a neat way of characterising the Foucauldian understanding of race articulated in these lectures – precisely as a machine, or as an element in a bio-political machine, which allows a power putatively dedicated to the optimisation of life to take life away. Of course, to call this understanding of race 'Foucauldian' invites the understandable objection that in several key respects it appears very much un-Foucauldian in its explicit linking of racism to the state form ('[o]nce the State functions in the biopower mode . . .')[44] and in its failure to account, in more

41 Foucault, *'Society Must be Defended'* 256.
42 ibid 255.
43 C. Guillaumin, *Racism, Sexism, Power and Ideology* (Routledge: London, 1995) 107.
44 Foucault, *'Society Must be Defended'* 256 (and see also 259: 'racism is bound up with the workings of a state'). In the years after the publication of *Discipline and Punish* Foucault was heavily criticised by Marxists for the fact that his theorisation of power relations as radically dispersed and as 'capillary' failed to take adequate account of larger-scale aggregations of power. (Of course, the criticism was not only made by Marxists. For a feminist-inspired criticism of Foucault on this point see Z. R. Eisenstein, *The Female Body and the Law* (Berkeley: University of California Press, 1988) 16–20.) Specifically, it was argued that a proper consideration of the state apparatus and the state's organisation and centralisation of violence were conspicuously absent from Foucault's analysis (see for example N. Poulantzas, *State, Power, Socialism* (trans. P. Camiller) (London: Verso, 2000) 44). Hence we see Foucault in this period attempt to justify and explain himself in interviews. He says, for example, 'I don't claim at all that the State apparatus is unimportant' and 'I don't want to say that the State isn't important; what I want to say is that relations of power, and hence the analysis that must be made of them, necessarily extend beyond the limits of the State' (Foucault, 'Body/Power' in *Power/Knowledge*

classic Foucauldian vein perhaps, for the subjectifiying aspects of the political technology of race (to the contrary, race is here narrowly conceived as a repressive function exposing to death, itself nevertheless understood broadly as 'the fact of exposing someone to death, increasing the risk of death for some people, or, quite simply, political death, expulsion, rejection, and so on').[45] At any rate, we arrive now at an understanding of the bio-political as a technique for managing populations that does not exclude killing as a limit but introduces it as a split within the field of lives to be governed. Foucault's examples tend towards the extreme. As we have seen, he discusses war and the death penalty, in which the split within the population, whilst aleatory, is nevertheless discernible. However, it is when he engages the hyperbolic instantiation of the bio-political state, the Nazi state, that this *caesura* vanishes, or rather collapses. In the Nazi state, disciplinary, bio-political and murderous technologies coincide: 'The Nazi State makes the field of life it manages, protects, guarantees, and cultivates in biological terms absolutely coextensive with the sovereign right to kill anyone, meaning not only other people, but also its own people . . . We have an absolutely racist State, and absolutely murderous State, and an absolutely suicidal State'.[46] What I want to examine here, however – using the model derived from Foucault of a bio-politics which distributes death – is how the contemporary liberal apparatus of criminal law functions in a similar way. I want to show how criminal law practises this bio-political division of life using sexuality as a principle of division and deploying the juridical *sanction* as its tool The two examples I use to begin to sketch this juridical bio-political conjuncture are the HAD and the criminalisation of sex.

The distribution of death through the criminal sanction

The HAD is, amongst other things, somewhat of a misnomer. For a start, it is not a 'defence' in its own right, but rather a particular narrative used to substantiate either a claim in provocation or in self-defence.[47] As most of the reported

55–62, 60; Foucault, 'Truth and Power' 122). This 'response to his critics' may go some way to explaining the focus on the state in Foucault's thematisation of racism in *'Society Must be Defended'*.

45 Foucault, *'Society Must be Defended'* 256.

46 ibid 260.

47 Although the terms are frequently used interchangeably in the literature on homophobia-related violence and criminal defences, it is useful to distinguish the related 'defence' of the 'Homosexual Panic Defence' (HPD) from the HAD because, whilst they refer to similar scenarios, there are still a number of salient historical, jurisprudential, medico-legal and discursive distinctions between the two concepts. To this end, whereas with the HAD evidence of an unwanted homosexual advance is led in support of either a defence of provocation or self-defence, the term HPD was originally employed by American academics and activists to refer to US cases in which a defendant would plead insanity, or diminished responsibility, in answer to the charge of murdering a gay male

litigation deploys the HAD in the service of a defence of provocation this is what I focus upon here.[48] If accepted by a criminal jury, the effect of a common law defence of provocation is to mitigate what would have been a conviction for murder to manslaughter (whereas a defence of self-defence secures the accused a full acquittal).[49] As traditionally and historically conceived, the excuse-based defence of provocation represents a 'concession to human frailty',[50] but by now even mainstream judicial commentators have been led to observe that 'the law's concession to human frailty was very much, in its practical application, a concession to male frailty . . . [and, more specifically, to] the frailty of those whose blood was apt to boil'.[51] From its normative roots in 'a world of Restoration gallantry' as a reparation of offended male honour,[52] to its more contemporary manifestation as a juridical defence of male sexual jealousy and the objectification of women, provocation has always acted as a 'profoundly sexed excuse for murder'.[53] Of course, the particular frailty catered to by the HAD-species of provocation is the frailty of the homicidal homophobe whose blood has been brought to a metaphorical boiling point by a supposed sexual advance – a sexual

victim, where that victim had made an unsolicited sexual advance upon the defendant. The plea rested on the rather dubious clinical basis of a psychological disorder entitled 'acute homosexual panic', a condition first identified by the psychiatrist Edward J Kempf in 1920. Kempf developed his theory whilst working in a government mental institution during and in the years following the First World War, studying the supposedly deleterious effects on returned soldiers and sailors of having been 'grouped together in same-sex environments for prolonged periods during the War'. According to the psychological literature, the standard script is that the subject who suffers from the disorder is in actual fact a 'latent homosexual' who is terrified of his attraction to other men yet is similarly terrified of heterosexuality. In Kempf's case histories, the disorder of 'acute homosexual panic' does not lead to the sort of brutal violence which typifies contemporary legal narratives, but rather the subject suffers from feelings of disgust and self-loathing more likely to manifest in self-harm and suicide than interpersonal violence. For a critical discussion of the HPD see K. S. Suffredini, 'Pride and Prejudice: The Homosexual Panic Defense' (2001) 21 *Boston College Third World Law Journal* 279, 288–92. The example of the HPD itself illustrates the crucial interrelation of juridical and extra-juridical discourses on sexuality, but I do not pursue that analysis here.

48 Although note the Victorian case of *R v Murley* (unreported, 1992), discussed in P. Johnston, '"More than Ordinary Men Gone Wrong": Can the Law Know the Gay Subject?' (1996) 20 *Melbourne University Law Review* 1152, in which both self-defence and provocation were pleaded and the accused was acquitted entirely.

49 The origins of the defence of provocation lie in the common law, but in many jurisdictions it has been modified by statute. For example see s 21 of the Crimes Act 1901 (NSW).

50 *Smith* [2000] UKHL 49 (Lord Hoffmann).

51 *Chhay* (1992) 72 A Crim R 1 at 11 (Gleeson CJ).

52 *Smith* [2000] UKHL 49 (Lord Hoffmann).

53 A. Howe, 'Reforming Provocation (More or Less)' (1999) 12 *Australian Feminist Law Journal* 127, 130. See also J. Morgan, 'Provocation Law and Facts: Dead Women Tell no Tales, Tales Are Told About Them' (1997) 21(1) *Melbourne University Law Review* 237 (reviewing relevant case law).

advance so disgusting as to have provoked the accused to kill. This exculpatory narrative of honour, disgust and corporeal intrusion has been used successfully in a number of different common law criminal jurisdictions and is typically deployed in two scenarios.[54] As the Australian sociologist of hate crime, Stephen Tomsen, has put it:

> The first of these fatal scenarios comprised a vicious gang attack in public space. Most often these were carried out at homosexual 'beats' or in a known gay precinct such as the Oxford Street/Darlinghurst area of inner-Sydney. The second general type of these crimes resulted from personal disputes and resulting violent conflicts that usually occurred between two men. Most typically, the survivor alleged that he was subjected to a sexual advance or a sexual attack by the deceased. These incidents tended to occur in private settings and often after episodes of drinking and socializing between male friends or acquaintances.[55]

The defence hence functions in the time-honoured fashion of victim-blaming by alleging that the allegedly gay victim 'provoked his own demise' by coming on to his attacker.[56] Of course, in a tactical sense an accused will often plead both self-defence and provocation simultaneously. Moreover, in a discursive sense, it is difficult to separate the affects of fear/apprehension (self-defence) and rage (provocation) in the courtroom deployment and judicial inscription of the HAD precisely because of the rhetorical ease with which homosexual desire is cast as predatory, abusive, and so forth.[57] And, as Tomsen's comments above make clear, the juridical retellings of homosexual advances are frequently poorly veiled *ex post facto* rationalisations for premeditated gay bashing or narratives superimposed upon a personal dispute the other side of which we never hear. But what concerns us here is not so much *what actually happened* in these cases but rather the somewhat different question of: what is the function and the effect of a juridical law which

54 For example, there was a rise in the number of HAD cases in the Australian state jurisdictions of New South Wales and Victoria in the 1990s, which culminated in the High Court of Australia's decision in *Green v The Queen* (1997) 191 CLR 334 which allowed the use of the defence in that case. For a structurallly similar New Zealand case on provocation see *R v Campbell* [1997] 1 NZLR 16. Both *Green* and *Campbell* feature disavowals of homophobia *per se* but an acceptance of the 'defence' of HAD where it is twinned with claims of child sexual assault. For more on this see my '"It forced me to open more than I could bear": HAD, Paedophilia, and the Discursive Limits of the Male Heterosexual Body' in *An Aesthetics of Law and Culture: Texts, Images, Screens* (ed. A. T. Kenyon and P. Rush) (Amsterdam: Elsevier, 2004) 53–72 at 65–67.

55 S. Tomsen, '"He Had to be a Poofter or Something": Violence, Male Honour and Heterosexual Panic' (1998) 3(2) *Journal of Interdisciplinary Gender Studies* 44, 46.

56 See A. Howe, 'More Folk Provoke Their Own Demise (Homophobic Violence and Sexed Excuses) – Rejoining the Provocation Law Debate, Courtesy of the Homosexual Advance Defence' (1997) 19(3) *Sydney Law Review* 336.

57 For more on this see Golder, 'It forced me to open more than I could bear'.

enshrines the view either that non-violent homosexual advances are sufficiently provocative as to exculpate an accused from a murder conviction or that such advances are so brutal as to constitute a threat against which an accused is justified in retaliating with lethal violence? That is, simply: what is the HAD?

According to a certain orthodox liberal view the HAD offends against principles of anti-discrimination, human rights and human dignity and its existence in the legislation represents an embarrassment to an enlightened modern criminal law which purports to treat legal subjects equally.[58] Others allocate to criminal law a more discursively constitutive role. The HAD surely represents, according to such a view, a 'judicial institutionalisation of homophobia'[59] – indeed, judgments of criminality here are surely inseparable from judgments of sexuality and the 'institutionalisation' of these views undoubtedly perform crucial discursive work.[60] But what I want to propose here is that the HAD can equally be understood from the perspective I have been developing above, namely as a bio-political technology that distributes death within a population. Here the sanction is a judicial letting-kill and the bio-political *caesura* revolves around the vector of sexuality. The state thus sanctions, in the sense of permitting, lethal violence against gay people both by partially excusing it through the operation of the defence of provocation and by sending a message that homosexual desire is to be reviled and a legitimate response to it is to kill. Thus gay men are exposed differentially through the work of law to a certain level of violence and their lives constituted as less worthy of being lived. In his analysis of the US Supreme Court decision of *Bowers v Hardwick*, to which I shall return again below, Kendall Thomas deploys a Foucauldian critique to link the 'private lawlessness'[61] of the homophobic vigilante with the state power that organises that violence by sanctioning it retrospectively and inciting it prospectively:

> [T]he body of the victim of homophobic violence is the environment for the practice of a brutal "bio-politics". The terrorisation of gay men and lesbian women through homophobic violence dramatizes two intersecting political

58 For example see J. Potter, 'Does the "Homosexual Advance Defence" Erode Equality Before the Law in Criminal Cases?' (2001) 3(1) *e-valuate* available at http://www.law.ecel.uwa.edu.au/ejournal/Volume%203/Articles%20Vol_3/potter.pdf (accessed 16 August 2002); and Kirby J's judgment in *Green* 53.

59 R. B. Mison, 'Homophobia in Manslaughter: The Homosexual Advance Defence as Insufficient Provocation' (1992) 80(1) *Columbia Law Review* 133.

60 For example, see work of the following two authors who stress the discursive construction of homosexuality and through legal discourse: Johnston, 'More than Ordinary Men Gone Wrong'; A. George, '"Roll a Fag and Go Free": Competing Discourses of Sexuality and Sexual Identity' (1995) 1(1) *Journal of Interisciplinary Gender Studies* 49; A. George, 'The Gay (?) Victim on Trial: Discourses of Sexual Division in the Courtroom' in *Homophobic Violence* (ed G. Mason and S. Tomsen) (Sydney: Federation Press, 1997) 46–57.

61 Kendall Thomas, 'Beyond the Privacy Principle' (1992) 92 *Columbia Law Review* 1431, 1482.

> relationships. The first is the internal relation between perpetrators of homophobic violence and their victims. The second is the external relation in which both victims and torturers stand to the political regime that variously incites, aids or allows homophobic violence to take place. This latter relation forces the recognition that homophobic violence at one and the same time expresses the power of the perpetrator of that violence and the power of the regime that the perpetrator represents. The person of the torturer (and the torturer's weapon) is the agency through which the strategy of the regime finds its substantive shape and force. If we were to use the conventional language of American constitutional law, we might say then that violence is inscribed on the bodies of gay men and lesbians and constitutes an extra-legal exercise of state power.[62]

Kendall develops an account of state violence which destabilises the traditional jurisprudential categories of the public and the private, arguing that the violence enacted on the bodies of gay men and women is a disavowed form of state violence. In his view, a wider notion of police power is needed to comprehend the different dimensions of homophobic violence condoned by the state. For my purposes here, I simply want to stress that when, as Gayle Rubin puts it, 'hoodlums commit sanctioned battery' (or worse),[63] the work of the sanction is not (only) found in the exercise of police and prosecutorial discretion but is in fact inscribed in the very form of law. Juridical mechanisms of the criminal law – here the venerable defence of provocation and, more specifically, the modern variant of the HAD – function as critical elements within a bio-political strategy of the distribution of death. If, in good Foucauldian fashion, it is crucial to insist that the work of policing sex is performed 'by the mental health professions, popular ideology, and extra-legal social practice',[64] then it nevertheless remains important to try to show how the juridical sanction *itself* is implicated in this process and how it performs a distributive bio-political role.

If the criminal law thus sanctions homophobic violence through the operation of the defences of provocation or self-defence, indirectly allowing a 'private lawlessness' to fill the space of a direct public enforcement, then so too can direct public enforcements generate violent effects (and affects) which transcend the given transgression being sanctioned. Here again Thomas's analysis, this time of homosexual sodomy laws, is instructive. In the article 'Beyond the Privacy Principle' cited above, Thomas takes aim at the privacy analysis adopted by the US Supreme Court to answer the question of the constitutionality

62 ibid 1468–69.
63 G. S. Rubin, 'Thinking Sex: Notes for a Radical Theory of the Politics of Sexuality' in *The Lesbian and Gay Studies Reader* (ed H. Abelove, M. Aina Barale and D. M. Halperin) (New York: Routledge, 1993) 3–44 at 22.
64 ibid 19.

of a Georgia homosexual sodomy statute[65] in the 1986 case of *Bowers v Hardwick*.[66] He argues that a concern to establish the constitutional limits of the state's regulation of private consenting sexual activity through the prism of the right to privacy (understood either as a spatial question, or as a right of intimate association, or indeed as a right to decisional autonomy) fails to comprehend the *real* mobilisation of power in these cases.[67] Thomas argues that cases such as *Hardwick* are not about the state failing to respect the privacy of the abstract rights-bearing individual but actually concern a more fundamental derogation from 'one of the most basic normative commitments of American constitutionalism: the physical security of the embodied individual'.[68] In Thomas's reading, homosexual sodomy statutes are part of a wider 'body politics' which legitimise homophobic violence:

> [L]aws criminalizing private homosexual sodomy belong to a constellation of public practices whose constitutional dimensions are best described, explained, understood and argued as a kind of 'body politics'. My task here is to show that the law against homosexual sodomy has been vexed from its inception by a persistent and pervasive practice of homophobic violence on the part of public officials and private citizens alike . . . [In short, m]y thesis is that homosexual sodomy statutes work to legitimize homophobic violence and thus violate the right to be free from state-legitimated violence at the hands of private and public actors.[69]

65 At the time, Ga. Code Ann. § 16-6-2 (Michie 1985) provided in relevant part that: 'A person commits the offence of sodomy when he performs or submits to any sexual act involving the sex organs of one person and the mouth or anus of another' and that such is punishable by 'not less than one nor more than 20 years'. For Thomas's unpacking of the theologic of 'sodomy', the scientism of 'homosexual' and their problematic conjoining in this instance see Thomas, 'Beyond the Privacy Principle' 1432–34, fn 4. That his eloquent discussion is confined to a footnote (admittedly of some sprawling two pages) should not render it marginal – suffice it to say my usage of the term in the text above should not be read as an endorsement, simply as a reflection of the court's categorisation of the issues.

66 478 US 186 (1986) (hereafter *Hardwick*).

67 The critique of privacy doctrine articulated by Thomas throughout 'Beyond the Privacy Principle' sustains a problematic distinction between the 'abstract' quality of privacy doctrine (see for example Thomas, 'Beyond the Privacy Principle' 1436, 1457) and the supposedly more corporeal, concrete, factic analysis of a 'body politics' for which Thomas advocates. Whilst I am in agreement with much of Thomas's analysis, I think the Foucauldian epistemological (and political) commitments upon which his text relies themselves trouble the very distinction between, on the one hand, abstract legal doctrine and, on the other, the daily, concrete reality of politics (and would insist that the former can, perhaps in subtle or attenuated ways, nevertheless go to constitute our experience of the latter). At any rate, the concrete does not appear as such, unmediated through discourses such as law.

68 Thomas, 'Beyond the Privacy Principle' 1435.

69 ibid 1435.

The direct state criminalisation of sexuality achieved by the kind of laws in *Hardwick* – and the explicit outlawing of the homosexual they produce – empowers state agents (and also private vigilantes) to harass and to perpetrate violence. In an attempt to show how the 'background biography of *Hardwick* resists translation into the language and logic of sexual privacy',[70] Thomas details Hardwick's initial encounter with Officer Torrick outside his place of work (an Atlanta gay bar), Torrick's issuing to him a ticket for public drinking, the assault on Hardwick three weeks later in which three unidentified men arrived outside his home to 'beat the hell out of [him]',[71] Torrick's arrest of Hardwick in his bedroom, and Hardwick's subsequent harassment by the police in jail. In Thomas's wider framing of the narrative in *Hardwick*, the case is hence 'not just a story about private homoerotic acts and their interdiction; it is also an account of the harassment, the humiliation, and the violence that await the mere assertion or imputation of homosexual identities and existences in the public sphere'.[72] And of course the effect of the interdiction directly spawns and authorises this violence – as Thomas puts it 'the coincidence of the law of homosexual sodomy and the lawlessness of homophobic violence' is of course not a coincidence at all but a coordination: 'the criminalisation of homosexual sodomy and criminal attacks on gay men and lesbians work in tandem'.[73] Such a view 'forces us to abandon [the] formalist assumption' that 'the punitive dimensions of homosexual sodomy statutes are restricted to those expressly set forth in the challenged statute'.[74] Rather, 'homophobic violence . . . radiates' from the interdiction,[75] which thus performs a wider, distributive role.

The direct sanctioning, the direct criminalisation, of sexuality not only authorises public and private violence directed towards the sexually outlawed but also performs a central bio-political role in the interaction with public health measures directed, for example, towards HIV and AIDS treatment at the level of the population.[76] Institutionalised homophobia and its legal supports obviously impede efforts at diagnosing and treating the virus. As Jorge Saavedra neatly puts it:

> MSM ['men who have sex with men'] remain hidden, they will be very cautious or refuse to get an HIV test, even if they feel they need it, and those seeking to reach them with services, from condoms and lubricants to

70 ibid 1439.
71 ibid 1438.
72 ibid 1442.
73 ibid 1469.
74 ibid 1475.
75 ibid 1475.
76 This is not of course to assert the neutrality or the purely ameliorative role of public health mechanisms, themselves clearly susceptible to a Foucauldian analysis (particularly along bio-political lines). I am simply concerned here to foreground the importance of the criminal sanction in its intersection with public health measures.

education and treatment outreach, can be harassed for supporting illegal activities.[77]

Whilst it is misleading to posit a monocausal relationship between the criminal sanction and rates of HIV infection within stigmatised sexual populations, nevertheless it is clear that the criminalisation (or conversely, the decriminalisation) of forms of sexual activity does have an effect on infection rates. As Bill Rutkin, then President of the Queensland AIDS Council, put it in 1990 in reference to the Australian State of Queensland's criminal laws (gay sex was decriminalised there in 1990): 'There can be no serious doubt that lives have been lost in Queensland because of the laws . . . if there had been State government support for behavioural change programs for gay men then, from November 1984, it would not be unreasonable to claim that 25 per cent of the cases of AIDS we now have wouldn't have occurred'.[78] I have done no more than sketch here the possible articulations of the bio-political criminal sanction with other mechanisms (such as public health measures) and with *infra*-state homophobic violence. My aim has not been comprehensiveness but rather to suggest possible lines of inquiry which might illuminate the 'tactical' bio-political role of law.[79]

Conclusion

I have argued in this chapter that the criminal law – through the mechanism of the *sanction* which can both allow and disallow – is a crucial dimension of contemporary bio-political apparatuses. From the reading of the first volume of *The History of Sexuality* and the last lecture of *'Society Must be Defended'* pursued in the pages above, bio-politics emerges not as a political technology solely devoted to the maximisation or the optimisation of life but precisely as a mechanism for the differential distribution of death. Bio-politics does not simply fail to prevent death; rather, as Foucault insists in his *Collège de France* lecture course for 1977–78, *Security, Territory, Population*, 'the death of individuals not only does not disappear, it must not disappear'.[80] If bio-politics thus differentially exposes or abandons certain others to the risk of death (and certain specified, literally 'sub'-populations as a whole to this risk) then this exposure or abandonment, I have tried to show, continues to be effected through the medium of the criminal law sanction. Whilst no Foucauldian approach to the criminal law would maintain a clear separation

77 J. Saavedra, 'Sex Between Men in the Context of HIV' The Aids 2008 Jonathan Mann Memorial Lecture in Health and Human Rights *XVII International AIDS Conference* (3–8 August 2008 Mexico City) (copy on file with author).
78 Quoted in D. Scammell, 'Law Reform Saves Lives: The Impact of Decriminalisation in Australia's Effective Response to HIV Among Gay Men' unpublished conference paper (copy on file with author).
79 Foucault, *Security, Territory, Population* 99.
80 ibid 42.

between the juridical and extra-juridical elements of the penal apparatus (for example, the juridical rule of the HAD is unthinkable without the historically stigmatising efforts of discourses such as psychiatry) nevertheless I have tried to demonstrate the important role that the criminal law sanction continues to perform in distributing death within a governable population. The juridical dimension of criminal law is hence not reducible to an epiphenomenon or supporting mechanism of more vital and determinative technologies of power which lie outside or beyond it;[81] rather, the criminal law sanction is a fundamental component of the bio-political apparatus.

In the course of seeking to explain the ongoing success of the prison in the face of its evident failure, indeed even the constant and paradoxical furnishing of the prison 'as its own remedy',[82] Foucault famously suggests in *Discipline and Punish* that 'the prison, and no doubt punishment in general, is not intended to eliminate offences, but rather to distinguish them, to distribute them, to use them'. He continues:

> Penality would then appear to be a way of handling illegalities, of laying down the limits of tolerance, of giving free rein to some, of putting pressure on others, of excluding a particular section, of making another useful, of neutralizing certain individuals and of profiting from others. In short, penality does not simply 'check' illegalities; it 'differentiates' them, it provides them with a general 'economy'. And, if one can speak of justice, it is not only because the law itself or the way of applying it serves the interests of a class, it is also because the differential administration of illegalities through the mediation of penality forms part of those mechanisms of domination. Legal punishments are to be resituated in an overall strategy of illegalities.[83]

The way of conceiving criminal law that I have argued for in this chapter, namely as a bio-political technique for the differential distribution of death, shares something with this description of penality as a distribution of illegalities. Far from a simple defining of the licit and the illicit, criminal law has a more complex distributive role to play in terms of allowing and disallowing certain practices, tolerating some and neutralising others. As hopefully emerges from the foregoing examples of the criminalisation of sexuality, criminal law does not simply attempt to punish transgression; nor does it aim, despite perceptions of a 'preventive turn' in criminal law, to prevent or pre-empt harm and violence *per se*, but rather it provides a mechanism for the differential exposure of some (others) to violence and death through the opening of a biological *caesura* within the population to be governed. This is just one of the ways in which law crosses what Foucault calls the 'threshold of modernity';[84] that is, its becoming-bio-political.

81 According to the argument made in Hunt and Wickham.
82 Foucault, *Discipline and Punish* 268.
83 ibid 272.
84 Foucault, *History of Sexuality* 142.

Chapter 6

Disassembling legal form

Ownership and the racial body

Brenna Bhandar[1]

In 1984, John Moore commenced legal proceedings against his physician, Dr Golde, Golde's employers (the Regents of the University of California system) and pharmaceutical corporations involved in the exploitation of the Mo cell line, derived from cells removed from his spleen.[2] Moore was being treated for hairy-cell leukemia, and Golde knew that the lymphokines[3] produced by Moore's cancerous cells were potentially very profitable. Moore's spleen was removed during the course of treatment, and he did not consent to the commercial exploitation of his bio-waste. The plaintiff's action lay in the tort of conversion, alleging that Golde, Quan (Golde's assistant) and the other defendants had effectively converted cells from his spleen into a commercially profitable cell line without his authorisation. The California Supreme Court found that Moore did not have an action in conversion, as he did not have a proprietary interest in his cells. *Moore v Regents* has been the focus of much scholarly attention, inviting as it does analysis of the rights of the individual to bodily integrity and dignity in the context of the biocapitalist exploitation of body parts;[4] the proprietary status of the cell line itself as a congealed network of hybridity (as both body part and intellectual product);[5] the central role of bio-waste in the burgeoning bio-medical life science industries of the 1980s;[6] and as a case in which reference to race and

1 My sincere gratitude to China Miéville, Sandro Mezzadra and participants in the McGill Faculty of Law Legal Theory Workshop for their very insightful comments on an earlier draft. The omissions and errors which nonetheless persist remain my sole responsibility.
2 *Moore v Regents* (1990) 51 Cal.3d 120.
3 Waldby and Mitchell note: '[l]ympokines are proteins used by the body's immune system and are of use and interest to many researchers. However, [they] are also notoriously difficult to produce in large amounts, and so Golde saw great economic potential in Moore's cells'. C. Waldby and R. Mitchell, *Tissue Economies: Blood, Organs, and Cell Lines in Late Capitalism* (London: Duke University Press, 2006) 88.
4 P. Rabinow, *Essays on the Anthropology of Reason* (Princeton: Princeton University Press 1996).
5 M. Strathern, 'Cutting the Network' in (1996) 2(3) *The Journal of the Royal Anthropological Institute* 517–35, 535.
6 Waldby and Mitchell *Tissue Economies.*

nation are utilised in order to illuminate newly emergent biotechnologies and their effects on the human.[7]

In my view, this case provides a moment through which to think about the relationship between legal forms of property ownership, the body of the legal subject, and the racial. I will take as my point of departure the notion that property ownership and the body of the legal subject to which ownership rights have historically attached are co-constituted through an analytic of the racial. The dispossession of Moore, a white male Alaskan engineer, of his body parts provides yet another moment (among so many) to think about how the disaggregation of the human body of the legal subject might provide an occasion for a radical interruption of the persistent fantasy of the self-possessed, unitary subject of rights. The dissenting judgment in *Moore v Regents*, that of Mosk J, explicitly invokes the spectre of slavery in arguing that Moore's self-possession of his body should be protected (see discussion below). The literal, biological disassembling of the body of the self-possessed 'I' threatens to place the proper legal subject of rights in extreme jeopardy, and this can only be safeguarded against by recognising a proprietary interest in one's self. Does the failure to preserve the integrity of John Moore's self-possession by the majority in *Moore v Regents* potentially unravel the legal forms of property ownership that simultaneously rely upon and constitute a notion of the legal subject whose body belies (and has perhaps, always belied) its own phantasm of being unitary?

From what moment, at which point do we enter this old story? That is to say, the disaggregation of the human body with the advent of biotechnologies and the commodification of tissue culture, genetic databases and other inscriptions of human life continue to raise a plethora of questions about the legal form of property, the networks of actors and objects that are productive of property, and the status (ontic, social, cultural) of the bodies (plant, animal, human) regulated by legal regimes of ownership. Questions of how technologies that embed proprietary invention within the biological organism itself collapse long-held distinctions between what is natural and what is made, what is social and cultural;[8] or how the device of the patent congeals entire networks of labour and their attendant social relations,[9] or shifts the temporal focus of ownership claims from past to future, may be of great utility in thinking about the shifting status of the human subject as it relates to the racial. Do emergent forms of property introduce new articulations of the body which, in turn, might provide a basis for reconfiguring legal subjectivity? Or does the abolition of the distinction between an ownership right that refers to an object and the object itself, which occurs with the emplacement of the right

7 P. Wald, 'What's in a Cell? John Moore's Spleen and the Language of Bioslavery' in (2005) 36(2) *New Literary History* 205–25.

8 A. Pottage, 'The Socio-Legal Implications of the New Biotechnologies' (2007) 3(3) *Annu. Rev. Law Soc. Sci.* 1–3.24.

9 M. Strathern, *Kinship, Law and the Unexpected: Relatives are Always a Surprise* (Cambridge: Cambridge University Press, 2005).

(over proprietary technology) within the body of the object perfect the 'archaic figure of *ius reale*', rather than reinventing the legal form of property altogether?[10] In other words, do emergent forms of property and their theorisations provide new frameworks through which to analyse long-standing and sedimented triangulations of the legal form of ownership, the body and the racial?

Moore's proprietary claim occurs in the realm of biotechnologies that begin to rewrite the human body as disaggregable and this represents a collapsing of ontological categories that repeats itself over and over, in different guises, from the time modern property law emerges in the colonial context. For instance, Best explores how the fugitive slave laws, by rendering ambiguous the distinction between slave as object of ownership and subjective agent who incurs a debt through refusing to gift her labour to the white master, lays the foundations for the disarticulation of the body and the recognition of intellectual property rights in such properties of the body as the voice.[11] Best writes:

> The figuration of the fugitive as debtor produces a willful subject against the express legal nullifcation of willfulness. To be precise, it projects a willful subject when the will-less is in suspension, fabulates a subject not owned when the owned escapes (to use the language of common law) 'absolute dominion,' fantasizes a person at the precise moment when the security of property is subject to greatest question.[12]

This is a moment where the distinction between slave as commodity and slave as a human person with volition is collapsed; the strict bounds of raciality are blurred as the 'Negro' becomes legal person, if only for a moment, if only to be held accountable within a logic of market exchange and legal positivism. In addition to the racial logic of slavery revealing the germ of its contradiction, the legal form of ownership itself is challenged as object of ownership becomes subject who is caught within the contractual relations of appropriation of labour, debt and abstraction of personality, some of the fundaments of property law.

In shifting our focus on property law and its fantasies of its own stability and the legal subject, who in its abstraction, 'does the dirty work of capitalist desires',[13] to a matter of legal form more generally, the question of the racial requires us to engage a post-colonial critique of capitalism.[14] The self-determining, autonomous

10 A. Pottage, 'Fiction Science and Proprietary Effect' in *Living Properties: Making Knowledge and Controlling Ownership in the History of Biology* (J.-P. Gaudillière, D. J. Kelves, H.-J. Rheinberger (eds)) (Berlin: Max Planck Institute for the History of Science, 2009) 230–32.

11 S. Best, *Fugitive's Properties: The Poetics of Law and Possession* (Chicago: University of Chicago Press 2004) 81.

12 ibid 8.

13 paraphrasing Best, *Fugitive's Properties* 63.

14 Cf D. Chakrabarty, *Provincialising Europe: Postcolonial Thought and Historical Difference* (Princeton: Princeton University Press. 2000); S. Mezzadra, 'Bringing Capital Back In:

'I' was forged during the 18th and 19th centuries in relation to beings who fell outside of the bounds of cognisability in a burgeoning capitalist economic and political system: those whose labour was unfree, enslaved, and those whose lands were viewed as non-productive wasteland. For Marx, the legal subject is essentially living a phantasmic existence, rooted in the violence of abstraction and the commodity form. However, Marx's critique of the chimerical nature of this subject has had to be stretched (as Fanon noted, discussed below) to account for the ways in which the alienation of labour (the precondition for assuming the status of legal-political subject) assumes a subject who is self-possessed, and also, how the capacity for self-possession and autonomy was thoroughly racialised and emplaced within a colonial logic.[15]

For instance, Fanon's devastating critique of the invention of settler and native explodes the distinction between form and substance, by repeatedly exposing how the *fact* of blackness (as both ontological category and lived experience) pervades the everyday life of the colonial subject. Fanon reveals the fantasy of the autonomous, self-possessed individual whose body is intact as always-already shattered and fragmented by a racial logic that relies on blurring the boundaries between beings (human subjects) and things (the animal, the slave as an instrument of production). What of the proper subject of the law, who finds quite literally its own body disaggregated by notions of the human inscribed as code? I seek to explore in the final part of the essay how (or whether) the racial is reconfigured with the disaggregation of the human body, the form essential to the political subjectivity of the self-determining autonomous I.

The first part of the chapter explores theories of the legal form as elucidated above, followed by a section on the relationship between the body and legal form. The final section of the chapter examines the judgment of *Moore v Regents of USC*, a case in which the litigant asserts a right to ownership over a cell line produced from cells taken from his body during medical treatment, a claim which is rejected by the majority judgment. In the conclusion, I consider the ways in which the racial is redeployed as the body of the legal subject is rewritten not as the sum of its parts but as cells, tissue culture, as code. I argue that the racial is continually being rewritten despite a moment of opportunity presented to us with the advent of various biotechnologies: to reveal (again) the fantasy of the self-determining 'I' as a means of diminishing its power in the legal and political field. Increasingly interrupted by biotechnologies, in the same moment that new forms of propertisation, accumulation and appropriation take shape within the law, we

A Materialist Turn in Post-Colonial Studies?' (2011) 12(1) *Inter-Asia Cultural Studies* 154–64; S. Mezzadra, 'How Many Histories of Labour? Towards a Theory of Post-Colonial Capitalism' (2011) 14(2) *Postcolonial Studies* 1–20; D. Ferreira da Silva, *Towards a Global Idea of Race* (Minneapolis: University of Minnesota Press, 2007).

15 G. Spivak, *A Critique of Post-Colonial Reason: Towards a History of the Vanishing Present* (Cambridge: Harvard University Press, 1999); Ferreira da Silva, *Towards a Global Idea of Race*.

seem to be in a moment that presents us with a space to reshape legal-political subjectivities along different lines.

Two theories of the legal form and some deficits

The question of the racial and its relationship to legal subjectivity is one that arises from our understandings of the legal form itself. For both Marx and Hegel, property lies at the basis of the legal form, yet what are the contours of the legal subject which they both assume in their theorisations of relations of ownership and contract? While Marx renders a critique of the phantasms that accompany the legal subject as property owner, Hegel posits ownership as central to the very becoming of the political-legal subject. The concept of form traverses the social, political phenomena that precede and exceed, that shadow the legal form itself. On a Marxist view, the legal form closely resembles the commodity form. The legal form mirrors and supports existing relations of production, property relations, and market forces. Because the legal relation's content is itself wholly determined by the economic relation,[16] there is no basis upon which one should, *contra* Kelsen (for instance), begin to theorise the legal form from an external vantage point of norms. Thus Pashukanis writes that: 'the legal relation is the cell-form of the legal fabric; only there does law accomplish its real movement. Compared to this, law as the aggregate of norms is merely a lifeless abstraction'.[17]

Abstraction functions as a more lively concept through its use, by Marx, as both a description and a critique of capital.[18] Marx's labour theory of value is premised on the idea that the particularities of different kinds of labour are abstracted and congealed in the commodity as homogenous labour, as a part of the process by which use values are created.[19] The abstraction of labour is the means by which use values are transmuted into exchange values. The violence of equivalence consists in the flattening of the differences between the labour necessary to produce different dimensions or aspects of a commodity, whereby concrete labour becomes the form of manifestation of its opposite, abstract human labour.[20] The abstraction of labour lies at the foundation of Marx's theory of commodity formation and, thus, the theory of the legal form elucidated by both Marx and Pashukanis.

As Marx explains, the violence of abstraction also lies in its rendering invisible the social relations that are necessary for the production of goods. The very expression of value (the value-relation of the products of labour within which the commodity appears) conceals a social relation:

16 E. Pashukanis, *Law and Marxism: A General Theory* (London: Pluto Press, 1989) 96.
17 ibid 85.
18 Chakrabarty *Provincialising Europe* 58.
19 K. Marx, *Capital Vol I* (London: Penguin, 1990) 135–36.
20 ibid 150.

> It is nothing but the definite social relation between men themselves which assumes here, for them, the fantastic form of a relation between things. In order, therefore, to find an analogy we must take the flight into the misty realm of religion. There the products of the human brain appear as autonomous figures endowed with a life of their own, which enter into relations both with each other and with the human race. So it is in the world of commodities with the products of men's hands.[21]

This is the definition of commodity fetishism, a fetishism which is mirrored in the faith instilled in legal rights and entitlements that are attached to the legal subject. And it is at this juncture that an analysis of the specificities and particularities of the individuals who alienate their labour and those who cannot, and therefore fall out of the bounds of cognisability in this theory of the legal (and commodity) form becomes necessary. The congealing of the multiple dimensions of labour and production in the commodity not only obscures certain forms of labour and the social relations to which they are attached,[22] but the very subjects of these forms of production. By defining property law, which lies at the basis of the legal form, only in relation to the institution of private property defined as a relation between owners in the most formal sense, 'jurists . . . exclude everybody but the owner from using and disposing of the object . . . In these abstract prohibitions, the concept of property loses any living meaning and renounces its own pre-juridical history'.[23] While we may want to question what constitutes the pre-juridical (and whether this simply means pre-capitalist), the critique of the way in which property law is defined solely in relation to market relations and subjects who have the power to alienate the object of ownership continues to be relevant as contemporary scholarship turns ever more attention to the affective, interrelational and social dimensions of propertisation and ownership.

That property becomes the central focus of the theorisation of legal form is of no surprise. Marx emphasised that the property relation is the fundamental basis of the legal system. Because property becomes the basis of the legal form 'only when it becomes something which can be freely disposed of in the market',[24] different ways of being and different beings themselves are cast out from this regime of private property and legal recognition. He who is a slave, as a mere commodity, can only become a subject with legal personhood when he is able to act as someone who can dispose of commodities and participate in the market.[25]

Defining legal personality on the basis of one's status as private property owner is nowhere more explicit than in Hegel's *Philosophy of Right*. For Hegel, private

21 ibid 165.
22 Pashukanis, *Law and Marxism* 113.
23 ibid 122.
24 ibid 110.
25 ibid 112 n 12.

property ownership was central to the constitution of the legal political subject. It was only through the recognition of one's will, externalised into the object of ownership, that one became a full legal person. The *Philosophy of Right* is an attempt to theorise the simultaneous unfolding and development of the individual person's struggle for freedom in relation with others, and finally, through the reconciliation of the individual and universal will as it is embodied in the ethical state. The realisation of the idea, or concept, is governed by an inherent rationality; one that moves from the immediate rationality of the individual human being to the external world and relations with others and is finally realised in its universal form. Property ownership is central to this unfolding when considering rights in their abstraction and is also retained and held intact within civil society.

Of prime import to the self-determining subject is the struggle to reconcile his subjective will with that of the universal will. The will is the means through which freedom is actualised; it is the vehicle through which thought 'translates itself into existence'.[26] The will is both the medium through which the self is reconciled to the universal – the will becomes one which has 'being in and for itself' – and the locus of the desire and thought that propels the self through its dialectical progression towards mutual recognition with others and reconciliation with the universal.[27]

The capacity and desire of an individual to externalise his will in an object establishes private property ownership as the necessary precondition of recognition by and of others and, relatedly, founds the distinction between rational human beings and human beings who have yet to realise their individual personality in its completeness. In order to become embodied as a rational human being, the subject must 'go out of himself' and 'educate himself inwardly, in order so that he may become rational "for himself"'.[28] The merely natural or immediate will is posited and embodied in an object and thus becomes capable of recognition by another being. In the movement of the 'absolutely free will' in its abstract state towards its embodied being as a personality in the 'real' world, property takes on a central role.[29] In order for the free will, the individual self-consciousness, to become a personality capable of holding legal rights, it must externalise itself in an object. Externalisation of the will in an object, and possession of that object (although that can take many different forms) is necessary for the free will to confront and relate to the external, 'real' world of things and, also, to take on a form that will be recognised by other individuals. Thus the abstract will becomes embodied and gains recognition as such by another individual through his own possession of objects.

26 G. W. F. Hegel, *Elements of the Philosophy of Right* (Allen W. Wood (ed)) (Cambridge: Cambridge University Press, 1991) 35.
27 ibid 52.
28 ibid 45.
29 G. W. F. Hegel, *Philosophy of Right* (trans. T. M. Knox) (Oxford: Clarendon Press, 1967) para 34.

The contradiction inherent in externalising one's will into an object already occupied and owned by another results in what Hegel refers to as a 'madness of personality'.[30] The madness of personality results when there is no mediation between my exclusive, individual will and that of another in a single object.[31] Ownership asserted by Europeans over land already occupied and used by aboriginal communities; ownership asserted over self-possessed human beings *as* objects to be owned makes it tempting to conclude that a madness of personality is an apt description for the colonial settler context, were it not for the ascription of lower or less developed states of consciousness to aboriginal communities or, for that matter, slaves. The will is crucial, as an enabling capacity, for the fulfilment of individuated human subjectivity. The slave has the capacity to reach this level of consciousness but not without engaging in a struggle for recognition. If the *Phenomenology of Spirit* and *Philosophy of Right* are understood as texts that unfold in a non-linear, non-chronological fashion, the slave, on the contrary, seems to be very much caught within a progressive *telos* of development in which advancement can only be made through risking his life in battle. The slave is not only understood as having a lower or lesser developed form of consciousness, but moreover, Mbembe's critique of this Hegelian politics of death reveals how this *telos* sets the scene for sovereign control over the bio-political reproduction and death of the racial subject in the post-colony.[32] While slaves have the capacity to fight for the realisation of truth through the coming into being of self-consciousness (as opposed to mere consciousness), it is beyond dispute that Hegel's play of world history places the colonial world as lagging behind Europe. The madness of personality is resolved by the force of property law that excluded colonised subjects from the bounds of the wilful, self-determining, autonomous 'I'.

The self-determining subject is, however, even in Hegel's own political-theology, a fractured, dislocated, disaggregated thing. It defies the absolute certainty, and thus the ontological closures that Hegel's dialectical logic is often accused of. Hegel, as the author of a dialectic of recognition that entails violent closures in ontological and phenomenological registers, is also author of a text in which a resolutely dislocated body appears as unhappy consciousness. Even before the

30 ibid para 62. The issue of owning property that is already owned by another, for Hegel, is an impossibility because the object of ownership already contains or is replete with the will of the original owner. I can use, in a partial or temporary sense, a thing, but this form of possession is to be distinguished from ownership (ibid para 62). The object contains a will that is impenetrable by my will. When I own something, that thing takes on an 'independent externality' and is not just limited to my presence, to my knowledge and will in the present time and space (ibid para 56). Recognition between two individual wills occurs through property; it is my individual will that is recognised through the medium of property by another individual will. Thus, there is a contradiction where two wills are present in the same object, and recognition is rendered an impossibility.

31 ibid para 62.

32 A. Mbembe, *On the Postcolony* (Berkeley: University of California Press, 2003).

arrival of unhappy consciousness, Butler reminds us that the emergence of the body in the master/slave dialectic occurs, and it occurs as a moment of alienation. The self recognises itself but also recognises that it is not itself. Butler argues that the 'self-recognition [of the bondsman] is derived from the radically tenuous status of the bondsman': he recognises himself in the forfeiture of the signature and the constant threat to his autonomy that the expropriation of the objects of his labour presents.[33] This body constitutes my life, notes Butler, but this body there is equally me. I am in other words, both here and there; echoing the fractured subjectivity that migrants and refugees, to think of one example, inhabit as a matter of course.[34] There is a spatial indecision that Butler speaks of that indicates a moment of being simultaneously embodied and alienated from oneself. In this moment, the self is not concerned with mastery but with trying to apprehend and give meaning to its split self; a split that is the very condition of its being. However, I refer to the ways in which Hegel forecloses these ruptures, particularly in relation to the body of the slave or non-Europeans, as discussed above.

Marx undoes this self-determining, autonomous 'I' who is co-emergent with capitalist relations of production. Noting that mutual recognition as legal subjects can only occur as owners of private property[35] Marx, and Pashukanis after him, illuminate the false foundation of the 'will' and 'freedom' of the legal subject in a capitalist liberal democracy. Commodity exchange itself presupposes a conscious act of will on the part of the owner of the commodity in the context of the market, even though the commodity itself 'acquires its value independently of the will of the producing subject'.[36] As the owner is constituted within and by a juridical frame, 'economic relations of ownership then give this subject a gift- (in compensation as it were) – a will, juridically constituted, which makes him absolutely free and equal to other owners of commodities like himself'.[37] Freedom and self-determination are inextricably linked and, indeed, expressed solely through market relations of exchange. This is what freedom means for the legal subject (or property owner).

The bounds of the self-determining, autonomous 'I' have been the site of contestation since its emergence in philosophical and political domains. Different forms of anti-colonial resistance have both attempted to stretch the bounds of the legal subject to include the colonised and to shatter them completely. The legal form, as dialectic, has been critiqued for failing to allow for the existence of a genuinely emergent plurality, rendering instead forms of legal pluralism that maintain the self-same identity of the sovereign, European, nation-state form or

33 J. Butler, *The Psychic Life of Power: Theories in Subjection* (Stanford: Stanford University Press, 1997) 39.
34 See B. Bhandar, 'Plasticity and Post-colonial Recognition: Owning, Knowing and Being' (2011) 22(3) *Law and Critique* 227–49.
35 Pashukanis, *Law and Marxism* 114; Marx, *Capital* 178.
36 Pashukanis, *Law and Marxism* 112.
37 ibid 114.

equivalent. It would be uncontroversial, I think, to argue that the legal form, as becomes manifest in a dialectic of recognition between nation states or between state and legal subjectivities that emerge in the modern colonial era, rely upon an analytic of the racial. In contemporary colonial settler contexts such as Palestine, for instance, the wasteland rationale used to appropriate the lands of others is still employed, reflecting the persistence of the notion of a proper subject of ownership who is quite thoroughly saturated with raciality. Colonial logics are deterritorialised and retemporalised repeatedly, all over the globe.

In thinking about the body to which the subject is attached, Marxist theories of the legal form enact a different scene of erasure. Fanon points to the fissures in Marxist philosophy that are revealed in Marx's disregard of the bodies that signify the racial and economic relations of the colony:

> The originality of the colonial context is that economic reality, inequality and the immense difference of ways of life never come to mask the human realities. When you examine at close quarters the colonial context, it is evident that what parcels out the world is to begin with the fact of belonging to or not belonging to a given race, *a given species*. In the colonies the economic substructure is also a superstructure. The cause is the consequence; you are rich because you are white, you are white because you are rich. This is why Marxist analysis *should always be slightly stretched* every time we have to deal with the colonial problem.[38]

The flight into the mystical realms of religion, a precondition for the realisation of a commodity fetishism which by definition obscures social relations between men is not afforded to the colonised. In the colony, economic relations never mask the violent social relations that characterise life there.

Fanon's observation that one must begin with considering whether the colonial subject belongs to a given species makes precisely the interjection into the notion of human subjectivity that is needed in an anti or post-colonial reading of Marx. He raises the biological dimension of being and here and elsewhere brings into focus the very constitution of the body of the colonial subject.[39] Marx's concept of species-being is subjected, and needs to be subjected to this sort of thorough shaking from the outside. How does the very notion of the human species need to be rethought in light of colonial violence? If the human person is only recognised as a legal subject through the externalisation of his will (which the colonised subject by definition lacks) in an object (which the colonised subject cannot own), to which species does the colonised belong? That the colonised subject is dehumanised and, indeed, animalised is not a particularly contentious claim.[40]

38 F. Fanon, *The Wretched of the Earth* (London: Penguin Books, 2001) 31 (emphasis added).
39 Bhandar, 'Plasticity and Post-colonial Recognition'.
40 Fanon, *The Wretched of the Earth* 34.

More specifically, the body of the colonial subject, the body of the slave, has always been fragmented in multiple ways. Skin as a site of desire, as a site of wounding, that has a political-economic and symbolic significance all of its own;[41] the dismemberment of the body that characterised colonial forms of domination in Africa;[42] the living death[43] that characterises the colonial condition and the fact of blackness[44] that shapes the lived experience of colonial subjects in a non-totalising but dramatic fashion,[45] are all instances of the myriad ways in which the colonial (and slave) body has been disaggregated by a racial logic of subordination with which, as I have attempted to show, propertisation and the legal form were thoroughly imbricated.

Before, however, attempting to imagine a different species-being that is not bound by the strictures of the self-determining 'I' of capitalist-colonial economic relations, a different kind of accounting of the subject needs to take place. The disaggregation of the body of the proper, autonomous self-possessed legal subject as a result of advances in the life sciences industries has placed the form of this subject at risk. The hyper-commodification of the body touches the subjectivity of the self-possessed 'I' that has hitherto had its fantasy of self-sovereignty protected by a legal form that assumed and relied upon it. In the following section, I offer an analysis of *Moore v Regents of USC*, taking note of how the California Supreme Court grappled with the challenge to Mr Moore's bodily integrity and assertion of ownership over materials derived from his body. In the conclusion, I return to the question of the racial logic that persistently haunts the legal subject and speculate on the productive challenges the disaggregation of the body of the legal subject might hold for legal-political subjectivities.

Moore v Regents: self-possession interrupted

In the case of *Moore v Regents of University of California*, the Supreme Court of California addressed the issue of whether John Moore, the plaintiff and appellant, had a legal cause of action for breach of the physician's disclosure obligations and for conversion.[46] The facts of the case, briefly, were as follows. John Moore underwent treatment for hairy-cell leukemia at the Medical Center of the University of California at Los Angeles (UCLA Medical Center) in 1976. The

41 F. Fanon, *Black Skin, White Masks* (trans. C.L. Markmann) (New York: Grove Press, 1967); E. Povinelli, *The Empire of Love: Toward a Theory of Intimacy, Genealogy, and Carnality* (Durham: Duke University Press, 2006).
42 A. Mbembe, *On the Postcolony*; A. Mbembe, 'Provincialising France?' (2011) 21(1) *Public Culture*.
43 Mbembe, 'Provincialising France?'.
44 Fanon, *Black Skin, White Mask*.
45 F. Moten, *In the Break: The Aesthetics of the Black Radical Tradition* (Minneapolis: University of Minnesota Press, 2003).
46 Conversion is a tort that protects against interference with possessory and ownership interests in personal property.

doctors who treated him were aware that certain blood products extracted from Moore during the course of medical testing for his condition were 'of great value in a number of commercial and scientific efforts' and that access to a patient whose blood contained these substances would provide 'competitive, commercial, and scientific advantage'.[47] Eventually, in that same year, one of the defendants, Moore's treating physician Golde, recommended that Moore's spleen be removed in order to slow the progress of the disease. Moore signed a consent form authorising the splenectomy; however, neither Golde nor Quan, another physician defendant, informed Moore of their plans to use parts of his spleen for research. Nor did they request his permission. In fact, Golde negotiated agreements for commercial development of the cell line (derived from Moore's cells) and the products to be developed from it. Golde became a paid consultant with the Genetics Institute and 'acquired 75,000 shares of common stock' in the company. The Genetics Institute also agreed to pay Golde and the Regents 'at least $330,000 over three years, including a *pro rata* share of [Golde's] salary and fringe benefits, in exchange for . . . exclusive access to the materials and research performed' on the cell line and products derived from it.[48] The deal that Golde reached with the Genetics Institute was very lucrative indeed. The university obtained a patent on Moore's cell line, which covered various methods for using the cell line to produce lymphokines. Moore estimated that the market for such products would reach a value of approximately US$3 billion by 1990.

The Supreme Court found that Moore did not have a cause of action on the basis of conversion, but that he did have a cause of action for breach of a physician's fiduciary duty to disclose. The Court considered whether the theory of conversion should be extended to apply to an individual's biological materials, and rejected this claim on three bases. The first was that 'a fair balancing of the relevant policy considerations counsel against extending the tort. Second, problems in this area are better suited to legislative resolution. Third, the tort of conversion is not necessary to protect patients' rights'.[49] The Court concluded specifically that the use of excised human cells in medical research did not amount to a conversion. The reasons for the rejection of the conversion claim are taken up most pointedly in Mosk J's dissenting judgment, which I discuss below. However, what is clear from the majority's rejection of this claim is that Moore's body parts were clearly being taken into the proprietary realm by the Genetics Institute and the physicians, but were taken out of his proprietary control. The bodily aspects of subjecthood travel into the realm of policy objectives and social goods and the commercial domain within which scientific innovation is lodged and sustained is hived off into a putative private realm. The body of the self-possessed legal subject in this instance becomes resolutely non-proprietary in relation to itself, while corporations engaged in the business of

47 *Moore v Regents* 120 at 126.
48 ibid 120 at 127.
49 ibid 120 at 142–143.

the life sciences potentially profit enormously from the bodily parts of the legal subject. One of the strongest justifications for rejecting the plea to extend the doctrine of conversion to apply to Moore's biological materials was the uncertainty that it would inject into the market of the life sciences and medical research:

> Indeed, so significant is the potential obstacle to research stemming from uncertainty about legal title to biological materials that the Office of Technology Assessment reached this striking conclusion: '[R]egardless of the merit of claims by the different interested parties, resolving the current uncertainty may be more important to the future of biotechnology than resolving it in any particular way'.[50]

The Court concluded that they

> 'need not, however, make an arbitrary choice between liability and nonliability. Instead, an examination of the relevant policy considerations suggests an appropriate balance: Liability based upon existing disclosure obligations, rather than an unprecedented extension of the conversion theory, protects patients' rights of privacy and autonomy without unnecessarily hindering research'.[51]

Recall that this case arose in the 1980s when the life sciences industry was in its adolescence and there was palpable fear about freezing the development of this market with potential litigation over the raw materials required to fuel the industry. The Court also cited *Diamond v Chakrabarty*,[52] finding that Moore's cells were factually and legally distinct from the patented cell lines and the products derived from it and, therefore, he had no property in the cell line.

Arabian J, in a concurring judgment, went much further than Panelli J in respect of the moral and ethical issues at stake in the claim. In very prosaic if not theological language, he found that the plaintiff 'entreats [the court] to regard the human vessel – the single most venerated and protected subject in any civilised society – as equal with the basest commercial commodity. He urges us to commingle the sacred with the profane. He asks much'.[53] Vehement in his conviction that human tissue should not be treated as a fungible article of commerce, he refused to 'deliver the majestic force of the law' to the ground beneath Moore's claim.

Mosk J, in a dissenting judgment, engaged property as a bundle of rights, and found that even where rights in relation to property are diminished, they remain an interest protected by property law.[54] He found that the same logic applied

50 ibid 120 at 143.
51 ibid 120 at 144.
52 (1980) 447 U.S. 303.
53 *Moore v Regents* 120 at 148.
54 ibid 120 at 166.

to Moore's interest in his own body tissue: 'even if we assume that section 7054.4 [of . . .] limited the use and disposition of his excised tissue in the manner claimed by the majority, Moore nevertheless retained valuable rights in that tissue. Above all, at the time of its excision he at least had the right to do with his own tissue whatever the defendants did with it: i.e., he could have contracted with researchers and pharmaceutical companies to develop and exploit the vast commercial potential of his tissue and its products'.[55] He reaffirmed the Court of Appeal's conclusion that to accept the position of the defendants, that they could own the plaintiff's tissue while the plaintiff himself could not, was rife with an irony that is legally untenable. Mosk J ultimately affirmed the self-determining and autonomous 'I' as having property in his or her body, and the right to alienate that property for his or her own economic benefit. The ethical imperative to protect the body from inhumane and degrading treatment must be vigorously defended, and it is here that he explicitly invoked the spectre of slavery: 'The most abhorrent form of such exploitation, of course, was the institution of slavery. Lesser forms, such as indentured servitude or even debtor's prison, have also disappeared. Yet their spectre haunts the laboratories and boardrooms of today's biotechnological research-industrial complex. It arises wherever scientists or industrialists claim, as defendants claim here, the right to appropriate and exploit a patient's tissue for their sole economic benefit – the right, in other words, to freely mine or harvest valuable physical properties of the patient's body'.[56]

The patenting of Moore's cell line was one instance of a growing 'tissue economy', which heralded the quite radical shift in notions of human life. No longer dependent on being a part of a whole, human body, human life existed in *in vitro* for the first with the cultivation of the HeLa cells.[57] The HeLa cells are referred to in a footnote in this judgment, although not by name. The subtextual reference to the HeLa cells in the majority judgment and the explicit reference to the institution of slavery in Mosk J's dissent, open onto a discussion of the place of the racial in the disaggregation of the body of this autonomous legal subject. If the body of the phantasmagorical autonomous 'I' has (also) always been fragmented, evinced most clearly by the body of the racial subject, does raciality as a logic implode, or is it reformulated in these moments when the fantasy is explicitly challenged by the rewriting of the body as cell lines, or as genetic code?

Conclusion: determining selves in an era of new bodily technologies

When the body comes to be produced differently, and very much not as signifier of the mind but as signifier of cell or code, how does this reconfigure the racial that

55 ibid.
56 ibid.
57 H. Landecker, *Culturing Life: How Cells Became Technologies* (London: Harvard University Press, 2007).

was tied to the onto-epistemological presupposition that privileged interiority and the self-same 'I'?[58] Biotechnological innovation makes it difficult to not take notice of how organisms, parts of bodies which are separated from the whole and continue a separate life of their own (immortal cell lines, for instance) fold exteriority into interiority, turning the outside into the inside and vice versa. As we see in *Moore v Regents*, the self-determination and freedom that are the preserve of the autonomous, legal subject are denied to him as the logic of new forms of capital accumulation and exploitation (now drawing on the material, physical resources of the body, rather than its expenditure in the form of labour) emerge with advent of biotechnologies in the life sciences. Indeed, Moore's very will to exert control over his bodily property, his freedom to contract in relation to his property, is denied; despite the fact that the sale of bodily parts (organs, blood, tissue) is not legally prohibited in the US, strictly speaking.[59]

The onto-epistemological edifice that the modern human subject assumes, as Ferreira da Silva reminds us, 'that particular bodies that signify the mind, whereas other bodies signify nature'.[60] With the disaggregation of the human body by biotechnologies, the nature/culture divide (transposing Ferreira da Silva's critique into a related idiom), is shored up by intellectual property laws that rely upon a distinction between invention and discovery.[61] This idea of self-determination is reconfigured by judgments dealing with body parts or life; the notion that one should be able to decide autonomously about what happens with one's very body and self is interrupted by a proprietary regime that maintains a conceptual divide between the natural and cultural. The difference here is that the subject who has always been assumed to be the natural progenitor of rights, self-determination and autonomy is undone by the imperatives of new forms of appropriation.

The legal form, however, still relies on the distinctions between the natural and the social, between nature/culture that built the edifice upon which the self-determining, autonomous 'I' sits, and ends up with sort of persistent jetlag that will not let newer inscriptions of the body live or die. Rather, they seem forced into a zombie state with raciality – as both a discourse and philosophical-scientific apparatus continuing to operate despite radical shifts in the relationship between human subjectivity and the body.

For instance, in the case of the HeLa cells, Hannah Landecker notes how the cell line of Henrietta Lacks, a young black woman who died of cervical cancer in the 1950s, comes to be described in popular and scientific journals in very racialised-sexist metaphors reserved for black women. As a part of the growing immortalisation of the human person through the culturation of cell lines *in vitro,*

58 Ferreira da Silva, *Towards a Global Idea of Race.*
59 See *Moore v Regents* (Mosk J).
60 D. Ferreira da Silva, 'No-bodies: Law, Raciality and Violence' (2009) 18(2) *Griffith Law Review*
61 A. Pottage and B. Sherman, *Figures of Invention A History of Modern Patent Law* (Oxford: Oxford University Press, 2010).

Lacks's cell line played a primary role as the first permanent strain of a human cell that could be used for experimental use.[62] Landecker notes how raciality and scientific innovation become fused with the discovery that HeLa cells had 'contaminated and overgrown many of the other immortal human cell culture established in the 1950s and 1960s'.[63] In 1967, geneticist Stanley Gartler announced to an audience that, having analysed 18 different cell lines, all had the same profile as the HeLa cell. Because the key piece of evidence was the 'profile for a particular enzyme called G6PD . . . a factor in red blood cell production', Gartler concluded that the type of G6PD variant present in all cell lines was a type 'found only in Negroes'.[64] Landecker observes that from this point onwards, the contaminating cell line is marked as black, and the contaminated as white.[65] From this moment onwards, race becomes a key aspect of the HeLa narrative, with metaphors of miscegenation used to describe cells in culture and the threat posed by contamination – one drop of HeLa was enough to take over any other culture.[66]

Drawing on an example from the realm of genetics, Donna Haraway describes how in the early 1990s the organisers of the Human Genome Diversity Project wanted to adjust the thinking of the mainline Human Genome Project by collecting hair-root, white blood-cell and cheek-tissue samples, to be held in the American Type Culture Collection, from over 700 groups of indigenous peoples on six continents. She notes that modernist perspectives distorted the definition of the categories of people from whom samples were to be sought, leading to a vision of dynamic human groups as timeless 'isolates of historic interest'. She notes that other potentially genetically distinct ethnic communities did not appear on the sampling list.[67] The subject/object divide, again, challenged by the very technologies used to map the human genome, such as recombinant DNA techniques, remain intact in the way that raciality is understood and signified. Blood remains the medium through which raciality is marked, echoing 19th century concepts of raciality that buttressed miscegenation laws and eugenics. The body – and changes in how human life is conceived of – could interrupt the legal form that wants to cling to late modern proprietary regimes of recognition (perhaps as it always could have), by harnessing the plasticity and instability manifest in the body and its parts. It is from a position of instability that political practices that disrupt the spatial fixity and the temporal closure of a singular, linear *telos*, which have characterised colonially embedded relations of being and property ownership, could emerge.

62 Landecker, *Culturing Life* 127.
63 ibid 168.
64 ibid 168–69.
65 ibid 169.
66 ibid 170.
67 D. Haraway, *Modest_Witness@Second_Millenium.FemaleMan_Meets_OncoMouse: Feminism and Technoscience* (London: Routledge, 1997) 249.

Chapter 7

Being, nothing, becoming

Hegel and the legal order

Tarik Kochi

Introduction

A number of what might vaguely be called 'antagonistic' theories of society and politics have taken on increasing currency within contemporary legal and political theory on the left today.[1] Drawing attention to the role of conflict, struggle and disagreement in the constitution and continuation of political and legal orders, these theories stand in contrast to standard versions of liberal legal and political theory which display a tendency to downplay the role of social, economic and political conflict.

Liberal theory often plays a double game of displaying naïvety towards, or ignoring many causes of, social conflict, and placing faith in the role of 'reason' to resolve and cure all antagonism. Presupposing that a number of base rules and institutions have already been set and guaranteed by reason's progress in history (ie private property, capitalist production and exchange, individual rights, 'liberal democracy'), liberal theory generally assumes that any remaining conflict may be resolved through the medium of Kantian-style reason and open communication between subjects within the public realm.[2] However, in 'hard cases' (ie militants, anti-democrats, religious fanatics, terrorists) where conflict cannot be pacified, those who do not acquiesce to a liberal political order are made to feel the brunt and force of coercive law. In this respect the liberal legal order generally attempts to shelter itself from disruption by quarantining conflict. What is agonistic, the grounds of antagonism and inquiry into these grounds are hidden and the liberal legal order protects itself by institutional, formal and rhetorical techniques that redescribe and repress sites of conflict and struggle.[3]

1 See for example: A. Schaap (ed), *Law and Agonistic Politics* (Farnham: Ashgate, 2009); W. Rasch, *Sovereignty and its Discontents* (London: Birkbeck Law Press, 2004).

2 I am speaking here generally of the liberal versions of legal theory presented by Rawls and Habermas. For general critiques of liberal legal theory see C. Douzinas, R. Warrington and S. McVeigh, *Postmodern Jurisprudence: The Law of the Text in the Text of the Law* (London: Routledge, 1991); V. Kerruish, *Jurisprudence as Ideology* (London: Routledge, 1991).

3 See more generally E. Christodoulidis, 'The Objection that Cannot be Heard: Communication and Legitimacy in the Courtroom' in *The Trial on Trial Vol 1*

In what follows I draw upon the philosophy of G. W. F. Hegel to present an alternative account of the nature of social conflict within society and its relationship to 'right' (*Recht*) – norms, ethics, law. Such an account challenges general liberal assumptions about the non-conflictual nature of human reason and presents instead a theoretical model which helps us better to understand the role of antagonism, struggle and violence within the creation of ethical norms, moral principles and legal orders. My interpretation focuses upon the theory of recognition (*Anerkennung*) as read primarily through a number of passages within the *Phenomenology of Spirit* (*PhS*) (1807)[4] and *Science of Logic* (*SL*) (1812–16).[5] This theory of recognition highlights the necessary relationship between epistemic conflict, power and norm formation. Recognition is implicit within any form of 'public reason' and underlies ethical and political acts directed towards the realisation of freedom. While I do not think that this reading of recognition is the only way in which we can understand the relationship between law and social conflict, such a reading still provides a relevant critique of some of the dominant assumptions held by liberal legal theory. Further, the theory of recognition remains relevant to considering how any radical politics may go beyond the liberal legal order. As a theory of freedom, recognition sets out some of the grounds and limitations for any such ethical and political act.

In the background of Hegel's theory of right – the temporal, social, political, economic and ethical aspects that constitute the modern legal order – is a theory of recognition. For much contemporary Hegel scholarship the disparate aspects of the theory of recognition have been drawn into the open and shown to form the theoretical basis of Hegel's account of the human, social-psychological world of spirit (*Geist*). Hegel cannot be understood without the reader comprehending the play and work of recognition within his texts. Against the standard accusation of Hegel's philosophy being closed, totalising and conservative, a reading of Hegel's philosophy which keeps the role of recognition in mind offers a view of a social world constantly in flux, caught in the movement of struggle, conflict, restlessness and contradiction.

Hegel presents a view of the social world upsetting itself, of aspects rising up, breaking free and returning to wreak havoc on thought, on belief, on material, only to be soothed until upset again. Hegel's dance of intersubjective recognition is the social world drunk on its own music, swirling like a dervish and then struck down by the existential crisis of a self alienated from itself and smacked up against an other who cannot be fully known. Such an account is one of the

(ed A. Duff et al) (Oxford: Hart, 2004) 179; S. Veitch, *Law and Irresponsibility* (Abingdon: Routledge-Cavendish, 2007).

4 G. W. F. Hegel, *Phenomenology of Spirit* (trans. A. V. Miller) (Oxford: Oxford University Press, 1977).

5 G. W. F. Hegel, *Science of Logic* (trans. A. V. Miller) (London: Allen & Unwin, 1969); G. W. F. Hegel, *The Encyclopaedia Logic: Part I of the Encyclopaedia of Philosophical Sciences with the Zusätze* (trans. T. F. Geraets, W. A. Suchting and H. S. Harris) (Indianapolis: Hackett, 1991).

driven, desiring and utterly pragmatic negotiation and formulation of social and ethical norms, being at one point a moment of receptivity and care and in another, sheer inwardness, self-assertion, exclusion. In this play, in this work, sits symbolic and material production, deeds – acts of positing – which shape and reshape the legal forms and logical formulas of the world. Some of these are held tight, set in their place, put to good use, while others rise up and fly off as grand reified creatures assuming independent lives. In between, beliefs are held, intellects lay claim to reason, and right, and bodies are ordered, negated and pushed around.

Thrown about, by this perspective the critic tries to make sense of it all, render the whole meaningful – to find a 'rose in the cross of the present' and to act so as to make freedom more actual (*wirklich*). At the same time, or at another, the critic, encountering the limits of philosophic thought is encouraged to lay down the concept in the face of the whole, to let the other go free, and step back as the cosmos churns, slaughters and passes by. Then, suffering hits a tipping point, revolution explodes, or a cat knocks over a bucket, and demand grips again – to cognise the world and re-cognise the outlines of ethics and social being.

Hegel's philosophy presents a theory of antagonism and perhaps his most famous example is the dialectical relation of recognition between master and slave contained within the opening chapters of the *PhS*. What might these passages, dressed in a convoluted style of expression, tell us about politics and law? How might they overcome some of the limitations inherent in the approaches taken by liberal theory? On one reading/reconstruction, Hegel's account divulges a relationship between epistemology and force and demonstrates the working of power-knowledge within the intersubjective production of ethical norms.[6] Hegel, following Spinoza, rejected a Cartesian (and later Kantian) strict dualism between mind and body. In this respect, Hegel's attempts in the *PhS* to set out a philosophical or scientific account of the 'experience of consciousness' situates the human intellect firmly within the physical realm and locates the physical-cognising body within the temporal realm of the social.

As a white European man working in a philosophical tradition still heavily influenced by Socrates, Plato and Aristotle, Hegel emphasised a particular historical role of 'reason' and saw philosophy's dual task as that of comprehending the world and (following Kant's critical philosophy) that of comprehending *how* we come to know the world. Yet, in a sense, not unlike Nietzsche, Hegel was also aware of the various forms of desire that underlie reason's (often self-interested, culturally contingent and manipulative) efforts to know the self ('know thyself') and to know the world. And from the outset within the *PhS* Hegel situates the cognitive or intellectual act by an ego to comprehend and claim 'knowledge' over an object (ie to construct meaning in relation to diverse phenomena) within the

6 See T. Kochi, *The Other's War: Recognition and the Violence of Ethics* (Abingdon: Birkbeck Law Press, 2009).

broader operation of 'desire' [*Begierde*],[7] and relates this desire to a plurality of conflicting desires within the social world.

At the beginning of the *PhS* Hegel develops something like a philosophical anthropology in which the determinations of meaning (sense and reference) posited or constructed by an ego take place within the very bodily realm of human desire. The ego is a desiring ego situated within a process of 'life'; it is a living thing, living in relation to other living things.[8] Within Hegel's anthropology the ego, as a living being, desires its preservation in the face of its environment and perpetuates its life through negating objects around it. The biological desire for self-preservation and security, with its echoes of Hobbes, motivates the ego's comprehension of the world (its reasoning) and it can be anticipated that a conflict between multiple egos might ensue in situations where they cannot agree on mutually satisfactory methods of joint preservation. Yet, something further is at work within Hegel's account, which pushes the ego forward; this is the desire of the ego to become '(self-)certain'.[9] Such a desire is not disconnected from the biological – for the ego to eat, it has to become certain of what is edible and what is not, what is fruit and what is a rock, of whether the fruit is best eaten now or later and of whether it should be accumulated for the sole benefit of the ego or shared amongst others.[10]

The desire for certainty, as a desire for greater knowledge, drives the ego. In one respect this desire can be understood as the ego's desire for certainty in its own being, a certainty that interlinks the symbolic and the material. The ego needs certainty, but life around it, the plurality of differences within phenomena (and within the manifold of phenomena which it seeks to unify into distinct, nameable objects[11]) consistently renders things uncertain. The ego's attempt to cognise being runs up against infinite difference, against negativity which reveals the limit of any cognition, against the limit of any symbolic utterance which both excludes and then vanishes into something other than it. Struck by uncertainty the ego reaches out in ongoing attempts to gain certainty in being, relating common aspects of

7 Hegel, *Phenomenology of Spirit* 105.
8 ibid 107.
9 ibid 104.
10 In this sense Hegel (*Phenomenology of Spirit* 12) talks of 'reason' as 'purposive activity'.
11 'The *Here pointed out*, to which I hold fast, is similarly a *this* Here which, in fact, is *not* this Here, but a Before and Behind, an Above and Below, a Right and Left. The Above is itself similarly this manifold otherness of above, below etc. The Here, which was supposed to have been pointed out, vanishes into other Heres, but these likewise vanish. What is pointed out, held fast, and abides, is a *negative* This, which *is* negative only when the Heres are taken as they should be, but in being so taken they supersede themselves; what abides is a simple complex of many Heres. The Here that is *meant* would be the point; but it *is* not: on the contrary, when it is pointed out as something that *is*, the pointing-out shows itself to be not an immediate knowing [of the point], but a movement from the Here that is *meant* through many Heres into the universal Here which is a simple plurality of Heres, just as the day is a simple plurality of Nows.' Hegel, *Phenomenology of Spirit* 64.

phenomena together as 'universals'[12] and then watches as these fall into pieces again – limited, inadequate, contradictory, indeterminate – the surety of being negated by infinite negativity.

The cognitive-ontological claim made by Hegel in the early chapters of the *PhS* is reformulated later in the *SL*, as 'being', 'nothing', 'becoming' (*Sein*, *Nichts*, *Werden*).[13] Being in its immediacy is shown to be indeterminate, inadequate (negative to itself), as cognition comes up against limit, finitude, difference, contradiction and prior assumption (presupposition) which negate any fixity, any stability, any certainty. Negativity pushes being forward, being is always not-yet, is unfinished, shown to be constantly becoming – becoming other than itself.

Further, there is a contradiction inherent in the attempt to think being. Being presupposes something else, nothing. Yet this is not identical, not reducible to it. Being, nothing, two markers which thought, turned in upon itself, cannot reconcile, cannot hold together peacefully, cannot somehow ignore. Thought is moved by this contradiction, it tries to make sense of it, of itself, by stretching out, by some form of speculative realisation, by thinking this as becoming or as something more; sometimes something suppressed, something reconciled. In any case thought (as the unity of thought and being) has to work, has to work against what is paradoxical within and at odds with itself. In this sense the attempt of the ego (or at a more abstract or formal level: 'thinking', 'reasoning' or 'reason') to come to terms with contradiction has to draw in differences in phenomena, construct universal terms of signification, to construct an account of being that has a more complex, nuanced, thick, concrete, determinate or 'speculative' character ('determinate being';[14] a 'concrete' rather than 'abstract universal'). Yet, this then is shown up as inadequate, indeterminate (as always presupposing something else – a missed step behind) and therefore needing to be cognised again, re-cognised.

For Hegel it is precisely this *act* of cognition (the act of the thinking thing, the ego, the subject) in its attempt to order or organise phenomena in a coherent way which helps to create its own split from the world, negating and excluding as much as it grasps or holds onto. Thought-determinations take place by way of negativity, by way of identifying and positing differences in phenomena, by way of distinguishing what something 'is' from what it is 'not'.[15] Further, negativity/

12 ibid 68.

13 Hegel, *Science of Logic* 82; Hegel, *Encyclopaedia Logic* 136–41. Importantly for Hegel, 'Being' and 'Nothing' represent contradiction residing at the constitution of thought. Rather than withdraw from contradiction (paradox, antinomy), as did Kant, Hegel argued that human thinking is antinominal, that it is characterised by contradiction. For an account of the necessary role of contradiction within human thinking, as it relates to metaphysics, logic and mathematics. See U. Petersen, *Diagonal Method and Dialectical Logic: Tools, Materials, and Groundworks for a Logical Foundation of Dialectic and Speculative Philosophy* (Tönning: Der Andere Verlag, 2002).

14 ibid 107, 145.

15 Hegel, *Encyclopaedia Logic* 147 (Addition) argues: 'The basis of all determinacy is negation (*omnis determination est negatio*, as Spinoza says)'.

negation contained and constitutive of the act of cognition institutes an inadequacy, a not-yet character, and operates as a motor which drives the cognising being forward (as becoming) in the attempt to grasp more adequately its own being which itself is becoming. A sense of this is given by Jean-Luc Nancy:

> The *subject* is what it *does*, it is its act, and its doing is the experience of the consciousness of the negativity of substance, as the concrete experience and consciousness of the modern history of the world – that is, also, of the passage of the world through its own negativity: the loss of references and the ordering of a 'world' in general (*cosmos*, *mundus*), but also, and thereby, its becoming-world in a new sense. It becomes immanent, and it becomes infinite. The world is only this world; it has no other sense, and it is in this way that it is the world of the history-of-the-world (history in the sense as movement of negativity, but it does not itself have a sense that would bring it to an end). At the same time – and it is this that is *time*, the concrete existence of negativity – this world, the realm of the finite, shelters and reveals in itself the infinite work of negativity, that is, the restlessness of sense (or of the 'concept,' as Hegel names it: restlessness of conceiving-itself, grasping itself, and relating-itself-to-itself – in German, *begreifen*: 'to grasp,' 'to catch hold of,' 'to comprehend'). It is in this way, in the restlessness of immanence, that the spirit of the world becomes. It neither seeks itself (as it were for itself an exterior end) nor finds itself (as it were a thing here or there), but it effectuates itself: it is the living restlessness of its own concrete effectivity.[16]

In this respect, what Hegel calls recognition – with its anthropology and its differing historical moments set out in the *PhS*, and its formal method described in the *SL* – is the ego's (always inadequate) attempt to see-into or (re)cognise being.[17]

16 J.-L. Nancy, *The Restlessness of the Negative* (Minneapolis: University of Minnesota Press, 2002) 5.

17 See G. Rose, *Hegel Contra Sociology* (London: Athlone, 1981). Rose notes that Hegel's theory of recognition attempts to combat what Hegel saw as inadequacies in Fichte and Schelling's attempts to use a notion of 'intellectual intuition' to explain Kant's otherwise 'inexplicable' transcendental unity of apperception and the causal efficacy of the will. She argues: 'In the Jena lectures of 1803-4 and 1805-6 Hegel gradually changed intuition, *An-schauen*, into re-cognizing, *An-erkennen*. "Re-cognizing" emphasizes the lack of identity or difference which is seen. *Anschauen*, to intuit or perceive, has the semantic disadvantage of sounding too immediate, too pre-critical, too successful. The "an", "into", becomes "re", "again" in *An-erkennen*. *Anerkennen* thus implies an initial experience which is misunderstood, and which has to be re-experienced. It does not imply an immediate, successful vision, but that the immediate vision or experience is incomplete, "*Das Bekannte überhaupt ist darum, weil es bekannt ist, nicht erkannt* [The well known is such because it is well known not known]." The familiar or well known, the immediate experience (*das Bekannte*), is a partial experience which has to be re-experienced or known again (*anerkannt*) in order to be fully known (*erkannt*). Hence "re-cognition" implies initial mis(re)cognition, not an immediate "seeing-into"' (at 71).

Never immediately successful, recognition takes place as mis-recognition and has to be repeated again and again, settling at times in relative stability and then upset once more. In this respect, the biological, symbolic and socially derived desires, passions and affects that push the ego in multiple directions are all channelled through what Hegel calls recognition – the cognitive acts of the ego that attempt to make sense of the world all the while struggling, being pushed about and undone by the operation and negativity which renders thought-determinations more determinate and highlights their inadequacy.[18]

The ego, driven by multiple desires, strives for a degree of certainty and does so via ordering phenomena in particular ways. It understands objects in the world as having a particular, determinate meaning. This particular, ordered meaning of phenomena excludes other possible different meanings which are negated by the meaning posited by the ego. In a formulation which Hegel takes from Fichte, the ego *posits* an ordered set of meanings (A) which excludes and negates the inclusion of other possible meanings (not-A). Yet, this ordered meaning given by the ego must come from somewhere – 'caused' by some other thought determination, another set of meanings or symbolic references. Against an individualist account of 'intellectual intuition' relied upon by Fichte, Hegel, influenced by Spinoza, sees an infinite variety of not-As already presupposed by and affecting any thought-determination posited by the ego. In this respect, when the ego posits itself, it posits a version of its own self-certainty and an order of a certain world which it derives from both its own act of cognition *and* from the social world of symbolic references given to it by its intersubjective participation in language, culture and history. In its ordering of the world for certainty, the ego simultaneously posits itself and the flux of external (other) symbols/meanings which it identifies as constituting part of itself. In this vein recognition operates as the mode of thought-determination

18 Instead of a Kantian gap or breach between phenomena and an unknowable 'thing-in-itself' Hegel thinks that this dual world view is inadequate and that Kant misunderstands the nature of this 'gap'. The gap is not between the knower and the unknown world, but is contained within the act of cognition itself as negativity and contradiction: as the limit point of each thought-determination shown up by another which it presupposes or which it contradicts. An ego, perpetually self-alienated from itself and the world through its own act of knowing. In one sense of this see for example S. Žižek, *The Sublime Object of Ideology* (London: Verso, 1989). At 205–206, Žižek argues: 'Kant still presupposes that the Thing-in-itself exists as something positively given beyond the field of representation, of phenomenality; the breakdown of phenomenality, the experience of phenomena, is for him only an "external reflection", only a way of indicating, within the domain of phenomenality, this transcendent dimension of the Thing which persists in itself beyond phenomenality.'

Hegel's position is, in contrast, that there is *nothing* beyond phenomenality, beyond the field of representation. The experience of radical negativity, of the radical inadequacy of all phenomena to the Idea, the experience of the radical fissure between the two – this experience is already *Idea itself as 'pure', radical negativity*. Where Kant thinks that he is still dealing with a negative presentation of the Thing, we are already in the midst of the Thing-in-itself – *for this Thing-in-itself is nothing but this radical negativity*.'

in which the ego draws for itself the boundaries of what constitutes its self and what constitutes its not-self – that is the delineation of what is included and affirmed in the notion of 'self' from everything other that is negated and excluded from self-identification.

One aspect of Hegel's philosophical project, following (and attempting to go beyond) Spinoza, is to show the fundamental interconnectivity of the differing aspects within a multiplicity of being: 'to see the finite within the infinite'; 'to see subject as spirit (*Geist*) and spirit as subject'; 'to see the true as the whole and the whole as the inter-relation of its parts'; 'to see the I as We and We as I'. Yet, within this project Hegel is also concerned to show how the human ego only identifies with fractured, limited aspects of the multiplicity of being within distinct temporal moments. In this respect any knowledge of the 'absolute' can only proceed impartially by way of re-cognising these fractured modes of identification that, held together, make up parts of the whole. As such, only particular, limited orders of meaning and conceptions of being are posited by egos within history as having an affirmative character and held up as 'truth' or as 'right' (that is, as 'individuality', as 'personality', as 'abstract right', as a particular rights claim), while others are negated and excluded. The mode of always inadequate self-identification within the ego, its claim to certainty or knowledge, is related then by Hegel to a normative ordering of thought in the world.

In the passages within the *PhS* which deal with the struggle for recognition Hegel shows how differing modes of the self-identification of the ego take place intersubjectively. Through reciprocal agreement, and by way of threat and physical force, normative orders of phenomena (truth and right) are posited socially and, once held in place, become the naturally assumed basis upon which further moments of recognition are grounded. Hegel demonstrates that while there is a more open approach in which an ego may recognise the way in which otherness is contained within itself and do so with speculative-philosophical and ethical results, there is also a mode of (mis)recognition which excludes otherness and does so through domination and violence. When thinking critically about law, both of these aspects of re-cognition have relevance to the consideration of the relations between knowledge and power, violence, struggle.

The ego which posits itself through its conception of the world (a particular order of meaning; a 'world view') is thrown into uncertainty when faced by another ego who challenges this view and posits another.[19] Seen from such an intersubjective perspective the act of cognition and the ordering of phenomena is shown to be 'normative'. Any intuition or cognition emerges as 'always already' social, that is, as an act which presupposes language and symbolism, culture and norms. What appeared earlier within Hegel's anthropology as solipsistic thought determinations of the certainty or 'truth' of the ego's being are shown to be normative claims about the nature of being – the nature of the world made by one subject in relation

19 Hegel, *Phenomenology of Spirit* 111.

to the claims of others. In this sense truth possesses an intersubjective, normative function.[20] The ego's enunciation to its other about how the world 'is' can be considered as also a normative statement made to the other about how it should ('ought' to) conceive the world.

Hegel's description of the moment of conflict between two egos, their subsequent duel or struggle to the death, the acquiescence of one to the power of the other and the resultant position of master and slave[21] positions cognition, knowledge and truth within the field of normative conflict and struggle. The positing of one normative conception of certainty/order rubs up against that posited by another and within this arise the possibilities of shared normative commitment and/or struggle, violence and domination. Where the parties can come to some agreement, acknowledge or recognise the validity of the claim made by the other, then a shared normative position emerges as a 'universal' which mediates and unifies their positions. This universal, contingent upon their continued recognition, affirmation and agreement expresses a shared normative position in relation to phenomena, in relation to knowledge and in relation to behaviour; it emerges as a joint truth, a collective conception of what counts as 'right'.

In the situation where there is disagreement, a lack of acknowledgement between the parties, where recognition is refused, then the 'universal' (truth/right) is put and held in place via struggle and force, and as such, truth and right represent the domination of one ego over the other. While in the latter example of struggle, the working of power is more visible as domination, power is still present in the former example of mutual recognition – it is the mutually complementary relations of power and force which constitute and sustain the position of the universal, and without this power contained within recognition, a particular universal of truth/right would fade.

Hegel's theory of recognition involves a philosophy of reflection upon otherness.[22] In the moment of confrontation between one ego and another, each positing their own certainty of truth/right, Hegel suggests the possibility of each ego reflecting upon the role and status of the other in relation to their own being. The appearance of the other challenges certainty of their initial conception of identity, and the ego is forced to render more certain what it views as the 'essence' of its identity in relation to the differences posed by the other. Challenged by the counter-claim of the other, what seemed special, abiding, certain in the

20 For differing views on this aspect of recognition see T. Pinkard, *Hegel's Phenomenology: The Sociality of Reason* (Cambridge: Cambridge University Press, 1994); R. Pippin, *Hegel's Idealism: The Satisfactions of Self-Consciousness* (Cambridge: Cambridge University Press, 1989); R. R. Williams, *Hegel's Ethics of Recognition* (Berkeley: University of California Press, 1997). On Hegel and law more generally see A. Norrie, *Law and the Beautiful Soul* (London: GlassHouse Press, 2005).

21 Hegel, *Phenomenology of Spirit* 113–116.

22 ibid 14. Hegel argues: '*Pure* self-recognition in absolute otherness . . . is the ground and soil of Science or *knowledge in general*'.

ego's conception of self-identity comes to be shown as a little more contingent, arbitrary, reliant upon grounds and distinctions that may not be wholly unlike those drawn by the other. What immediately might have appeared to be independent, self-contained, shows itself in the other's voice, the other's argument, the other's threat, to be more relative, thus presupposing and dependent upon so much that is present in the other. Within such reflection, for Hegel, the posited immediate 'essence' (*Wesen*)[23] of self-identity of the ego falls into 'existence' (*Existenz*)[24] – as the ego's thought determinations are shown to be dependent and grounded upon other grounds, shown up as purely relative and relational in their being, as always already containing infinite difference and otherness within the self. Hegel argues:

> Existence is the immediate unity of inward reflection and reflection-into-another. Therefore, it is the indeterminate multitude of existents as inwardly reflected, which are at the same time, and just as much, shining-into-another, or *relational*; and they form a *world* of interdependence and of the infinite connectedness of grounds with what is grounded. The grounds are themselves existences, and the existents are also in many ways grounds as well as grounded.[25]

In this respect the moment of mutual recognition involves a 'speculative' realisation on the part of the ego that its identity already contains within it aspects of the other and that its being is really a relational, interdependent existence, a form of social being (*Gemeinwesen*) – the 'I that is We and We that is I'.[26] For Hegel, the speculative re-cognition of social being has an ethical result: the ego which now sees the other as part of itself affirms the other as if it were itself. The ego in recognising the other attempts to limit its negation of the other and views its pursuit of self-certainty as now a project which can only occur through mediation with the other. As the ego's positing of an order of the world is inherently normative its freedom to posit itself can only be realised through normative agreement with the other. The form and content of the ego's freedom is then entirely contingent upon the mutual recognition between the ego and its other and as such, for Hegel, mutual recognition is necessary for freedom to become actual.

What Hegel calls, 'actuality' (*Wirklichkeit*)[27] can be understood as the bringing into realisation the freedom of being. As being is the contingent, interrelated, and interdependent flux of existence – namely social being – freedom only becomes actual through speculative acts of (re)cognition and material acts of the collective

23 Hegel, *Science of Logic* 394; Hegel, *Encyclopaedia Logic* 175.
24 ibid 481, 192.
25 Hegel, *Encyclopaedia Logic* 192–93.
26 Hegel, *Phenomenology of Spirit* 110.
27 Hegel, *Science of Logic* 541; Hegel, *Encyclopaedia Logic* 213.

positing of egos (mutual recognition).[28] It is in this respect, grounded in the *PhS* and *SL*, that Hegel can say in the *Philosophy of Right* (*PhR*) (1820) in relation to 'right': 'What is rational is actual; and what is actual is rational. (*Was vernünftig ist, das ist wirklich; und was wirklich ist, das ist vernünftig*)'.[29] What is rational (or reasonable) is the realisation of the freedom of being which can only occur if the ego gives up its immediate solipsistic tendencies towards self-certainty and instead finds itself in, and gives itself to, the radical project of mutual recognition: the positing of itself in and through its others; the re-cognition of its truth claims as shared and negotiated normative commitment; the acknowledgement of the shared power that underlies the constitution of moral norms and political institutions; the speculative comprehension of its always already social being. From this perspective, Hegel's theory of recognition stakes a claim for what is necessary to realise the freedom of being. Mutual recognition – egos who affirm the other in their selves, equally – as the realisation of the freedom of social being – expresses a speculative idea. In Rousseau this idea is called the 'general will'; in Marx and Lenin it is called 'communism'.

Yet, as soon as this idea comes to the surface it falls away again into epistemic error, limit and negativity that characterises the *mis* of misrecognition. In recognising the other, each ego affirms aspects of the other but misses, ignores, overlooks other aspects which are then given no positive affirmation. When the other appears to the ego, particular aspects of its phenomena shine out, are held as essential and the other is known as this shape of appearance (*Erscheinung*). Each act of recognition only grasps one form of appearance of the other and as such misses, suppresses and negates other aspects of the other's existence. As such, every mutual act of recognition only cognises one particular appearance or form of (social) being; and each intersubjective ethical positing, only grasps one particular and limited (although 'valid', and not a mere 'semblance') appearance of being and posits only one corresponding, inadequate form or right.

From this perspective there is a certain ethical-cognitive demand within recognition to push beyond its own limitations and failings. Each attempt to name the 'real' of the other (or the 'real' of ethical relationship between egos) misrecognises the part for the whole, misrecognises one mode of appearance for the multiplicity of inter-grounded existence, raises the other as an object, a 'thing', something which is held up as distinct, special and independent when it is in fact merely one possible inter-subjective cognitive formulation amongst many others. In this respect, the ethical-cognitive work of recognition is the continued effort of undoing the moment of *reification* that creeps into cognition. This moment can be thought of as that in which the ego 'forgets' that the appearance of the object that it sees (the shape of the other ego) is always already the product of intersubjective

28 On the relation between Hegel's logic and recognition see the discussion in P. Dews, *The Limits of Disenchantment: Essays on Contemporary European Philosophy* (London: Verso, 1995).
29 G. W. F. Hegel, *Elements of the Philosophy of Right* (ed. A. W. Wood, trans. H. B. Nisbet) (Cambridge: Cambridge University Press, 1991) 20.

recognition – the collective process of cognitive positing, symbolic description and norm formation (and material production). This forgetfulness[30] treats a particular appearance as a 'fact', as some 'natural' occurrence and as possessing some stable form of being, rather than always already being the human product of intersubjective, co-cognitive becoming.

In this sense, recognition could be thought as a form of 'attentiveness'[31] to the ego's constant forgetting of the inter-subjective grounding of its cognition. That, what is 'real' or 'actual' (within this ongoing to and fro between being and becoming, between essence and existence, between appearance and actuality) is only ever the mutual self-grounding of cognition within inter-subjectivity itself. Hegel's position suggests a speculative standpoint or activity which constantly acknowledges and attempts to overcome a tendency to forget, that thought and being are dependent upon and produced by the praxis of inter-subjective recognition. It is an uncovering and an awareness of the position that any normative or symbolic formulation is necessarily contingent upon the broader *onto-logical concept (Begriff) of recognition* as such.

As much as a notion of 'right' develops out of the shared speculative standpoint of mutual recognition and the inter-subjective positing of a shared set of norms that are held up as 'laws' historically, culturally and politically, this positing contains within it a moment of wrong.[32] Within the *PhS* Hegel describes this in terms of the struggle for recognition where one ego confronting another refuses to acknowledge the validity of the normative position of the other and misrecognises its own grounding within the inter-dependency of social being. The ego pushes its own limited view of certainty upon the other and through force and the threat of death sets up a limited 'universal' of right and truth, which is also a regime of mastery and domination.[33]

In this sense, for Hegel, right and forms of law emerge also out of misrecognition and disagreement between egos over how the world should be normatively

30 This 'forgetfulness' is shaped also by capitalist ideology and the pervasiveness of the commodity form (fetish-character and the production of subjectivities within the market) and shaped also by various disciplining procedures. In Hegelian parlance these might be called historical shapes or forms of spirit (*Geist*).

31 On this forgetting and attentiveness of recognition in relation to the operation of reification see A. Honneth, 'Reification: A Recognition-Theoretical View' Tanner Lectures on Human Values, University of California, Berkeley (14–16 March 2005) available at http://www.tannerlectures.utah.edu/lectures/documents/Honneth_2006.pdf (accessed 21 January 2012)., Honneth continues: 'Reification in the sense of "forgetfulness of recognition" therefore means that in the course of our acts of cognition we lose our attentiveness to the fact that this cognition owes its existence to an antecedent act of recognition' (at 130).

32 This sense of a 'wrong' is somewhat different to the notion of the 'wrong of law' as set out by Valerie Kerruish. My reading does, however, share with her a certain spirit of the Altona interpretation of Hegel. See V. Kerruish, 'But What's It Got To Do With Law?' (2009) 4 *Dillemata* 81.

33 Hegel, *Phenomenology of Spirit* 115.

ordered. Right and law appear as much through mutual recognition, as through conflict and struggle. The formation of norms does not take place purely as moments of moral meditation by way conscience and public reason (Kant, Rawls) or by free and open communication between subjects (Habermas) but are constituted via misrecognition, conflict and struggle over which particular norm is to have precedence in shaping a particular social order. A form of speaking, a mode of description, posited without attentiveness to the demands of the other negates an alternative formulation and sets up a regime of power-knowledge upon which further aspects of a normative structure may be built. And yet, within this framework, even when an ego is attentive, the speech act, the normative description, may still carry out a 'violence of the word'[34] by one against the other. In such a sense, what might initially look like the happy act of mutual recognition seems again troubled by the *mis* of mis-recognition, the moment of domination and negation in what was intended as a positive affirmation. A crushing in the embrace.

Pared down, recognition reveals itself as fundamentally problematic, especially when it comes to attempting to draw the line between where open mutual recognition ends and where the conflict of mis-recognition begins. Attempting to judge these distinctions, cognition is plunged back into positing thought-determinations based on 'quantity', 'quality', 'degree' and 'measure' which fall into claims about the 'essence' of that something (conflict, domination, force) that can only be 'determined' as such by the shared standpoint of mutual recognition. At the point when this shared standpoint over what constitutes the nature of the 'thing' (the boundary between mutual and mis-recognition) cannot be reached and shows itself as disagreement, then the whole process of recognition and the attempt to realise the freedom of being is characterised by the conflict, struggle and counter-positing of knowledge and experience.

Where open mutual recognition ends, and the conflict of mis-recognition begins, is a central problematic that troubles the attempt to realise the freedom of being. Even when the speculative, onto-logical concept of recognition is drawn upon by the ego as a guiding *praxis* or attentiveness in its dealings with the other (that is, mutual recognition as right, as equality, as communism), there is no guarantee that the participants will still not fundamentally disagree over the meaning of this notion and its translation within the temporal moment. When the onto-logical real is only recognition as such, then there is no recourse to another transcendental principle or meta-language (or ethical, messianic or romantic orientation to the absent 'thing-in-itself') that might guide the act of recognition in any particular direction. In this respect, for Hegel, the project of norm formation – right and truth – does not and cannot escape disagreement

34 Cf J. Derrida, 'Violence and Metaphysics: An Essay on the Thought of Emmanuel Levinas' in *Writing and Difference* (trans. A. Bass) (Chicago: University of Chicago Press, 1978).

over how phenomena ought to be interpreted or over how human bodies and behaviour ought to be arranged.

In locating disagreement within norm formation Hegel views the shapes of right and law which have 'appeared' historically, as norms that have been co-constituted (posited, rendered actual) via *both* mutual acknowledgement and by way of struggle, mastery and domination. Even what looks like a shared norm cannot escape what can be termed an 'ethics of exclusion' in which one normative formulation between a group of subjects necessarily negates the inclusion of an alternative normative perspective. Negation troubles law and ethics and any act which attempts to posit a shared, 'universal' norm, necessarily excludes a contradictory position which cannot be accommodated. In this respect, negativity haunts the attempt to realise the freedom of being – the dissident, the forgotten, the internal enemy, the minority of one, the aspect of otherness ignored and not captured by recognition, returns to unsettle the stability and right of any collective project. To realise the freedom of being these moments of otherness cannot be ignored but must be brought into the operation of recognition, and yet, with every act of (mis)re-cognition some aspect of phenomena, somebody, some form of life, some perspective is left behind, negated.

Understood in this manner, as much as Hegel's *PhR* sets out moments of mutual recognition as the historical positing of a 'right', something is excluded and denounces such a right as inadequate and a wrong. In the moment of love in the family,[35] in the thin universality of individual legal rights within the market-orientated civil society[36] and within the 'solidarity'[37] held by citizens within the state,[38] each of these is simultaneously a 'wrong' describing the domination of patriarchal family relations, the unfreedom and exploitation of the market, and a rampant nationalism that devalues the human and asserts its rights through war. Between rights and wrongs Hegel paints an image of history in which particular norms are built through shared normative agreement between some and defended against others. Right and the constitution of particular norms within law is largely the product of bargain and struggle. In this same vein we can think of modern day human rights[39] and rights of collective self-determination[40] as neither natural nor the product of a non-violent reason, but as the historical outcome of struggle which displaced alternative conceptions and were brought about through violence and force. Just like the economic institution of slavery, pointed to by Hegel in

35 Hegel, *Philosophy of Right* 199.
36 ibid 220.
37 To use the reformulation made by Honneth. See Axel Honneth, *The Struggle for Recognition: The Moral Grammar of Social Conflicts* (trans. Joel Anderson) (Cambridge: Polity Press, 1995).
38 Hegel, *Philosophy of Right* 275.
39 See C. Douzinas, *The End of Human Rights: Critical Legal Thought at the Turn of the Century* (Oxford: Hart, 2000).
40 See B. Bowring, *The Degradation of the International Order? The Rehabilitation of Law and the Possibility of Politics* (Abingdon: Routledge-Cavendish, 2008).

the master–slave relationship,[41] these normative formulations are sustained by force and are the outcome of the cognitive and material power that is the intersubjective positing and ordering of the ego.

Any assumption by liberal legal theory that is, has, or can overcome conflict and social antagonism through the public use of reason (in either Rawlsian, Habermasian or other varieties) cannot be sustained, simply because antagonism (negativity, contradiction) cannot be purged from inter-subjectively-grounded reason. Right and law, even when historically or 'empirically' shown to be grounded on a temporal moment of mutual affirmation between members within a group (a social contract or general will) and reaffirmed by 'public debate' and 'democratic participation' does not constitute a social existence outside of conflict, outside of wrong. Right and law carry within them moments of negation and exclusion. Every positive right, every positive law has been brought about in some sense or other through a process of struggle, force and empowerment, over and against an alternative normative formulation held by others.

Right and law take place as struggle and conflict, and this sense comes close to the formulation by Foucault that 'politics' (and we can add to this 'law') is 'war by other means'.[42] Yet, there is something lacking in the Foucauldian formulation, a certain over-determination that gives too much emphasis to the side of struggle, to the side of war, violence and domination and has difficulty accounting for positive moments of affirmation between subjects in the process of norm formation.[43] Such a Foucauldian formulation perhaps reduces every thought, every act, every bodily motion and conjugation of a verb, to 'war' and turns the becoming of being into war.

In contrast, Hegel's formulation of the social in terms of recognition (while lacking Foucault's numerous other important insights into processes of discipline

41 On the colonial context of recognition and the formation of 'right' as the struggle against colonial slavery see S. Buck-Morss, 'Hegel and Haiti' (2000) 26(4) *Critical Inquiry* 821. She continues (at 852) she argues: 'Beyond a doubt Hegel knew about real slaves and their revolutionary struggles. In perhaps the most political expression of his career, he used the sensational events of Haiti as the linchpin in his argument in *The Phenomenology of Spirit*. The actual and successful revolution of Caribbean slaves against their masters is the moment when the dialectical logic of recognition becomes visible as the thematics of world history, the story of the universal realisation of freedom. If the editor of *Minerva*, Archenholz, reporting history as it happened, did not himself suggest this on the pages of his journal, Hegel, longtime reader of them, was capable of that vision. Theory and reality converged at this historical moment. Or, to put it in Hegelian language, the rational – freedom – became real. This is the crucial point for understanding the originality of Hegel's argument, by which philosophy burst out of the confines of academic theory and became commentary on the history of the world'.

42 M. Foucault, *Society Must be Defended* (trans. D. Macey) (London: Penguin Books, 2004) 15.

43 For a critique of Foucault from perspective of recognition see A. Honneth, *The Critique of Power* (trans. K. Baynes) (Cambridge, Mass.: MIT Press, 1991).

and governmentality) is less bleak and does not condense the social to purely antagonism, war or the violence of power relations. Importantly, Hegel holds onto this moment and shows how forms of right cannot come about without some aspect of negation, without some aspect of struggle. Yet, Hegel also holds up a perception of right, and an aspect of legal order, which is not reducible to struggle and domination. These are the reciprocal moments of recognition in which something is positively affirmed in the other by attentive, re-cognising subjects. A sphere of ethical life (*Sittlichkeit*) brought about and sustained by mutual *acts* of recognition. Further, the logic of contradiction and restlessness of negativity within Hegel's formulation renders any conservative identification of what 'is' with the whole of right a joke. Hegel sees the demand for the 'actual' or 'real' of freedom as always upsetting and attempting to overturn the inadequacy of any historical appearance of right. The demand of right, is the demand that what is inadequate in any historical appearance of right/law – that is its wrong – be negated, overcome, and a more concrete sense of right – as the freedom of (social) being – be made more actual.

Grounded on the onto-logical concept of recognition, there remains a demand for law and for ethics to attempt to realise, or to bring into actuality, the freedom of being. On the interpretation of Hegel I have taken, this remains an open possibility and is no way grounded upon a philosophy of history. Yet, within a highly antagonistic view of reason and the social, this possibility is questioned by the role of negativity itself. As such, the possibility of mutual recognition can be thought to sit between three prominent images given by Hegel in the *PhS*. The first is of the modernist act of the French revolution in which the ethical act of constituting/positing a new political order of freedom as an 'event' resulted in liberation and, also in uncontrolled violence of negativity and terror.[44] The second is the somewhat neurotic figure of the beautiful soul, who, so attuned to the violence of negativity that accompanies any ethical act, withdraws purely within itself and is unable to act at all, for fear of negating itself, its principles and anyone else.[45] The third is the tragic position of Antigone, whose attempt to act ethically is torn apart by the inherent contradictory demands within ethics and who, nonetheless, acts in the knowledge that her choice will bring about her own destruction.[46]

The ethical-cognitive act guided by the onto-logical concept of recognition is forced to walk endlessly between these different positions. So also have critics and philosophers walked and continue to walk in the to and fro between these positions, shuffling back and forth between acts of political radicalism and the caution of the beautiful soul.[47] Between, on the one hand, calls to act in 'fidelity to the event' so as to constitute a new speculative political order of freedom and equality and,

44 Hegel, *Phenomenology of Spirit* 355.
45 ibid 383.
46 ibid 267.
47 A critical legal theory seemingly caught between the disciples of Badiou and Derrida.

on the other hand, the decrial of the impossibility of any such politics and its fall into the mastery of modernist philosopher-kings and the 'metaphysics of presence', sits the uncomfortable truth of Antigone – that the political/ethical attempt to make right actual cannot escape contradiction, negation or destruction.

Whether this third position remains within modernity and within capitalism, as a farcical rather than a tragic act – the farce of choice within the market (between Coke and Pepsi), within liberal parliamentary politics (between 'progressive' and 'conservative'), within the university (between publication in a 'top journal' or securing a research grant) – is an open question. While the attempt to make such distinctions cannot hope to escape a certain folly of mis-recognition, an attentiveness to the nature of social antagonism itself perhaps offers some line of guidance and maybe hope. The act responds not merely to an antagonism that offers competing or contradictory choices, but to a more fundamental antagonism which can only be overcome through the risk of self-destruction and death. An attempt to make actual the freedom of social being – right – judged and risked against the death and destruction that constitutes the extent of law's wrong.

Chapter 8

Faith and resignation

A journey through international law

*Jason A. Beckett**

The fate of international law is not a matter of re-employing a limited number of professionals for more cost-effective tasks but of re-establishing hope for the human species.

Martti Koskenniemi

All international lawyers have a critical engagement with law. For the 'mainstream' the critique tends to focus on the (non-)enforcement of public international law (PIL), the *mala fides*, non-compliance and manipulations of states; their 'abuse' of the legal project. From this perspective, law is good and politics is bad; and states are political actors only slightly constrained by law. Law is the attempt to speak right to might, or truth to power; the lawyer's role is to facilitate this with ever-greater efficacy.

The 'mainstream' is characterised by a faith in the legal project but is not a discourse without *esprit critique*. At times, individual laws, or interpretations and applications of law, are recognised and portrayed as unjust. However, this injustice is generally identified and criticised in strictly legal terms, by reference to other laws, which could, and *should*, have been adopted instead.

Consequently, if anything could be said to characterise the mainstream, it would be the idea that *generally speaking* PIL is just, fair and beneficial to all; at the least the system is the best that we can realistically have, whilst always working towards an even more just system. Vaughan Lowe captures this sensibility perfectly in his claim that, 'after all, the system works for most of the time'.[1]

Whilst for the mainstream, international law is relatively determinate and overarchingly good, for the newstream,[2] international law is radically

* I would like to thank Henry Jones and Stefano Bertea for their comments; and Anne-Charlotte Martineau for her support, for our discussions, and for reading and commenting upon earlier drafts. Anastaziya Tataryn and Ramy Basily provided timely support at a late stage, for which I am also most grateful. Naturally, all errors of form and substance remain mine alone.

1 V. Lowe, 'Book review of *From Apology to Utopia*' (1990) 17 *Journal of Law and Society* 384, 386.

2 It is difficult to settle on a specific signifier for the critical project as regards PIL. I will use the terms newstream, CLS and the crits more or less interchangeably, based on little more than aesthetic considerations.

indeterminate[3] and *overwhelmingly bad*. The poles are inverted: from a generally efficacious, relatively determinate and tolerably just legal order to an indeterminate and unjust order of legally sanctioned domination.

From a critical perspective, the *esprit critique* of the mainstream project is best understood as reformist rather than truly critical: a piecemeal process of incremental improvement rather than a radical rethinking of the international legal project. This is simply insufficient, because, for crits, the system does *not* work most of the time! As Marks has put it:

> International law . . . has failed and goes on failing millions, not 'on occasion', but overwhelmingly and systematically . . . if we live in a world of chaos and conflict, that is not in spite of international law [but] because of it.[4]

In simpler terms, the world is a catastrophe. This world, the world existing beneath the benevolent gaze of PIL is a world where 50,000 human beings die *quite unnecessarily* every single day.[5] Consequently the critical project attempts to grapple with – to isolate, identify, analyse and alter – the role of law in this world.

Initiation into the critical legal project can be (and was for me) a slow and painful process. It is a process of recognising one's commitment to law as an act of faith; and then seeing the naïveté of that faith, attempting first to redeem and then to abandon it, before settling into a resigned acceptance of law's simultaneous impossibility and necessity. In this chapter, I wish to outline this journey, as well as the map of the critical legal project which it reveals.

Prologue: the structure of enquiry

In *Fear and Trembling*, Kierkegaard offers an understanding of faith as a process or journey, which can be understood in four distinct phases. My project is to transpose the structure developed by Kierkegaard to the critical project in international law – the move from (i) a naïve faith in law, through (ii) an internal *esprit critique*, manifested in the attempts first to reform and then to redeem the legal system, to (iii) 'resignation' to the legal form, and, finally, to (iv) an attempt to transcend the epistemological and structural shackles of legality. This journey is punctuated by a series of crises of understanding and of faith; crises which open the paths to new understandings of international law, but which also limit both the legal *and* critical projects.

The point of interest is not simply that PIL does not function as a technical system and does not provide justice. Rather, the vital point is that it *cannot* operate

3 By which I mean, *inter alia*, that compliance cannot be distinguished from non-compliance; nor implementation from manipulation; nor use from abuse.

4 S. Marks, 'International Judicial Activism and the Commodity-Form Theory of International Law' (2007) 18 *European Journal of International Law* 202.

5 T. Pogge, *World Poverty and Human Rights* (Cambridge: Polity, 2008) 222.

in a technical manner[6] and it *cannot* provide justice. It is in responding to these impossibilities that the critical project faces its greatest challenges and must find its fate. The reformist impulse of the mainstream or idealist *esprit critique* comes from the realisation that PIL *is not working*. The critical spirit comes from the realisation that *it cannot work* or that the standard of what *counts as working* must itself be altered or abandoned.

Consequently, I explore the idea that the failings of international law are not solely the product of the bad faith with which it is made and applied. Instead, they stem from the *impossibility* of a universally inclusive justice. Within law there can be no New Jerusalem,[7] for the very structure of formal equality not only defines justice but it also *precludes* justice. As a result, critique cannot be adequately founded on an implicit belief in a just tomorrow; it must instead find a foundation[8] which is *neither* an appeal to substantive justice *nor* an appeal to a procedural inclusion and consensus.

My enquiry is driven by the observation that all too often PIL allows us to be *irresponsible*, to avoid responsibility for our actions or actions taken on our behalf.[9] This is manifested in two related concerns:

1. What prevents us from perceiving the irresponsibility of our actions?
2. How can we act responsibly in a world without universal justice or truth?

Unless great care is taken, *critique itself* can be as inimical to responsibility as the very laws being critiqued.

(In)determinacy and (in)justice

Greater attention must be given to the dynamic between apparently good law and the catastrophic state of the world. PIL fails millions, systematically. Structurally induced poverty causes the deaths of 50,000 human beings *daily*. That is 350,000 human lives lost weekly and 1,050,000 (over *one million* human deaths) every three weeks or 18,000,000 human deaths annually.[10] These deaths occur under the benevolent gaze of PIL. Worse, these deaths occur in an international political-economic regime *structured by*, and implemented through, PIL.

6 Actually, this claim is too strong. *If* we were willing to use law to pursue a single interest without compromise (ie as a blatant weapon of class or religious conflict) and to override all opposition then we could, perhaps, reduce it to a mathematical functionality.
7 G. Rose, *Mourning Becomes the Law: Philosophy and Representation* (Cambridge: Cambridge University Press, 1996) 36.
8 Following eg Deleuze and Foucault, it may be necessary to go further and to posit critique in the *absence* of a foundation.
9 S. Veitch, *Law and Irresponsibility: On the Legitimation of Human Suffering* (Abingdon: Routledge-Cavendish, 2007).
10 Pogge, *World Poverty and Human Rights* 222.

Despite this, the mainstream position is clear: 'The world needs international law'.[11] The mainstream *esprit critique* perceives legal failings as unfortunate anomalies calling for intra-legal reform. The system itself is perceived as generally just, efficacious and tolerably fair. This image can be maintained in either of two ways. The first is simply to ignore reality; poverty is an unfortunate fact, lying outside the competencies of PIL. It (a never examined, contextualised or even quantified 'it') is someone else's problem. The second is to frame these deaths as the result of illegalities or 'gaps' in international legal regulation.

This is the naïveté characteristic of faith. If the law is generally good then its adherents are able simply to ignore the catastrophe, to fail to see poverty, exploitation, degradation, human suffering and death on this massive scale, because these things are *too unlawful to exist.* They simply do not appear within the epistemic horizons of law's faithful. Hard though it may be to believe, many maintain this position. If we focus only on the (sacred) legal texts, then we need not see – we can avoid thinking about – the bigger picture outside. We can focus solely on each death, or each group of deaths, avoiding the pattern they represent, refusing to perceive them as systematic. We need only ask how the individual deaths were 'caused' (in the *legal* rather than the structural sense) and whether anyone was 'responsible', the question being whether any laws were broken?

This, however, raises an important question of a very different order: what does it *mean* to say that a law was broken? Sadly, this vital methodological question is generally overlooked by mainstream international lawyers. But it must be engaged, because answering it not only allows us to understand the law's implication in these deaths but it also offers a key to the riddle of legal indeterminacy: for every human death, in response to the tragedies of poverty, exploitation and war, we can *always* craft a legal argument for justice. As long as we possess an appropriate political sensibility we can *always* portray these occurrences as unlawful.

I should acknowledge here that in my own 'mainstream/dogmatic' phase (my period of legal faith)[12] I was far more apt to impose my politics subconsciously on my legal analysis than I am now in my 'critical/political' mode. The politics of law are easiest to overlook when they are agreed with – or imposed – by the interpreter. The complexity of legal reality can so easily be buried under a web of non-recognition and denial; the comforting delusion of a legal rationality:

> And something fragile and superficial will be built on top of this . . . seething mass which is sometimes murky and sometimes bloody: a growing rationality . . . a rationality which, as we move upwards and as it develops, will

11 V. Lowe, *International Law* (Oxford: Oxford University Press, 2007) 1.

12 J. A. Beckett, 'New War, Old Law: Can the Geneva Paradigm Comprehend Computers?' (2000) 13 *Leiden Journal of International Law* 33; J. A. Beckett, 'Interim Legality: A Mistaken Assumption? An Analysis of Depleted Uranium Munitions Under Contemporary International Humanitarian Law' (2004) 3(1) *Chinese Journal of International Law* 43.

> basically be more and more abstract, more and more bound up with fragility and illusions, and also more closely bound up with the cunning and wickedness of those who have won a temporary victory.[13]

This 'temporary victory' can be either institutional or personal (and thus pyrrhic). In the former guise, it underwrites claims to a so-called 'rule of recognition', the idea that there is a consistency to legal judgments. In the latter guise, it simply stands for each interpreter's unacknowledged (and often unconscious) imposition of their own politico-ethical values into the acts of law identification and interpretation.

> The legal thinker will insist that *Le hors de texte, c'est moi*. This risk is great because our legal texts (quite paradoxically) constitute each of us as privileged individual selves. And the thing is: it is extremely difficult to give up this exceedingly flattering self-image. It is a very addictive self-image.[14]

The tendency to impose idiosyncratic ethics onto law remains even when, acting out their *esprit critique*, the mainstream lawyer recognises that the law itself and/or the way it was interpreted and applied *was/is* bad. For example, when they perceive specific cases of trade law causing poverty and human misery, they can say 'that is wrong'; but they can also say 'that is *illegal*'. Many would claim, for example, that trade law is (or ought to be) subject to human rights law, and thus poverty breaches the rights to health, education and even life.[15] This position allows us to say, simultaneously, 'trade law is/was bad' *but* 'the law is good' because it was human rights *law* which 'proved' that trade law was bad.

However, it is *also* the case that trade law *itself* could have been interpreted and applied differently through a purely internal reference to its alternate bases in social justice.[16] Likewise, IMF policies could be criticised by reference to internal guidelines, the organisation's statutes etc.[17] Finally, this result could be achieved quasi-externally through a 'trade and . . .' argument. These so-called linkage

13 M. Foucault, *'Society Must be Defended': Lectures at the Collège de France 1975–76* (London: Allen Lane, 2003) 54–55.

14 P. Schlag, '*Le hors de texte, c'est moi*: on the Politics of Deconstruction' (1990) 11 *Cardozo Law Review* 1631. *Le hors de texte* is literally rendered as 'the outside of the text' and, in Schlag's deconstructive argument, it is here that the meaning to be imposed upon the text is constructed, and here that the interpreter – in true Louis XIV style – proclaims his own absolute sovereignty. The text, the law, means what I say it means!

15 T. Pogge, 'Recognized and Violated by International Law: The Human Rights of the Global Poor' (2005) 18(4) *Leiden Journal of International Law* 717.

16 M. Koskenniemi, *From Apology to Utopia: The Structure of International Legal Argument*, 2nd edition (Cambridge: Cambridge University Press, 2007) 607–608.

17 eg IMF, 'Poverty Reduction and Growth Trust' available at http://www.imf.org/external/pubs/ft/sd/index.asp?decision=8759-%2887/176%29 (accessed 28 November 2011).

debates attempt to generate coherence in international law by 'interpreting' its various branches in accordance with one another.[18] Thus the mainstream has at least one way of condemning the *specific* law as illegal and two ways of showing it was incorrectly implemented: injustice may have occurred but this was (we are told) in spite of the law and certainly not because of it.

We see this paradigm – which could be labelled 'eclectic pragmatism' or 'principled interpretation' – in the Dworkinian enterprise of 'making the law the best it can be'. Legal formalists will disagree, arguing that we can simply describe the law 'as it is'. However, one of the few points on which the Dworkinians are correct is that there is no such thing as 'the law as it is'.[19] To perceive law, we must impose our own values and this can be done *either* consciously or unconsciously.[20]

In either guise, stability is perceived/created *precisely* by the interpreter taking their values so seriously that they read them automatically into the law. This manner appears to promote justice and to suppress indeterminacy by showing the 'illegality' of competing, even actualised interpretations. The problem, of course, is that different interpreters of the law can equally impose their values onto the law, showing that yet another result 'ought' to have been reached. As Schlag has noted:

> While [Dworkin's] theory does authorise his politics, *in a sense*, it also authorises virtually anyone else's politics.[21]

The outcome is a self-fulfilling quest to exonerate the law by demonstrating the illegality of each injustice. The assumed aim of this process must be that once something has been demonstrated to be unlawful (and especially to be a breach of human rights) then it has been exposed to the healing light of legal judgment and legal justice, and will consequently disappear of its own accord. And yet, 18,000,000 people continue to die annually; it seems that only the visibility of these deaths recedes.[22]

18 J. A. Beckett, 'Fragmentation, Openness, and Hegemony: Adjudication and the WTO' in Meredith Kolsky Lewis and Susy Frankel (eds) *International Economic Law and National Autonomy* (Cambridge: Cambridge University Press, 2010) 44.

19 See eg O. Raban, 'Dworkin's "Best Light" Requirement and the Proper Methodology of Legal Theory' (2003) 23(2) *Oxford Journal of Legal Studies* 243.

20 I offer an expanded version of this critique of positivism in J. A. Beckett, "Rebel Without a Cause? Martti Koskenniemi and the Critical Legal Project' (2006) 7 *German Law Journal* 1045; J. A. Beckett, 'The Hartian Tradition in International Law' (2008) 51 *The Journal Jurisprudence* 53; J. A. Beckett, *The End of Customary International Law? A Purposive Analysis of Structural Indeterminacy* (Saarbrucken: VDM Verlag Dr Muller, 2008).

21 Schlag, 'On the Politics of Deconstruction' 1662.

22 Indeed, Foucault has suggested that law (and legitimacy) operate like spotlights, focusing bright attention on a small circle of phenomena, whilst relegating everything else to the obscurity of shadows. See Foucault, *'Society Must Be Defended'* 54–55, 70. Kelman

Alongside this perpetuation of injustice there is a strictly formal paradox, in that good mainstream lawyers, in seeking to discover the singularly just law, *generate* the very indeterminacy they believe they are suppressing. This is exacerbated by a tendency towards law-proliferation: the propagation of ever more laws and treaties.[23] Poverty has already been portrayed as a breach of human rights and yet it remains stubbornly persistent. How can this be? Obviously what these people need is a *more precise* human right: a right to food, to water, to development! Nice though this thought is, I suspect that what the starving, the degraded, the impoverished, the 'wretched of the earth' would prefer is some actual food and water; some physical shelter and some real medicine; not simply rights thereto.

Unfortunately the human rights/just law project can but paraphrase Brecht somewhat brutally: 'we could not give them bread; we could only explain that they had a right to bread'.[24] This, of course, would be more of a problem if these wretched had to be encountered as anything more than stories or statistics; but it is less of a problem when they are reduced to the fleeting role of illustrating the (self-evident) justice of the law and the (few) remaining flaws which need to be ironed out in it.

Worse from a legal perspective, however, is the apparent connection between the pursuit of justice and the proliferation of indeterminacy. This is impossible to ignore even *within* the self-contained paradigm of pure legal analysis.

Radical indeterminacy is: *the simultaneous justice and injustice of the law*. This generates both the indeterminacy and the apparent marginalisation of PIL. People complain about 'illegality' when they mean 'my interpretation was not adopted'.[25] They can then complain that 'the law' (their interpretation) was not enforced. This facilitates the use of law to criticise the world, but not to change it. Similarly, Mattei can talk of an 'illegal rule of law',[26] and many commentators like to speak of the courts getting the law *wrong*.

Justice is not really the issue. The law is always just, even though it is also always unjust. The pursuit of just law simply exacerbates indeterminacy or, rather, brings a greater part of it into relief.

('*Trashing*' (1984) 36 *Stanford Law Review* 293) makes a similar point in noting law's tendency to 'foreground' certain issues, whilst 'backgrounding' everything else; whilst Rasch (*Sovereignty and Its Discontents* (London: Birkbeck Law Press, 2004)) talks of law's capacity to invisibilise.

23 D. Kennedy, *The Dark Sides of Virtue: Reassessing International Humanitarianism* (Oxford: Princeton University Press, 2004).

24 B. Brecht, 'The Young Comrade' .

25 See eg C. Mieville, 'Multilateralism as Terror: International Law, Haiti and Imperialism' (2009) 18 *Finnish Yearbook of International Law* 63, 73–74.

26 U. Mattei and L. Nader (eds), *Plunder: When the Rule of Law is Illegal* (Oxford: Blackwell, 2008).

An important limit to radical indeterminacy

Although possible to shroud in plausible deniability, radical indeterminacy affects both treaty and customary PIL. It is inherent in the rules of interpretation[27] and exacerbated (or brought into focus) by the linguistic compromises inherent in international negotiations. Indeterminacy also inheres deeply in customary international law (CIL), where disputes continue to rage albeit often silently and invisibly over what counts as a norm of CIL.[28]

Of course, all of this is denied by the mainstream self-image and disguised by the tendency of each interpreter to impose his or her own values onto law as a stabilising force. Consequently, legal decisions are presented as determinate, as *determined by law*. Crits, following Unger, have termed this move 'false necessity'.[29] However, the analysis of false necessity is radically incomplete and must be allied to an examination of 'false contingency'.[30] Put very simply: just because a legal judgment could textually, or in theory, have gone completely the other way, does *not* entail that that could happen in reality.

At first glance then, false contingency looks like an 'antidote' to false necessity; a medicine to cure the 'dread disease'[31] of radical indeterminacy. This seems especially true when false contingency is 'institutionalised' and equated to what Koskenniemi has called 'structural bias'. Koskenniemi claims that specific international institutions possess specific structural biases and that these allow an informed observer accurately to predict the outcomes of specific disputes *regardless* of the radical indeterminacy of legal norms.[32]

In such a situation, the institution in question will present the law as determinate and clear; *and* as having led to, even *caused*, the decision reached. This is 'false necessity'; however, it is also what the mainstream purport to examine as interpretative determinacy: 'recourse to values already embodied within the system to determine which interpretation best makes sense systemically'.[33] This is said to reveal a coherent 'segmental expression of policy which underlies discrete areas of the legal system'.[34] But the apparent similarity between structural bias and intra-systemic coherence is far from an identity. The coherent 'segmental expressions' on which the formalists focus and from which Dworkinians extrapolate

27 Beckett, 'Fragmentation, Openness, and Hegemony' 56–57.

28 J. A. Beckett, 'Countering Uncertainty and Ending Up/Down Arguments: *Prolegomena* to a Response to NAIL' (2005) 16(2) *European Journal of International Law* 213; Beckett, *The End of Customary International Law?* especially ch 4.

29 R. Unger, *False Necessity: Anti-necessitarian Social Theory in the Service of Radical Democracy* (London: Verso, 2004).

30 S. Marks, '*False Contingency*' (2009) 62 *Current Legal Problems* 1.

31 D. Bederman, 'Book review of *From Apology to Utopia*' (1990) 23 *New York Journal of International Law and Politics* 228.

32 Koskenniemi, *From Apology to Utopia* 598–608.

33 I. Scobbie, 'Towards the Elimination of International Law: Some Radical Scepticism About Sceptical Radicalism' (1990) 61 *British Yearbook of International Law* 339, 350.

34 ibid.

readings of law in its 'best light', are nothing more than *ex post facto* rhetorical justifications for decisions reached for entirely different reasons. It is these *underlying* and *unacknowledged* reasons which form the structural bias and which bring apparent stability to the decision-making process. Bringing these to light may enable the articulation of a rule of recognition, but one far less savoury than the formulations usually offered suggest.

False contingency, moreover, is a wider concept than structural bias and continues to apply outwith what could be understood as the formal institutional structure of PIL. Here it refers to the law as *that which actually occurred.* And what actually occurs is systematic, consistent and deeply implicated in those 18,000,000 annual poverty related deaths. In other words, false contingency points to the law's *implication* in those situations condemned as *illegal.*

One necessary implication of the radical indeterminacy thesis is that those actions and situations *construed* as unlawful were also lawful. They were constructed through law. Even if poverty breaches human rights, it is law which causes poverty (laws in the form of IMF impositions, WTO free trade agreements, TRIPs + bilateral agreements, the international sale of the arms needed to oppress, the patenting of life-saving medicines or the production and *transnational* sale of sweatshop clothing/food/sugar/coffee). So poverty cannot really be 'illegal'. Likewise, law saturates the US prison camp at Guantanamo Bay.[35]

Consequently, marginalised claims of illegality – the claims of academics, students, activists, human rights crusaders etc that such conduct 'breaches international law' – also function to *disguise* the fact that PIL was, in fact, (also) being *applied.* Claims of illegality thus deflect attention from the concurrent reality of legal regulation, of *legality.* This is the reality of false contingency: despite 'impeccable legal arguments' being offered for their illegality, poverty and exploitation continue to be regulated and facilitated by law, in an endemic and systematic manner.

One final wrong in the quest for right

Because the legalist quest for justice subconsciously posits a series of false necessities which serve unintentionally to disguise a systematic false contingency, it becomes inherently futural – even eschatological – in structure and function. That is to say, this project posits a utopian future where all rights are upheld and justice, peace, prosperity and happiness are shared by all – a future where the 'developing world'[36]

35 F. Johns, '*Guantanamo* Bay and the Annihilation of the Exception' (2005) 16(4) *European Journal of International Law* 613; Lord Steyn, 'Guantanamo Bay: The Legal Black Hole' (2004) 53 *International and Comparative Law Quarterly* 1.

36 An interesting misnomer for a large collection of countries systematically precluded from development. See eg S. Marks, 'Human Rights and the Bottom Billion' (2009) *European Human Rights Law Review* 37; S. Marks, 'Human Rights and Root Causes' (2011) 74 *Modern Law Review* 57–78.

has finally learned to abandon its barbarism, corruption and inefficiency, and to follow the lead, and tutoring, of the 'civilised', developed world.

This generates a focus on:

(i) further refining and polishing the cherished, ideal(ised) future; and/or
(ii) analysing why 'the rules', 'human rights' and/or 'PIL' norms are being 'breached'.

The first possibility ignores reality, whilst the second misrepresents reality. More importantly, however, *both* foci function to insulate the proposed Utopia from scrutiny and critique. Alone or in combination, they serve to exonerate the rules advocated, and because those rules embody the 'justice' imposed onto indeterminate international law by their zealous advocates, they serve to exonerate *us*; our justice, and our civilisation.

Because our interpretations are based on a situated and unreflexive ideal of justice, by projecting them into law and then focusing on technicalising law (that is, ensuring their implementation or coherence as critique) we insulate our own conceptions of ourselves, of civilisation and of justice from critique and consideration.

Consequently, in an interesting double movement, the ideal is sheltered from its own empirical impossibility whilst the blame for poverty is squarely located with the poor themselves. I call this process the *localisation of pathology*. The causes of poverty are posited at the local level: corrupt and unrepresentative governments, inadequate political, economic and physical infrastructures, poor education, geographic misfortune, cultural backwardness or even barbarism. All of these contrast point-for-point with our cherished self-image as transparent, democratic, developed, educated, blessed by nature and civilised. It is this self-image we seek to protect.

Yet the vast majority of the world's natural resources are extracted from the 'developing world', whilst the vast majority of said resources are consumed in the developed world. This seems prima facie curious. Moreover, for everyone in the world to live an 'average British lifestyle' would require the resources of 3.1 Planet Earths.[37]

The questions then could be posed very differently; the pathologies located at both the international level (PIL), and at the doors of their beneficiaries, *we* the developed, civilised, and just peoples of the world. After all, if third world governments are corrupt, who bribes them? And is it not the world economic system which precludes investment in their economic and physical infrastructures? (And just why do so many (ex-)colonies share a physical infrastructural design

37 See BBC, 'Britain Now "Eating the Planet"' available at http://news.bbc.co.uk/2/hi/science/nature/4897252.stm (accessed 28 November 2011) and it is worth noting that the Brits do not live in the most profligate of styles – the Americans, Canadians and Australians all out-consume us (head for head) quite significantly.

running from the resource deposits in their centres to harbours on their shores?[38]) Were the inadequate political structures not inherited from us, the (ex-) colonial masters? Such questions could go on indefinitely.

What is beyond dispute, however, is that it is *we* the citizens of the North who benefit, daily and drastically, from the very suffering which we like to sentimentally condemn as unjust:

> How can love of humanity appeal as a motive to nations whose love of luxury is built on the inhuman exploitation of human beings, and who . . . have been taught to regard these human beings as inhuman?[39]

It must also be recognised that we have developed the structure and mechanisms of PIL precisely to disguise and deny these facts. As Gerry Simpson has demonstrated, the purpose of a war crimes tribunal is less to establish the guilt of the accused than the innocence of the accusers,[40] thus unmasking such trials as 'simply vindications of the international community'. Likewise, the purpose of international law and human rights is less to alleviate the conditions of the poor than to justify and legitimise those of the rich.

The mainstream understanding of law allows attention to be diverted away from the structural causes of poverty and human suffering, past and present. Instead there is only a lament that they *will not* be like us. They are not like us – but they could be if only *they would* choose to be like us. This is the dynamic of identity superimposed onto the dynamic of difference – it generates a false necessity from a false contingency:

> False Necessity: *they should be like us* (we are the standard, that is unquestionable).
>
> False Contingency: they are not impoverished by accident. *They cannot be like us*: we will not allow it!

Moreover, if they were like us then we would have to stop being like us. There are insufficient resources for that. Our lifestyles are *subsidised* by their suffering.[41] Thus we strive to avoid sympathy.[42] We avoid understanding them as them; *and we avoid understanding us as us!* Instead, we continue to dream of – and thus imagine in(to) legal/futural reality – the *ever-expanding pie* necessary to accomplish the human rights utopia.

38 A. Anghie, *Imperialism, Sovereignty, and the Making of International Law* (Cambridge: Cambridge University Press, 2005).
39 W. E. Burghardt Du Bois, 'The African Roots of War' available at http://www.library.umass.edu/spcoll/digital/dubois/WarRoots.pdf (accessed 28 November 2011) 712.
40 G. Simpson, *War, Law and Crime: War Crimes Trials and Reinvention of International Law* (Cambridge: Polity, 2007) 88–91.
41 Marks, 'Human Rights and the Bottom Billion'; Marks, 'Human Rights and Root Causes'; Pogge, *World Poverty and Human Rights* 222.
42 Marks, ibid.

This myopic fascination with just laws and new rights allows us to overlook:

(i) the generation of a profusion of competing legal norms and regimes, and thus of radical indeterminacy;
(ii) the law's *implication* in that systemic human suffering condemned as illegal; and
(iii) the fact that by uncritically imposing *our* unreflected conception of justice, we indulge in nothing more than self-justification.

In trying to represent the law either positivistically 'as it is' (and as it is 'ignored') or through natural law as 'the best it can be', the mainstream structurally precludes itself from acknowledging the dynamics, forces and structures causing PIL to do what it in fact does; as it is in fact applied, not ignored.

The quest for just law generates indeterminacy, marginalisation and solipsistic self-justification. This forlorn quest perpetuates injustice. We benefit from that injustice and define our own justice in response to the need to deny that fact. This occurs because of the basic indeterminacy of justice itself. As such, it could simply be an ordering problem: a need to harmonise the various demands of justice.[43] Alternatively, it could be solved by the discovery of the one true justice: the universal justice to which a universal law should aspire.

If such universality could be discovered, then the mainstream project of a determinate, just and technical law could be redeemed. However, if it could not, then that project would be revealed as an attempt to redeem the ideal of law in the face of the world and thus as an untruthful effort to pursue particular politics under a fraudulent claim to the universal. This 'fact' would remain true irrespective of whether the project was carried out in cynical bad faith, in innocent ignorance or in psychological denial. But then again:

> You already know that. So do I. It is not knowledge that we lack. What is missing is the courage to understand what we know and draw conclusions.[44]

Redeeming the law (again)

The most obvious response to the 'crisis' of bad law is to seek to develop good law: a system which is determinate, or at least determinable, and just. The laws we happen to have may be unjust, but law itself remains just, indeed the embodiment of justice. What we need are better rules, better rule-making procedures and, of course, better institutions to apply and enforce those rules.[45]

43 I. Berlin, *Liberty* (Oxford, Oxford University Press, 2002) 290–91.
44 S. Lindqvist, *Exterminate All the Brutes* (London: Granta, 1997) 172.
45 I think this version of idealist redemption is most clearly illustrated by my own attempts to overcome indeterminacy in 'Ending Up/Down Arguments' op cit, and perhaps in Thomas Pogge's substantive critiques, of exploitation under law eg *World Poverty and Human Rights*.

This moves us towards the culmination of the redemptive stage of the legal faith. There would be little point in a just law which remained fundamentally indeterminate, nor in a determinate law which remained fundamentally unjust. But, sadly, the redemptive project is doomed to failure on both fronts. Indeterminacy is a structural feature common to both language and the liberal legal project.

Furthermore, injustice is not simply a product of bad faith and power politics. Rather, injustice too is an inexorable fact in a pluralist world. All rules, all justices, exclude: perfection and universal inclusion cannot be achieved:

> Ethics and metaphysics are torn halves of an integral freedom to which they have *never* added up.[46]

There can be no universal justice: 'Whoever claims humanity wants to cheat'.[47] This would be difficult to demonstrate exhaustively,[48] but can be glimpsed schematically by considering the twin alternatives for seeking justice: Rawls and Habermas.

Rawls's system is solipsistic in the extreme: universalising a specifically American conception of human nature and human needs, and extrapolating a universalised justice therefrom. In MacIntyre's memorable phrase: 'What is claimed to be a systematic theory is, in reality, an incoherent bundle of personal intuitions and bygone social conditions'.[49]

Habermas's theory is more nuanced, but ultimately suffers the same fate: control over the conditions of discourse is tantamount to control over the outcomes of discourse. Habermas claims that 'the conception of human rights does not have its origins in morality [but] is distinctly juridical in character'.[50] Human rights are not particular, because they are not derived from moral claims. Instead, human rights are 'rationally justifiable'[51] and this forms the 'fundamental discourse principle': 'Just those action norms are valid to which all possibly affected persons could agree as participants in rational discourse'.[52]

This, however, is predicated upon problematic assumptions. It assumes the commensurability of different value systems under a rational ordering, and it

46 Rose, *Mourning Becomes the Law* 9.

47 The quote, often attributed to Schmitt, in fact comes from Proudhon, and thus quite the opposite end of the political spectrum.

48 But for an excellent attempt see Rasch, *Sovereignty and Its Discontents.* See also J. A. Beckett, 'Conflicting Orders: How Peace is Waged' (2007) 20 *Leiden Journal of International Law* 281; and J. A. Beckett, 'The Violence of Wording' in *No Foundations: The Journal of Extreme Legal Positivism* 8 (May 2011) 3.

49 J. Murphy, *Retribution Reconsidered: More Essays in the Philosophy of Law* (London: Kluwer, 1992) 145.

50 Rasch, *Sovereignty and its Discontents* 55.

51 ibid 56.

52 J. Habermas, *Between Facts and Norms: Contributions to a Discourse Theory of Law and Democracy* (Cambridge, Mass.: MIT Press, 1996) 107.

assumes the possibility of neutral, rational, discourse. Isaiah Berlin has long established the fallacy of the first assumption[53] and, on the second, a sceptical William Rasch has pondered:

> What is rational discourse? What are its rules and whom and what does it exclude? And if such discourse does exclude things and people, in what way can it be the basis for universally valid legal norms?[54]

Perhaps, however, the impossibility of just law can be best demonstrated by an allegory and a paradox.

Neutrality is impossible between competing value-systems, or competing ontological assumptions: one cannot argue for one's ontology, but only assume it.[55] I turn to religion to illustrate this point, allegorically. Imagine a family of Jehovah's Witnesses – mother, father and son – sadly involved in a car accident. The mother and father are unharmed but the child is grievously injured. Jehovah's Witnesses believe[56] blood transfusions to be a mortal sin; perhaps even a soul-destroying one:[57] a denial of Heaven, and a cause for eternal damnation.

UK law recognises this, and allows Jehovah's Witnesses to refuse such treatment – *if* they are over 16. If they are under 16 they cannot refuse; nor can a parent refuse on their behalf. A less than sensitive law, causing both (presumed devout) parents great distress here: to call an ambulance, and see invasive medical treatment, a mortal sin, inflicted upon their child? To fail to report the accident, commit a crime, and watch their child die in agony, denied treatment?

This is easy, conceptually, to resolve: we can imagine a more sensitive law, one which allowed the parents to report the accident, call an ambulance and have palliative treatment for their child, until his (now easier, pain-free) death.

However, what if one parent – let us say the mother – has a crisis of faith (Eve eats the apple): rejects the very idea of heaven, hell and damnation; just wants her son to live? The father remains devout; the child lapses into unconsciousness. To call an ambulance would be to save her child, and damn his: 70 years of life for eternity in hell? A vastly premature earthly death for eternal life, in paradise? Or just life, with no afterlife whatsoever? Who to favour, which (imagined) law to

53 On the impossibility of which see Berlin, *Liberty* 290–91.

54 Rasch, *Sovereignty and its Discontents* 56.

55 ibid 107.

56 I hate this word, and use it for convenience only. The denigration of religious faith and *knowledge* to mere *belief* is a key component of the secular-rationalist subordination of religion; a cornerstone of the Enlightenment quest for epistemic (and, ultimately, political) hegemony. This is hinted at, but under-developed, in Robert Darnton's excellent 'Philosophers Trim the Tree of Knowledge: The Epistemological Strategy of the *Encyclopedie*' in his *The Great Cat Massacre: And Other Episodes in French Cultural History* (Harmondsworth: Penguin, 1985).

57 Perhaps this is an overstatement on my part, but please bear with me. For the purposes of the allegory, it is the point, not the detail, which is important.

decide neutrally here? Where is the just, or impartial, position from which a decision could be made?

Alas! No originality of position, no intensity of pondering behind a veil of ignorance, will reveal a neutral or just answer; nor will 'rational discourse' – however well meaning, however extended in time – fare better. The problem is simply intractable and the basic tractability of problems is a key hidden assumption of both Rawlsian and Habermassian methods.

And thus to the paradox: Habermassians turn to procedural solutions, because rules created without procedures are necessarily solipsistic. However, procedures cannot operate without rules and rules cannot be created without procedures. It is this basic circularity – perhaps rendered tautologically – which seals the common fates of any attempt at eschatological escape via Habermas as much as via Rawls.

Indeterminacy II: the birth of resignation

Eventually, and perhaps tragically, we come to realise that law is no more capable of moral/rational redemption than is religious faith. At this point we must face the profound crisis of faith in legality. Perhaps we may acknowledge, alongside Martti Koskenniemi, that it is a good thing that PIL is radically indeterminate,[58] or perhaps we may acknowledge, with Gillian Rose, that 'the *aporia* is the Janus face of the universal'.[59] In whatever way we look at it, we come to recognise that law *cannot* be universal, inclusive, just or determinate. The 'ideal legal form' is impossible, or fatally flawed.

However, we may also realise that the legal form is nonetheless necessary and that without it, 'many of the criticisms we make of international conduct would make no sense'.[60] For our 'other' techniques of judgment are themselves built upon the juridical structure of formal equality. Thus we enter the phase of resignation: law is impossible and necessary. It is simultaneously a tool of injustice and yet the very definition of justice. The two most obviously attractive options – to 'fix' law or to abandon it completely – are simply not available.

Tools and traps: being resigned to law

The first two steps in my critical journey (recognising bad law and then undertaking reformist and indeterminacy suppressing efforts to generate good law) maintained the orthodox assumption that law is a tool to be used; that the academic task is to define and refine that tool in order to maximise its utility. The resigned approach is altogether more complicated.

58 Koskenniemi, *From Apology to Utopia* 591.
59 Rose, *Mourning Becomes the Law* 10.
60 M. Koskenniemi, 'International Law in Europe: Between Tradition and Renewal' (2005) 16 *European Journal of International Law* 113, 119.

This approach starts from twin assumptions:

(i) that the universal position is impossible; and
(ii) that this impossibility can only be observed from the presumption of the universal position.

The juridical *both* effects and limits normative perception. From this perspective, law is less a tool than a trap: the juridical form is the 'iron cage'[61] of modernity and of modern thought.

This is interesting for two distinct reasons. First, it highlights the limits of the technicalisation debate, in the sense that there can be no right answers outside of the technical paradigm. Secondly, it demonstrates that the dichotomy between resignation to – and abandonment of – the legal project, is not merely political, but rather epistemic and even ontological in nature. The question is not simply whether we should abandon the juridical model but whether we can escape it.

The problem is that ethics, politics and justice, all analytics and discourses of power are built on the juridical: each uses the tripartite structure of claim, counter-claim and rule:

> 'Whoever says humanity wants to cheat' is a useful reminder that a universal law, too, has no voice of its own . . . But it builds on a distinction between honesty and cheating that presupposes the existence of the universal standard.[62]

Although the universal position dreamed of from Solon to Kant[63] to Habermas[64] is unattainable, the structure of universality retains its hegemony over modern (rational) thought. The structure cannot be realised, but only in its name is critique possible. Consequently, we must join (Camus's) Sisyphus in a never ending struggle toward an impossible goal. However, the movement of resignation is not paralysed; nor is it despondent. It is realistic about the boundaries within which 'progress' or 'emancipation' can be attained:

> [F]rom the fact that there is no authentically universal position, it does not follow that all positions are the same. Indeed, were this the case, we would have no reason to take the realist critique seriously, no basis to distinguish between honesty and cheating.[65]

61 M. Weber, *The Protestant Ethic and the Spirit of Capitalism* (London: George Allen & Unwin, 1930).
62 Koskenniemi, 'Between Tradition and Renewal' 118.
63 Foucault, *'Society Must be Defended'* 53.
64 Rasch, *Sovereignty and its Discontents* 49–59.
65 Koskenniemi, 'Between Tradition and Renewal' 119.

Resignation to the impossibility of universal justice does not then equate to moral relativism; or rather it does so in a very particular sense. Moralities remain relative not only to one another, but to something else, to a 'missing third',[66] which gives them context and intelligibility:

> Here it takes three to make a relationship between two: the devastation between posited thought and posited being, between power and exclusion from power, implies the universal, the third partner, which allows us to recognise that devastation. The aporia or gap is the Janus-face of the universal.[67]

For the resigned, the universal is empty.[68] It is a gap, an unfillable space, which reminds us of the inadequacies – the situatedness, exclusions, and biases – of *all* concrete claims to the universal (including, especially, our own). It is a space from which we are forced to recognise the contingency of any claim to the universal and thus forms a defence against narcissism and hubris. Justice, truth, the universal and humanity have all been used as cloaks for particularistic violences.

However, it is vitally important to realise that this has not always been done in bad faith, although it often is. This is where three parallel critiques of justice intersect:[69]

1. 'We', the powerful/developed have defined justice to suit our own interests.
2. Nonetheless, we fail to live up to the demands of even that justice.
3. This does not alter the fact that universal justice does not exist.

Empty justice and abstract humanity offer responses to all three critiques. First, we must judge ourselves as we would judge others.[70] Secondly, and simultaneously, we must launch a critique of the very standards to which we claim to hold ourselves and others. Living up to our own standards – unlikely as that is – is far from enough, nor is it even close to a sufficient condition to justify our imposing those standards on others. Finally, however, we must recognise that the critique of situated justice will only ever lead to another situated justice.[71] To paraphrase Samuel Beckett, we must learn not only to fail and fail again but to fail *better*.

66 Rose, *Mourning Becomes the Law* 10.
67 ibid.
68 See also E. Laclau, *Emancipation(s)* (London: Verso, 1996).
69 Contrary to popular opinion, mathematicians tend to the conclusion that parallel lines *do* in fact meet, in eternity or at infinity; exactly where we might locate justice. See eg http://www.math.colostate.edu/~renzo/MathDay.pdf (accessed 21 January 2012).
70 As we have known at least since Adam Smith, this is hard to do, as humans (at least in our societies) tend toward narcissism and, as a consequence, so do their societies: this creates a self-perpetuating loop, a mutually reinforcing cycle of narcissism and justification.
71 Gillian Rose refers to this difficult and painful task as 'thinking in the wake of disaster; *without* generating any fantasy of mending the world.' See Rose, *Mourning Becomes the Law* 9.

It is the pursuit of success that has blinded even those acting in good faith to the dangers of apparently universal justice. The pursuit of such (necessarily false) universals has desensitised adherents to the reality of their actions. This is what I term *concrete* humanity and precisely what I wish to oppose with the resignation of empty, *abstract*, humanity:

> Because of its anxiety that our sentimentality be left intact [concrete humanity] leaves us at *the beginning of the day*, in a Fascist security of our own unreflected predation.[72]

Concrete humanity is that of those who perceive themselves as good, civilised, moral, superior – as bearers of the universal spirit. It is the humanity that underwrote the invasions of Iraq and Afghanistan, Blair's total lack of repentance, Obama's 'good war' (holy war?): that humanity claimed by those who want to cheat. Abstract humanity is the absent-presence which brings that cheating into perspective. Wars – including so-called lawfare – waged in the name of concrete humanity are waged without responsibility: the end is so great that it can *always* justify the means. As Rasch has noted: 'Used politically . . . the term 'humanity' takes the form of a particularly brutal weapon'.[73]

Or in the Secretary of State Madeleine Albright's infamous response to the charge that the UN sanctions regime had killed 500,000 Iraqi children: 'I think this is a very hard choice, but the price, we think the price was worth it'.[74]

However, it is also humanity, abstract humanity, which identifies brutal weaponry as unacceptable; it is abstract humanity which identifies the killing of innocents as wrongful. There is an apparent paradox – superbly illustrated by the Milgram experiment – that it is what humanity facilitates that humanity condemns as wrong. How could 75 per cent of Milgram's test subjects bring themselves to electrocute a perfect stranger to death? Humanity, concretised in the pursuit of science. What is wrong with electrocuting a perfect stranger to death? Humanity, it is in*humane*.

Like the universal (which facilitates and identifies cheating) humanity has two manifestations. The movement of resignation is the refusal to accept the first manifestation as complete, while acknowledging the impossibility of attaining the second. Our actions should be held to our particular legal manifestations of the universal (eg Human Rights law), but compatibility with such norms is never sufficient, as the law must always reach beyond them: relativising itself against abstract humanity; it is this gap which manifests the always absent justice.

72 ibid 48.

73 Rasch, *Sovereignty and its Discontents* 32.

74 J. Pilger, 'Paying the Price: Killing the Children of Iraq' available at http://johnpilger.com/videos/paying-the-price-killing-the-children-of-iraq (accessed 28 November 2011).

The radical rejectionists

There will, however, always be those for whom resignation is insufficient: Kierkegaard's knights of faith in (anti-)legal form. Thus, the final movement in the journey of faith would be an attempt to transcend the legal form altogether, to abandon equality and legitimacy, and to seek new epistemic-evaluative grids through which to realise an authentic justice. This encapsulates the sense of law as 'part of the problem' – the iron cage to be escaped or the juridical form as the perfect example, indeed the *cause*, of the failed metaphysics of classic philosophy. As Rose notes: 'The dismissal of "metaphysics" is accompanied by the unabated search for a *new ethics*'.[75]

We can give this position names: faith, authenticity, existentialism; and scholars: Schmitt, Jaspers, Sartre, Foucault, Derrida (whose ontology of the 'to come' could fit in either rejectionist or resigned movements), Rasch, Luhmann and perhaps Teubner. Describing the project is altogether more awkward. It shares with resignation the pursuit of responsibility, and the eschewal of technicalisation. However, it allies this with a claim of possible epistemic liberation from the hegemony of legitimacy: of hierarchical order.

Consequently, abandonment is an embodied thought experiment – an attempt to learn to see, think and evaluate the world differently – to truly realise the ideal of 'equal but different' to overcome 'the prejudice of equality'.[76] It questions the truth of the claim that justice is impossible and that legitimacy must be rejected as an analytic grid, arguing that this is true only within the epistemic order of the juridical. Can we, however, escape the epistemic hegemony of the juridical?

This might be facilitated by abandoning the technicalising project. But we cannot abandon this too far, lest we render ourselves incapable of responsibility. This would be to posit the self as so radically free that it could no longer be evaluated in terms of standards. With no way to assess or assume responsibility, this position would ultimately perpetuate injustice:

> The dominant CLS paradigm['s] . . . affirmation of a radical individual subjectivism . . . seek[s] to canonize or elevate the radically free individual subject.[77]

This would be the subject that *just knows* its own justice (the subject of Kierkegaard's *Either/Or*) and that justice would be equally well insulated from examination or critique. The noble attempt to 'provoke the grief of encountering the violence

75 Rose, *Mourning Becomes the Law* 1.
76 T. Todorov, *The Conquest of America: The Question of the Other* (New York: Harper & Row, 1984) 165.
77 Schlag, 'On the Politics of Deconstruction' 1642.

normally legitimised by the individual moral will'[78] cannot be accomplished by the radically free individual moral will. It requires a structure, a situation, a *logos*, a rationality. For without rationality, 'no argument could be devised, no analysis could be conducted, and no conclusion could be urged'.[79]

True faith – beyond even Camus's existential absurdity (which is really a movement of resignation[80]) – can end only in the asylum, or back in the same naïve religious faith it sought so hard to evade. 'God is dead', but it is only through law that we can aspire to Nietzsche's admonition to 'make ourselves worthy of His murder'. The 'true faith' of abandoning law replicates precisely that intoxicating promise through which naïve faith precluded responsibility:

> If Fascism [unreflected faith in law] promises beginnings of the day, representation exposes the interests of the middle of the day; then the owl of Minerva, flying at dusk, may reflect of the remains of the day – the ruins of the morning's hope, the actuality of the broken middle.[81]

There is a direct parallel between the mainstream desire to subsume or submerge individual responsibility under the impartial technical expertise of legal regimes, ethical laws, or inter-disciplinary scienticity and the critical attempt to free ourselves from such structures completely. Each move reflects the same basic narcissism and denial: either we read our desires into the law or we impose them consciously onto reality. In both cases, the desires perpetuate unreflexively the particular social interests we sought to escape, and in both cases we shield those interests from analysis and critique.

The difference, then, is reduced to the archaic grandeur of the latter posture. If the search for justice under naïve faith leads to an exalted marginalisation, 'the hubris of martyrdom',[82] then the imposition of ungrounded justice in the name of true faith can amount only to the hubris of, well . . . hubris I guess.

Moreover, the push to true faith, the abandonment of law tends to founder of its own accord regardless. The precondition of equality for the act of judgment is re-established. Think, for example, about non-universalist understandings of PIL – like Rawls's tripartite division (civilised, decent, barbaric)[83] or understandings which do not treat all alike, but which nonetheless seek refuge in a higher-order distinction which does embody formal equality: the very division on which inequality of treatment is predicated, *itself* embodies equality.

78 Rose, *Mourning Becomes the Law* 54.
79 ibid 7.
80 'To an absurd mind Reason is useless, and there is nothing beyond Reason.' See A. Camus, *The Myth of Sisyphus* available at http://www.scribd.com/doc/3223928/Albert-Camus-The-Myth-Of-Sisyphus (accessed 28th November 2011) 19.
81 Rose, *Mourning Becomes the Law* 42.
82 M. Koskenniemi, 'The Politics of International Law – 20 Years Later' (2009) 20 *European Journal of International Law* 7, 14.
83 J. Rawls, *The Law of Peoples* (London: Harvard University Press, 1999).

A return to resignation

Thus, I find myself returning to resignation because self-critique, and the necessary analysis of our own humanity, claims to justice, can only occur within a paradigm of universality.

To oppose anarchic, individual love or good to civil or public ill is to deny the third which gives meaning to both – this is the other meaning of the *third city* – the just city and the just act, the just man and the just woman.[84]

For love is not enough and good is not individual.[85] Law frames our understanding of our actions and those of others. The juridical form – claim, counter-claim, rule – structures our rationality as much as our ethics. Although we know this rule form is flawed, resignation tells us it is inescapable.

Despite its empirical impossibility, this model structures our understanding of civilised order, and thus law constructs its own conditions of acceptability. Ultimately, we can criticise actions only on the basis that they could not be emulated by others in analogous situations.[86] If every situation were truly unique, every action truly singular, then every judgment would be truly subjective, with neither context nor meaning.[87] Being responsible 'is not therefore solely [an act] of infinite love: it is a finite act of political justice'.[88]

The task of those of us resigned to law is therefore always 'To present [a] rational order which throws into relief the specific act of injustice perpetrated by the current representatives of the city'[89] and, more importantly, of those claiming to represent the *Cosmopolis*. Although capable of founding positive action, resignation is inexorably a stance of critique and undermining, of the destabilising of certainties and the inculcation of doubt and anxiety: the only true defences against narcissism, solipsism and uncontrolled irresponsibility.

Ultimately then, critical legal studies (CLS) require law, and so does critical thought generally. The critical project must always be 'a protest against arbitrary power . . . not a protest against power and law as such'.[90]

Good and bad faith: narcissism and impossibility

Perhaps the most important fault line in critical thinking then is that between those who attribute law's implication in the catastrophe of reality solely to bad faith and

84 Rose, *Mourning Becomes the Law* 26.
85 *Pace* The Beatles 'Love is All you Need'.
86 *See* Beckett, 'Conflicting Orders'; J. A. Beckett, 'Mercy, Particularity, the Map from the Void' (2007) 93(2) *Archiv für Rechts und Sozialphilosophie* 217.
87 M. Koskenniemi, '"The Lady Doth Protest Too Much": Kosovo, and the Turn to Ethics in International Law' (2002) 65 *Modern Law Review* 159, 173.
88 Rose, *Mourning Becomes the Law* 25.
89 ibid 26. This passage fits more easily in the body of Rose's work, I believe, referring to *a* rather than *the* rational order.
90 ibid.

those who see impossibility lurking behind bad faith. However, there must also be a degree of circularity here, for I am often asked how the desires of the resigned differ from those of the idealists.

If law is necessary, then we must strive for good law, however that may be defined. However, if *we* have been the beneficiaries of 'bad' law then the move to good law will 'disadvantage' us. Thus narcissism is unveiled as a proximate enemy of the CLS movement; and the possibility of critique as 'projection' or self-justification comes to light.

It seems to me to be common in 'critical' or 'progressive' circles to demand that something is done about the law, about world politics and the economic system. NGOs are challenged to do more, even as they critique governments and transnational corporations, demanding that they in turn do more: drop the debt; accept corporate social responsibility; clean up your act; respect rights; pay fairly. Yet it is also apparent that this demand is always projected *elsewhere*. The problem is real, but it is someone else's to solve.

This is where narcissism enters the equation: it resides in our belief in our own goodness but, much more importantly, in our sense of *entitlement* to our standards and ways of living. But, if the governments of the North and West are not to pay for the elimination of poverty and degradation in the South and East, then who is? Who is to finance debt-relief, decent wages and infrastructural development?

Logically, of course, the answer is 'us' – the mass of those who have benefited. Our duty, as Pogge has noted, is not to help the Third World but to stop hurting it/them. Our sense of our own righteousness must be destabilised; but this is an area where critique comes close to implication. Even if we were to assume the possibility of a better law, of a fair world, would we – citizens of the North; dreamers of the *Cosmopolis* – pay the price willingly? Would we, *could* we, learn to accept the extent to which the poverty of others *subsidises our own lifestyles*?

Would we confront the ways in which we have developed laws, as well as critiques of those laws, which function only to disguise this subsidy, this implication? To maintain a 'fascist security of our own unreflected predation'?[91] *Dare* we take responsibility? The parallel between the mainstream love of law and the critical love of critique – where each projects the problems elsewhere and exempts the self from analysis – is the frontier that critical thought generally, and the international newstream in particular, must confront.

William Rasch once observed, sadly, that 'to be human is to be corrected'. But if to be Western is to be subsidised, and to be justified, then perhaps it *is* correction that *we* need; to live up to our own claims of humanity.

91 ibid 48.

Chapter 9

Economy or law?

Vincent Keter

It seems that the most prominent result of the global 'financial crisis' that began in 2007, in tandem with the astonishing volume of narrative produced about it, has been that everyone has been proven right whilst everyone else has been proven wrong. Each narrator offers their own assemblage of the facts to reach different conclusions. This effect is no doubt owing to orthodox economic theory, which despite attempts to dignify itself with the garb of scientific speculation, has revealed itself as primarily the continuation of politics by other means.

This substitution was convenient for politics, which had in the course of the bloody travails of the 20th century repeatedly lost the ability to project its ideals. Economic theory promised a purely technocratic answer to social distribution leaving politics to managerial detail. As an intellectual adventure this movement was always destined to encounter the centuries-long recurrence of economic failures that were invariably attended by economists describing the dynamics of past crises and nursing prescriptions for reform in the conviction that 'this time is different'.[1] As an insight into humanity, economic theory has delivered at best only an impoverished offering: a spectacle of human nature as self-interested caprice. The laws that science has culled from the empirical world have at least the benefit of a common field of reference and thus remain open to falsification. Economic 'data', notwithstanding its comfortingly numeric presentation, is riddled with the opacity of human agency; politicised measurement; and, in some cases, the disinformation of colossally fraudulent accounting. Economic algebra, as the basis of a policy doctrine, is the mirror image of scientific socialism and has the same implications for the notion of democratic accountability. Money, and its distribution, can never be anything other than political questions.

Whilst it is obvious that the content of law is politically determined, a consensus with a long historical development has sedimented the liberal view of legal structure and form as transcendent. This idea has endowed law with the authority and independence to convene a social contract and embody that in a constitution

1 C. M. Reinhart and K. S. Rogoff, *This Time is Different* (Princeton: Princeton University Press, 2010).

within which politically heterogeneous views can compete. Traditionally, in liberal jurisdictions, economic policy is never primarily a legal matter, since to allow law to determine the economic distributions of the constituted state would contaminate legal transcendence with political difference. Liberal law may adjudicate on the consequences of economic and social decisions but it cannot make them. Under the rule of law, that is the role of politics. The idea that economic governance is no longer to be regarded as a political matter is therefore bound to have implications for the foundations of social contract and law. Economics as technocratic scientism acquires a position of transcendence above both law and politics. The social bond of consent in law appears to tolerate this elevated role for economic activity, as a state of nature, but perhaps only to the extent that theory can make economic activity appear as nature or the tides which lie outside the scope of human legislation. If that appearance fails then the current crisis may well prove different, not because it represents a different kind of financial or economic crisis against historical example, but because it may evolve into a crisis in the liberal social contract.

The range of economic writings on the crisis, narrating its causes and setting out prescriptions for future policy, clearly replicate historical political movements. Adherents of economic liberalism, who currently enjoy political dominance in Europe and the US, point to high levels of public debt and seek an intensification of neoliberal social and economic policy in the hope of attracting investment that will deliver economic growth. The discretionary control of these hoped for investments lies in the hands of the interests behind globally mobile capital which must be propitiated. This economic liberal movement is weakly moderated by concerns for regulatory reform in the financial sector, based on an analysis of the causes of the crisis as lying in financial sector predominance and a few specific activities of participants in financial markets.

Orthodox opposition to these views comes from social liberals with a melancholic attachment to the economic policy consensus that reigned during the three decades after the Second World War. They speak the language of demand management and social investment, calling for macroeconomic interventions to support growth in consumption that may finance a return to redistributive economic policy. Social democratic observers worry that markets on the whole have become under-regulated and trace the causes of the crisis to imbalances between capital and labour that have decisively resolved in favour of capital. In general they seek the restoration of social market and industrial policy. This entire range of opinions assumes stability in the social contractual underpinning of the rule of law and alternatives are staked within that frame. How safe is that assumption? On this question economics has nothing to say. Each position conceals different ideas about what the social contract has promised and what it entails. In most cases, these understandings remain confined within the strictly limited picture of humanity in terms of the play of interests in market systems.

An economic-liberal social contract can be identified that emerged in the late 1970s clearly resting on the motive of aspiration and the promise of social mobility.

It depicts the economic sphere as a zone of liberty where all individuals may pursue their desires for self-advancement. As Amartya Sen observes, all social contractual offerings must select a basis of equality to remain socially plausible.[2] The necessary axis of equality for neoliberalism is portrayed as being ultimately a question of equality of opportunity and freedom to pursue social mobility; which may be progressed through education, experience and personal merit. It is left to the individual which opportunities they wish to value and pursue and no implicit hierarchy is imposed, such that aspirations toward, for example, a career fulfilling social objectives, are no more worthy than financial speculation or rent seeking enterprise. The role of social and economic policy is to improve access for all citizens to these opportunities. As it transpired, an important element in sustaining popular support for this political programme promoted the ownership of property. Many economic liberals like to think of the system as a whole as the 'property owning democracy'. Citizens could improve their life prospects through investment, particularly in home ownership, pensions and education. Aspiration also evoked an expectation of enriched lifestyle in terms of higher quality goods and services. The difference between this recent formulation of economic liberalism and the 19th century version, which simply privileged the interests of those with capital over those without it, was the way in which it promised the benefits to all who were willing to work hard and shoulder the burden of responsibility. The idea of a property owning democracy was distinguished from perilous comparisons to the 'rent seeking society' of mercantilism by assurances of the self-regulating properties of free markets. These would generate efficiencies that would benefit all members of society. Into the bargain, Europeans could keep their welfare state settlements.

In order to deliver on these promises, neoliberal economic policy took a series of decisive steps. A crucial decision was taken to deregulate financial and labour markets. In due course, financial sector organisations developed ways of increasing their profit margins in deregulated jurisdictions and so tended to gather in financial centres such as London or New York. Initially, one of their important activities was to receive surpluses from the oil producing nations and lend them to developing economies. Whilst this ultimately proved disastrous for those developing economies, there were nevertheless many benefits for the countries that hosted international finance. Domestic corporations gained a foothold in foreign markets that were prised open by programmes of structural adjustment following national debt default. This provided new sources of cheap labour and imports, as well as impetus for the creed of globalisation and free trade. The financial sector flourished and this increased tax revenues to their host states. Many Asian countries, fearful of debt, re-engineered their economies toward exports which they sold at low prices to consumers in the West. They accumulated surpluses which the Western banks were then able to lend to their customers who bought cheap imports (a colossal

2 A. Sen, *The Idea of Justice* (London: Allen Lane, 2009).

form of vendor finance) or bought property in a bubble as well as taking on increasing levels of debt. Monetary policy could keep interest rates on this debt artificially low without risking inflation in consumer prices as a result of cheap imports and diminishing domestic wage demands, which were replaced by easy access to credit. Thus it appeared that the promises of economic liberalisation were delivering, albeit heavily debt financed. Interest rates and inflation remained low. Receipts from the financial sector grew allowing increased public spending on welfare. It is now clear that this state of affairs was mediated by financial innovations that made credit unsustainably elastic and provided a fictional experience of wealth.

The reductions in employment protection law were advanced under the efficiency goal of 'labour market flexibility' that would reduce the 'barriers to entry' at the expense of 'labour market insiders' in favour of new participants, such as women and younger people. At the same time organisations would be free to adapt employment composition to changing technological and market conditions. This would also allow employees who had been 'outsourced' to quickly gain re-entry into work. Labour market participation among women increased albeit predominantly in temporary or part-time work associated with low levels of job security. As a result of labour market reforms, the workforce became more exchangeable and employment prospects less secure. This development unfolded at the same time individuals were being aggressively encouraged to take on long-term debt commitments by the agents of deregulated finance. Prior to 2008, high levels of employment prevailed and so neoliberal governments also started reducing legal entitlements to social security. Progressive globalisation also allowed companies to replace domestic labour with selective relocation of their operations to cheaper wage environments abroad.

The financial arrangements that neoliberalism introduced were sometimes called 'Bretton Woods II' or the 'Great Moderation'. While they lasted, politicians appeared to have achieved a kind of alchemy whereby they could appease all constituencies. On the one hand they could entertain the business lobbies and praise their entrepreneurial zest; at the same time, on the other hand, they could claim to be holding dear the interests of the lower economic strata in maintaining public spending on welfare and easier access to work as a result of labour market efficiency. Political interests appeared to have homogenised and so politics found a new managerial role, busying itself with the finer points of policy and local issues. Political culture decayed into a centrist compact and celebrity drama. The onset of the crisis did not much alter political landscapes in terms of the consensus on economic policy. If anything, it intensified that consensus, solidifying the appearance of a political class rotating office between colour factions. Of course, there are many neoliberals who now regret how things developed and look back on financial deregulation with a view to reform. Their policies have left their constituents in a severely compromised position. This is increasingly being felt in various forms of labour and welfare discipline, which politicians must enforce within a very limited range of perceived options.

Here we encounter social liberals pushing in from the margins, roused by the wealth of evidence from the financial crisis that now makes the academic theory and economic policy of the Washington Consensus look pretty silly. The starting point is usually a comparative analysis of current events through the lens of the last great economic calamity in the 1930s. From this period emerged a social liberal approach that was pioneered by Keynes. At that time societies were not so extensively financialised and the experience of total war had focused attention on social needs. Global capital movement was restricted by nationalist fragmentation and a set of international policy accords known as Bretton Woods. Within this framework national economies enjoyed some freedom of movement in relation to commissioning public debt and spending to promote an increase in aggregate demand and therefore economic activity and growth. In the spirit of those times social liberals now call for fiscal intervention to achieve the same ends. These views, as dignified as they are by towering figures and grand laurels, have had a meagre response from electorates or those in charge of practical governance.

However, they do offer credible warnings about how events might unfold, based on some unarguable propositions. Simply put, the stated goal of neoliberal incumbents of reducing public debt through sharp reductions in government spending has little precedent in past experience of the impacts of economic policy. Usually such spending reductions increase the burden of debt on a state because they result in economic decline or stagnation. Unlike private household debt, public debt cannot be controlled simply by offsetting reductions in spending. This is because public income is dependent on tax revenues that are in turn dependent on the economic performance of the tax base. This performance is unlikely to be improved by withdrawing demand from an economy through public spending reductions.[3] But valid as this insight may be, no coherent political programme or lasting settlement appears to follow from it, while populations and their governments remain supine to the tender mercies of international money markets. Post-crisis Keynesians, such as those grouped with the Institute for New Economic Thinking, have made noble attempts to champion reason with a new (nicer) economic scientism, but they remain marginal in their impact. They confer with psychologists, political scientists and sociologists but have no particular interest in legal or constitutional issues. Legal and political approaches allied with social liberal economists confine themselves to the disproportionate impacts of austerity measures on identity groups and their legal rights in anti-discrimination and human rights law.

A more sustained critique of neoliberalism comes from the social democratic tradition. These commentaries are primarily political and in general adopt the economic theory perspectives of social liberal economists, whilst collating

3 V. Chick and A. Pettifor, 'The Economic Consequences of Mr Osborne, Fiscal Consolidation: Lessons from a Century of UK Macroeconomic Statistics'(6 June 2010) available at www.debtonation.org/wp-content/uploads/2010/06/Fiscal-Consolidation1.pdf (accessed 28 November 2011).

economic facts that trace the relationship between capital versus labour and the distribution of income and wealth in society. At present their most pressing concerns are focused on traditional social democratic preoccupations with welfare provision and the prospects of workers in the labour market. They make the central point that capital has gained the upper hand over labour. Legal scholarship in this area has mostly focused on the erosion of labour law protection under neoliberal policies and institutions. With social liberals, social democrats are often prone to converge on the flippant insight that neoliberal institutions are still neoliberal, even after the financial crisis.

More fundamental lines of legal inquiry consider the impact on the rule of law from the intense deregulation and regulatory arbitrage that neoliberalism created. For example, Alain Supiot suggests that labour interests have lost ground against capital for reasons that have moved beyond the purely ideological: regulatory arbitrage and financialisation undermined the rule of law.[4] For Supiot, this is essentially a doctrinal issue. The ideology of neoliberalism, in privileging the economic sphere, is anti-democratic, to an extent that resembles scientific socialism. The application of this doctrine means that the law-making function of government has become scientistic 'governance' tearing down the distinction between 'is' and 'ought'. Law, despite its normative vocations, is viewed by neoliberal doctrine in regulatory terms as merely a participant in regulatory systems. This view is naturalistic and displaces normative questions with false prescriptions for regulatory efficiency, as if a medical model applied to social and economic systems could resolve moral or ethical dilemmas. This provides a deeper diagnosis of the economic crisis of 2008 as symptomatic of a crisis in law and institutions. His analysis starts with the observation that markets rest upon the guarantees of the law in matters of contract and property ownership. Neoliberalism sought to dismantle this institutional framework through 'financial deregulation and the promotion of competition between different systems of labour and environmental law'.[5] This critique of market fundamentalism draws upon the work of Karl Polanyi, who pointed to the fictitious commoditisation of land, labour and money.[6] This is primarily a legal fiction that allows for the formation of contractual and property rights so that they may circulate in markets. Labour law and environmental law are needed to realign these fictions with reality, to protect natural resources and to 'sustain the long-term operation of labour markets over successive generations'.[7]

These necessary social democratic elements of the legal system have been undermined by neoliberal reforms. Of course neoliberal governments have enacted some direct restrictions on labour rights and have tended to privilege

4 A. Supiot, 'A Legal Perspective on the Financial Crisis of 2008' (2010) 149(2) *International Labour Review* 151–62.

5 ibid 152.

6 K. Polanyi, *The Great Transformation* (Boston: Beacon Press, 1944).

7 Supiot, 'A Legal Perspective on the Financial Crisis of 2008' 153.

economic competitiveness over environmental protection. But, more significantly, extensive implications arise from the effect of financial deregulation in the context of globalisation. The laws protecting labour and the environment were inevitably constructed at a national level within the bounds of national constitutions. The global mobility of capital that neoliberal deregulation accelerated has created a market in legal systems. Thus law itself has become commoditised. In both political decision-making and the construction of international law and institutions, economic competitiveness has taken precedence over social and environmental concerns. As a result, the interests of global capital engage in regulatory arbitrage among competing national legal protections, in other words a 'race to the bottom'. This amounts to an attack on the rule of law. There is evidence that international legal institutions such as the European Court of Justice have supported this process. Other international institutions also actively participate. For example, the World Bank provides explicit support for regulatory arbitrage by publishing a league table comparing different national regulatory regimes as part of its 'Doing Business' programme.

The growth of global finance and international trade has also revealed another way in which the rule of law is undermined. Both trade and finance are reliant on contracts that extend credit to consumers and enterprise. The legal meaning and coherence of these contracts rests in the prudential obligations and benefits of financial risk. Financial innovations found ingenious ways of obscuring underlying financial risk and redistributing it in ways that ultimately collapsed in the socialisation of losses. Thus the legal mechanisms in credit transactions lose their ability to stabilise credit systems. In addition, these costly dysfunctions are cast onto society. The agents of finance in their international zone of mobility and immunity escape the losses that they have legally commissioned and thus appear to have transcended the rule of law.

Supiot traces the rise of regulatory arbitrage to the economic theories of Hayek in the formation of neoliberal doctrine. This saw the 'spontaneous order of the market' as having superior benefits to democratic process. It was therefore essential that economic process should be set free from the domination of politics. This led to decades of policy and legislative measures that sought to depoliticise economic governance. The result has been that social interests have been overcome, rather than finding any enduring expression in the total market order. Supiot's conclusion is that the doctrines of the International Labour Organization need to be reasserted in international governance, distilled in the statement that 'lasting peace can be established only if it is based on social justice' and that, if they are not, society will face a resurgence of xenophobia.[8]

These, and other calls for a return to social democratic values, have been overtaken by wider effects. Concerns about regulatory arbitrage are now mainstream. However, the reimposition of regulatory controls over finance faces

8 ibid 160.

a collective action problem. Ever since the age of mercantilism the doctrines of economic competitiveness have applied between nations and the financial crisis has heralded resurgence in mercantile policy that is manifesting itself in various ways, such as 'currency wars' and global commodity price inflation. There were moments in the heat of the crisis as global financial meltdown was contemplated when the neoliberal doctrine appeared to face suspension; then central banks intervened with massive liquidity operations. That set off a series of competitive currency devaluations as countries sought to rebalance their failing economies. Commodity price inflation, which many suspect was stoked by quantitative easing through a flight to commodity investment, has gained new impetus from rising oil prices. In that configuration the ILO is nowhere to be seen. Unless one entertains the hope of a geopolitical mechanism for social contractual renewal, the international scene now seems like an even more barren field for a social democratic springtime than ever before.

Consideration of prospects for the rule of law and democratic renewal then returns to within national boundaries. There are some small indications of labour activism in countries such as China that accumulated financial surpluses; but the authoritarian nature of that regime does not bode well for them. In the West, a pervasive effect is the penetration by financialisation deep into the social fabric. As Lapavitsas points out, in the run up to the crisis the financial sector increasingly acquired contractual rights to take profits directly from household incomes.[9] There are many other ways in which financialised governance has displaced democratic accountability and the rule of law. Financialisation expresses its own regulatory objectives in a host of scientific management techniques applied to every aspect of daily life that escape constitutional and democratic accountability. These range from credit reference checks to the impact of money market imperatives on education, public sector employment and service provision. Financialisation has facilitated an aggressive return to a mercantile 'rent seeking society', rather than self-regulating markets under the rule of law. Under the dominance of the rentiers' axioms, knowledge is strictly subordinated to risk calculation. The 'knowledge economy' becomes de-autonomised in the scientific management of knowledge.[10]

The growth of finance under deregulation amounted to a deep regression in the rule of law, one not limited to the impact of regulatory arbitrage on social rights and the environmental law. The doctrines of neoliberalism have become instrumentalised in contingencies that force the selective suspension of legal development. Neoliberal economic theory became instrumentalised in the behaviour of financial markets when those theories came to be relied on extensively

9 C. Lapavitsas, 'Financialised Capitalism, Direct Exploitation and Periodic Bubbles' (May 2008) available at www.leftlibrary.com/lapavitsas1.pdf (accessed 28 November 2011).

10 P. Wilby, 'The Awful Truth: Education Won't Stop the West Getting Poorer' *Guardian* (28 February 2011) available at http://www.guardian.co.uk/commentisfree/2011/feb/28/education-jobs-middle-class-decline (accessed 28 November 2011).

by market participants to guide their trading activities.[11] The theories increasingly determined rather than predicted market behaviour. In a similar way, neoliberal doctrine has moved beyond the influence of ideology on governance that is open to electoral franchise and parliamentary debate; it has become sedimented in economic and financial contingency to the extent that the representative function of neoliberal ideology in politics has been displaced by an immunised principle of determination. The goal of current neoliberal policy in the grinding march of episodic crises is not fundamentally ideological. Economic liberal politicians are not striving primarily to save banks or the orthodoxies of efficient market hypotheses. They are desperately fighting to save the neoliberal social contract that has secured them political tenure for the past three decades. It is not purely a matter of regulatory or ideological capture. They are condemned to keep the dream alive or perish. Many of the dynamics behind the financial crisis that analysts now regard as important (for example loose tax regimes for debt-funded speculation) are traceable to the social contractual basis of neoliberalism: the property owning democracy.

Whilst debate has focused on economic prospects, the underlying questions concern the prospects for democracy. Rancière recalls the emergence of the *demos* in Athenian democracy out of laws that liberated people from debt bondage to oligarchs.[12] Applied to contemporary realities, this raises questions about the impact of high levels of personal and public debt on democratic freedom of action. The concept of 'responsibility' in debt bondage situations takes on an entirely different connotation to notions of aspiration and social mobility. Rancière also notes that Aristotle's philosophical formulation of justice in exchange preserved an axis of oligarchs and aristocrats within a geometric distribution. It now appears that the contractarian principle has become more about these exemptions than government by consent. Whilst economic liberalism was moderated by social liberalism and social democracy, these ends were achieved through liberal law. Through the legal fictions of commoditisation, the liberal definition of the *demos* in political life was crucially limited to the economic interests of labour and citizen participation in systems of social insurance – which have now become financialised. It appears that neoliberal doctrine has simply revived the concept of aristocratic virtue and fused it as a property of wealth, calling for its liberation. The financial crisis has revealed that the financialisation which ensued has had profound implications for both social insurance and the economic interests of labour. We have to ask: which road has led to serfdom?

This in turn appears to undermine some fundamental assumptions of liberal democracy. In some cases the prospects for democracy seem particularly eclipsed. On questions of economic and social policy, countries such as Greece and Ireland

11 D. Mackenzie, *An Engine Not a Camera, How Financial Models Shape Markets* (Cambridge, Mass.: MIT Press, 2006).

12 J. Rancière, *Disagreement: Politics and Philosophy* (Minneapolis: University of Minnesota Press, 1999) 6.

have witnessed their democracies rapidly transform to the status of 'mandated territories with limited sovereignty' under the conditions of European Central Bank and International Monetary Fund banking sector bailouts delivered via sovereign accounts.[13] Across European nations social resources are being cannibalised on the grounds that this is necessary to avoid a similar fate. In the UK, popular anger over disproportionate banking sector bonuses achieved pre-electoral promise but not post-electoral action. In addition, legislating for increased individual debt burdens to fund higher education is the antithesis of neoliberalism's aspirational promises. At the same time there is little evidence that positions on such issues are the subject of great party-political difference.

This evidence of plutocratic capture is not simply a matter of political ideology, still less conspiracy. Ideology may still serve to project the view that the economic crisis is a 'natural' disaster rather than a consequence of political decisions that enjoyed widespread political support at the time. But such propositions are now more a question of securing popular compliance within a web of contingency, rather than a question of rational belief. These effects are traceable beyond ideology to levels of anti-social economic overdetermination that are absent from the social contractual fundamentals that both liberalism and social democracy have projected. In the meantime, the sorcery of central bank intervention is losing its magic as conditions of ongoing credit contraction meet rising cost-push inflation. Have these interventions merely postponed a crisis in the social contract?

The ideology that placed aspiration at the centre of political discourse encouraged greater social reflexivity among individuals, who have decisively abandoned the culture of deference that characterised previous eras. Reflexivity is now increasingly developing into resistance. In the past, liberalism tamed the political instability that emerged out of economic crisis amid high levels of income inequality by the creation of a buffer class whose economic and social aspiration was called upon to unify society. But a repeat of this dynamic is precisely foreclosed by the instrumentalised contingencies of neoliberalism, owing to the economic autarchy and imperial expansion that it would necessarily require. Neoliberalism has undermined the status and power of those in the middle economic strata and opened them up to the embrace of globally mobile financial capital which has simply made their aspiration contingent on debt finance, compressing them back down in the income distribution.

As social discipline slowly advances, possibly taking on identity and public order dimensions, it may transpire that liberalism's end point is anything but liberal. Liberalism ushered in much that people consider valuable: universally enfranchised parliaments, civil and political rights, and principles of non-discrimination; but ultimately it bound its societies to an external agency. No one can predict the

13 C. Douzinas, 'Europe and the End of Politics' available at http://www.newleftproject.org/index.php/site/article_comments/europe_and_the_end_of_politics (accessed 28 November 2011).

course of economic events or, indeed, whether liberalism's liberties will survive financialisation. Neoliberals still hope for the happy ending that economic history has repeatedly failed to deliver. The deeper the negative dynamics of financialisation penetrate, the more social liberal and social democratic alternatives are rendered inoperable; whilst the social aspirations encouraged by neoliberalism are comprehensively disappointed for all but a few and particularly for the young. If political risks do escalate into a breakdown of the liberal social contract, what are the implications for the rule of law? Does not the failure of liberal law to preserve its social contractual guarantees under these conditions end up facing either a continued decay into increasingly illegal discipline or a necessary return to the principles of radical natural law; isonomia; unvarnished by contractarian or market-based ideology, as the only other (far from technocratic) basis of legal transcendence?

Part III

Futures of critical legal thinking

Chapter 10

Before the law, encounters at the borderline

Elena Loizidou

> Law is an order of human behaviour . . . Law and force must not be understood as absolutely at variance with one another. Law is an organisation of force.[1]

Before the law

I ask: 'What do an anarchist, a mulla and a Taoist, have in common? Let us see', I tell myself, bringing to mind the stories that I am about to narrate below. I continue: '. . . all three tell us about being *before* the *law* . . .' and I recall: '. . . all three find a way to pass *through* the law and its various guises (magistrates and mayors, customs and immigration officers)'. The importance of these stories, as we shall see, lies in what they convey about law and its relation to life. These three vignettes allow us to see some of the operations of the juridical order, its ability to order life forcefully, how we fail to render the juridical order inoperative but also, and more importantly (and this may sound like a paradox), how we go on to explore parallel lives to the ones that the juridical order organises. This chapter sees these particular encounters at the borderline as exchanges with law that reveal to us that our existence may not necessarily need to be verified or recognised by law. Life, our life, may exceed the borders of law. This may of course only be seen, understood, or even imagined, if we begin to see the law not as the means and the end to our existence but rather as a prop and, while we may not be able to wish its existence away, we are certainly able to tease the form of life that the juridical order ossifies at the back or on the side of our focus in the world.

As we are well aware, stories about being *before* the *law* are not unique. We just need to surf the web, listen to the news on the radio, watch television, talk to our neighbours and friends or skim through the newspapers and we encounter a plethora of them. Many of them are stories about celebrities breaking the law (George Michael, Boy George, Paris Hilton), or their previous court orders (Lindsay Lohan) and others report the stories of ordinary folk that break the law by allegedly engaging in housing benefit fraud, anti-social behaviour or homicide. Such encounters with the law, unlike our three stories –as we shall see – invest in the law the monolithic power of ordering (forcefully as even Kelsen points out) human activity and do not really

1 H. Kelsen, *General Theory of Law and State* (Clark: Lawbook Exchange, 2009) 3, 21.

tell us much about the operation of law (it is taken for granted that law is an instrument of ordering life and as such it must be obeyed otherwise sanctions will be imposed) nor about whether and to what extent any of the transgressors of law have or manage to have parallel lives to the ones that are ordered by law. Put another way, their life stories or their names are being absorbed by the juridical order and its pervading discourses.

We can say with safety that very few of such stories can reach the status of a story that would render academic reflection with the legal academy by either social-legal theorists or critical legal theorists. There is for example the relatively recent story of O. J. Simpson[2] that we may say belongs to the genre of 'before the law'. O. J. Simpson was put on trial but acquitted for the murders of Nicole Brown Simpson (his wife) and Ronald Goldman (allegedly his wife's lover). The trial attracted so much attention primarily because it reflected the inability of the US to address racism.[3] Nevertheless, while we can attest to the legal, cultural, racial and gender ripples that the O. J. Simpson trial has created in the latter part of the 20th century, it has not been as effective as the two-page parable by Kafka entitled 'Before the Law'.[4] The parable, as you probably know, was published in 1919 for the first time as a free-standing literary piece and forms an integral part of Kafka's novel *The Trial*. Kafka's 'Before the Law' produced copious reflections by both critical and non-critical lawyers,[5] as well as critical theorists and philosophers.[6]

2 See for example: A. Howe, 'Imagining Evidence, Fictioning Truth – Revisiting (Courtesy of O. J. Simpson) Expert Evidence in the Chamberlain Case' (1997) 3(1) *Law Text Culture* 82; S. Kadri, *The Trial: A History from Socrates to O. J. Simpson* (London, New York: Harper Perennial, 2005); M. Valverde, 'Social Facticity and the Law: a Social Expert's Eyewitness Account of Law' (1996) 5(2) *Social & Legal Studies* 201; C. Lassiter, 'The O.J. Simpson Verdict: A Lesson in Black and White' (1996) 1 *Michigan Journal of Race and Law* 69; C. H. Weston, 'Orenthal James Simpson and Gender, Class, and Race: In That Order' (1995) 6 *Hastings Women's Law Journal* 223.

3 For a sophisticated account of this see S. Felman, 'Forms of Judicial Blindness, or The Evidence of What Cannot Be Seen: Traumatic Narratives and Legal Repetitions in the O. J. Simpson Case and in Tolstoy's The Kreutzer Sonata' (Summer 1997) 23(4) *Critical Inquiry* 738.

4 F. Kafka, 'Before the Law' in *The Trial* (London: Penguin Modern Classics, 2000) 167.

5 See for example G. Dargo, 'Reclaiming Franz Kafka, Doctor of Jurisprudence' (2006-7) 45 *Brandeis Law Journal* 495; D. E. Litowitz, 'Franz Kafka's Outside Jurisprudence' (2002) 27 *Law and Social Inquiry* 103; H. van Houtum, 'Waiting Before the Law: Kafka on the Border' (2010) 19(3) *Social & Legal Studies* 19 285; B. Carlsson and M. Baier, 'A Visual Self-Image of Legal Authority: "The Temple of Law"' (2002) 11(2) *Social & Legal Studies* 11 185; J. R. Elkins, 'Lowell B. Komie of Chicago – Writer and Lawyer' (2001) 25 *Legal Studies Forum* 1; M. Aristodemou, 'Studies in Law and Literature: Directions and Concerns' (1993) 22 *Anglo-American Law Review* 159; I. Ward, 'From Literature to Ethics: The Strategies and Ambitions of Law and Literature' (1994) 14(3) *Oxford Journal of Legal Studies* 389; L. J. Moran, 'Gothic Law' (2001) 10 *Griffith Law Review* 75; R. A. Posner, 'Remarks on Law and Literature' (1991–92) 23 *Loyola University of Chicago Law Journal* 181; C. Douzinas and A. Gearey, *Critical Jurisprudence: The Political Philosophy of Justice* (Oxford: Hart Publishing, 2005) 336–62.

6 See for example T. Adorno, *Notes on Kafka's* 'Prisms' (Cambridge, Massachusetts: MIT Press, 1967) 243; G. Agamben, 'Form of Law' in *Homo Sacer: Sovereign Power and Bare Life*

The parable of 'Before the Law', as you may know, tells the story of a man from the country who lived his whole life before a doorkeeper, so as 'to come to know the fleas in [the doorkeeper's] fur collar'[7] and even plead with the fleas to enable him to convince the doorkeeper to allow him an audience with the law, and to discover at the end that he is not to be admitted but rather to have the door of law be shut for him forever. However, as we shall see later on, in this part of this chapter the parable maybe interpreted in ways that can obliterate the taste of inevitability and despair that my transmission of it so far conveys. Why then, we may ask, has Kafka's literature achieved such acclamation? There are of course many reasons. Jason Baker suggests that 'critics have celebrated [it] for its universality',[8] albeit one that scripts down 'a universe with different rules than those governing our reality'.[9] Benjamin also confirms that Kafka's work captures a different universe without losing its universal applicability. Benjamin focuses on a particular character that keeps featuring in Kafka's literature, the figure of the assistant. He points out that Kafka's most eminent figures, 'the assistants',[10] '[have] a firm place in the world'.[11] With the assistance of Benjamin's observation of Kafka's literature we may also suggest that Kafka's parable 'Before the Law' depicts through the figure of the 'man from the country' the paradoxical position that we may have in the world, in relation to the law, a position that reveals our non-relation to the law. Perhaps this is the universality that this parable captures. Its popularity demonstrated by the plethora of critical readings we have inherited may well be because of the oblique, dense and difficult to interpret prose. Dargo informs us through Harold Bloom that Kafka used dense prose because he did not want to be interpreted.[12] Of course, this stirred up the desire for interpretation and the search for signification in Kafka's work.

Whatever is the case, my intention here is not to try to reinterpret this parable. The above digressions are offered as a way of introducing the different account of life and law that the three stories I will talk about shortly reveal. Before proceeding to introduce these stories, however, I would like to focus briefly on a recent retelling of 'Before the Law'. This retelling is given to us by Giorgio Agamben in his world-noted book *Homo Sacer*. I do so for primarily two reasons. The first reason is because

(Stanford: Stanford University Press, 1998) 49–62; W. Benjamin, 'Franz Kafka: On the Tenth Anniversary of His Death' in *Illuminations* (Glasgow: Fontana/Collins, 1979) 111–40; G. Deleuze and F. Guattari, *Kafka: Toward a Minor Literature* (Minneapolis: University of Minnesota Press, 2006); J. Derrida, 'Before the Law' in *Acts of Literature* (ed D. Attridge) (New York, London: Routledge, 1992) 181–221; J. F. Lyotard, *The Postmodern Condition: A Report on Knowledge* (Minnesota: Minnesota University Press, 1992); S. Sontag, *Against Interpretation* (London: Penguin, 2009) 3–14.

7 Kafka, 'Before the Law' 167.

8 J. Baker, 'Introduction' in F. Kafka, *Metamorphosis and Other Stories* (Dover, 1996) xv.

9 ibid.

10 Benjamin, 'Franz Kafka' 116.

11 ibid 117.

12 Dargo, 'Reclaiming Franz Kafka' 500.

Agamben offers an interpretation that generates an understanding of the parable beyond one that attempts to find a hidden meaning in a text. Agamben's critique of the parable is in line with, I would like to suggest, Susan Sontag's understanding of the role of critique and consequentially that of the critic. For Sontag excavating secret meanings of literary or artistic work fails to acknowledge that the 'merit'[13] of the work lies somewhere else. As she claims: '[t]he function of criticism should be to show *how it is what it is, even that it is that what it is*, rather than to show what it means'.[14] What is she gesturing towards then? Sontag wants us to see that the merit of a work may lie for example in what it does, in how it affects its public. I want to suggest that Agamben's reading of the parable focuses precisely in what the figures of the parable, 'the man from the country' and the doorkeeper, do and, in this sense, it provides us with a nuanced understanding of the relationship of law and man. The second reason for engaging albeit briefly with Agamben's presentation of the parable is interlinked with the first reason. For Agamben, as we shall see below, the parable *shows* how the law may be rendered inoperational or how the man from the country manages to close the door of law forever. The parable holds for him a way out of law and specifically the juridical order. This shift from meaning (what is the meaning of law?) to one of an indication of what we can do to law is a significant shift in the retelling of 'Before the Law', a shift that I will depart from, but which I follow to some extent (at least in the motif of the encounter at the border) in order to understand what is done to law when we encounter it at the borders and how or whether life can be 'freed' from the formality of law, despite its presence.

So let us now turn briefly to Agamben's reflection on the parable in *Homo Sacer*. Agamben begins his retelling by agreeing with interpretations of the parable (including that of Derrida) that suggest as he points out that: '[n]othing – and certainly not the refusal of the doorkeeper – prevents the man from the country from passing through the door of the Law if not the fact that this door is already open and that the Law prescribes nothing'.[15] Taking this as his starting point, he turns his attention to the problematic of the operation of law in the parable. In doing so his focus is on the effects of law, and specifically the effects of law on life. Like Derrida he tells us that law's foundations are based on 'nothing',[16] without grounds that may legitimise its practices. To this effect for Agamben law is just pure form. But law's pure form, Agamben will have it, does not mean that the law is non-operational. On the contrary, Agamben notes whether the law is pure form or 'nothing' it still operates, and in its operational mode it succeeds, as he argues, in making life indistinguishable from it.[17] Or, to put it differently, this ungrounded law can absorb into its jurisdiction (forcefully) any form of life (social, political,

13 Sontag, *Against Interpretation* 9.
14 ibid, original emphasis.
15 Agamben, *Homo Sacer* 49.
16 ibid 51.
17 ibid 55.

ethical, aesthetic). This observation that he brings to the parable is of significance. It allows us to begin thinking of ways in which we can undo this capturing of life by law. But before attending to the undoing of the 'coincidence' of law and life, let us take a step back and see how Agamben understands the juridification of life. How, then, does this 'coincidence' of law and life comes about? Law captures 'life' through formality; through a series of questions of authorisation ('can I see the doorkeeper of the law?' (as in the parable), 'can I have my rights recognised?'). This juridification of 'life' has two dimensions. On the one hand, if one is recognised by 'law' something is captured within its formal requirements (which may not necessarily be specific: an example of an unspecific formal requirement is that arrests can be made on the grounds of reasonable suspicion that some criminal activity is taking place or is about to) and, on the other hand, life can be captured by law through excluding it or abandoning it, for example by not allowing a refugee to attain asylum status. In this second instance 'life' is banned or abandoned, but the very abandonment takes place through the operation of formal laws. The man from the country, the protagonist of the parable, is *shown* to be abandoned outside the legal parameters through the very application of law (refusal of authorisation of entry into law without explanation). If you recall, the doorkeeper refuses entry without justification. Hear his words: '. . .just try going in despite my interdiction. But take note: I am powerful'.[18] The only justification we have for not allowing the man from the country through the door of the law is that the doorkeeper is powerful; no explanation is given as to where this power comes from, or we may say that this power comes from the form of law. The man from the country is thus 'abandoned' or left to his own devices. This legend, and the 'form' of life that is shown to be at play, 'resembles life in the state of exception'.[19] The 'state of exception', a state whereby the law includes 'life' by banning it or excluding it (displaced people fleeing from war zones at nation borders would be an example of such a category) according to Agamben has become the rule in our contemporary setting. Of course this may appear to be a very pessimistic state of affairs; one whereby we may see no way out, and where 'life' is constantly reduced to its bio-political with no access to what we understand as the 'good life'. Agamben, through Kafka's 'Before the Law', meditates on how we may undo or free 'life' from the formalities of law, undoing it from law's codes, formulaic gestures, authority and, moreover, bringing about a 'real'[20] state of exception. As he asks: '. . . how, first of all, is one to conduct oneself before such a 'form of law'. . .?'[21] The answer to the question as he sees it does not lie with either demanding more legality, in the forms of legal rights or legal procedures, or policing the law for any abuses or merely stating that the law has no grounds. If we are to untangle 'life'

18 Kafka, 'Before the Law' 167.
19 Agamben, *Homo Sacer* 52.
20 W. Benjamin, 'Theses on the Philosophy of History' in *Illuminations* (Glasgow: Jonathan Cape 1970) 259.
21 Agamben, *Homo Sacer* 52.

from the nets of a forceful law, and the 'virtual' state of emergency that sustains it, our conduct could be so as to make real the inefficacy of law. Our conduct should be such as to have the legal door shut. And the man from the country's conduct is *imagined* as achieving precisely this. Here is how Agamben tells the story:

> If it is true the door's openness constituted, as we saw, the invisible power and specific 'force' of the law, then we can imagine that all the behaviour of the man from the country is nothing other than a complicated and patient strategy to have the door closed in order to interrupt the Law's being in force. And in the end, the man succeeds in his endeavor, since he succeeds in having the door of the law closed forever (it was, after all, open 'only for him'), even if he may have risked his life in the process (the story does not say that he is actually dead but only that he is 'close to the end').[22]

The freeing of 'life' from the stifling and suffocating captivity of legal formality, if we are to follow Agamben's imagination, requires the shutting of a door, the shutting of our *aspirations* that we may have of law (after all, the door is already 'open') and it requires imaging of ways in which it can be achieved and the risk of one's life, risk to be in our abandonment. This of course requires very different forms of conducts, as each one of us has to close the door of law. And Agamben ends his chapter on Kafka's parable by offering a set of diverse modes of conduct (via Kojève and Bataille) through which or by which we can begin imagining how we can achieve the shutting of the door of law that was made for us. The man from the country is imagined – we do not really know whether this has happened or not and we will never really know – to have achieved this through his persistent formal request to be before the law. And in Bataille's outlook, the 'law' may be 'consumed' in the moment, through man-creating forms like laughter or luxury.[23] As Agamben points out at the end of his recounting of Kafka's parable, law can be rendered inoperative in a variety of ways, and we need to keep open our eyes and our imagination to the ways in which this is achieved or is possible to be achieved.

This chapter now explores, through 'The Smuggler' (a joke attributed to the Mulla Nasruddin,[24] a celebrated figure in Turkey but also beyond[25]), an encounter that the 19th century anarchist Pierre-Joseph Proudhon narrates having had with the mayor of Toulon[26] and Bertolt Brecht's poem the 'Legend of the Origin of the

22 ibid 55.
23 ibid 61.
24 See I. Shah, *The Exploits of the Incomparable Mulla Nasrudin* (London: The Octagon Press, 1983) 6.
25 The Mulla is part of the cultural myths of many countries: Greece, Albania, Serbia and Romania all have their own Mulla Nasruddin anecdotes.
26 D. Guérin, *No Gods, No Masters: An Anthology of Anarchism* (Oakland, Edinburgh: AK Press, 2005) 42–44.

Book Tao-Tê-Ching on Lao-Tsû's Road into Exile',[27] a different relation to law and life than the one Kafka points to in the parable and which Agamben so powerfully extrapolates. These are not stories of how one manages to shut the door of law as Kafka's parable is telling us, Agamben suggests, but rather they are stories about seeing that the door is closed (seeing that the law has the tendency, which is more exaggerated when the state of exception becomes the rule, to capture life in its claws) and where one proceeds to live one's life, to build one's life, under such a premise. The underlying problematic that prompted me to present these stories lies with the following questions. To what extent and how we can undo the capturing of 'life' from the claws of law without necessarily having to close its door of law forever, but rather in recognition that the door of law may not be locked forever – it may remain constantly ajar, our companion and a prop? And if we take this as our premise, that the door of law remains always ajar, what can we learn from its operations? These three stories, as you will see, do not convey the same values. Our three protagonists here have different aspirations for their lives, and their acts and words are demonstrations of this. But I see that all three of them show us different aspects of the operation of law and our ability to deossify life from its stones. This is not to render unimportant Agamben's rendition of the relationship between law and life and the necessity of undoing, but rather to see whether different stories of encounters 'before the law' provide us with an alternative relation to law and life and possibilities for deossifying life from the claws of the juridical order.

The Mulla

Mulla Nasruddin's tales form an integral part of the cultural traditions of the Middle East. He is the protagonist of a variety of humorous stories as the wise fool. The editor of *Islamic History*[28] informs us that between the 15th and 18th centuries his stories, along with the Arabian Nights, were often recited at the tea houses popular amongst men in all three Islamic Empires: the Ottoman Empire in the Middle East, the Balkans and Northern Africa, the Safavid Empire in Greater Iran and the Mughul Empire in South East Asia. The stories of the Mulla (or *Hodja* in Turkish)[29] expose 'absurdities of social conventions'.[30] (While the

27 B. Brecht, 'Legend of the Origin of the Book Tao Tê Ching on Lao-Tsû's Road into Exile' in *Bertolt Brecht: Poems 1913–1956* (ed J. Willet and R. Manheim) (New York and London: Methuen, 1976).

28 L. S. Etheredge (ed), *Islamic History* (New York: Britannica Educational Publishing, 2010) 177.

29 The Mulla Nasruddin takes on various disguises. Sometimes he is presented as a Sufi, other times he appears as a court adviser and some others as a smuggler as we can see in our anecdote.

30 D. Haase (ed), *The Greenwood Encyclopedia of Folktales and Fairy Tales* (Westport Connecticut: Greenwood Press, 2008) 662.

Mulla's stories have been predominantly developed and become popular in the Middle East, they have also been celebrated and absorbed by outside jurisdictions. Idries Shah informs us that the Greeks, for example, have adopted him into their folklore.[31]) And indeed his stories are known to me through my maternal grandmother, who was Greek-Cypriot. She used to narrate them to me at bedtime and I can still recall the laughter that ensued from hearing them.

'The Smuggler' is the particular anecdote that concerns me here. We see the Mulla Nasruddin engaged in border-crossing for the purposes of commerce. Here it is:

> Time and again Nasruddin passed from Persia to Greece on donkey-back. Each time he had two panniers of straw, and trudged back without them. Every time the guards searched him for contraband. They never found any.
>
> 'What are you carrying, Nasruddin?'
>
> 'I am a smuggler.'
>
> Years later, more and more prosperous in appearance, Nasruddin moved to Egypt. One of the customs men met him there.
>
> 'Tell me, Mulla, now that you are out of the jurisdiction of Greece and Persia, living here in such luxury – what was it that you were smuggling when we could never catch you?'
>
> 'Donkeys.'[32]

The anecdote could be part of an instruction manual on how to pass through customs and excise with prohibited goods without being caught or, if we push it to its limit, it could be presented as a generalised story about how to 'transgress' borders. It would be far-fetched, however, to suggest that this anecdote is a parable about how to shut the door of the law. This anecdote does not by any stretch of the imagination resemble Kafka's parable. But its lack of resemblance may still offer an insight into the mechanisms of law, subjectivisation and life. Let us see what we can learn from it.

You may recall that in his essay 'Ideology and Ideological State Apparatuses',[33] Althusser explains how the subject is a product of ideology. Individuals, he explains, are interpellated or hailed by ideology into subjects. The example that he uses to transmit this happening to us is familiar to most of us. It is the one of the policeman who hails a passer-by and the passer-by turns around. This turning around signifies that the passer-by recognises that the hailing is being addressed to him/her. And

31 I. Shah, 'Introduction' in *The Exploits of the Incomparable Mulla Nasrudin* (London: The Octagon Press, 1983) ix.

32 Shah, *Exploits* 6.

33 L. Althusser, 'Ideology and Ideological State Apparatus (Notes Towards an Investigation)' in *Lenin and Philosophy and Other Essays* (New York: Monthly Review Press, 2001) 85–126.

in turning around, he is turned also from a concrete individual into an abstract subject, the product of ideology. The example points to one of the paradoxes of subjectivisation:[34] our subjectivisation is maintained through a doing that one, the individual, '*freely*' enters into subjectivisation, '*freely*' turns around to address the call of the police, or that it is his/her choice to have or enter into a family. This doing, as you can see, exposes a paradox: it exposes that one is only '*free*' to his or her own subjection.

We see Nasruddin time and time again, subjected to the hailing of the border control customs officer: 'What are you carrying, Nasruddin?' The repetitive character of the question, its content, along with the searching of his donkey, propels us to think that such questions could be considered as being interpellative as they implicitly appear to be saying: 'Hey you; I know you are trafficking something illegal, you are a criminal'. And this contention gets stronger when we hear Nasruddin replying each time: 'I am a smuggler'. His answer is given in recognition not only of the fact that the question is addressed to him as a subject but that it is also addressed to him as a transgressive subject, that is, as a trafficker. And consequently it appears that in returning an answer to the question, Nasruddin, as Althusser suggests, can be seen as being exemplary of this paradoxical position; that when being interpellated we are made to think that we act freely, we turn for example out of our own and only accord. We may pause, however, for a second and reconsider to what extent Althusser's claims in relation to interpellation are in operation in this case. Nasruddin, in declaring himself to be a smuggler, manages to avoid the claws of law. We are told that he lives a prosperous life in Egypt. Moreover, we are also informed that – years afterwards – a customs official inquisitively asks him what was he smuggling, confessing both a suspicion of his acts of transgression and an inability to unveil them. How are we to understand that part of the story? It appears that Althusser's concept of interpellation limits our understanding not only of how we are formed as subjects but of what would be the relation between law and life. It is with this in mind that I turn to Judith Butler's understanding of interpellation.

Judith Butler reminds us that Althusser's explanation fails to see that our formation through power is not only formative but it can also be *performative*.[35] If you recall, Althusser talks predominantly about the hailing, or calling, or naming (interpellation) as an action that explicates that we are 'always already subjects'. The calling in itself exposes 'the existence of ideology' and, as Althusser puts it: '[t]he existence of ideology and the hailing or interpellation of individuals as subjects are one and the same thing'.[36] But Althusser fails to notice that it is interpellation *per se* that brings the subject into being, or he fails to recognise that

34 For more on the paradoxes of subjectivisation see E. Loizidou, 'The Body Figural and Material in the Work of Judith Butler' (2008) 28 *Australian Feminist Law Journal* 29–51.

35 J. Butler, *Bodies that Matter: On the Discursive Limits of 'Sex'* (New York and London: Routledge, 1996) 122.

36 Althusser, *Ideology* 118.

the subject does not pre-exist his/her calling into being. In doing so, at the same time he fails to notice that the speech act of naming somebody is effective, is performative. If interpellation is also performative, as Butler suggests, it can have a variety of effects. It can indeed produce obedience but it can, at the same time, produce an array of disobedient acts.[37] It can make someone run away; it can activate 'the refusal of the law in the form of the parodic inhabiting of conformity that subtly calls into question the legitimacy of the command, a repetition of the law into hyperbole, a rearticulation of the law against the authority of the one who delivers it'.[38] The effect of Butler's intervention in the Althusserian concept of interpellation is significant on numerous accounts. By focusing on the variety of effects that can be produced through interpellation, she also dismantles or at least questions the power that Althusser gives to the law: 'it calls into question the monotheistic force of its own unilateral operation'.[39] This anarchic moment, where the subject playfully subjects itself to the law, and simultaneously defies it through giving back to its command more than it has asked, showing to it that it is not the only source of producing effects – or to put it in more post-structuralist terms, exposing its fantasmatic grounds (the monotheistic force of its own unilateral operation) – is also an instance of an opening of a different sociality and subjectivity than the one inferred by Althusser. 'Ideology and Ideological State Apparatuses' is concerned with how the production of social relations is reproduced. This reproduction – or the instance of reproduction – is heavily ordered or secured by ideology and its apparatuses, by a centralisation of power and its capacity to form us through the practice of interpellation, our sociality and our subjectivity therefore unquestionably being bound in ideology. The ideological class struggle that he points to is a struggle about the assumption of power, of who will occupy the central position and therefore command the reproduction of ideology in general. Ideology, along with its structures, process or rituals, does not vanish, but remains. Butler's anarchic reading provides a different alternative. The parodical or hyperbolic effects of disobedience convey in its doing or action or playfulness (without denying that it is a product of power) a sociality that does not want to assume or have a stake in the law or assume the power that brings it into being, but rather to experiment in a different organisation of life, one that undoes our understanding of centralist power or authority. This type of action/practice is a repetition which, as she writes, can be read as an affirmative response to the violation[40] of being named (a violation that she names after Spivak's 'enabling violation'[41]). More precisely, being named (even if in injurious terms – an enabling violation) brings one into being, an act that also gives the possibility to one to undo the violation, to reclaim a name or reinvent a name. The important point that is

37 Butler, *Bodies* 122.
38 ibid.
39 ibid.
40 ibid 124.
41 ibid 122.

made here is that a violation does not always catch us in the circle of violence, the only response to which will be one of violence itself or a constant repetition of a trauma.

In the tale of Nasruddin we may see how interpellation is effective. Narsruddin, playfully (he is known to be a jester as well as a Mulla), by inhabiting the name of a smuggler, teases out not so much the fact that ideology or its apparatuses (law, custom and excise officers) are not present but rather that their existence is not founded upon anything more than ritual of the performance of an authority and that their operation is limited. The 'Ideological State Apparatuses' *is* limited in this case to the operation of searching. The 'Ideological State Apparatuses', personified by the customs officer, operates as hands in action, bereft of any thinking. We may even say that if the law's hands thought, they would have noticed that what was being smuggled was not hidden, that what was being smuggled was the carrier of legal goods, namely the donkey.

The verb 'to search' has a variety of uses. One of these relates to the examination of the contents of the inside of a structure in order to find something that is concealed or lost.[42] Another use refers to searching as the practice of 'mental introspection'.[43] If we focus on the first meaning or use of the word that the dictionary provides, the word 'search' coincides with what Nasruddin reveals to us when he is asked to be searched. It is a physical action that tries to reveal something hidden. It does not require any reflective or introspective thinking. The law or the customs officers appear to be engaged in the first use of the word 'search' rather than in the second. That search has a blind spot. If the function, or if one of the functions, of law is 'searching', searching for truth, for illegality, by moving its hands through bags, structures or evidence, then it fails to see that it is its whole structure or vessel, that the very thing that is illegal it is the 'law' itself, that which (to paraphrase Kelsen) forcefully organises human affairs. And as this type of searching, a physical act that puts aside thought, the operation of law can be seen as not only forceful but also being thoughtless.

Nasruddin's performative speech act, 'I am a smuggler' allows us to see not only how the law is forceful but also that it is thoughtless. The operation of law is precisely a continuous physical movement that constantly attempts to grab hold of life or one's livelihood. At the same time, however, it is this very thoughtlessness of law that allows one to 'invent' ways of securing one's livelihood, of going on to have a prosperous life, as happened with the Mulla Nasruddin. The Mulla's life may resemble that of a commodity trader or capitalist but the story also shows that law may not after all be able to grasp 'life' fully in its claws. It may be that something like the 'economy' may potentially be able to totalise the sphere of life.

42 Oxford English Dictionary, 'search' available at http://www.oed.com (accessed 18 April 2011).

43 ibid.

On the road into exile

In his 1939 poem 'Legend of the Origin of the Book of Tao Tê Ching on Lao-Tsû's Road into Exile', Bertolt Brecht tells the legend of how the Taoist book *Tao Tê Ching*[44] came to be written. The stories about who Lao-Tsû was are as varied as the stories about when the 81 verses of the *Tao Tê Ching* were written. The most widespread story about Lao-Tsû tells us that he came from a noble family but that he rejected his noble origin and the privilege that came with it, and worked as an archivist 'of the royal library at Loh'.[45] When Lao-Tsû reached the age of 70 and his bones were 'getting brittle', Brecht tells us he took the road to exile out of China to die.[46] At the time:

> In his country goodness had been weakening a little
> And the wickedness was gaining ground anew.[47]

The verses indicate that what brought Lao-Tsû to self-exile was an unhappiness with the state of affairs in China. China at the time was being transformed through Confucian thought. Unlike Taoist cosmology and practices which hold strong, anti-authoritarian, anti-centralisation of government and anti-juridification beliefs, Confucian thought supported the modernisation of the country which included juridification and centralisation of government as a way of bettering the country's operation. Lao-Tsû, as the legend suggests, sends himself into exile as a response to these unhappy changes that were taking place. The *Tao Tê Ching* was written on the borders after what we may call today a migration border officer asked Lao-Tsû to write his thoughts for the future; or as the poet has the border official saying:

> Write it down. Dictate it to your boy there.
> Once you've gone, who can we find out from?[48]

As a result of this request we have a written record of one of the most important books on Taoist philosophy. The *Tao Tê Ching* is written in poetic form and is concerned with providing advice to ruling kings on the art of government. Its 81 verses are divided into two parts: verses 1–37 (the 'Way') and verses 38–81 (the 'Virtue'). The 'Way' refers to all 'reality' before coming into existence or being. As such 'reality' is presented as being undifferentiated. If we are to attempt to undertake the crude act of translating this nutshell account of the 'Way' into Western philosophical thought we can perhaps say that it may be adjacent to the

44 Lao-Tsû, *Tao Tê Ching* (trans. Robert Hendricks) (New York: The Modern Library 1993).
45 P. Marshall, *Demanding the Impossible: A History of Anarchism* (London: Fontana, 1993) 54.
46 Brecht, 'Legend' 314.
47 ibid.
48 ibid 315.

metaphysical impetus to keep word and deed inseparable. While the 'Way' presents us with an undifferentiated cosmos, the 'Virtue' explains how this undifferentiated energy exists in everything created. At times the 'Virtue' refers to a sense of morality.[49] Nevertheless, despite Lao-Tsû's preference for the unwritten, the *Tao Tê Ching* gets written because of an encounter that he had with the law or, more precisely, with a customs officer, at the borders of China. Unlike our previous story, however, what we are about to find out about law and life does not come about due to interpellation but rather through a command. As Walter Benjamin informs us, for Brecht it was not so much the encounter with the law or the 'command' of the law that intrigued him in this encounter (and in Taoism more generally), but rather the attribute and operation of friendliness in this cosmology.[50] And as he elaborates: '[i]t might be untrue to say that friendliness is the actual content of the book *Tao Tê Ching* but it would be entirely true to say that, according to the legend, without the spirit of friendliness the book would never have been handed to us'.[51] Before we proceed to unpack how Benjamin explains the operation of 'friendliness' and its contribution in the writing of this book, which was written in seven days, let us have a look at how the customs officer, or at least how Brecht imagines the customs officer, is commanded by Lao-Tsû to memorialise his teachings:

> 'What valuables have you to declare there?'
> And the boy leading the ox explained: 'The old man taught.'
> Nothing at all, in short.
>
> Then the man, in cheerful disposition
> Asked again: 'How did he make out, pray?'
> Said the boy: 'He learnt how quite soft water, by attrition
> Over the years will grind strong rocks away.
> In other words, that hardness must lose the day.'[52]

Why are these verses significant in understanding how friendliness unfolds? Both Benjamin and the commentary on Brecht's poems in *Bertolt Brecht: Poems 1913–56* point out that the kernel of the poem lies in Brecht's appreciation of verses 43 and 78 of the *Tao Tê Ching*. These verses talk explicitly about the ability of softness, associated in the book with water, to transform hard surfaces. As the *Tao Tê Ching* is written as advice to those that govern, the metaphoric use of these materials, water and rock, and the ability of the former to transform the latter carries in it a lesson: rulers should govern as if they are not governing. Hendricks explains: 'The ideal ruler works to make it possible that all his people will grow to maturity in good health and will feel free to be who or what by nature they are, yet he claims

49 R. Hendricks, 'Preface' in Lao-Tsû, *Tao Tê Ching* xxiii.
50 W. Benjamin, 'Commentaries on Poems by Brecht' in *Understanding Brecht* (trans. A. Bostock) (London, New York: Verso, 1998) 43–74, 72.
51 ibid 72–73.
52 Brecht, 'Legend' 314–15.

no credit for all that he does'.[53] The idea of friendliness is not apparent in these verses; nevertheless, what they demonstrate is that the art of government includes a certain sensibility that requires an appreciation of simplicity and a practice of letting things be or become as they wish to. Friendliness is an attitude to life. In a variety of Brecht's writings, as Benjamin points out, friendliness manifests itself in a series of gestures that do not tie either the one that gives or the one that receives to any formality. They just take place. And moreover these gestures: '. . . are to be found at the hardest moments of existence: at birth, at the first step into life and at the last one, which leads out of life'.[54] Friendliness, like water, may take away the hardness of life. And the request by the customs official is made politely but firmly after he hears that the old man was able to fend for himself effortlessly, like the way the water makes hard surfaces or stone erode. And while this request was made with some self-interest it was also wrapped in a desire for the thoughts of Lao-Tsû to be left behind for future generations.[55] In the custom officer's request or command, Lao-Tsû recognises a friendliness and he responds in kind. But his friendliness, or the friendliness that the poem unfolds, is not unqualified.

Benjamin suggests that the poem exposes three facets of friendliness: (i) 'friendliness is not dispensed without forethought'[56] (the customs official deserved an answer because he asked politely, modestly and not only for his sake but also for the sake of future generations); (ii) 'friendliness does not consist of doing small things casually but of doing the very greatest things as though they were the smallest'[57] (this specifically refers to the delay by seven days that Lao-Tsû has to make to his journey to fulfil a friendly request); and (iii) 'friendliness does not abolish the distance between human beings but brings the distance to life'.[58] When Lao-Tsû finishes his writing he leaves without looking back.

What do we learn then from this encounter about law and life? Here the law, or the customs official as the law, reveals himself in his capacity beyond the form of law. His question, which appears as a command, is expressed softly, cordially, filled with desire and thirst for knowledge. His gestures do not serve the austerity of authority nor do they remain within the realm of what his position commands (searching people that pass through borders), but rather reveal if anything the unnecessary use of the grammar of officialdom. Lao-Tsû had nothing to declare or, if he had something, it was a declaration of who he was and what he did in his life. The grammar of officialdom, we may say, cannot cope with such confession.

53 Hendricks, 'Preface' xxvi.
54 Benjamin, 'Commentaries' 74.
55 Note that it was only after the boy tells the man about the water's ability to grind rocks down, to transform with its persistence the hardest surfaces, that the request comes. We may also say that Brecht's poem is in some respects his way of telling us that to govern we may not need to hold tight to form.
56 Benjamin, 'Commentaries' 72–73.
57 ibid 73.
58 ibid.

And it is at this point, this breaking point, that the officer becomes friendly. And in so doing, he gets Lao-Tsû to write his body, his story, his thoughts; to write the way to exile. But this happens precisely because we experience at the border the transformation of an apparatus into a man. Like the water, the thoughts of Lao-Tsû transform the border official. And, if we learn something from this, it is that the road out of law takes patience (after all, Lao-Tsû takes seven days to pass the border), persistence and some obedience, which comes out of friendliness – the friendliness that Lao-Tsû taught and the friendliness that the official showed. Life may perhaps fail to be captured by the formality of law, through friendliness.

The compositor

In our final story that brings us 'before the law', we have as a protagonist, Pierre-Joseph Proudhon, the father of anarchism. Proudhon was born in 1809 and died in 1865. He was an autodidact and a self-styled anarchist[59] and a political thinker who is well known for politicising anarchism, poverty and social inequality through writings that thrived on paradoxical statements. His first widely-received essay, 'What is Property?' (1840), has coined the phrase 'property is theft', an example of his paradoxical way of thinking. He was an avid writer and during his short life (he was only 56 when he died) he wrote 40 books, 14 volumes of correspondence and 11 notebooks. Proudhon's work stresses the economic struggle as the primary struggle of freedom, with the political following. The exchange that I refer to below is found in Daniel Guérin's *No Gods, No Masters: An Anthology of Anarchism*,[60] which Guérin informs us is from the 'Lettres à l'Academie de Besançon' (1837).[61]

As one can see even from this early correspondence, a correspondence that precedes the revolutionary Proudhon, his major concern was not with justice or politics but with the economy and, more specifically, with economic inequality. So here is how the story goes. Proudhon arrived in Toulon looking for casual work. There was none. Inspired by the uprisings of workers in Paris he decided to confront the local authorities. He asked to see the mayor, who answered to the name Monsieur Guieu but who Proudhon tells us was 'known as Tripette or Tripatte, a former attorney of law . . .'[62] When he encounters the mayor, Proudhon tells him:

> Here, monsieur . . . this document [his passport] cost me two francs and, following information supplied with regard to me by the police superintendent of my district, along with two known witnesses, it promises me and enjoins the

59 Guérin, *No Gods, No Masters*; Marshall, *Demanding the Impossible*.

60 Guérin, *No Gods, No Masters* 41–44.

61 The French version of this letter is available at http://dwardmac.pitzer.edu/anarchist_archives/proudhon/letters/letters.html (accessed 19 January 2012).

62 Guérin, *No Gods, No Masters* 43.

> civil and military authorities to afford me assistance and protection should the need arise. Now, you will know, Mr Mayor, that I am a printer's compositor, that since Paris, I have been searching for work, without success, and that I am down to the last of my savings. Theft is punished and begging prohibited; not everybody can live off their investments. That leaves work, a guarantee of which, it seems to me, looks like the only thing likely to fulfil the purpose of my passport. Consequently, Mr Mayor, I have come to place myself at your disposal.[63]

To this demand and offer the mayor responded by saying that Proudhon failed to recognise what it meant to be in a possession of a passport. He failed to read it as a warranty for defence or security in case a criminal act against him was committed, and not as an access to employment. Proudhon persisted in his line of questioning:

> Forgive me, Mr Mayor, but in France the law protects everyone, even the guilty whom it cracks down upon. The gendame does not have the right to strike a murderer who stabs him, except in self-defence. If a man is put in prison, the governor cannot seize his effects. The passport, as well as the record book, for I carry both, suggests something more to the working man, or it means nothing at all.[64]

To this persistent questioning, the mayor responded that the only thing he could do is award him 15 centimes per league, and that '[His] powers go no further'.[65] Proudhon pointed out to the Mayor that his solution was no solution at all.[66] If he returned back to his abode he would be still unemployed as there was no work there and it would consequently cost the state money. But he also proceeded to ask his advice about whether there is a particular employment path that would make it more possible for him to find work. To this mayor replied: 'To take yourself off Monseiur'.[67] Proudhon informs us that after this he took to the road for two years, studying the world. And his experiences have proven valuable for his anarchist writings that followed.

Proudhon's encounter with the law is self-explanatory. On the one hand it reveals its semi-openness (I will address your request by both seeing you and sending you away) of the door of law, and on another level it opens a road to a life without the law or more precisely without the need for authorisation (anarchism). But at the same time this biographical note reveals a particular inefficacy or impotency of law, of law's inability to address or provide life-affirming answers to social, or social-economic plies like the question of unemployment. The law or the

63 ibid.
64 ibid.
65 ibid.
66 ibid 44.
67 ibid.

sovereign (in the sense of the decision-maker in each instance) has no mechanisms to do so and, moreover, its solutions (providing money to return back to his town of abode where there is no work, a costly state solution) show us not just that the foundations of law are fantasmatic but perhaps that its role, its functions or operations, are to sustain 'nothing' – sustain the *status quo*. Proudhon's persistent, courageous, even naïve questions to the mayor enable him to take the route of discovery, self- and social-discovery, that would enable him later on to write and propagate his anarchist beliefs and work towards building a better social world.

In the end

What happens when we find ourselves on the borders of law? Many things can happen. The three stories, produced in different forms, a legend, a poem that is based on a legend and a biographical note, provide us with various avenues in which the law is encountered and bypassed. All three open our eyes paradoxically to the myopia of law and its desire: its failures and limits, and its inability to deal with criminality (in the case of the Mulla Nusraddin), with its desire for a philosophy that tries to provide an outlook that is not ossified by the formality of law (in the case of Lao-Tsû), and its limited ability to address social and economic reality (as in the case of Proudhon). This may have been said over and over again by so many legal scholars and in so many different ways. But what all these writings do not to tell us is that despite the law we go on to live our lives parallel to it. We may encounter some discomfort or delay before reaching our destination but this may not always be a bad thing. The door of law may not be locked forever – it may remain constantly ajar, our companion and a prop to the way. This chapter may not have revealed too much about the law but I hope it has revealed something about life. I hope it has paved some thoughts for how our lives can be lived in parallel with the law and how we may not necessarily capture life completely in the claws of a petrified legal institution. And this can be done in so many ways: with cheekiness (the Mulla Nasruddin), friendliness (Lao-Tsû), or with courageous naïvety (Proudhon), and not only.

Chapter 11

Life beyond law

Questioning a return to origins

Matthew Stone

Introduction

Critical legal theorists typically have a complicated relationship with the law. Often dysfunctional, sometimes painful, it can be a difficult marriage. Whilst such theorists show a persistent and unconditional scepticism and cynicism over the pretensions of law, nevertheless it is the lens through which we think, and usually what we also spend copious time teaching. It is therefore worth questioning whether this relation is one born out of pragmatic necessity or out of a *desire* of law: a law free of failure, miscarriage and exploitation. Are we critics because we hate law or because we love it? This is not something I will attempt to answer, but it points us towards an important issue for critical legal theory, especially in the present context in which the methods and subjects of legal critique have greatly furcated and multiplied since the CLS of 30 years ago. It is a matter that addresses the questions we ask and the answers we seek. What, if anything, do we want from law?

Proceeding from this question, this chapter is mindful of the continuing adoption of continental philosophy in interdisciplinary legal studies. This in turn is arguably distinct from the work proliferated in the 1990s, when figures such as Foucault and Derrida were read as deconstructing, decentring, and perhaps even delegitimating law.[1] On the contrary, we now see a move away from the textual and the discursive towards much more overtly philosophical, and frequently political, questions.

Critical legal theory was commonly thought of as adopting a technique of taking law outside the privileged territory of jurisprudence, exposing the thinking

1 The example of Foucault is a particularly good one. Whilst in the 1990s Foucault was interpreted as dismissing the place of law in his power/knowledge work (see A. Hunt and G. Wickham, *Foucault and Law: Towards a Sociology of Law as Governance* (London: Pluto Press, 1994)), it has been argued more recently – and probably quite rightly – that Foucault's *oeuvre* in fact accommodates a notion of law threaded throughout his many analyses (B. Golder and P. Fitzpatrick, *Foucault's Law* (Abingdon: Routledge, 2009)). Similarly, even Derrida has recently been the subject of a much more philosophical approach to law in Jacques de Ville's *Jacques Derrida: Law as Absolute Hospitality* (London: Routledge, 2011).

of law to other disciplines, thus moving away from the question of fundamental legal essence and into a multiplicity of new enquiries on the presence and production of legality outside of the law's institutional form. But it may be possible that we are also now seeing a converse position, in that theory is being mobilised in a return to central questions of law and law's origin, soul or guiding spirit.

It is therefore necessary to ask what it means to be critical when we return to such questions. With what is probably a rather cavalier disregard for the obvious pitfalls of reductive categorisation, I tentatively suggest there are principally two critical methods available here. The first is to focus critique deep in the theoretical heart of law. Giorgio Agamben provides us with a good example of this strategy, arguing that the very structure of modern sovereignty – and therefore the configuration of modern legality – is predicated on the constitutive exclusion of depoliticised or 'bare' life.[2] This is, then, a critical theory of law in that it shows how the very legitimacy of law, that which makes law *law*, depends upon the legal disenfranchisement, the non-legality, of embodied *Homo Sacers*, those who have been reduced to bare life. The basis of what we recognise as law is thus revealed to be inextricably political and indeterminate. Thus, we see the arrival of quintessentially critical legal themes within a work of political philosophy.

The second method operates in a different fashion, arguing that for all the failings of our real, tangible laws, there is still some underlying Law-with-a-capital-L to which we can aspire. This law – however intangibly it might be theorised – may then serve as a plumb line by which the actually existent laws of case and statute can be critiqued. A more familiarly critical way of adopting this second method is exemplified by some thinkers gathered loosely around an enquiry into the 'law of the law'. Gilbert Leung, in this very volume, enquires into an originary law of freedom, for instance. Further afield, Golder and Fitzpatrick have investigated the manner in which the law of modernity has sought to ground itself once detached from natural or theological foundations. Following Foucault, they are able to critique the law's attempt to moor itself to the truths of the human sciences through disciplinary and biopolitical practices. Developing Foucault's notion of critical ontology (an approach predicated on the rupture and transgression of the limits imposed upon beings) the authors trace a law of the law based on the 'very contestation of [the law's] determinate position'.[3] This refers to the responsive character of law, its capacity to underpin our sociality without being founded upon a static structure of meaning. Golder and Fitzpatrick thus address the question of law's foundation to theorise the radical possibility of a law that is detached from God and the rational logic of truth or consensus. Their project is one that turns to the question of foundation to ask of the nature of law in the space opened by their

2 G. Agamben, *Homo Sacer: Sovereign Power and Bare Life* (Pittsburgh: Stanford University Press, 1998).
3 Golder and Fitzpatrick, *Foucault's Law* 110.

critique of modern juridical practices. In this manner they retain a vigorous critical method in their tracing of 'Foucault's law'.

The above examples are presented as productively critical methods of adopting an overtly philosophical approach to central questions of law. There is, however, another direction in which this form of enquiry into law's foundations can manifest, which moves towards the idea of the investment of a direct *authority* in a higher or deeper law. It is this type of approach, which will be delineated in greater detail below, that is the subject of this chapter. The principal concern is that in theorising a privileged space as some kind of intangible origin of laws, we are in some instances potentially witnessing a turn to a new form of natural law theory which risks the subordination of critical capacities to an imperative to delineate law's underlying normative essence. This would not entail the assertion of some rational or religious dogma to underlie the expression of laws but might for example be based upon a model of ethics or justice. Of course, theorists who tread close to this method might disagree; for instance, Jacques de Ville's recent article in which he wrote of a 'higher law' articulated in Heidegger and Derrida's reading of the Anaximander fragment. This higher law, we are told, is the transcendent source of both positive *and* natural law,[4] the latter differentiated by what de Ville argues is its dependence upon a form of Platonism.[5] Indeed, it is important to emphasise that I am not trying to claim an equivalence between this way of returning to origins and the persistently buoyant writings in *traditional* natural law circles that still pervade Anglo-American legal theory.[6] Far from seeking to find a 21st century home for Aquinas or Augustine, the method I am seeking to identify typically finds the essence of law in a process of radical differentiation or in otherness, rather than in a static foundation. The nuance of de Ville's higher law claims that it 'precedes the notions of presence and absence' and takes the form of 'unconditional justice, the gift without return, or absolute hospitality'.[7] Yet, in posing this 'law' as the source of all laws, it becomes questionable to maintain its categorical distinction to the outlook of the natural lawyer, if we indulge ourselves by thinking that the latter might exist in more expansive terms than a simple Platonism.

The need for caution in the reserving of a non-legal foundation, or 'higher law' for that matter, as the basis of laws has been amply expressed by others already. Gillian Rose, writing of Levinas, counsels against the diremption of his ethics that would see it separated and elevated away from the hard work of politics.[8] Writing in a more directly legal context, Panu Minkkinen has warned that we risk losing

4 J. de Ville, 'Rethinking the Notion of a "Higher Law": Heidegger and Derrida on the Anaximander Fragment' (2009) 20(1) *Law and Critique* 59, 77.
5 de Ville, 'Rethinking the Notion of a "Higher Law"' 60.
6 eg A. M. González, 'Natural Law as a Limiting Concept: A Reading of Thomas Aquinas' in A. M. González (ed), *Contemporary Perspectives on Natural Law: Natural Law as a Limiting Concept* (Aldershot: Ashgate, 2008) 11–25.
7 de Ville, 'Rethinking the Notion of a "Higher Law"' 77.
8 G. Rose, *The Broken Middle: Out of Our Ancient Society* (Oxford: Blackwell, 1992).

the possibility of critique if we retreat from concrete law, and from the difficult questions of law's possibility and impossibility.[9] The theoretical arc of this approach plots a flight into law's abyssal origin, spirited on by the hope of discovering law's redemptive encounter with ethics, goodness and justice. Having exited a century defined by our enduring attempts to destroy each other in war, proceeding into another which has been so far dominated by violent dogmatisms, hegemonic uncertainty and economic collapse, it is barely surprising that theory turns to demand a more hopeful relation with law. But, to echo the caution expressed by Rose and Minkkinen, it should be asked to what extent these approaches retain a critical apparatus capable of engaging in the political exigencies of our times.

There are two threads to the argument in this chapter. The first (and 'meta-') argument is that we should be cautious, although not dismissive, about this return to the question of law's foundation where the redemptive power of origin is presented as authority. This approach risks addressing the problem of law's failure by replacing law with a more foundational (or natural) law, creating the sort of diremption forewarned by Rose. In arguing that such approaches risk abandoning the theoretical apparatus necessary to engage meaningfully and critically with exigent political problems – such as those posed by the phenomenon of biopolitics – I move to my second point. This is to argue for a way of adopting a critical space that allows for a distance to be taken from law whilst avoiding the problem of diremption. I seek to make this argument with a specific claim about the anti-biopolitical potential available in a reading of the philosophy of Emmanuel Levinas.

The essence of law

I have so far only tentatively hinted at the approach that I suggest seeks the redemption of law by reinvesting authority in themes such as ethics and justice. I dwell upon a specific example in greater detail in this section, which is Oren Ben-Dor's *Thinking About Law*.[10] This recent monograph is a lengthy exposition of the place of law in the philosophy of Martin Heidegger or, perhaps more accurately, a Heideggerian approach to thinking law. Its selection for more focused attention in this chapter is also influenced by the sustained critique it makes of the present state of critical legal scholarship (although in fairness, it is important to note that the ferocity of Ben-Dor's stance may have been tempered in more recent comments[11]). As will be seen, Ben-Dor's position is that established trends of legal critique are erroneous or, at the very least, devalued in that their methods lack a critical depth that he argues can only be attained by entering into fundamental ontology.

9 P. Minkkinen, 'Right Things: On the Question of Being and Law' (1996) 7(1) *Law and Critique* 65.
10 O. Ben-Dor, *Thinking About Law in Silence With Heidegger* (Oxford: Hart, 2007).
11 O. Ben-Dor, 'Introduction: Standing Before the Gates of the Law?' in Oren Ben-Dor (ed), *Law and Art: Justice, Ethics and Aesthetics* (Abingdon: Routledge, 2011) 1–29 at 3.

Ben-Dor wishes to explicate to us how to think about law, and extols the importance of thinking the *being* of law specifically. It is here that the attack on critical legal studies is located: dominant modes of legal critique are at fault for failing to think the being of law because they situate their critical method at the ontic, rather than ontological, level.[12] (For those unfamiliar with this terminology, the ontic refers to the existence of things, whereas the ontological concerns the being of things. An ontic mode of understanding is therefore limited to understanding what exists, but to ask what it *is* means asking of its being, and is ontological. The distinction also entails that the ontic is limited to the terrain of the visible, as it concerns existent entities, whereas the ontological, which addresses the being of these entities, is necessarily concealed.)

Like others, Ben-Dor is interested in the law's origin. Following Heidegger, when he poses the imperative to 'think back to the origin of law',[13] this origin he speaks of is not literally historical, but ontological. It is the 'primordial saying of law which is before all other sayings'.[14] If the basic Heideggerian concept of *Dasein* is of a (human) entity that 'understands itself in its own being',[15] Ben-Dor's project is to bring law into the analysis of *Dasein*. To this end he makes the argument that *Dasein* is 'spoken' by law in its thinking about law, and that '[t]he Being of law is an aspect of that which is innermost essential to *Dasein*'.[16] In other words, law is an irrefutable component of the relationship between Dasein and its being in the world.

Turning back to the question of origin, the nuance of this inquiry allows Ben-Dor to make a crucial and perhaps, at first sight, provocative claim that '[t]he essence of law is not legal'.[17] By this, he is arguing that law's 'essence' lies in its mysterious unfolding rather than our more accustomed notion of essence as a graspable and predetermined structure of meaning. The 'legal' should be understood as the ontic level of laws and legal concepts, where legal subjects and their potentially culpable actions are understood by their correspondence to preset legal ideas. It is from here that Ben-Dor can move to make claims about alterity and ethics, questioning the way in which ethical duties might purport to found legal relations at the deeper ontological level. He attacks theories of ethics that prescribe responses to 'others', which he identifies in a polemically critical reading of Emmanuel Levinas.[18] Such theories, he claims, anticipate the

12 Ben-Dor, *Thinking About Law* 88.
13 ibid 83.
14 ibid.
15 M. Heidegger, *Being and Time* (trans. J. Macquarrie and E. Robinson) (Oxford: Blackwell, 1962) 32.
16 Ben-Dor, *Thinking About Law* 92.
17 ibid 119.
18 The argument goes as far as to claim that Levinas's philosophy has inflicted 'immeasurable' harm upon humanity (ibid. 287). It has already been noted elsewhere that Ben-Dor does not adopt the sort of charitable reading of Levinas that he claims we should extend to Heidegger (L. Wolcher, Review of *Thinking About Law in Silence With Heidegger* (2009) 72(6) *Modern Law Review* 1035 at 1043).

encounter with the other, as well as the ethical response of the subject, and therefore emplace ethics within the realm of the ontic. In this sense, a legal theory that aims to critique law with reference to a predetermined ethical norm is simply asking for one ontical position to be replaced with another. It is for this reason that Ben-Dor argues that critical legal theory is rarely critical enough, the gravest offenders being those supposedly 'dominant'[19] analyses of Levinas (although those working in the area of law and psychoanalysis are also singled out for attack[20]). Indeed, with a turn of phrase that coincides with the title of this collection, Ben-Dor's critique of Levinasian critical legal thinking is that it is 'merely critical *legal* thinking',[21] the italics signalling the pejorative context.

The essence of law is nevertheless articulated in an ethics that Ben-Dor locates not in a response to the distant other, but in the ontological unconcealment of the mysterious near. The alterity of the other is determined not by its separation but rather by its 'strange togetherness',[22] and this ontological closeness is constitutive of a more sincere ethics. 'Ethics is letting oneself be claimed by being together with other *Daseins*.'[23]

There are different ways of interpreting the normative thrust of Ben-Dor's argument. On one level, there is a very clear imperative: we need to be silent. The errant chatter of (critical) legal theory leads us away from the fundamental question of law's being, and it is only in poetic silence that (law's) being can speak. Silence does not connote the absence of speech. Rather, to be silent is to refrain from stepping immediately into pre-given representations, and instead 'listening before articulating'[24] and reflecting on the irruptive saying of language that allows us to approach the being of law.

A further dimension of normativity is somewhat more overt. If critical legal thinking is defective when it fails to transcend the level of the ontic, then the ontological and its expression in an ethics of togetherness may serve as the catalyst for genuine critique (or at least, the means by which critique can be judged). Yet the conclusion to which this route leads is an eerie affirmation of the undeclinable command of law. This is perhaps no more stark than when Ben-Dor writes: '[t]o this essence [of law] that comes straight from Being, *Dasein* owes an absolute and unconditional obedience and authority'.[25] What we see here presented in the most explicit terms is the marriage of law's non-legal foundation with authority. The question thus becomes not merely of the being of law, but also the law of being.

19 Ben-Dor, *Thinking About Law* 30.
20 ibid 108–114.
21 ibid 285.
22 ibid 335.
23 ibid 334.
24 ibid 360.
25 ibid 162.

This is reasonable in the sense that law itself is arguably a structure of command. But one must be careful to recognise that it is not merely law that is being attached to authority, but also law's origin – which, as Ben-Dor is at pains to point out, is not itself law. When, in this manner, the non-legal essence or origin of law is posited as authority, we find ourselves veering towards the natural law territory outlined above, notwithstanding the considerable nuance of Ben-Dor's precise analysis of Heidegger. Remembering that Ben-Dor's argument develops an attack on critical legal scholarship, it is worth reflecting briefly on why the critical community has so far neglected this sort of deep meditation on law's being. Reaffirming the supremacy of law and our correlative duty of obedience, may, on its own terms, be philosophically sound, but it would represent a departure from the commonly understood objectives of critical legal thinking. For many scholars in this discipline (maybe those whose marriage to law cannot be rekindled with a renewal of vows), the point is not to divine a higher law but to delegitimate and attack law in its entwinement with ideology and dominance. With this in mind, one might be reminded of an anecdote of Gillian Rose's. She questioned why, at an academic talk proclaiming the mass disempowerment effectuated by the anaesthetising effect of the popular media, the audience cheered rapturously.[26] Her answer was that this dystopian prognosis legitimated a desire for an absolute alternative, a boundless and just political community. By returning to the question of law and in doing so surrendering to an ontology of togetherness, are we not similarly entertaining a trope that legitimates our disengagement from the work of politics?

Ben-Dor's critique of critical legal thinking is instantiated in the greatest detail in his claim that Levinasian ethics have become dominant in conceptualising the origin of law. Whether this extent of pervasion is accurate or not, one can indeed find examples of this form of argumentation that Levinas's insight for law is the way that law, and specifically legal adjudication, should strive to meet the impossible demand of doing justice to multiple others.[27] But it would be a mistake to believe that this is a representative or exhaustive account of how such a model of ethics can inform a critical engagement with law. On the contrary, I would like to argue, with a response to Ben-Dor's argument, that Levinas's philosophy presents us with a trajectory of critique free from reliance upon a reversion to the question of origins. For instance some, myself included, have focused on the way that Levinas's ethics describe not the foundational guiding star of law, but the mechanism internal to the resistant political subject capable of challenging the prevailing legal and political arrangement.[28] In other words, Levinas need not lead us back

26 G. Rose, *Mourning Becomes the Law: Philosophy and Representation* (Cambridge: Cambridge University Press, 1996) 36.

27 eg D. Manderson, *Proximity, Levinas and the Soul of Law* (London: McGill-Queen's University Press, 2006).

28 eg S. Critchley, *Infinitely Demanding: Ethics of Commitment, Politics of Resistance* (London: Verso, 2007); M. Stone, 'Levinas and Political Subjectivity in an Age of Global Biopower' (2010) 6(1) *Law, Culture and the Humanities* 105.

to the centre in a search for origin and ground, but may provide a theoretical space in which critique and resistance can be thought outside and against law. In pushing on my argument about the role of theory in returning to the question of law, I want to focus on a specific issue, namely that of biopolitics. It is my claim that the problematic of biopolitics, which is exemplary of the sort of political exigency that critical legal thinking must tackle, cannot be addressed adequately by this return to the question of law's origin.

Excursus on biopolitics

Biopolitics is a curiously indeterminate concept, given its ubiquity. To provide a concise summary of theoretical positionings, and beginning with Foucault's version, biopolitics figures in a particular historical configuration, namely in the way that power has changed since the incorporation of the monolithic sovereign. It should barely be necessary to rehearse his argument, which holds that the sovereign's protective power to kill its own subjects or outsiders has been supplemented first by disciplinary and then biopolitical mechanisms.[29] Discipline is addressed to the individual, and looks backwards, seeking where possible to correct the subject in accordance with a particular normativity. Biopolitics is addressed to society as a whole, and looks forward, seeking to minimise risk with reference to statistics, projections, plans etc.

Given the following gained by Agamben in the legal academy over the past decade, a similarly concise restatement of his work will be sufficient. In purporting somewhat boldly to 'correct' or 'complete' Foucault's thesis,[30] and rather than arguing that sovereignty has been supplemented with new forms of power, Agamben argues that there is a biopolitical kernel in the very structure of sovereignty itself. This is the way in which sovereignty is predicated on the distinction between bare life (*zoe*) and political life (*bios*). As mentioned briefly at this chapter's beginning, sovereignty maintains itself by a process of differentiation between the internal political life and the constitutively excluded bare life. The more polemical aspect of Agamben's argument is found in the claim that this distinction is increasingly suspended. Rather than finding particular identities to be *Homo Sacer*, Agamben argues that the rendering of bare life is open to be applied to all people.[31] Thus, what unites Foucault and Agamben from a legal perspective is the way they conceive of norms (and here norms should be understood as encompassing, but not limited to, law) colonising life.

29 See for example *The Will to Knowledge: The History of Sexuality Vol 1* (London: Penguin 1998); *'Society Must be Defended': Lectures at the Collège de France 1975–76* (London: Penguin 2004); *Security, Territory, Population: Lectures at the Collège de France 1977–1978* (Basingstoke: Palgrave Macmillan, 2007).

30 Agamben, *Homo Sacer* 9.

31 ibid especially ch 7.

Since the establishment of these two authoritative voices, there has also been a growing attention towards the work of Roberto Esposito, the translations of whose writings are slowly emerging in English. He recognises the risk of biopolitics becoming 'not only the instrument but also the object of a bitter philosophical and political fight'.[32] Esposito's project is an important one: to help avert theories of biopolitics descending into a detached scholastic battle between Foucault and Agamben, or even worse an unquestioning acceptance of one to the exclusion of the other, and to help us understand the unifying motivations and insights of these theories. To illustrate, he seeks to address perceived weaknesses in Foucault's position. Specifically, there is an unresolved antinomy in Foucault's method in respect of biopolitics' relation with modernity. On the one hand, one could adopt a 'continuist' interpretation, finding that a genocidal trajectory is woven into the very fabric of modernity. On the other, there is the discontinuist position, which finds biopolitics to be necessarily weaker than Foucault seems to want us to believe, in that it would mean life is always capable of resisting.[33] If Foucault's weakness is an underdeveloped concept of life's relation with the political, which holds him back from negotiating this aporia, then Esposito seeks to address this with the concept of immunity. Biopolitics is an expression of the way that modern society follows a logic of immunisation. The weaving of 'immunarity' from the individual body into the social and the political can be traced back to the institution of the sovereign: individuals' immune tendencies to see them attack each other as a means of self-preservation, but as this also attacks the community as a whole, the immune reaction is incorporated into the sovereign. In this sense, the constancy or contingency of biopolitics is not at issue, as biopolitics can be understood as a manifestation of the modern paradigm of immunarity.

If a pertinent challenge of critical legal theory is to expose the manner in which legality permeates life, and does so in a way that its politics is hidden behind a false veil of necessity or truth, then the critique of biopolitics by legal scholars becomes paramount. If we are to take seriously the points being made in biopolitical debates, we have to recognise the claim that it is not enough to return to the question of untainted legal origins, to divine the ethical and pre-legal origin of law. What biopolitics reveals is the manner in which it is increasingly difficult to understand law in any useful capacity except in its connection to power. I would question the adequacy of holding that critique is flawed if it fails to adopt a political enquiry into the nature of law beyond politics. To take seriously the insights of Foucault, Agamben and Esposito, notwithstanding their differences, is to reveal the necessity of thinking law in its *fundamental* complicity with disciplinary and biopolitical practices.

32 R. Esposito, *Bios: Biopolitics and Philosophy* (trans. Timothy Campbell) (Minneapolis: University of Minnesota Press, 2008) 14.

33 Esposito, *Bios* 43.

Resistance and ethics

The final part of this chapter will illustrate how Levinas's ethics, rather than reifying some ethical foundation of law, can be applied to theorise a mode of resistance to law's connection with biopolitical practices. This section holds no ambition to resolve the theoretical differences between Heidegger and Levinas. Attempting to reconcile two philosophical positions whose separation can be traced back at least to the time of Parmenides is, mercifully, beyond the scope of this chapter.

Levinas's philosophy is born out of a dissatisfaction with Heidegger, but it would be a mistake to assume that the two had precisely the same understanding of basic notions such as being. As I will argue, it is from Levinas's alternative engagement with the question of being, and the complicity of ontology with power, that we receive a philosophical apparatus capable of engaging with law's entanglement with biopolitics, an apparatus that I argue is not made available in the same way if one persists with a return to the authority of the non-legal origin of law. Ultimately, Levinas's depiction of subjectivity caught in a traumatic struggle between imprisonment and emancipation will explain that ethics, justice and compassion need not be pursued in the guise of an originary law, but instead in modes of resistance. Levinas allows us to think a form of fractured escape from law. As will be argued, this is not an escape of diremption that takes one outside of the work and demands of politics. It is an escape that opens up a site of critique, but one which never fully detaches itself from legality.

The significance of Levinas in this context has already been signalled, albeit without full exploration. Slavoj Zizek, hardly Levinas's most sympathetic reader, describes the latter's work as 'radically antibiopolitical'[34] in the manner in which it attempts to transcend a philosophical meditation on life. The same point has been made by Esposito, who suggests that a logic of immunarity is traced by Levinas in his critique of identity and enclosure.[35] But there remains little written directly and substantially on the relation between Levinas, law and the concept of biopolitics, the latter having gained much greater momentum only after his death in 1995.

If the problem traced in this chapter so far has been the adoption of ontology as the base of authority, it is helpful to proceed now by looking at how Levinas thought of being. In his early works *On Escape*,[36] *Existence and Existents*[37] and *Time and the Other*,[38] written in the 1930s and 1940s, Levinas is manifestly engaged in a critical dialogue with Heidegger, characterising being as burdensome and imprisoning. The simple being of the world, bare existence itself, is what he calls

34 S. Zizek, 'Neighbors and Other Monsters: A Plea for Ethical Violence' in S. Zizek, E. L. Santer and K. Reinhard (eds), *The Neighbor: Three Inquiries in Political Theology* (London: University of Chicago Press, 2005) 134–90 at 149.

35 Esposito, *Bios* 141.

36 E. Levinas, *On Escape* (Stanford: Stanford University Press, 2003).

37 E. Levinas, *Existence and Existents* (Pittsburgh: Duquesne University Press, 2001).

38 E. Levinas, *Time and the Other* (Pittsburgh: Duquesne University Press, 1987).

the 'there is' [*il y a*] or 'being in general'.[39] Whilst those who have continued to extend Heidegger's project, such as Jean-Luc Nancy, have pursued the nexus between ontology and community with claims such as '[t]he co-implication of existing is the sharing of the world',[40] Levinas thought that being thrown into a worldly situation of being guarantees nothing so utopian:

> Being is essentially alien and strikes against us. We undergo its suffering embrace like the night, but it does not respond to us. There is pain in being.[41]

Being is a burden for Levinas. It provokes the very opposite of inspiration, motivation and vitality, and weighs upon every being as if it presents an obligation articulated in curiously legal terms: 'in weariness existence is like the remainder of a commitment to exist, with all the seriousness and harshness of an unrevocable contract'.[42] Already Levinas desires resistance against the authoritative capacity of being.

For Levinas, identity and freedom are not found in ontology nor in the rejection of ontology, but in a desire to escape from it. The realm of ontology is impersonal and anonymous, invading and submerging experience, and is like the lonely reign of the night that dominates the insomniac.[43] When submitted to the reign of general being, or the 'there is', there can be no drawing in of a subject being for itself. There is no absolute escape from being; one is 'without the possibility of withdrawing into sleep as into a private domain'.[44] The denial of identity that is effectuated by being is characterised negatively by Levinas, in contrast with the togetherness of *Mitsein*, or being-with, in Heidegger. Being provokes fear, a fear of unindividuated anonymity, a fear delivered by a bond where one is touched but not addressed. It is a fear of being swamped in and swallowed by being itself – swallowed by togetherness – whereby there would be nothing left of oneself, one's irreconcilable alterity.

For Levinas, there is therefore something oppressive about the prioritisation of being. He did not accept the idea that an underlying togetherness of being was an adequate means of understanding alterity. His is a philosophy predicated not on a deep, Parmenidean oneness, but on difference. As such one can understand his claim that an ethical response to radical otherness is a kind of 'first philosophy', occurring prior to ontology. Thus, whilst law may be influenced or steered by ethics, his work evinces a deep cynicism over the capacity of ontologies to sublate difference into togetherness, other into same, people into law.[45]

39 Levinas, *Existence and Existents* 52.
40 J.-L. Nancy, *Being Singular Plural* (Stanford: Stanford University Press, 2000) 29.
41 Levinas, *Existence and Existents* 9.
42 ibid 12.
43 ibid 52.
44 Levinas, *Time and the Other* 49.
45 E. Levinas, *Otherwise than Being or Beyond Essence* (Pittsburgh: Duquesne University Press, 1998) especially 162–65.

In contrast to those that wish to use Levinas to pose a different, ethical foundation to law, I believe that he is better read as a critic of law's entwinement with ontology. In this context one should understand the law to be more than a proscriptive code of rules but also a fabric of meaning that allows us to make sense of ourselves, others and the world around us. If a return to legal origins resembles an attempt to study a natural law of being, then Levinas can be understood as providing a much more radical theoretical apparatus with which this approach can be critiqued. What he reveals is the way that the ontological character of legal authority – irrespective of whether its ontic content is benevolent or malign – has a capacity for the dominance over life. The more we recognise what could be termed 'legal ontology', law's move away from proscriptive code and towards biopolitical regulation, the more one can see with the help of Levinas the pitfalls of this return to origin, and a need for a means of understanding law on the basis of resistance rather than obedience.

Levinas's idea of subjectivity is posited in an 'ethical' predisposition to transgress the order of being, which is achieved through an analysis of time and language. If subjectivity is something other than the articulation of an ontology, and if time itself should be meaningful, there must be a dimension of language that does not defer to a sedimented and temporally synchronous structure of meaning (what Levinas calls the 'said'), and which instead articulates diachronic time in the form of a 'saying'.[46] It is in this saying that the subject responds to its originary, constituent relation with what is beyond the order of being and command of law.

It might be asked at this point whether the subject is thus dissolved into nothingness or, perhaps even more terrifyingly, elevated above the terrain of law into an implausible seat of holiness and righteousness. This is a question Levinas turns to in *Otherwise than Being*. Western philosophy, he argues, is characterised by its exposition of consciousness as 'self-possession' and 'sovereignty'.[47] Even the fundamental ontology of Heidegger, which addresses the concealed, encircles the 'thematic exposition of being'[48] despite its imperative not to grasp and to know absolutely. If one's subjectivity is constituted by the other – or to put it another way, if one exists through the other – then it is understandable that Levinas would call this relation 'substitution'. One is 'substituted' for the other, because it is through the other that one's subjectivity is lived. In this sense, 'identity is inverted'.[49] Substitution denotes the manner in which the subject finds itself *in* the other, in the torsion and trauma of being structured as the other in the same. As Levinas puts it in a particularly (and rarely) succinct passage, '[i]n substitution my being that belongs to me and not to another is undone, and it is through this substitution that I am not "another", but me'.[50] Therefore, Levinas adduces a seemingly paradoxical

46 ibid 45–48.
47 ibid 99.
48 ibid.
49 ibid 115.
50 ibid 127.

idea of subjectivity whereby the traditional characteristics of the individual (autonomy, self-grounding, sovereignty) are affirmed, but only as artificial constructs that are founded not on the self, nor an intangible yet unifying concept of being, but instead founded on the substitutive relation with the other. Levinas therefore allows us to think about our subjective relation with the law in a manner that does not posit a law of being or of ethics, yet simultaneously bequeaths a space in which the subject can be theorised in a mode of necessary resistance.

Ethics, immunity and allergy

The biopolitical paradigm sees the attempt to correlate life with norm. We should therefore be dissatisfied with an authoritative ontology of law as a means of engaging with biopolitics. It is precisely the turn to the 'is' that enables the biopolitical project, in its conflation of norms with facts, politics with science, and ultimately power with knowledge. One should not forget the considerable nuance of Heidegger's own philosophy, and the crucial difference between his fundamental ontology and the basic ontology defined as a mere study of being. Yet we might heed Levinas's lack of surprise that such a philosophy could be instrumentalised by National Socialists in events that would become the apogee of biopolitics in the 20th century.[51] A legal ontology not only fails to provide a domain of resistance against law, but its placing into proximity of law and the authority of being opens it to the gravest risk of abuse.

Turning back to Esposito, it can be recalled that the biopolitical process of normalisation takes effect through practices of what he describes as immunarity. For example, in the legal context we can understand, at a local level, the attempts made to correct or expunge criminal deviance and, at an international level, the claims to legitimacy of pre-emptive wars wrought in the name of preventing terrorist attacks. But predating Esposito's writing on immunity and contagion, as well as Derrida's on the autoimmune, Levinas was explicating a concept of the allergic as early as 1961. To illustrate the centrality of these themes to his work, Levinas described nothing less than the entire thrust of *Totality and Infinity* to be the explication of the 'non-allergic' relation with alterity.[52] With the idea of allergy, Levinas revisits a metaphor of illness he began when using the notion of nausea. Whereas nausea marks the visceral malaise in the lonely contemplation of being as one's centre of gravity,[53] allergy refers to the reaction against an other whose alterity has become contorted. Allergy is, of course, a type of autoimmune reaction, whereby the attempt of the body to protect itself against alien matter comes to form an attack on the body itself. For Levinas this form of allergy arises when the relation with the other becomes mediated through an understanding of

51 E. Levinas, 'As If Consenting to Horror' (1989) 15(2) *Critical Inquiry* 485.
52 E. Levinas, *Totality and Infinity: An Essay on Exteriority* (Pittsburgh: Duquesne University Press, 1969) 47.
53 Levinas, *On Escape* 68.

being (perhaps for our purposes, through a law of being). It is through this process that we see the supreme biopolitical danger: the way in which otherness becomes ontologised as otherness, turning into otherness itself, such that difference can take on the form of degeneracy.[54]

Transposing this bio-logic from the corporeal body to the social body, a standard reading of social contract theory might hold that allergy is the natural state of war, where individuals' instinct for survival renders greater risk and uncertainty for the social as a whole.[55] It would then be the erection of the state and the institution of law that purports to cure allergy, allowing for the mediation of individual drives. Levinas would invert this reading. For him, the human condition in its pre-legal, pre-state and pre-ontological format is a state of peace. It is in the institution of shared meanings, of ontology, rules and laws, that the possibility of war emerges. For it is only then that alterity can be reduced to sameness, and that ontological violence can be wrought. As Levinas himself put it, '[w]ar presupposes peace, the antecedent and non-allergic presence of the Other'.[56] Allergy arises at the ontological level, in the flux of beings in search of their being. Peculiarly, Levinas would agree that there is togetherness in this state of war: not a togetherness of finality or unity, but a togetherness of egos pitted against each other.[57]

Earlier in this chapter I explained how Levinas's idea of the subject arises out of the inadequacy of being, and the subject's constitutive desire to be otherwise. Having now considered how Levinas's entire philosophy can be regarded as an attack on allergy, it is apparent that this may be harnessed as a deep critique of the complicity of authority and existence, and the reduction of the 'ought' to the 'is', which underlie the mechanics of contemporary biopolitics. The Levinasian subject that I have traced in the latter half of this chapter is predicated on an impossible demand to escape law, not to divine the authority of a purer law in the guise of ethics or being. In this sense, the subject does not merely enjoy a critical distance from the law, but operates *as* the critique of law: the ethical subject in its relation to law is the critical subject. In this manner, Levinas offers a method whose critique is based not on a philosophical enquiry into law's essence, but on the identification of a space in which life can be shown to flourish beyond, or perhaps against, the law. Just like the critics' dysfunctional marriage to the law, this is a resistance that will never escape legality; and what is more, it is all the better for it.

54 It is worth noting here the clear parallels with Foucault's analysis of biologised difference in *'Society Must be Defended'* op cit.

55 Cf Esposito's reading of the relation between immunarity and theories of the social contract in *Bios*, eg at 58.

56 Levinas, *Totality and Infinity* 199.

57 Levinas, *Otherwise than Being* 4.

Chapter 12

Notes for a novella of the future

Oscar Guardiola-Rivera

Introduction: critique and Latin American philosophy

Born in Argentina but settled in Mexico after the military placed a bomb in his house, the life and work of Enrique Dussel exemplifies the emancipatory, cosmopolitan and experimentalist spirit of Latin American philosophy. From its origins in the convergence between the critique of imperialism inaugurated by Bartolomé de Las Casas and the realism of the resistant practices of pre-Columbian indigenous peoples in the 16th century, Latin American thought has placed the situation of subordinated peoples in the emergent world system of modernity at the centre of its reflections.

Latin American philosophy seeks to go beyond the situation of subordinated and dehumanized peoples, and to engage in the creation and recreation of the world in reality and imagination. The modern world system, its past, present and future, has been from the outset the spatial and temporal basis of Latin American philosophy's analysis and critique. Its subject matter has been the encounter between Europeans and non-Western peoples, as the former plundered their way into history and accumulated potency through the dispossession of the latter.

Latin American critique focuses on the effects that the accumulation of potency on the one side, and dispossession or impotentiality on the other, have on the relationship between history and the writing or narrativization of history. The tale according to which there are two sorts of peoples, those who are exposed to the horizon of accumulation and enjoy the privilege of living historically, on the one hand, and those who are not, on the other, exemplifies the kind of narrative that is the focus of Latin American philosophy's critique. This specific form of critique points out how the tale of the two sorts is repeated in a varied number of contexts and disciplines even though it belongs to no context or discipline in particular (it moves from philosophical geography to modern law and development economics; and from Francisco de Vitoria to Adam Smith, Immanuel Kant, Hegel and contemporary accounts of law and development). To sum up, Latin American critique unveils the operation of a generic measure of value across historical contexts and epistemic disciplines; it denounces such a generic measure of value as contrary to the priority of truthfulness and the right of peoples to create their own means of intellect and make history. Moreover, Latin American philosophy identifies the functioning of a discursive element that seems unchanging amidst the flux and chaos of modern history and epistemology with the operation and effects of money, the ultimate accumulation fetish, the totem that breaks all taboos, which makes everything possible for man but his self-creation.

Money decrees the horizon of the possible, insofar as it gives to the one who possesses it the power to acquire everything he or she desires. In that sense it is the law of the law and the only right that cannot be suspended (the right to acquire), which makes all other human rights a de facto sub-set of the right of capital. But in the process money as capital destroys the very possibility of the possible, in the sense that the drive to accumulate reduces the range of what is to what can be (ie the object of desire); as if actuality emerges exclusively from potentiality, chance or probability. But what is possible in reality is much more than what is given at any point in time or available to the desiring subject; there is the improbable, for instance, truth or the unknown, the gift, and the whole range of objects beyond human desire – which are infinite. Put otherwise, the range of what is includes what cannot-be, for actuality emerges also from impotentiality. More simply, reality comprises not just what is available here and now but the process of self-creation, which Dussel calls 'life' in order to emphasize that it is a mode of the infinite. This raises the following question: what is life conceived of in the mode of impotentiality and the infinite?

Although Dussel does not answer this question directly, we can use his work in alliance with other southern voices such as Frantz Fanon or Boaventura de Sousa Santos, and even some strands of American Pragmatism, and Hegelianism in order to pave the way towards an answer. Thus, for instance, southern critical voices put forward an analogy between life in the mode of impotentiality and the "mindless bodies" of the enslaved and the colonized, or their persistent situation of subordination and the invisibility of their ways and knowledge. In my work, I have proposed there is more than an analogy between the operation of money as capital *vis-à-vis* the future (including future generations and the sustainability of the planet) and the destruction of such futures. Conversely, what is needed from critique is a model of construction in the age of greed and wreckage. While European criticism seems stuck between the models of destruction and subtraction (or 'negative dialectics') and considers that everything else would be near-magical synthesis or liberal compromise, I argue Latin American critique and other southern voices provide a model for the work of salvage and montage in their engagement with the operations of money as fetish. Money-as-fetish, or 'money that begets money' de-realises the future; for in making everything that is desirable available to the one who has money, it makes reciprocity – the bond between two or more people, the future and the planet – irrelevant. Pre-columbian societies, like most so-called 'traditional' societies, were organised around a principle or a maxim of reciprocity. In accordance with this maxim, everything that exists does so as a gift; time and space are themselves donated to humans and therefore are priceless.

They cannot be acquired or accumulated, at least not without fundamentally undermining the integrity and orientation of human beings who engage with the planet and the future in their process of self-creation in time and space, historically.

Put another way, the condition for that process to continue is that there is space and there is time; that there is a future. This abstract condition becomes concrete in the set of relations that connect present generations with their ancestors or with the planet as such, and in the set of obligations that exist *vis-à-vis* future generations. That so-called 'Western' societies have such a difficulty responding to their obligations with the young and with future generations, or the planet as such, as is becoming increasingly clear nowadays to the youth of Europe, is evidence of the problematic tension that exists between the right to acquire and right (what is right: the priority of truthfulness over acquired truth and the right to exist and to create a future). The current situation of the youth in places like Europe, the Middle East, Chile or the US, which is the result of the present articulation between global political and economic structures, also reveals a tension between the power of the particularity of he or she who has money to acquire everything he or she desires and the universality of history as collective creation and self-creation. This is precisely what has been captured so succinctly and correctly in the slogan used by Occupy movements all over the globe: 'we are the 99 per cent', in contrast with the 1 per cent that controls the vastness of economic and political resources in our money-centred world. Crucially, the right invoked here is not predicated of actually existing beings and their object-subject relations (which is why it must be distinguished from "rights" in general and "human rights" in particular). Rather, it refers to action that emerges from impotentiality, to the acts of those who live in the mode of impotentiality, poverty, invisibility or inexistence. We're better off speaking of "post-human rights" (ie future generations, the planet) and of relations that do not belong to the set of subjects and available objects.

The set of relations and obligations referred to above, which do not belong to the set of relations between potent acquiring subjects and the objects available to them, has been described by anthropologists and other observers of societies where money plays a marginal role as operating under the 'Principle of Gift-giving'. It is in accordance with such a principle that one can accurately describe the whole of culture and knowledge as a commons that cannot be appropriated (without fundamentally undermining the process of culture's self-creation) because of its prior orientation towards truthfulness and the rights of future generations and the planet as such. Socrates exemplified that principle in antiquity, for instance, when he offered his poverty as evidence of innocence before the Athenian tribunal that decided upon the accusation of corruption made against him in 390 BC. Seventeenth century Peruvian indigenous critic Waman Puma de Ayala developed his arguments against colonization in the 1615 *New Chronicle and Good Government* on the basis of such a principle. And UN High Commissioner for Human Rights Navi Pillay appeals to a similar principle when she says that "for the UN, health care, education, housing, and the fair administration of justice are not commodities for sale to the few, but rather rights to which all are entitled without discrimination.[1]

That their societies based upon such a principle were under threat of extinction became quite clear to those who witnessed the rise of world money between the 15th and the 18th centuries, as I have explained in my book *What If Latin America Ruled the World?* (Bloomsbury, 2010), when silver and gold flowed from Spanish America to Europe and from there to the rest of the world. For they saw that the condition for the ascent of money in Europe was the sacrifice of human life in the mines and the plantations everywhere else. Then, and only then, when silver and gold became acceptable as the embodiment of mutual trust and confidence all over the world thanks to the quality, amount and continuous production of the mines of Mexico and Peru, money abandoned its marginal position and came to occupy the central standpoint that has become so familiar to us moderns, and it is from such a high position, from such aloofness and abstraction, that it can subsume all other aspects of social life. And yet, this does not mean that money has the final word. It may be true that money talks, as we say colloqually, but it does not have the last word. It belongs to humanity, which from the standpoint of the future, can always pass judgment upon the current situation and suspend the dehumanisation of mankind.

This means that the future of mankind is not secured (it cannot be presumed as a matter of necessity; rather, contingency reigns) but also, that it is the nature of that contingency that needs to be considered. For it is divided into two, just as humanity itself appears divided into two (for instance, as the '99 per cent' and the '1 per cent'). On the one hand, contingency appears confused with chance, risk, uncertainty and all the other probabilistic avatars of choice and acquisition. On the other hand, contingency appears in the form of gift and gift-giving, what emerges and is created and around which we gather as a community and imagine the when and how of communism.

Enrique Dussel's liberation philosophy receives and transforms this legacy, amplifying Latin American philosophy's preoccupation with subordination and the concrete situation of the modern world system. While western political philosophy (and its side-projects, legal theory and economic theory) has been mostly concerned with the faculty of judgment – that is to say, with reason and its limits, chief among them historical finitude – Latin American philosophy has experimented with the generative powers of imagination and prosopoetic acts: the when and how of communism, liberation, the act of reading, love, and reciprocity, all of which bring nothingness into being. If you prefer to borrow the language of mathematics, the matter of Latin American philosophy is a conjecture (what

1 N. Pillay *The Tunis Imperative: Human Rights in Development Cooperation in the Wake of the Arab Spring. Statement by Ms. Navanethem Pillay United Nations High Commissioner for Human Rights to the United Nations Chief Executives Board*, Fall Session, 2011, New York, 28 October 2011, available at http://rconline.undg.org/wp-content/uploads/2011/11/HC_Statement_to_the_CEB_Final_Format_1.pdf

if . . .?) but one that has to do with the definition of what is priceless or infinite and cannot be appropriated, for it belongs to the general economy of reciprocal relations (as opposed to non-reciprocity of property and money-based relations).

Because of this, although hitherto ignored by the mainstream of Western philosophy, Latin American thought, amplified and illustrated in the work of Dussel, could contribute to the revitalisation of some crucial tenets of the critical tradition.

It is thus possible to understand his work as revolving around two questions: 'what is war?' and 'what is money?' It could also be argued that the force of his writings and teachings (I tend to enjoy his live performance and conversation as much, if not more, than his vast compositions – comprising memoir, history, theology and philosophy) comes from what is perhaps the most creative and indefatigable political impulse of human beings: the principle of hope. In exploring this in its many forms, Dussel joins the tradition of mystical nomads such as Ernst Bloch and Walter Benjamin. He recovers for the purposes of modern criticism the older legacies of las Casas and Waman Puma de Ayala, and links these with the language and experimentalism of the Latin American magical realism of the 1970s. This is the tradition of storytelling on an epic scale, not only because of its size and ambition but, most important of all, because it emphasises the creation of a new world in which what Bloch called 'the anticipatory element' functions as a technology guaranteeing its eventual – or as Dussel would say, kairotic – realisation.

Dussel engineers new concepts rather than discovering them. He bequeaths us hopeful images of the past, the present and the future. The tales of hope amidst generalised hopelessness often sound epic, in the sense of the ancient sagas and cosmologies. They evoke a distant time of a García Marquezian Macondo, in an effort to push philosophical imagination and political practice to their outmost limits of improbability: towards 'a poetry of the future'.[2] It is in that spirit that I engage in the following narrativization, which focuses on the question of multiple political subjectivity and the positive capacities of impotentiality, or the 'political power of the people', to use Dusselian parlance. This philosophical narrative takes the form of a series of notes for a novella of the future, but in the specific situation of a promised (empathetic) global community held back by the sort of fetishism that the excessive nature of money and the rise of the conquering ego have introduced into modern society.

Plunder as historical and narrative motif

Let's imagine a future in which historians conclude that what appeared to humanity as the history of liberal institutions, laws and the 'free market', was in fact an invasion from the future 'by an artificial intelligent space that must assemble itself

2 A. Merrifield, *Magical Marxism* (London: Pluto Press, 2011) 10; K. Marx, *The Eighteenth Brumaire of Louis Bonaparte* (Rockville, Maryland: Wildside Press, 1963) 18.

entirely from its enemy's resources'.[3] Our future historians would say that in so far as money communicated addiction, capital propagated virally 'replicating itself through host organisms whose boundaries it breached and whose desires it reprogramed'.[4] Each one of us, as subjects of will,[5] would be designated as 'host organisms' of this virus. Capital, considered as an invading digital virus from the future, would replicate itself through us, collectively, by tapping into our innermost desires and reprogramming them. Put otherwise, in our times money is not simply an object of accumulation but a force that although created by men reacts back upon them impacting the most fundamental levels: those of intelligence and will. It took language away from intelligence and left in its stead a pictorial world of images and spectacle; and it turned the will to live into will to will, the sort of flat desire that is incarnated in money and referred to when it is said the 'money begets money' ad infinitum.

Money is an agent of replication, the communicating agent of addiction. It is desire incarnate. Another way to put this would be to say that in our time money is 'the flesh' or the sublime substance that the various rituals surrounding the monarch's particular physiology attempted to shape and manage in the pre-modern past.[6] It follows that moneyed bodies, potentially each one of us, have come to be divided into a political body (the incarnation of fundamental will that Dussel speaks of) and an infinitely desiring body (the incarnation of the will to will, to have and consume that Dussel does not speak of, but which foreshadows his thesis of the fetishisation of power in our time). I see any worthy meditation on politics today ultimately as a consideration of the fundamental dilemma confronting 'the people's two bodies'.[7]

The stakes of modern political philosophy are related not only to the transition from royal to popular sovereignty which follows the cycle of 18th and 19th century revolutions in Europe and the Americas, which can be grasped by following the transformation from the political theology of royal sovereignty into the bio-political pressures of popular sovereignty, as Eric Santner observes. The stakes of modern political philosophy are also closely tied to the transition from cosmological debt to state and private debt. In cosmological debt, we were all subject to an obligation to reciprocate each other and living nature for the gift of time and space bequeathed to us equally and gratuitously (either as cosmic gift or divine grace). Individual and collective will were shaped by the injunction that life should continue and to continue in life. In this way, will was understood as linking up the past/present with the future. Accordingly, individual and collective actions were

3 N. Land, 'Machinic Desire' (1993) 7(3) *Textual Practice* 471–82 at 478. Also in *Fanged Noumena: Collected Writings 1987–2007* (Falmouth:, Urbanomic, 2011).

4 Land, 'Machinic Desire' 479.

5 E. Dussel's 'political community' in *Política de la Liberación Vol II* (Trotta, 2009) 13.

6 E. Santner, *The Royal Remains* (Chicago: University of Chicago Press, 2011) ix–x.

7 ibid xi–xii and Dussel, *Política de la Liberación Vol II* at 48; the latter distinguishing between will-to-live and its perverse side or will-to-power.

forward-looking: a politics of life (inventing and reinventing life, or constitutive). Concretely speaking, action and *praxis* took place in common and its object/result was 'the commons' (memory and common space). However, with state and individual debt no such imperative of mutual recognition shapes our most mainstream interactions. Instead recognition coexists with and is marginalised by the demand of constant enjoyment, mimicry and envy which is introduced by the power of money. This acts as a universal leveller and translator, with each and every single one of us assuming the dignity of a prince. Our will becomes the will of the prince, individually distributed through a covenant, as in the case of the Hobbesian 'state by institution' (giving origin to parlamentarian or representative democracy) or imposed, as in the case of the 'state by acquisition', also described by Hobbes.[8] In both cases, as Hobbes points out, will is constituted (in the sense of being represented or substituted). Collective and individual action would then become backward-looking, geared towards the maintenance of what has been constituted.

To be more precise, the pressures that shape our modern will, incarnated in our moneyed bodies (turn between wants and desires, sympathy and envy, abundance and scarcity) pertain not only to questions concerning the foundation of political authority 'but more generally to those concerning the patterns and procedures whereby human beings come to be vested with the authority of the various 'offices' they occupy and the ways in which such (. . .) transferences of symbolic authority, are ultimately legitimated'.[9] In this situation, capital, standing in the place of God as ultimate sovereign and universal equivalent, impacts upon us as some sort of normative injunction to want more, to accumulate more and to be frugal, in contrast to other sorts of people who lack symbolic authority – the damned, who are prodigal and hence unable to contemplate a horizon of accumulation and live historically.

Correspondingly, the domain of magic and religious life, previously associated with notions of cosmic gift, original guilt and dignity based on reciprocal recognition, is contracted into what eventually becomes the 'private life' of citizens, while the reach of religious meanings and values expands into the sphere of political and economic life. This double movement of contraction and expansion may seem contradictory. The contradiction is dispelled once we realise that, although in modernity religious practices seem confined to the domestic realm, in fact it is money which alienates humanity and comes to occupy the place left empty by religion. Put otherwise, it is not the case that religious meanings dissapear from modern society but rather they are displaced by monetary meanings.

But there is something else at stake in this historical transformation, and not only the onset of secular modernity. Two different conceptions of history and contingency, of end times, and of how to respond to signs of societal crisis or

8 T. Hobbes, *Leviathan* (Harmondsworth: Penguin, 1968) 223 ff.
9 Santner, *The Royal Remains* xii.

catastrophe mark the distinction between the public life of the gift-giving community and the private realm of the citizen consumer. Strictly speaking, this is a contrast between two cosmologies and their respective symbolic forms.

The key point is that cosmology in general and Christian cosmology and its theologico-political symbolic form in particular, is vigorously involved with the act of giving. More precisely, the object of all cosmologies is time (and by implication all that is in time) as a gift. In that sense, the theme of our discussion is that of the ethical and political consequences of the act of giving.

In Christian theology, the measure (that is, the value) of this act 'is determined by the emphatic limit of the act of giving in the sense of the Divine which is Revelation, or the epistemological Gift'.[10] And what is specific to Christian revelation – the epistemological gift contained in the symbolism of the Bible and natural law, which include the laws of nations as understood by Renaissance Europe – is that it 'abstains from excess and ceases to be radical in itself and in the act of donation'.[11]

I would add to Reza Negarestani's observation about the significance of the act of donation in European Christendom, that it makes sense not in the abstract but in the specific context of a Europe responding to the emerging centrality of money and finance (debt, credit etc). To say that the act of gift-giving 'ceases to be radical' means that, unlike what happened in so-called 'traditional' societies, money has ceased to be marginal or secondary to other forms of trust and solidarity in this specific society. Rather, money becomes so central that it instals itself in the hearts of European conquerors to the point where, as Columbus put it, 'its owner is master of all he desires' (quoted in Guardiola-Rivera 2010: 54). It 'abstains from excess' in the sense that it satisfies the needs of man; it becomes, as Admiral Columbus said, the key to paradise.

In contrast, for the way of life of, say, Amerindians, the gift is radical because it is exorbitant (in the sense that time as well as nature and its resources are outside the cycle of exchangeability); it cannot be paid back or counter-balanced, and it is external to satisfaction insofar as it cannot be reduced to a particular content or measure of value. Put simply, time/nature is priceless. To speak of 'end times', catastrophe, historical rupture, revolution or apocalypse from this perspective is to stress the pricelessness of time and of all that was given to man; it is not a 'when', but rather, the event that attests to the immensity of the ultimate act of giving. The point is this: that as a matter of essence, the ultimate gift cannot be appropriated.

If the gift of the gods (or God) were to satisfy man, or position itself as exchangeable, it would put man on an equal footing with God (or the gods); it would make man (some men, as German philosopher Ludwig Feuerbach put it)

10 R. Negarestani, 'Apocalypse in the Wake of Refractory Impossibility' in *Collapse. Philosophical Research and Development Vol II* (Falmouth: Urbanomics, 2007) 296.
11 ibid.

gods to themselves and to others. And this would bring human being to extinction, to an existential inferno (Frantz Fanon's 'zone of non-being' inhabited by the slave, the poor and the colonised), epistemological decadence, farcical violence and ontological eradication. I have argued elsewhere that Amerindians understood this all too well; in fact, they experienced it. And they use this knowledge nowadays, the result of the exercise of a cognitive and imaginative faculty of reading disasters as signs, in order to mobilise themselves collectively as a political subject, as happened for instance during the 2000 Water Wars in Bolivia.

More generally, this contraction of the public life of the gift-giving community into the private life of the citizen-consumer, which was at the same time an expansion of the religious into politics and economics can be observed in the operation of two crucial institutions: the political-legal state of exception and the unending drive to consume. Neither the state of exception (understood as the virtual state of war) nor unending consumption (the clash of each man against another and of all against all) were cases of a conflict 'between weapons or fists' but one driven by imitation or mimicry: 'there are presentations, manifestations, signs', exchanged as in a theater of representations, or 'a sort of unending diplomacy between rivals that are naturally equal'.[12]

In both cases, the community of reciprocal recognition was superseded by a society of *doppelgänger* that admire and envy one another in equal measure. Such a society would have to immunise itself against the potential escalation inherent in the virtual war of all against all brought about by the leveling power of money. And this, as both Thomas Hobbes and Adam Smith recognised, was the origin of the demonic *doppelgänger* that the former called the 'Leviathan'. In the case of Leviathan, 'the means of self-preservation, of individual and communal immunisation themselves become infected with their own drive of self-preservation and begin, in the manner of compulsive *doppelgänger*, to attack the life at issue'.[13]

This is precisely what Dussel theorises as the 'fetishisation of power' – the prosthetic extension of nature into a political technology that acquires a life of its own and strikes back at the will to live of the community through the institution of a social contract or imposition and acquisition. This is sovereignty as forced choice.[14] What Dussel does not acknowledge is that the fetishism of power has as one of its most decisive conditions of possibility the emergence of world-money as general equivalent. But he is in good company here: neither Hobbes, Foucault, Habermas nor any of the theorists of governmentality and instrumental reason, have acknowledged the deep relation that exists between the state of unending warfare (exception) and incessant, insatiable consumption (enjoyment, accumulation, innovation).

12 Foucault, *'Society Must Be Defended: Lectures at the Collège de France 1975–76'* (London: Penguin Books, 2004) 92.

13 Santner, *The Royal Remains* 15 (*à propos* of Esposito) and E. Santner, *On Creaturely Life* (Chicago:University of Chicago Press, 2008) 52–53.

14 Santner, *The Royal Remains* 17.

If they had noticed this relationship and considered it in terms of the formation of the will of the modern subject, they would have stumbled upon two crucial insights: first, that the question of will-formation and subjectivity in modernity is inseparable from the event of discovery and conquest. The clash, on the one hand, between the conquerors' dream of redemption in gold, blood and gift-giving communities (especially in the Americas after the 15th century) and, on the other, the realisation by conquering societies of the existence of communities organised without a single point of accumulation or unending consumption. The second insight is that the consequences of this encounter would take the form of catastrophe on one side, and something quite close to psychosis on the other. I mean the real prospect of world destruction, on the side of the Amerindians, and the delusions of world destruction on the side of European money-based societies.

The madness of modern politics

We must come to terms with the fact that our (modern) subjectivity has very little to do with the citizen *qua* rational consumer dreamt of by John Stuart Mill and others. *Homo economicus* – the idealised agent always behaving with rational self-interest – would turn out to be not just misinformed or irrational at times but actually always already bonkers. Of course, in this respect our hypothetical historians of the future would be discovering something that sales and advertising people – as well as a few economists and psychologists – have known pretty well since the 1950s. This is something that so-called 'traditional societies' had recognised long ago and made the basis of their collective organisations and political institutions: that when it comes to money, we are more than a little bit crazy. We are plain mad. This is so because money, having the capacity to substitute all substitutes, may actually take the shape of whatever it substitutes. This means it can become the measure of all things. It also means money quantification can be profoundly arbitrary. Money, to put a spin on the well known definition proposed by historian Niall Ferguson, is desire incarnate.[15] This is to say that money-measure (as price) has nothing to do with the nature of the object of desire (the product) and everything to do with the representations we exchange (the signs, emphatic expressions). It has everything to do with the wiles and deceitful expressions we communicate to one another in order to provoke a certain reaction from one another. Put another way, 'we are in a theatre where presentations are exchanged', in a relationship of mutual and simultaneous envy and admiration in which there are no limits. This is the realm of reciprocal or mimetic action.[16]

Money as the price system that emerged in post-renaissance Europe allowed for complete indifferentiation, or at least insufficient differences. Because money appears endowed with boundless powers of acquisition. Discreetly and efficiently,

15 N. Ferguson, *The Ascent of Money* (Harmondsworth: Penguin, 2009).
16 Foucault, *'Society Must Be Defended'* 91; see also Girard, *Sobre Clausewitz* (2010) 36.

these powers can acquire and transform anything, turning all values upside down. What makes money attractive is not so much the yearning to accumulate, as the idea that it could be converted into all sorts of things depending on want or desire. Money's unlimited capacity to convert or substitute creates a feeling of possibility and offers an unlimited array of choices. But also, for the same reason, money acquires a sort of dangerous magic: it is capable of buying what ought not be sold. In *What If Latin America Ruled the World?* I call this feeling, and the image of boundless possibility that accompanies it, 'the dream of the conquerors'. We must remember that colonisers such as Francisco Pizarro were not just soldiers and adventurers; they were also financiers and entrepreneurs. In the vision of the city of gold and the mountain of silver, they saw the opportunity of escaping from the strict hierarchies that organised post-medieval monarchical European society. This is why their idea of the Americas approximated a utopian vision that combined the wonders of the ancient world with the promises of a return to paradise: this would be a land of opportunity, where one could start anew because its untold riches would allow for the absenting of all 'natural' differences. As they say, money is the big equaliser.

In this the European monarch confronted its 'first death', the threat posed by money to undo its dignity, which from then onwards could be bought and redistributed among all those who had the property to do so. The conquistadors of New Spain and New Granada in the 15th and 16th centuries, the *bourgeois* merchants and gentrified landowners who cut off the head of the king in the English revolution of the 17th century and the *bourgeois* French revolutionaries of the 18th century would each establish the artifice of the sovereign ruler who thereby becomes their representative or substitute. Their relationship would from then on be one of substitution, and therefore one that fundamentally relocates the space of the sacrificial (the religious) in society and re-enacts it (in the death/life of the king and the executive decision over the state of exception). But equally important (and much less noticed) is the fact that European monarchy faced a 'second death' in the hands of those who took the recent discovery of communities without sovereign in the Americas as proof that subjection (to the monarch and to divine law) was unnatural and could be or should be done away with. This started of course with the Amerindians, who responded to the threat of cultural catastrophe and annihilation with ideas and practices of rebellion and liberation that aimed at relocating in the modern situation the age-old distinction between the priceless and what can be bought and sold. It is from within this response that the very term 'fetish' arose as a critical weapon. Hence the possibility of the accusation of 'fetishism' as a critique of Dussel's two senses of power: as a denunciation of the forced choice of sovereignty, and as a critique of the excessive nature/power of money.

Dussel's second sense of power points out that the disruptive force of non-difference that money brings into society also introduces a virtual state of unending warfare within it. The same principle that explains the arbitrariness of the price system operates also in the calculus of probabilities and the exchange of representations that Thomas Hobbes (whom I have alluded to before) considered characteristic of what he called 'the state of war' in his Leviathan. He correctly observed that the absence of natural differences was the element in which the war of every man against every man took place.[17] And, as he pointed out, this was the situation that the state (the juridical-political apparatus) would attempt to push back into prehistory and into its margins. But he never seemed to make the link between the state of war brought about by the absence of differences (which creates uncertainties, risks, hazards, and therefore the will to fight on both sides) and the disrupting/levelling power of money.

What our historians of the future would discover is precisely the continuous operation of that force in our historical, civic, societies. They would point out that 'the dream of the conquerors' sharply contrasted with the suspicion that the use of metal as desire incarnate generated among so-called traditional societies (the ones Hobbes thought would be consigned to pre-history after the emergence of the state). That suspicion was nearly universal among such societies; they actively sought to contain the use of metal as the existing and active concept of value, or condemned it as an irredeemable perversion of otherwise perfectly normal commercial relations. Instead, they dreamt of a world in which time and space were gifts from nature to man and therefore invaluable, posing strict limits to the realm of prices. This fundamental difference would be captured in political apparatuses without a centre of accumulation (which early Spanish chroniclers in the Americas called *behetrías*) and in tributary systems through ritualised warfare and sacrifice. In these societies, conflict resolution mechanisms were based upon the idea of a constitutive (cosmic) debt: that time is the cosmic gift *par excellence.* Time would therefore be the principle of the generous (as opposed to the profitable) and obligatory exchange, since all receive it for free. Whoever uses what he has thus received in order to draw profit from it is guilty of unforgivable abuse. It would be unthinkable for the gift relationship to be transformed into a commercial relationship.

In contrast, from the moment profit is present, there is a temporal interruption (deferral), because whoever appropriates a gift without returning it thus breaks off an internal movement of circulation. This is the case for all lending with interest or time-deferral (as in the case of insurance). This temporal deferral allows for the appropriation of time. The sovereign would be, precisely, he who decides on the appropriation of time or, as Carl Schmitt put it, on the time of exception. Considering money and consumption as deeply related to the state of exception (the fetishised form of power that is the object of Dussel's criticism) places him on a par with Jacques Lacan's writings on the logic of the signifier, according to which a (master) signifier comes to represent the subject for all other signifiers.

This logic can be grasped as the formalisation of the structure of unending war and sovereignty in Hobbes, in Adam Smith's consideration of the dynamic of

17 Foucault, *'Society Must Be Defended'* 90.

admiration and envy, in Michel Foucault's analyses of governmentality (and neoliberalism), or in Habermas's critique of instrumentalism. In fact it can be traced all the way to their contemporary heirs: Giorgio Agamben, Roberto Esposito, Martin Beck Matustik and Eduardo Mendieta. This is the continent of thought that Enrique Dussel's critique of political reason has opened up for us. It is truly a Macondo of the mind that dares to engage in 'the creation of a new and sweeping utopia of life, where no one will decide for others how to die . . . and where peoples condemned to one hundred years of solitude will have, at last and forever, a second opportunity on earth'.[18]

Historians of the future describe our current legislative arrangements

Our historians of the future would understand that the demand to 'enjoy life' that is so central to our societies is connected with money as an agent of addiction. In so far as money can take the form of all things, it subjects us by demanding of us 'to be real', only that its reality principle appears in the concrete form of the price system. But it is the price system that is the norm and the principle of its suspension. The price system, as we know, emerges from the convergence of mathematical-scientific, monetary quantification, economic implementability and, decisively, methods of forecasting (surveys, mapping, visitation, *conocimiento por cuestionarios*, probability thinking and scenario planning, whose object is chance, risk, probability etc). The convergence between these three operations produces a kind of knowledge of the unknown, built entirely upon the image of journeys of discovery and exploration. This is why, if capitalism turns out to be a conquering virus from the future, which incrementally virtualises everything (it de-metallises money in the direction of credit finance, it de-realises productive force in the direction of speculation) its only possible mode of operation would be time travel.

Put otherwise, capitalism assembles itself by cannibalising the past, tearing it asunder and then using the not-quite-alive pieces in order to give itself a body (not quite a 'living body', but an 'undead' one – like a zombie or Frankenstein's monster) that can operate in the present and reproduce itself into an unending future. Literally, it has to travel back into the past, tear it asunder and then reorganise the pieces under its aegis. At this point you may have realised that my novella of the future, just like every sci-fi dystopia I can think of, resembles some well known narratives of conquest and plunder. If it is true that the production of knowledge of the unknown (as the norm) has as its model the image of the journey of discovery and exploration, then the condition of possibility for the production of that sort of knowledge is the production of an 'other' – a space, a time, a subject or population that is, in some fundamental respect, unknown.

18 G. García Márquez, 'Nobel Lecture' Nobelprize.org. available at http://www.nobelprize.org/nobel_prizes/literature/laureates/1982/marquez-lecture.html (accessed 30 November 2011).

To be fundamentally unknown means, as Kant would put it, to be a 'thing-in-itself', a stone-like object that is in practice inert (in the sense that it is moved by a force external to itself, but cannot move itself). What defines an 'other' as such is the lack of what social scientists call agency. An 'other' is produced both as a lacking object and/or a subject of lack. What does this mean? Notice that in utopian and dystopian narratives of journey and exploration, the result of finding or 'discovery' is never the total eradication of the encountered eco- or belief systems, but rather, a reorganisation or reassemblage in which the systems that do not sufficiently resemble those of the expansive force are marginalised. This is a movement that takes place both in space and time. On the one hand, a 'centre' emerges *vis-à-vis* its margins or 'peripheries'. On the other hand, spatial marginalisation with respect to a centre means also backwardness in time. What follows next is a process of subjectivation, which consists of moving people and things 'from the savage margins to the civilised centres'.[19] Put otherwise, this is integration by conversion. This is precisely how the idea of identifying the margin with the past began to emerge, but also, a certain idea of history as progress specific to post-renaissance Europe. That idea was a response to the need for the consolidation (integration, organisation, unification) of (the manifold of experienced) differences and the integration of an as yet unknown fourth part of the world into European consciousness. It was a solution to a problem of management of information: to turn an objectively unworkable mass of information (a manifold, experienced by the European mind as traumatic, that is, both as threat and promise) into a manageable, unitary source of knowledge. The solution involved judging the unknown and unfamiliar in terms of what was actually familiar and well known.

In accordance with such a criterion, experienced differences could be measured in terms of values, and values in terms of chronological, linear, evolution or ascent. Although it would not be possible for us finite beings to contemplate or experience the totality of the manifold of differences or the totality of possible cases, it would be possible to index all actual and possible cases in terms of the uncertainty of things to come, to survey the future in order to identify and interpret signs of radical variation or difference and contain them. If radical variance can be contained, then it would be possible to expect that the persistence and evolution of what is will continue unimpeded in the future. Evolution is guaranteed. In this respect, the regimes of production of knowledge of the unknown are profoundly historicist, both in the sense that they take stock of our finitude and that they locate themselves within a narrative of evolutionary linear time. But their condition of possibility, although historical, has become contextless. The production of other spaces, times and peoples as fundamentally unknown or perhaps even unknowable operates as the frame within which all narratives of linear evolution unfold.

19 W. Mignolo, *The Darker Side of the Renaissance. Literacy, Territory and Colonization* (Michigan: University of Michigan Press, 1995) 247.

The question of price as norm is not a matter of an unknown quantity, but rather, to quote British philosopher Nick Land once more, a matter 'of a quantity that operates as place-holder for the unknown, introducing the future as an abstract magnitude'.[20] If price is the norm of our times, this is so because it posits itself in the place of the future, or rather in its stead as a substitute for the real future. And it can do this by turning all different futures (actual or possible) into a case of its own present and its iteration in the imagined future, and all presents into a case of its own past. Such different presents and futures become the 'exception' that confirms the norm: the norm of the norm, the law of the law.

I have also said that this was a problem of 'management' of information. This was not metaphorical. It meant that we were not confronting merely an epistemological problem but, as I hope I have made clear, that this was a cognitive problem that emerged together with a practical question: a question of government, the management of the world. The world became a practical problem only after 1492, which is to say that the question of 'how to govern the world' (and the peoples and things of the world) only arose as a problem in the context of conquest and plunder and only from the viewpoint of the agent in need of justification for an act of conquest and plunder. This act would subsequently produce both material and subjective scarcity: extraction and expropriation of resources by force (plunder) and lack of agency on the part of the peoples conquered and plundered (inert consent). Referring to this double whammy (to the capacity for free action, non-marginal or non-dependent activity) Simón Bolívar spoke in his 1815 Letter from Jamaica of the peoples of Spanish America as being in a situation 'even below slavery'. He was actually quoting John Milton's *Samson Agonistes*. In doing so he not only linked up the memory of Amerindian loss and permanent rebellion – the Lascasian spirit – to the memory of the struggles for the commons at the time of the English Civil War. He was also making a case for the illegality of the ruling law by highlighting the fact that the law of that law actually condemned whole parts of the world and its peoples – specifically, the Americas – to a permanent state of exception. They were caught between human and non-human states, in a situation of systematic exposure to that paradoxical domain in which law has been suspended and recourse to naked force been allowed in the name of preserving law (guaranteeing the evolution of what is and so on).

That situation is war, as the only law ruling human relations. It is a war in which the means of war turn into ends in themselves, and in which the only aspiration becomes the reciprocal annihilation of the other (which, following Fanon, Sartre and Foucault I do not hesitate to call 'racial war'). This is an important extension of the Lascasian critique that prefigures the discovery of total and unpredictable hostility, or the mimetic violence operating in the regime of truth (or knowledge production) of Christendom. It is also the basis, in modernity, for a radical discourse and practice of human rights. The first of these rights is the right to revolution in a process of decolonisation, legalised later on as a controversial

20 Land, 'Machinic Desire'.

but crucial (from the viewpoint of the colonised) right to self-determination or autonomy (to use the language of Miltonianism, in which Bolívar is clearly embedded). Moreover, it seems prescient if we reconsider it from the vantage point of the events that would mark 'the long 19th century' of global history, all the way up to the Second World War and the second half of the 20th century.

The derivation of a right to revolution and universal autonomy in the real future, out of an understanding of the present situation as a normalised state of exception – a racial war condemning the victims of history to a station 'even below slavery' – constitutes the basis of the democratic spirit of republican institutions in French, Spanish and, later on, Portuguese America. It is also the source of their strength; strength identified with the universal and anti-historicist nature of the prescription of equality and absolute recognition at the core of French, Spanish and Portuguese American institutions. This raises at least two questions: first, the question of the sort of violence involved in or invoked by the practice of the right to revolution (anti-racial violence, war against slavery, and so on); and, secondly, the question of 'rogue' others: that for all the discussion of 'weak', 'failed' or 'rogue' states out there, our own states 'over here' often come to operate routinely as rogues. Clearly, in that capacity, they threaten us too. The question was summed up in the debates following the fall of the Weimar Republic in the words of Carl Schmitt, channelling the spectre of Thomas Hobbes and thus also that of the English Civil War and the struggle for the commons: '*Protego ergo obligo* is the *cogito ergo sum* of the state'. I protect therefore I obligate.

But what makes Bolívar's 19th century derivation of the right to revolution in the spirit of las Casas truly original, is that from the outset he made it clear that the question or set of questions concerning the basis of political and legal institutions could not be differentiated in the era of the global market, from the issue of planetary evaluation through price and money. This was, as he saw it in the context of the expansion of British trade, the other candidate for a universal prescription. On the one hand, racial war was the means through which the production of the other as a condition of possibility for the management of the unfamiliar future could be accomplished. He saw that war played a fundamental role in the opening of markets and the establishment of terms of trade worldwide, that it would remain a constant whether in the hands of the increasingly triumphant British or in those of up-start Americans. Political liberation would not be complete because the global economy was itself a political venture, an art of government. British capitalism, as Bolívar saw it from Jamaica, was the future, conquering and colonising both the present and the past.

On the other hand, we must ask the question that Bolívar never asked himself but which is implicit in his references to las Casas, the near-extinction of Amerindian culture and the question of the *ergo sum* of French, Spanish and Portuguese Americans. I am not talking about the issue of the 'cultural identity' of Latin America or Latinos, which I consider a red herring. Rather, I am referring to the question of the need of capitalism, already evident in the 19th century, constantly to produce an 'other' (which is not, I repeat, a cultural other) in order to reproduce itself as the arbiter of history and time: to exoticise the Amerindian yesterday or the Latino in the US today and to turn them into 'the enemy', in the process turning our epoch into the time of total hostility and total competition, two phenomena that may not be as separate as we would like to think or, to sum up, our time as a time seemingly void of hope (a time of unending scarcity both material and ideal).

Therefore, we end up with two questions: 'what is war?' and 'what is money?', originating a third: if hope is indispensable for the projects of human flourishing, how is hope, once it has been lost, found? I believe the latter is the sort of question that is specific to Latin America and to Latin American institutions. It goes beyond the law of price (the language of financial capitalism as scientific theodicy) and in the direction of what I would like to call, after Latino philosopher Eduardo Mendieta and post-secular thinker Martin Beck Matustik, redemptive critical theory.

The possibility of redemptive critical theory, arising from a meditation on material scarcity, hinges upon our ability to ask the question 'is there anything priceless?' and to remember (in an act of recognition of the memory of the Amerindian and the African Latin-American) that all cultures throughout time, 'traditional' and not, have sought to separate what is priceless from the sorts of human or social relations that can be subject to the rules of commercial exchange. If this is as close to a universal common (public) value and distinction as you can get, then there may be a correct intuition behind it.

Chapter 13

Towards a radical cosmopolitanism

Gilbert Leung

Introduction

Cosmopolitanism as an expression of human unity is commonly traced back to the noble philosophy of the Ancient Stoics. It is a highly seductive and malleable concept, appealing to both reason and sentiment, which is perhaps why every era since has witnessed its redeployment in one form or another. The decades either side of the second millennium are no exception, with the publication of countless books and articles devoted to the idea. It has been variously understood as a philosophy of moral concern, the political necessity for world citizenship, the inspiration for global democracy, the future of post-national law, an extant sociological fact, and so on. Yet it is not without its critics, with one of the main reservations being the ease with which Stoic-inspired cosmopolitanism is aligned with imperialism through, for instance, the imposition of norms and institutions upon the 'global citizen'.

Given the ethical and political stakes involved, this chapter will begin to explore the possibility of what might provisionally be called a 'radical cosmopolitanism' that does not revolve around a formal logic of human unity. Although, for some, it may seem impossible to conceive of cosmopolitanism fully outside Stoic discourse, it so happens that history provides us with at least one conspicuous opportunity. Long before the Stoics, Diogenes the Kynic (*kyon* [gen. *kynos*] 'dog', whence cynic), a figure associated with an oft-scorned movement of *provocateurs* in Ancient Greece, had already identified himself as *kosmopolitēs*. What could this have meant for a 'buffoon without shame or scientific satyr' and for whom, Nietzsche exhorts, 'the higher man must prick up his ears'?[1] The answer to this question is made all the more difficult because, to paraphrase Hegel, the Kynics had no philosophy worthy of note.[2] Nevertheless, it is this question that will constitute the point of departure.

1 F. Nietzsche, *Beyond Good and Evil* (trans. R. J. Hollingdale) (London: Penguin Books, 2003) 53.
2 G. W. F. Hegel, *Lectures on the History of Philosophy* (trans. E. S. Haldane and F. Simson) (Lincoln: University of Nebraska Press, 1995) 487.

Kynicism as point of departure

Let us first re-emphasise that cosmopolitanism, contrary to popular perception, has at least two possible ancient histories.[3] One we know hails from the Stoics and has been well documented. Although we cannot uncontroversially attribute the beginning of Stoic cosmopolitanism to the Old Greek Stoa, namely Zeno and Chrysippus, a recognisable cosmopolitan line is clearly visible in the later Roman Stoa, from Cicero to Seneca to Marcus Aurelius. In the Middle Ages, Renaissance and Enlightenment it can be further traced through, for example, Dante, Erasmus and Kant respectively; while today it is present in the thinking of Habermas, Nussbaum and Appiah, to name but a few. The particular characteristics of this line are the general acceptance, either explicitly or implicitly, of the idea of a common humanity within a community of mankind and the sharing of normative commitments between its members. Admittedly, such a one-line characterisation is crude and conceals the nuances with which various thinkers have imbued the concept. All the same, it offers a convenient way to identify a specific line of thinking, whether it be Cicero's prioritising of the 'class of duties grounded in human fellowship',[4] Kant's formulation of *ius cosmopoliticum* as 'a universal right of humanity'[5] or Nussbaum's advocacy of a cosmopolitan education to teach us – and particularly US citizens – to be 'citizens of a world of human beings'.[6]

The other cosmopolitanism hails from the Kynics. Standard histories tend to conflate Kynic and Stoic cosmopolitanism, attributing to Diogenes the Kynic the invention of the term cosmopolitanism, while crediting the later Stoics with its philosophical development as a concept of human unity. But Roman Stoicism and Greek Kynicism are very different ways of thinking, and their cosmopolitanisms are also likely to be different. On being asked where he came from, Diogenes is said to have replied: 'I am a citizen of the world [*kosmopolitēs*]'.[7] The problem from an historical point of view is that there is no further textual reference as to what he meant by this, nor is there any subsequent development in the history of ideas as to what a specifically kynical cosmopolitanism might be. In order productively to think this alternative provenance, it is necessary to impute meaning into Diogenes's statement and effectively to reinvent kynical thought for today.

3 G. Leung, "A Critical History of Cosmopolitanism" (2009) 5(3) *Journal of Law, Culture and the Humanities* 370.

4 M. Tullius Cicero, *On Duties* (ed Miriam Tamara Griffin and E. Margaret Atkins) (Cambridge: Cambridge University Press, 1991) 62.

5 I. Kant, *Political Writings* (ed. H. Reiss, trans. H. B. Nisbet) (Cambridge: Cambridge University, Press 1970) 108.

6 M. Nussbaum, 'Patriotism and Cosmopolitanism' in *For Love of Country?* (ed J. Cohen) (Boston: Beacon Press, 2002) 6.

7 Diogenes Laertius, *Lives of Eminent Philosophers* (trans. R. D. Hicks) (Cambridge: Harvard University Press, 1925) 63.

Diogenes fully embraced the appellation Kynic (*Kyon* = Dog) and even introduced himself as such to Alexander the Great. When Alexander asked what he had done to deserve such a name, he replied: 'I fawn on those who give me anything, I yelp at those who refuse, and I set my teeth in rascals'.[8] He saw himself as the kind of dog that all like to praise but with whom no one dared go hunting.[9] He poured scorn on his contemporaries: he called the school of Euclides bilious, Plato's lectures a waste of time and the demagogues the mob's lacqueys.[10] His main weapons were an acerbic wit, biting humour and a fearless exercise of free speech (*parrhesia*), the latter he considered 'the most beautiful thing in the world'.[11] When he saw someone being led away by temple officials for stealing a bowl, he quipped: 'The great thieves are leading away the little thief'.[12] On hearing Plato's definition of man as a featherless biped, Diogenes presented a plucked foul with the words 'Here is Plato's man'.[13] And when Alexander wished to honour him by granting any favour, Diogenes asked him to '[s]tand out of my light'.[14] In sum, kynicism focuses on practice and performance rather than theory, laughter rather than convention and free-spiritedness and risky provocations rather than the disciplinary structures of paradigmatic thought. Kynic references written on the dog's tail – that is to say, in a manner influenced by a kynic heritage – by the first Stoic Zeno were erased from the library at Pergamum by the later Stoic Athenodorus because they were an embarrassment to the school.[15] It comes as no surprise that Cicero openly declared: '[t]he reasoning of the Cynics must be entirely rejected; for it is hostile to a sense of shame, and without that nothing can be upright and nothing honourable'.[16] If it is true that Diogenes was the first to call himself a cosmopolitan, it is quite certain that he did not mean it in the sense later invoked by Cicero when he paraphrased Terrence's famous line: 'I am a human being; I think nothing human alien to me'.[17] Diogenes, by his own admission, was 'Socrates gone mad' and it is unlikely that his cosmopolitanism followed any formal logic of human unity.[18]

Given the social realities of the ancient Greek world, it is also likely that his contemporaries would have thought cosmic citizenship the maddest idea of them all and merely another of his jocular provocations. They would have been right, of course, but perhaps this was precisely the point. As Branham has noted, kynical

8 ibid.
9 ibid 35.
10 ibid 27.
11 ibid 71.
12 ibid 47.
13 ibid 43.
14 ibid 45.
15 M. Schofield, *The Stoic Idea of the City* (Cambridge: Cambridge University Press, 1991) 4.
16 Cicero, *On Duties* 57.
17 ibid 30.
18 Laertius, *Lives of Eminent Philosophers* 55.

humour can act as a philosophical enthymeme that entails the bridging of a logical gap through a movement between alien codes or frames of reference.[19] Through this movement there is a tendency to cross established boundaries, eliciting laughter through thwarting expectations and the presentation of incongruity. Diogenes's world citizenship is underpinned by a tacit premise, namely that a resident of Athens need not be subject to its laws and mores if s/he answers to a higher cosmic law. For Diogenes, it was the Athenian citizen who was the barbarian and not the foreigner at the gates. Diogenes's claim to world citizenship is spiked with impudence and irreverence. Whether one smiles at his cheekiness or scoffs in incredulity, one could say that Diogenes's claim to be a cosmopolitan was more than a mildly humorous quip. It was arguably a political event, the birth of a radically new idea.

In beginning to rethink this political event as a 'postkynical' radical cosmopolitanism, it is first necessary to distinguish it from what some today call 'strong' cosmopolitanism. Strong cosmopolitanism follows the line from the Stoics. It focuses on the principle that each individual is the equal object of moral concern and takes this principle all the way to the end by making a claim for the existence of related duties owed equally to every person, regardless of their closeness in relation, and for such duties to be guaranteed by universal legislation from some form of world government. This is contrasted with 'weak' cosmopolitanism, which also promotes the merit of equal moral worth but without specifying any particular global institutional framework in which it may best be implemented. Moreover, the myriad combinations in-between tend to relate to the challenges the idea poses to the continuing dominance of state-centred sovereignty and imbricated nationalisms. Even if the breaking down of nationalisms and the erosion of state sovereignty through the promotion of cosmopolitan (human) rights is a 'radical' enough project to be going on with for some, this does not equate to a postkynical radical cosmopolitanism, which in principle cannot be based on the idea of human unity or a concomitant idea of rights and duties. To stay true to spirit, it must begin from an irruption of freedom that challenges the normative and cultural constraints of the *polis*.

The law of freedom or Kant with Diogenes

Diogenes put freedom above all else, especially freedom from what he saw as the arbitrary constraints of the *polis*.[20] Yet such an absolute freedom is the most paradoxical of ideas and almost impossible to invoke in theory without being trapped in a web of contradictions. Even at the most elementary level, Diogenes freed himself from the normative constraints of the *polis* but then subjected himself

19 R. Bracht Branham, 'Diogenes' Rhetoric' in *The Cynics* (ed R. Bracht Branham and M.-O. Goulet-Cazé) (Berkeley: University of California Press, 1996) 99.
20 Laertius, *Lives of Eminent Philosophers* 73.

to the cosmic realm, implicitly binding himself to a prototypical form of natural law. Perhaps this is why Diogenes refrained from high theory, resisting the quagmire of linguistifications and preferring instead to materialise freedom in his everyday existence. If this led to scandalous behaviour, so much the better, from Diogenes's point of view.

This difficulty in thinking freedom continues in modernity and can clearly be seen in the work of Immanuel Kant. Kant brought the Enlightenment project of *bourgeois* emancipation to its apex by making freedom the supreme principle, equating it with pure reason and encapsulating it within a unified concept of autonomy (self-legislation). To make moral decisions, to legislate for ourselves, we must be free to do so, otherwise we would be mechanically determined entities subject to the causal laws of nature. Moreover, if there is to be any form of beginning rather than an infinite regression of causes, he reasoned that there needed to be a first cause that was not in itself determined by another cause. This is why he was compelled to assume '*an absolute spontaneity of causes*'.[21] That things could begin on their own, that is to say, independently, became a key factor in his conceptualisation of freedom and the moral law. In order properly to discern the necessity and universality of a specific moral obligation (categorical imperative), practical reason has to be pure, *a priori* reason, independent of material experience. If it were not, it would be contaminated by alien forces or emotional inclinations that would interfere with one's freedom. At this point, paradoxes start to re-emerge: the moral law is determined by a freedom that itself has no cause, which means it becomes a non-determined determination. This is why he deemed it necessary to relate freedom to a causality that accords with immutable laws of a 'special kind'.[22] Perhaps more importantly, the moral law obliges us to use our autonomy to suppress every natural impulse or desire, every sense of affection or movement in sympathy, all for the sake of freedom.[23] Kant starts off by postulating freedom and extracts an immense *pathos* from it, but in the end this freedom is dispensed with entirely. As Adorno has noted, there is nothing left of 'even the miserable freedom to do the wrong thing and behave like an utter swine'.[24]

Despite the paradoxes and risks inherent in any attempt to define freedom, it is possible today to think freedom differently: not as a concept with some predetermined or posited content, but as a concept released from its own signification – in other words, to think the 'sense' of freedom without reserve. Jean-Luc Nancy has contributed one of the most sophisticated analyses in this regard. While acknowledging that Kant's moral law quite justifiably offends many of our

21 I. Kant, *Critique of Pure Reason* (trans. W. S. Pluhar) (Indianapolis: Hackett Publishing Company, 1996) 475.
22 I. Kant, *Groundwork of the Metaphysics of Morals* (trans. M. Gregor) (Cambridge: Cambridge University Press 1997) 52.
23 T. Adorno, *Problems of Moral Philosophy* (trans. R. Livingstone) (Stanford: Stanford University Press 2001) 71.
24 ibid 133.

sensibilities because of its coercive intent, Nancy provocatively suggests that the categorical imperative is nonetheless much nearer to us than we suspect and gives Kant credit for thinking the necessity of freedom's unconditional prescription.[25]

Freedom, for Nancy, is incomprehensible, but this does not mean it is inconceivable. Kant, for instance, conceived its incomprehensibility in terms of a spontaneous causation, implying the existence of a cause without a cause.[26] For Nancy, freedom is neither spontaneous nor causal, neither empty nor full, neither a fixed essence nor an eternal presence. Freedom is 'what of presence comes to presence'.[27] Moreover, in freedom's coming to presence, there is nothing before and nothing at the moment of freedom. Instead, 'freedom consists in not consisting, without contradiction'.[28] Only in this way can it be truly free, that is, free even from itself.

At the same time, Nancy does not underestimate the significance of Kant's unveiling of freedom as the *ratio essendi* of the moral law.[29] For Nancy, this does not mean that freedom founds the law from a position external to it but that freedom is necessary for the realisation of the law insofar as the law cannot be addressed to a subject who is not free. Nature is not free and is therefore not subject to the moral law. Nature cannot do otherwise. But humanity is ostensibly free. We can do otherwise and our freedom to do so implies an inherent capacity for transgression, which in turn implies the existence of a thing to be transgressed. This thing is the moral law, that which is necessarily addressed to us in virtue of our freedom.

There is thus only one categorical imperative, namely to make one's principle of action accord with the form of universal law. Kant inferred from this a number of duties, such as the duty against taking one's own life, the duty against lying to obtain a loan or even the duty not to waste one's life in idle enjoyment like 'South-Sea Islanders'.[30] The latter example, in particular, betrays as much condescension as it does protestant work ethic, lending support to Hegel's criticism that the imperative does not produce a determinate content purely from itself and that such a content is instead presupposed in order for it to be productive.[31]

But what if it is precisely through an infinite lack of content, the absence of any sanction, threat or reward, that the imperative gains its categorical force. According to Nancy, the imperative prescribes nothing but the absolute necessity to make law

25 J.-L. Nancy, *A Finite Thinking* (ed. S. Sparks) (Stanford: Stanford University Press, 2003) 134–35.
26 Kant, *Critique of Pure Reason* 475.
27 J.-L. Nancy, *The Experience of Freedom* (trans. B. McDonald) (Stanford: Stanford University Press, 1993) 172.
28 ibid 81.
29 I. Kant, *Critique of Practical Reason* (trans. W. S. Pluhar) (Indianapolis: Hackett Publishing Company, 2002) 5.
30 Kant, *Groundwork of the Metaphysics of Morals* 31–33.
31 G. W. F. Hegel, *Elements of the Philosophy of Right* (trans H. B. Nisbet) (Cambridge: Cambridge University Press, 1991) 163.

addressed to freedom. The imperative is therefore not the same as a legal regulation since the latter is characterised by a determinate force within a limited jurisdiction.[32] Instead, the imperative is an originary law of freedom whose force haunts the very act of thinking. It does not strictly found humanity, yet one could say, on an ontological level, that it 'destines' being.[33] This means that the law addressed to freedom destines what 'in the individual, is not individual' and what is not strictly individual is one being addressed by the other.[34] In this sense the imperative can be seen as an 'other' law, one whose relation to freedom is both synchronic and asymmetric – law and freedom lie together and in excess of each other. In this way, the law infinitely calls out to infinite freedom, a form of address that has the quality of a correspondence without end. Being is under obligation, not in the sense of a banal moralism or legalism encrusted onto being, but through the 'ethical' deposing of being itself. The ethical here is understood in a Heideggerian sense, where *ethos* equates to abode. The abode of being is, however, less a form a permanent residence than it is an active residing. Ethics becomes the basic activity of being, which leads Nancy to claim, quite disconcertingly for some, that respect for the imperative can never be lost.[35]

The idea of no longer being free to lose respect might generate a sense of claustrophobia, of being confined, trapped or even oppressed. In a manner reminiscent of Emanuel Levinas's concern for the otherwise than being, one might ask how, if one cannot lose respect, it is possible to transgress the law or to be an outlaw. Moreover, if transgressiveness is that quality of freedom to which the law is addressed as a fact of reason, does not the inability to lose respect for the law contradict this fact? Nancy tackles these concerns through an unleashing of aporetic perplexity. If freedom is the condition of possibility of the law, then it must equally be the condition of possibility of the outlaw. We are therefore compelled to conclude that 'the law prohibits the one to whom it is addressed from obeying it from the outset, without stumbling'.[36] In effect, respect for the law guarantees the very possibility of the outlaw, one who corrupts the grounds of the maxim and shuns the legislature of freedom.

The obligation to respect the imperative is thus an originary law or law of the law, although this does not mean one cannot lose respect for a *particular* law or set of laws, whether they be cultural prohibitions or state legislation. Nancy suggests such laws can easily be seen as irrelevant or bad and that one might decide not to follow them in the name of some other law.[37] He does not explicitly suggest that this other law is the imperative and he may simply have in mind one arbitrary set of norms as opposed to another. Nevertheless, there is an implicit suggestion here

32 Nancy, *A Finite Thinking* 140.
33 ibid 151.
34 ibid.
35 ibid 146.
36 ibid 140.
37 ibid 145–46.

that to lose respect for specific laws is merely the realisation of the obligation to respect the law enjoined to freedom. To lose respect for particular laws to the extent that it invites legal sanction does not make one an outlaw, but surprisingly, quite the reverse.

Returning once again to kynicism, could one not impute a law of freedom into the kynical disrespect for the laws and conventions of the *polis*? If Diogenes's predicament was the timeless paradox of being bound to an other law through his love of freedom, not only does this other law (henceforth considered in the same light as the sublimity of the imperative) oblige him to make law addressed to freedom, but the making of the law also turns him into a sovereign law-maker, that is to say, it makes him autonomous in the literal Kantian sense of self-legislating. As with all forms of sovereign legislation, what is legislated repeals prior conflicting law, at least from the point of view of the sovereign. This, of course, leads to a clash between top-down and bottom-up sovereignties, a condition in which a revolutionary politics can germinate.

Kant himself did not countenance resistance against the sovereign laws of the state. His cosmopolitan right – linked to his general doctrine of right involving, *inter alia*, positive laws as well as their justification according to moral law[38] – applies to a cosmopolitan order that takes the form of a pacific federation of states and is limited to the condition of universal hospitality, namely 'the right of the stranger not to be treated with hostility when he arrives on someone else's territory'.[39] Despite this, we can now begin to think of cosmopolitan right not only in terms of a philosophy of perpetual peace but also in terms of a call to political resistance that is enjoined on the very force of the imperative to make law addressed to freedom. In a sense, this amounts to thinking Kant with Diogenes, turning Kant into an irreverent dog and Diogenes into a purveyor of lofty theory. Perverse as this may seem, it may just provide the key to thinking what a radical cosmopolitanism can mean today.

Acosmic cosmology

While Nancy helps us to rethink the paradox of freedom and law in Kant, he has been quite unequivocal in his criticism of classical Stoic/Kantian cosmopolitanism which for him 'disappropriates and de-signifies sense, tearing it to shreds'.[40] Cosmopolitanism for Nancy is a concept that envelops the world/cosmos in its entirety. In doing so, the cosmos in cosmopolitanism does not relate to *the* cosmos as such, but to a particular view of it, a world view, that is the 'end of the world as viewed, digested, absorbed, and dissolved in this

38 Kant, *Political Writings* 132–33.
39 ibid 105.
40 J.-L. Nancy, *The Sense of the World* (trans. J. S. Librett) (Minneapolis: University of Minnesota Press, 1997) 3.

vision'.[41] That cosmopolitanism designifies sense means there is a making sense of the world through signs pointing to it and from a position apart from or in transcendental relation to it, amounting to a general imposition of what can only ever remain a partial and incomplete vision. Cosmopolitanism thus becomes another name for what Nancy eventually calls globalisation, the uniformity or general equivalence of a world at its end.

Against the idea of globalisation, Nancy develops the notion of *mondialisation*. Although the two terms are similar in that they can mutually refer to the adoption of general networks of communication, economic exchange, legal regulation, and so on, globalisation tends to focus on the idea of an integrated totality, like the idea of the global village, while *mondialisation* is oriented towards world-forming, the world in expansion and the 'horizon of a "world" as a space of possible meaning'.[42] Nancy shifts the emphasis from concepts such as nature, earth, universe and even cosmos, which have become the 'name[s] of significations that have been surveyed, tamed and appropriated',[43] towards a sense that is one of abandonment and freedom in becoming. For Nancy, there is only mythology that stands above the world, giving it sense, thus making the world and cosmos its object of sense. In this regard, cosmopolitanism is a mythological totality *par excellence*. Ontologically speaking, the world no longer 'has a sense, but it *is* sense'; that is to say, '*sense* is structured as *world*'.[44] This sense of the world is, at the very minimum, a being-towards, that is to say, the flux of entities or existents toward each other, where being makes sense as itself.[45]

That said, Nancy does not completely dispense with the idea of cosmos but proposes a related idea that comes closer to the idea of *mondialisation*. It is the idea of an 'acosmic cosmology' whose sense is not inscribed from above but excribed from within, a mere opening of a space that is in the process of coming towards us.[46] This opening 'open[s] on nothing but its own distance from nothing, within nothing, its "something" having been thrown there from nowhere to nowhere . . .'.[47] The acosmic cosmos is neither a nihilism of pure nothingness nor a chaos which comes before or after cosmos. Rather, it is the affirmation of cosmos in its freely becoming, the truth of cosmos after the death of God, the cosmos that traces by itself the limit that nothing else delimits.[48] For Nancy, it is precisely a thinking of an acosmic cosmology that is needed in opposition to metaphysical cosmologies.[49] By extension one might say that it is an acosmic cosmopolitanism that is needed to

41 J.-L. Nancy, *The Creation of the World or Globalization* (trans. F. Raffoul and D. Pettigrew) (Albany: State University of New York Press, 2007) 43.
42 ibid 27–28.
43 Nancy, *The Sense of the World* 41.
44 ibid 8.
45 ibid 7.
46 ibid 37.
47 ibid.
48 ibid 38.
49 ibid.

counterpose the imperious logic of cosmopolitanism. One way to begin to do this is through the idea of *creatio ex nihilo.*

What is left of creation after the death of God, when, as Nietzsche proposes, 'belief in . . . God has become unbelievable'?[50] What can creation mean when we no longer presuppose a first creator, as Kant does, and when we affirm the closure of metaphysics by resisting any inscription of *mythos*, reason, foundation, or principle? *Creatio ex nihilo* is Nancy's answer. *Creatio ex nihilo* is neither the cosmos produced from nothing nor its miraculous appearance from nothing. Rather, it is the nothing growing (*croissant/creo/cresco*) as something: 'In creation, a growth grows from nothing and this nothing takes care of itself, cultivates its growth'.[51] This secularisation of creation amounts to a radical materialism insofar as it has no roots. It ruptures the deepest core of nihilism and opens the space for that which comes to presence. This is why *ex nihilo* contains the same ex- of ex-istence, which, inspired once again by Heidegger, relates being to projection or thrownness as opposed to an insistent timeless presence.[52] Creation is the infinite crescendo of existence, a 'provenance without production' and, as such, a 'provenance without a *pro-*'.[53] Creation is the ~~pro~~venance of cosmos, literally *coming* to presence in acosmic efflorescence.

Creatio ex nihilo relates back to the law of freedom because, to recall, there is nothing at the moment of freedom. Freedom depends on nothing and there is nothing that limits or conditions it. Only in this way can freedom be truly free, that is to say, free for freedom in its being free from freedom.[54] *Creatio ex nihilo* might thus be seen as the primordial activity of freedom. It is ex-istence thrown from nothing in an endlessly free beginning. Nancy more precisely describes this activity as an intensification of the nothing to the point where it bursts like a flash of lightening: 'it is the strike of the one *time*, the existing irruption of existence'.[55] Kant posits a spontaneity of causes that presupposes a first creator who acts freely. In contrast, *creatio ex nihilo* is creation without a creator since necessity and freedom arise together and in excess of each other. Bearing in mind there is nothing at the moment of freedom, a no-thing that is moreover in-finite, the moral law addresses itself to the infinite essence of freedom's finitude. This means that law does not call out to a fully evacuated nothingness; rather, it calls out to a self-deepening nothingness that irrupts as something. In this *schema*, the acosmic cosmos might be considered another name for freedom while *creatio ex nihilo* intimately connects itself to the law of freedom in the form of an acosmic cosmopolitan law, a law of creating the law that takes place continuously in the site of the *polis* to come.

50 F. Nietzsche, *The Gay Science* (trans. J. Nauckhoff) (Cambridge: Cambridge University Press, 2001) 343.
51 Nancy, *The Creation of the World* 51.
52 ibid 71.
53 ibid 66.
54 Nancy, *The Experience of Freedom* 81.
55 ibid 82.

All this suggests affirming radical cosmopolitanism acosmically. If we consider cosmopolitanism by itself, there are two ways in which the cosmos and *polis* can relate to each other: first, along the Stoic line, the *polis* can be seen as co-extensive with the cosmos, turning it into the universal or global city; secondly, along the Kynic line, the cosmos can be seen as in tension with and against the *polis*, where any claim to cosmopolitanism is a claim to a cosmic allegiance against the insularity of the *polis*. An acosmic cosmology provides a third option. If, in kynicism, the cosmos borders onto the *polis* and then expands outwards to cosmic infinity then, in postkynicism, the acosmic cosmos not only borders onto the *polis* but it also haunts the *polis* from within. The integrity of the *polis* is compromised by an outside that is already inside. A parallel line of thinking can be seen in certain forms of psychoanalysis. Julia Kristeva, for example, has argued that what is foreign is not simply the stranger that lies beyond our borders but the stranger that also lies within, that which frightens us as a manifestation of our 'erotic, death-bearing unconscious'.[56] Kristeva goes on to advocate a form of cosmopolitanism that makes the foreigner the basis of our common humanity, a consciousness of the stranger within, making us all foreigners. Likewise, the acosmic cosmos as the zero point of infinite freedom is a way to think the radical alterity of what is foreign or strange in relation to the *polis*. But unlike Kristeva, the acosmic cosmos is not a subtext to the possibility of a treatment (that is, consciousness of one's own uncanny strangeness) that would lead to a cure (that is, a cosmopolitan community of strangers). The acosmic cosmos is in immanent tension with the *polis*, giving rise to the flux of conflict and harmony or antagonism and friendship that is constitutive of the political nature of our being-together. The *polis* is in the process of formation and deformation as it moves towards an unknown future and is created anew as an event of freedom. In such a radical cosmopolitanism, the *polis* is stripped bare before revolutionary potentiality.

Conclusion

We have moved far from the conventional understanding of cosmopolitanism. The higher, prototypical form of natural law to which Diogenes subjected himself more than two millennia ago has been recast in terms of the respect for the law of freedom or, more precisely, the infinite demand to make law addressed to freedom. Amounting to a sovereign act of creation from nothing, the ushering in of the new, radical cosmopolitanism becomes the site of the *polis* to come.[57] It profoundly confronts any nationalist obsession or claim to global panacea and operates against

56 J. Kristeva, *Strangers to Ourselves* (trans. L. S. Roudiez) (New York: Columbia University Press, 1991) 192.

57 The general idea of a 'cosmopolitanism to come', inspired in part by Jacques Derrida, has been particularly well developed by Costas Douzinas. See C. Douzinas, *Human Rights and Empire: The Political Philosophy Cosmopolitanism* (Abingdon: Routledge-Cavendish, 2007) 291–98.

any topological, telelogical or normative finality. Radical cosmopolitanism, so conceived, is at root entwined with acosmic alterity and the concomitant *praxis* of free being. Instead of one world, it is the affirmation of the constituent power to create a world. No longer a traditional cosmopolis, it is or it becomes *political cosmogenesis*.

Bibliography

Adorno, T. 'Notes on Kafka' in *Prisms*, 243–71. Cambridge, Massachusetts: MIT Press, 1967.

Adorno, T. *Problems of Moral Philosophy.* Translated by R. Livingstone. Stanford: Stanford University Press, 2001.

Aeberhard, P. 'A Historical Survey of Humanitarian Action' (1996) 2(1) *Health and Human Rights* 30.

Agamben, G. *Furio Jesi, Lettura del 'Bateau Ivre' di Rimbaud.* Quodlibet, 1996.

Agamben, G. *Homo Sacer: Il Potere Sovrano e la Nuda Vita.* Giulio Einaudi, 1995.

Agamben, G. *Homo Sacer: Sovereign Power and Bare Life.* Pittsburgh: Stanford University Press, 1998.

Agamben, G. *Il Regno e la Gloria.* Nerri Pozza Editore, 2007.

Agamben, G. *Infancy and History.* London: Verso, 2007.

Agamben, G. *Means Without End: Notes on Politics.* Minneapolis: University of Minnesota Press, 2000.

Agamben, G. *Ninfe.* Bollati Boringhieri, 2007.

Agamben, G. *Nudities.* Stanford: Stanford University Press, 2010.

Agamben, G. *Potentialities.* Stanford: Stanford University Press, 1999.

Agamben, G. *Profanations.* New York: Zone Books, 2007.

Agamben, G. *Remnants of Auschwitz: The Witness and the Archive.* Translated by D. Heller-Roazen. New York: Zone Books, 2002.

Agamben, G. *Stanzas: Word and Phantasm in Western Culture.* Minneapolis: University of Minnesota Press, 1993.

Agamben, G. *State of Exception.* Chicago: University of Chicago Press, 2005.

Agamben, G. *The Coming Community.* Minneapolis: University of Minnesota Press, 1993.

Agamben, G. *The Idea of Prose.* Albany: State University of New York Press, 1995.

Agamben, G. *The Open.* Stanford: Stanford University Press, 2004.

Agamben, G. *The Sacrament of Language.* Cambridge: Polity, 2011.

Agamben, G. *The Signature of All Things: On Method.* New York: Zone, 2009.

Agamben, G. *The Time that Remains: A Commentary on the Letter to the Romans.* Stanford: Stanford University Press, 2005.

Agamben, G. et al. *Democracy – In What State?* New York: Colombia University Press, 2011.

Althusser, L. *Lenin and Philosophy and Other Essays.* New York: Monthly Review Press, 2001.

Anghie, A. *Imperialism, Sovereignty, and the Making of International Law.* Cambridge: Cambridge University Press, 2005.

Arendt, H. *Crises of the Republic*. Harmondsworth: Penguin, 1972.

Arieff, A. 'Political Transition in Tunisia' *Congressional Research Service*, 2011 available at http://fpc.state.gov/documents/organization/161570.pdf (accessed 11 November 2011).

Aristodemou, M. 'Studies in Law and Literature: Directions and Concerns' (1993) 22 *Anglo-American Law Review* 157.

Badiou, A. *Ethics: An Essay in the Understanding of Evil.* Translated by P. Hallward. London: Verso, 2001.

Badiou, A. *The Century.* Translated by A. Toscano. Cambridge: Polity, 2008.

BBC. 'Britain Now "Eating the Planet"' (15 April 2006) available at http://news.bbc.co.uk/2/hi/science/nature/4897252.stm (accessed 28 November 2011).

Beckett, J. A. 'Conflicting Orders: How Peace is Waged' (2007) 20 *Leiden Journal of International Law* 281.

Beckett, J. A. 'Countering Uncertainty and Ending Up/Down Arguments: *Prolegomena* to a Response to NAIL' (2005) 16(2) *European Journal of International Law* 213.

Beckett, J. A. 'Fragmentation, Openness, and Hegemony: Adjudication and the WTO' in *International Economic Law and National Autonomy*, edited by M. Kolsky Lewis and S. Frankel, 44–69. Cambridge: Cambridge University Press, 2010.

Beckett, J. A. 'Interim Legality: A Mistaken Assumption? An Analysis of Depleted Uranium Munitions Under Contemporary International Humanitarian Law' (2004) 3(1) *Chinese Journal of International Law* 43.

Beckett, J. A. 'Mercy, Particularity, the Map from the Void' (2007) 93(2) *Archiv für Rechts und Sozialphilosophie* 217.

Beckett, J. A. 'New War, Old Law: Can the Geneva Paradigm Comprehend Computers?' (2000) 13 *Leiden Journal of International Law* 33.

Beckett, J. A. 'Rebel Without a Cause? Martti Koskenniemi and the Critical Legal Project' (2006) 7 *German Law Journal* 1045.

Beckett, J. A. *The End of Customary International Law? A Purposive Analysis of Structural Indeterminacy*. Saarbrucken: VDM Verlag Dr. Muller, 2008.

Beckett, J. A. 'The Hartian Tradition in International Law' (2008) 51 *The Journal Jurisprudence* 53.

Beckett, J. A. 'The Violence of Wording' in *No Foundations: The Journal of Extreme Legal Positivism* (May 2011).

Bederman, D. 'Book review of *From Apology to Utopia*' (1990) 23 *New York Journal of International Law and Politics* 217.

Ben-Dor, O. ed. *Law and Art: Justice, Ethics and Aesthetics.* Abingdon: Routledge, 2011.

Ben-Dor, O. *Thinking About Law In Silence With Heidegger.* Oxford: Hart, 2007.

Benjamin, W. 'Commentaries on Poems by Brecht' in *Understanding Brecht*, translated by A. Bostock, 43–74. London, New York: Verso, 1998.

Benjamin, W. *Illuminations.* Glasgow: Jonathan Cape, 1970.

Benjamin, W. *Reflections.* New York: Schoken Books, 1978.

Benjamin, W. *Selected Writings Volume 1 1913–1926.* Cambridge, Mass.: Harvard University Press, 1996.

Berlin, I. *Liberty*. Oxford, Oxford University Press, 2002.

Berman, P. *Power and the Idealists: The Passion of Joschka Fischer and its Aftermath.* New York: Soft Skull Press, 2005.

Best, S. *Fugitive's Properties: The Poetics of Law and Possession.* Chicago: University of Chicago Press, 2004.

Bhandar, B. 'Plasticity and Post-colonial Recognition: Owning, Knowing and Being' (2011) 22(3) *Law and Critique* 227.

Bix, B. *Jurisprudence: Theory and Context.* London: Sweet & Maxwell, 2009.

Bowring, B. *The Degradation of the International Order? The Rehabilitation of Law and the Possibility of Politics.* Abingdon: Routledge-Cavendish, 2008.

Boyle, J. ed. *Critical Legal Studies.* New York: NYU Press, 1994.

Bracht Branham, R. 'Diogenes' Rhetoric' in *The Cynics,* edited by R. Bracht Branham and M.-O. Goulet-Cazé, 81–104. Berkeley: University of California Press, 1996.

Brecht, B. 'Legend of the Origin of the Book Tao-Tê-Ching on Lao-Tsû's Road into Exile' in *Bertolt Brecht: Poems 1913–1956,* edited by J. Willet and R. Manheim, 314–316. New York and London: Methuen: 1976.

Brown, M. and J. Pratt, *Dangerous Offenders: Punishment and Social Order.* London: Routledge, 2000.

Brown, W. *Politics Out of History.* Princeton: Princeton University Press, 2001.

Brown, W. *States of Injury: Power and Freedom in Late Modernity.* New Jersey: Princeton University Press, 1995.

Buck-Morss, S. 'Hegel and Haiti' (2000) 26(4) *Critical Inquiry* 821.

Burghardt Du Bois, W.E. 'The African Roots of War.' available at http://www.library.umass.edu/spcoll/digital/dubois/WarRoots.pdf (accessed 28 November 2011).

Butler, J. 'Benjamin's Critique of Violence' in *Political Theologies,* edited by L. Sullivan and H. de Vries, 201–219. New York: Fordham University Press, 2006.

Butler, J. *Bodies that Matter: On the Discursive Limits of 'Sex'.* New York and London: Routledge, 1996.

Butler, J. *Gender Trouble: Feminism and the Subversion of Identity.* London: Routledge, 1990.

Butler, J. 'Sexual Inversions' in *Foucault and the Critique of Institutions,* edited by J. Caputo and M. Yount, 81–98. University Park, Penn.: Pennsylvania State University Press, 1993.

Butler, J. *Subjects of Desire: Hegelian Reflections in Twentieth-Century France.* New York: Columbia University Press, 1987.

Butler, J. *The Psychic Life of Power: Theories in Subjection.* Stanford: Stanford University Press, 1997.

Camus, A. *The Myth of Sisyphus.* available at http://www.scribd.com/doc/3223928/Albert-Camus-The-Myth-Of-Sisyphus (accessed 28 November 2011).

Carlsson, B. and M. Baier. 'A Visual Self-Image of Legal Authority: "The Temple of Law"' (2002) 11(2) *Social & Legal Studies* 185.

Casarino, C. *In Praise of the Common: A Conversation on Philosophy and Politics.* Minneapolis: University of Minnesota Press, 2008.

Chakrabarty, D. *Provincialising Europe: Postcolonial Thought and Historical Difference.* Princeton: Princeton University Press, 2000.

Chandler, D. 'The Road to Military Humanitarianism: How the Humanitarian NGOs Shaped a New Humanitarian Agenda' (2001) 23(3) *Human Rights Quarterly* 678.

Chandler, D. 'War Without End(s): Grounding the Discourse of Global War' (2009) 40(3) *Security Dialogue* 243.

Chick, V. and A. Pettifor. 'The Economic Consequences of Mr Osborne, Fiscal Consolidation: Lessons from a Century of UK Macroeconomic Statistics' (6 June 2010) available at www.debtonation.org/wp-content/uploads/2010/06/Fiscal-Consolidation1.pdf (accessed 28 November 2011).

Chomiak, L. 'The Making of a Revolution in Tunisia' (2011) 3 *Middle East Law and Governance* 68.

Christodoulidis, E. 'The Objection that Cannot be Heard: Communication and Legitimacy in the Courtroom' in *The Trial on Trial, Vol 1*, edited by A. Duff et al, 179–202. Oxford: Hart, 2004.

Christofferson, M. S. 'An Antitotalitarian History of the French Revolution: François Furet's *Penser la Révolution francais* in the Intellectual Politics of the late 1970s' (1999) 22(4) *French Historical Studies* 557.

Cicero, M. T. *On Duties*. Edited by M. T. Griffin and E. M. Atkins. Cambridge: Cambridge University Press, 1991.

Clemens, J. 'The Abandonment of Sex: Giorgio Agamben, Psychoanalysis and Melancholia' (2010) 13 *Theory & Event* 1.

Connolly, W. 'Beyond Good and Evil: The Ethical Sensibility of Michel Foucault' (1993) 21(3) *Political Theory* 365.

Cornell, D. et al (eds) *Deconstruction and the Possibility of Justice*. London: Routledge, 1992.

Cover, R. 'Violence and the Word' (1986) 95 *Yale Law Journal* 1601.

Critchley, S. *Infinitely Demanding: Ethics of Commitment, Politics of Resistance*. London: Verso, 2007.

Dargo, G. 'Reclaiming Franz Kafka, Doctor of Jurisprudence' (2006–2007) 45 *Brandeis Law Journal* 495.

Darnton, R. *The Great Cat Massacre: And Other Episodes in French Cultural History*. Harmondsworth: Penguin, 1985.

de Certeau, M. *The Practice of Everyday Life*. Berkeley, University of California Press, 1988.

de Ville, J. *Jacques Derrida: Law as Absolute Hospitality*. London: Routledge, 2011.

de Ville, J. 'Rethinking the Notion of a "Higher Law": Heidegger and Derrida on the Anaximander Fragment' (2009) 20(1) *Law and Critique* 59.

Deleuze, G. *Two Regimes of Madness*. New York: Semiotext(e), 2006.

Deleuze, G. and F. Guattari. *Kafka: Toward a Minor Literature*. Minneapolis: University of Minnesota Press, 2006.

Derrida, J. 'Before the Law' in *Acts of Literature*, edited by D. Attridge, 181–221. New York, London: Routledge, 1992.

Derrida, J. 'Force of Law: The 'Mystical Foundation of Authority'.' in *Acts of Religion*, edited by G. Anidjas, 228-298. London: Routledge, 2002.

Derrida, J. *Politics of Friendship*. London: Verso, 2005.

Derrida, J. *Specters of Marx*. London: Routledge, 1994.

Derrida, J. 'Violence and Metaphysics: An Essay on the Thought of Emmanuel Levinas' in *Writing and Difference*, translated by A. Bass, 79–153. Chicago: University of Chicago Press, 1978.

Dews, P. *The Limits of Disenchantment: Essays on Contemporary European Philosophy*. London: Verso, 1995.

Diamantides, M. 'Ethics in Law: Death Marks on a "Still Life", A Vision of Judgement as Vegetating' (1995) 6(2) *Law and Critique* 209.

Douglas, S. 'Between Constitutional Mo(nu)ments: Memorialising Past, Present and Future at the District Six Museum and Constitution Hill' (2011) 22 *Law and Critique* 171.

Douzinas, C. 'Athens Revolting: Three Meditations on Sovereignty and One on its (Possible) Dismantlement' (2010) 21(3) *Law and Critique* 261.

Douzinas, C. 'Europe and the End of Politics' available at http://www.newleftproject.org/index.php/site/article_comments/europe_and_the_end_of_politics (accessed 28 November 2011).

Douzinas, C. 'Greece can fight back against neoliberals' *Guardian* (27 April 2010) available at http://www.guardian.co.uk/commentisfree/2010/apr/27/greece-imf-eu-welfare-state (accessed 26 November 2011).

Douzinas, C. *Human Rights and Empire: The Political Philosophy Cosmopolitanism.* Abingdon: Routledge-Cavendish, 2007.

Douzinas, C. *The End of Human Rights: Critical Legal Thought at the Turn of the Century.* Oxford: Hart, 2000.

Douzinas, C. and A. Gearey. *Critical Jurisprudence: The Political Philosophy of Justice.* Oxford: Hart, 2005.

Douzinas, C., P. Goodrich and Y. Hachamovitch, eds. *Politics, Postmodernity and Critical Legal Studies: The Legality of the Contingent.* London: Routledge, 1994.

Douzinas, C. and R. Warrington. *Justice Miscarried: Ethics and Aesthetics in Law.* London: Harvester Wheatsheaf, 1994.

Douzinas, C., R. Warrington and S. McVeigh, *Postmodern Jurisprudence: The Law of Text in the Texts of Law.* London: Routledge, 1991.

Dussel, E. *Política de la Liberación, Vol II.* Trotta, 2009.

Düttmann, A.G. 'Never Before, Always Already: Notes on Agamben and the Category of Relation' (2006) 6 *Angelaki: A Journal of the Theoretical Humanities* 3.

Eisenstein, Z. R. *The Female Body and the Law.* Berkeley: University of California Press, 1988.

Elkins, J. R. 'Lowell B. Komie of Chicago – Writer and Lawyer' (2001) 25 *Legal Studies Forum* 1.

Epstein, K. and K. Iveson. 'Locking Down the City (Well, Not Quite): APEC 2007 and Urban Citizenship in Sydney' (2009) 40(3) *Australian Geographer* 271.

Eribon, D. *Michel Foucault.* Translated by B. Wing. Cambridge: Harvard University Press, 1991.

Esposito, R. *Bios: Biopolitics and Philosophy.* Translated by T. Campbell. Minneapolis: University of Minnesota Press, 2008.

Esposito, R. *Categorie dell'Impolitico.* Il Mulino, 1999.

Etheredge, L. S., ed. *Islamic History.* New York: Britannica Educational Publishing, 2010.

Fanon, F. *Black Skin, White Masks.* Translated by C. L. Markmann. New York: Grove Press, 1967.

Fanon, F. *The Wretched of the Earth.* London: Penguin Books, 2001.

Felman, S. 'Forms of Judicial Blindness, or The Evidence of What Cannot Be Seen: Traumatic Narratives and Legal Repetitions in the O. J. Simpson Case and in Tolstoy's The Kreutzer Sonata' (Summer 2007) 23(4) *Critical Inquiry* 738.

Ferguson, N. *The Ascent of Money.* London: Penguin, 2009.

Ferreira da Silva, D. 'No-bodies: Law, Raciality and Violence' (2009) 18(2) *Griffith Law Review* 212.

Ferreira da Silva, D. *Towards a Global Idea of Race.* Minneapolis: University of Minnesota Press, 2007.

Fitzpatrick, P. (ed) *Dangerous Supplements: Resistance and Renewal in Jurisprudence.* London: Pluto, 1991.

Foley, C. *The Thin Blue Line.* Verso, London, 2008.

Foucault, M. *Birth of Biopolitics: Lectures at the Collège de France 1978–79.* Translated by G. Burchell. Basingstoke: Palgrave Macmillan, 2008.

Foucault, M. *Discipline and Punish: The Birth of the Prison.* Translated by A. Sheridan. Harmondsworth: Penguin, 1991.

Foucault, M. *Essential Works of Foucault 1954–1984, Vol 1: Ethics, Subjectivity and Truth.* Translated by R. Hurley et al. Edited by P. Rabinow. Harmondsworth: Allen Lane/ Penguin, 1997.

Foucault, M. *Power/Knowledge: Selected Interviews and Other Writings 1972–1977.* Translated by C. Gordon et al. Edited by C. Gordon. Brighton: Harvester Press, 1980.

Foucault, M. *Security, Territory, Population: Lectures at the Collège de France 1977–78.* Translated by G. Burchell. Basingstoke: Palgrave Macmillan, 2007.

Foucault, M. *'Society Must be Defended': Lectures at the Collège de France 1975–76.* Translated by D. Macey. London: Penguin Books, 2004.

Foucault, M. *The Archaeology of Knowledge.* Translated by A. M. Sheridan Smith. London: Routledge, 1972.

Foucault, M. 'The Mythical Leader of the Iranian Revolt' in *Foucault and the Iranian Revolution*, edited by J. Afary and K. Anderson, 220–23. Chicago: University of Chicago Press, 2005.

Foucault, M. *The Order of Things: An Archaeology of the Human Sciences.* London: Routledge, 2002.

Foucault, M. 'The Subject and Power' in *Readings in Contemporary Political Sociology*, edited by K. Nash, 8–26. Massachusetts: Wiley-Blackwell, 2000.

Foucault, M. *The Will to Knowledge: The History of Sexuality, Vol 1.* Translated by R. Hurley. Harmondsworth: Penguin, 1998.

Foucault, M. 'What is Critique?' in *What is Enlightenment? Eighteenth Century Answers and Twentieth Century Questions*, edited by J. Schmidt, 382–98. Berkeley and Los Angeles: University of California Press, 1996.

Foucault, M. and G. Anquetil, 'The Moral and Social Experience of the Poles Can No Longer Be Obliterated' in *Essential Works of Foucault 1954–1984 Vol 3: Power*, edited by J. Faubion, 465–73. New York: The New Press, 2000.

García Márquez, G. 'Nobel Lecture' available at http://www.nobelprize.org/nobel_prizes/literature/laureates/1982/marquez-lecture.html (accessed 30 November 2011).

Garland, D. ''Governmentality' and the Problem of Crime: Foucault, Criminology, Sociology.' (1997) 1 *Theoretical Criminology* 173.

George, A. ''Roll a Fag and Go Free': Competing Discourses of Sexuality and Sexual Identity' (1995) 1(1) *Journal of Interdisciplinary Gender Studies* 49.

George, A. 'The Gay (?) Victim on Trial: Discourses of Sexual Division in the Courtroom' in *Homophobic Violence*, edited by G. Mason and S. Tomsen, 46–57. Sydney: Federation Press, 1997.

Golder, B. 'Foucault and the Unfinished Human of Rights' (2010) 6(3) *Law, Culture and the Humanities* 354.

Golder, B. '''It forced me to open more than I could bear'': HAD, Paedophilia, and the Discursive Limits of the Male Heterosexual Body' in *An Aesthetics of Law and Culture: Texts, Images, Screens*, edited by A. T. Kenyon and P. Rush, 53–72. Amsterdam: Elsevier, 2004.

Golder, B. 'What is an Anti-Humanist Human Right?' (2010) 16(5) *Social Identities* 651.

Golder, B. and P. Fitzpatrick. *Foucault's Law.* Abingdon: Routledge, 2009.

González, A. M. 'Natural Law as a Limiting Concept: A Reading of Thomas Aquinas' in *Contemporary Perspectives on Natural Law: Natural Law as a Limiting Concept*, edited by A. M. González, 11–25. Aldershot: Ashgate, 2008.

Goodrich, P. *Languages of Law: From Logics of Memory to Nomadic Masks.* London: Weidenfeld & Nicolson, 1990.

Goodrich, P. *Law in the Courts of Love: Literature and Other Minor Jurisprudences*. London: Routledge, 1996.
Gordon, R. 'New Developments in Legal Theory' in *The Politics of Law: A Progressive Critique*, edited by D. Kairys, 281–93. New York: Pantheon Books, 1990.
Grigg-Spall, I. and P. Ireland, eds. *Critical Lawyers' Handbook*. London: Pluto Press, 1992.
Guérin, D. *No Gods, No Masters: An Anthology of Anarchism*. Oakland, Edinburgh: AK Press, 2005.
Guigni, M. and F. Passy, eds. *Political Altruism? Solidarity Movements in International Perspective*. Maryland: Rowman and Littlefield Publishers, 2001.
Guillaumin, C. *Racism, Sexism, Power and Ideology*. London: Routledge, 1995.
Haase, D., ed. *The Greenwood Encyclopedia of Folktales and Fairy Tales*. Westport Connecticut: Greenwood Press, 2008.
Habermas, J. *Between Facts and Norms: Contributions to a Discourse Theory of Law and Democracy*. Cambridge, Mass.: MIT Press, 1996.
Hagan, A. 'New Home in Illinois: A "Boat Family" Finds Sanctuary in the U.S.A.' (July 1980) *The Rotarian* 29.
Halberstam, J. 'Imagined Violence/Queer Violence: Representation, Rage, and Resistance' (1993) 37 *Social Text* 187.
Hamacher, W. 'Affirmative, Strike, Benjamin's "Critique of Violence"' in *Destruction & Experience*, edited by A. Benjamin and P. Osborne, 110–38. Manchester: Clinamen Press, 2000.
Haraway, D. *Modest_Witness@Second_Millenium.FemaleMan_Meets_OncoMouse: Feminism and Technoscience*. London: Routledge, 1997.
Hariman, R. 'Political Parody and Public Culture' (2008) 94(3) *Quarterly Journal of Speech* 247.
Hegel, G. W. F. *Elements of the Philosophy of Right*. Edited by A. W. Wood. Translated by H. B. Nisbet. Cambridge: Cambridge University Press, 1991.
Hegel, G. W. F. *Lectures on the History of Philosophy*. Translated by E. S. Haldane and F. Simson. Lincoln: University of Nebraska Press, 1995.
Hegel, G. W. F. *Phenomenology of Spirit*. Translated by A. V. Miller. Oxford: Oxford University Press, 1977.
Hegel, G. W. F. *Philosophy of Right*. Translated by T. M. Knox. Oxford: Clarendon Press, 1967.
Hegel, G. W. F. *Science of Logic*. Translated by A. V. Miller. London: Allen and Unwin, 1969.
Hegel, G. W. F. *The Encyclopaedia Logic: Part I of the Encyclopaedia of Philosophical Sciences with the Zusätze*. Translated by T. F. Geraets, W. A. Suchting, and H. S. Harris. Indianapolis: Hackett, 1991.
Heidegger, M. *Being and Time*. Translated by J. Macquarrie and E. Robinson. Oxford: Blackwell, 1962.
Hibou, B. *The Force of Obedience: The Political Economy of Repression in Tunisia*. London: Polity Press, 2011.
Hobbes, T. *Leviathan*. London: Penguin, 1968.
Honig, B. *Democracy and the Foreigner*. Princeton: University of Princeton Press, 2001.
Honneth, A. 'Reification: A Recognition-Theoretical View,' Tanner Lectures on Human Values, University of California, Berkeley (March 14–16 2005) available at http://www.tannerlectures.utah.edu/lectures/documents/Honneth_2006.pdf (accessed 12 January 2012).

Honneth, A. *The Critique of Power.* Translated by K. Baynes. Cambridge, Mass: MIT Press, 1991.

Honneth, A. *The Struggle for Recognition: The Moral Grammar of Social Conflicts.* Translated by J. Anderson. Cambridge: Polity Press, 1995.

Honwana, A. 'Youth and the Tunisian Revolution.' *SSRC Conflict Prevention Forum,* 12 available at http://webarchive.ssrc.org/pdfs/Alcinda_Honwana,_Youth_and_the_Tunisian_Revolution,_September_2011-CPPF_policy%20paper.pdf (accessed 29 November 2011).

Horvath, R. '"The Solzhenitsyn Effect": East European Dissidents and the Demise of the Revolutionary Privilege' (2007) 29(4) *Human Rights Quarterly* 879.

Howard, R. and J. Donnelly. 'Liberalism and Human Rights: A Necessary Connection' in *The Human Rights Reader: Major Political Essays, Speeches and Documents From the Bible to the Present,* edited by M. Ishay, 272–76. New York: Routledge, 1997.

Howe, A. 'Imagining Evidence, Fictioning Truth – Revisiting (Courtesy of O. J. Simpson) Expert Evidence in the Chamberlain Case' (1997) 3(1) *Law Text Culture* 82.

Howe, A. 'More Folk Provoke Their Own Demise (Homophobic Violence and Sexed Excuses) – Rejoining the Provocation Law Debate, Courtesy of the Homosexual Advance Defence' (1997) 19(3) *Sydney Law Review* 336.

Howe, A. 'Reforming Provocation (More or Less)' (1999) 12 *Australian Feminist Law Journal* 127.

Hunt A., and P. Fitzpatrick, eds. *Critical Legal Studies.* Oxford: Blackwell, 1987.

Hunt A., and G. Wickham. *Foucault and Law: Towards a Sociology of Law as Governance.* London: Pluto Press, 1994.

Hutchinson, A., ed. *Critical Legal Studies.* New Jersey: Rowman & Littlefield, 1987.

Hutchinson, A. and P. Monahan. 'Law, Politics and Critical Legal Scholars: The Unfolding Drama of American Legal Thought' (1984) 36(2) *Stanford Law Review* 199.

Ireland, P. and P. Laleng. *Critical Lawyers' Handbook II.* London: Pluto Press, 1997.

Ivison, D. *The Self at Liberty: Political Argument and the Arts of Government.* Ithaca and London: Cornell University Press, 1997.

Jackson, B. *Law, Fact and Narrative Coherence.* Roby: Deborah Charles, 1988.

Jackson, B. *Making Sense in Law: Linguistic, Psychological and Semiotics Perspectives.* Liverpool: Deborah Charles, 1995.

James, I. 'On Interrupted Myth' (2005) 9(4) *Journal for Cultural Research* 331.

Johns, F. '*Guantanamo* Bay and the Annihilation of the Exception' (2005) 16(4) *European Journal of International Law* 613.

Johnston, P. '"More than Ordinary Men Gone Wrong": Can the Law Know the Gay Subject?' (1996) 20 *Melbourne University Law Review* 1152.

Kacem, M. B. 'A Tunisian Renaissance: Interview with Mehdi Belhaj Kacem' available at http://www.lacan.com/thesymptom/?page_id=1046 (accessed 11 November 2011).

Kadri, S. *The Trial: A History from Socrates to O. J. Simpson.* London, New York: Harper Perennial, 2005.

Kafka, F. *Metamorphosis and Other Stories.* New York: Dover, 1996.

Kafka, F. *The Trial.* London: Penguin Modern Classics, 2000.

Kalyvas, A. 'An Anomaly? Some Reflections on the Greek December 2008' (2010) 17(2) *Constellations* 351.

Kant, I. *Critique of Practical Reason.* Translated by W. S. Pluhar. Indianapolis: Hackett Publishing Company, 2002.

Kant, I. *Critique of Pure Reason.* Translated by W. S. Pluhar. Indianapolis: Hackett Publishing Company, 1996.

Kant, I. *Groundwork of the Metaphysics of Morals.* Translated by M. Gregor. Cambridge: Cambridge University Press, 1997.

Kant, I. *Political Writings.* Edited by H. Reiss. Translated by H. B. Nisbet. Cambridge: Cambridge University Press, 1970.

Kelman, M. '*Trashing*' (1984) 36 *Stanford Law Review* 293.

Kelsen, H. *General Theory of Law and State.* Clark: Lawbook Exchange, 2009.

Kennedy, D. *The Dark Sides of Virtue: Reassessing International Humanitarianism.* Oxford: Princeton University Press, 2004.

Kennedy, D. *Sexy Dressing Etc.: Essays on the Power and Politics of Cultural Identity.* Cambridge, MA.: Harvard University Press, 1993.

Kennedy, D. 'The Stakes of Law, Or Hale and Foucault!' (1991) 15(4) *Legal Studies Forum* 327.

Kenny, K. "The Performative Surprise": Parody, Documentary and Critique' (2009) 15(2) *Culture and Organization* 221.

Kerruish, V. 'But What's It Got To Do With Law' (2009) 4 *Dillemata* 81.

Kerruish, V. *Jurisprudence as Ideology.* London: Routledge, 1991.

Khilani, S. *Arguing Revolution: The Intellectual Left in Postwar France.* Newhaven and London: Yale University Press, 1993.

Kochi, T. *The Other's War: Recognition and the Violence of Ethics.* Abingdon: Birkbeck Law Press, 2009.

Koskenniemi, M. *From Apology to Utopia: The Structure of International Legal Argument,* 2nd edition. Cambridge: Cambridge University Press, 2007.

Koskenniemi, M. 'International Law in Europe: Between Tradition and Renewal' (2005) 16 *European Journal of International Law* 113.

Koskenniemi, M. "The Lady Doth Protest Too Much": Kosovo, and the Turn to Ethics in International Law' (2002) 65 *Modern Law Review* 159.

Koskenniemi, M. 'The Politics of International Law – 20 Years Later' (2009) 20 *European Journal of International Law* 7.

Kouchner, B. 'Morals of Urgent Need' in *Assisting the Victims of Armed Conflict and Other Disasters,* edited by Fritz Kalshoven, 55–59. Dordrecht: Martinus Nijoff Publishers, 1989.

Kouchner, B. Jonathan Mann Lecture, Harvard University (6 March 2003) available at http://ww.harvardfxbcenter.org/resources/.../FXBC_WP15—Kouchner.pdf (accessed 19 January 2012).

Kristeva, J. *Strangers to Ourselves.* Translated by L. S. Roudiez. New York: Columbia University Press, 1991.

Lacan, J. *Ecrits: A Selection.* Translated by B. Fink. New York: W. W. Norton, 2002.

Laclau, E. *Emancipation(s).* London: Verso, 1996.

Laertius, D. *Lives of Eminent Philosophers.* Translated by R. D. Hicks. Cambridge: Harvard University Press, 1925.

Land, N. 'Machinic Desire' (1993) 7(3) *Textual Practice* 471.

Land, N. *Fanged Noumena: Collected Writings 1987–2007.* Falmouth: Urbanomic, 2011.

Landecker, H. *Culturing Life: How Cells Became Technologies.* London: Harvard University Press, 2007.

Lao-Tsû. *Te-Tao Ching.* Translated by R. Henricks. New York: The Modern Library, 1993.

Lapavitsas, C. 'Financialised Capitalism, Direct Exploitation and Periodic Bubbles' (May, 2008) available at www.leftlibrary.com/lapavitsas1.pdf (accessed 28 November 2011).

Lassiter, C. 'The O. J. Simpson Verdict: A Lesson in Black and White' (1996) 1 *Michigan Journal of Race and Law* 69.

Leung, G. 'A Critical History of Cosmopolitanism' (2009) 5(3) *Journal of Law, Culture and the Humanities* 370.
Levinas, E. 'As If Consenting to Horror' (1989) 15(2) *Critical Inquiry* 485.
Levinas, E. *Existence and Existents*. Pittsburgh: Duquesne University Press, 2001.
Levinas, E. *On Escape*. Stanford: Stanford University Press, 2003.
Levinas, E. *Otherwise than Being or Beyond Essence*. Pittsburgh: Duquesne University Press, 1998.
Levinas, E. *Time and the Other*. Pittsburgh: Duquesne University Press, 1987.
Levinas, E. *Totality and Infinity: An Essay on Exteriority*. Pittsburgh: Duquesne University Press, 1969.
Lévy, B.-H. *Barbarism with a Human Face*. Translated by G. Holoch. New York: Harper and Row, 1979.
Lindahl, H. 'The Opening: Alegality and Political Agonism' in *Law and Political Agonism*, edited by A. Schaap, 57–70. Aldershot: Ashgate, 2009.
Lindqvist, S. *Exterminate All the Brutes*. London: Granta, 1997.
Litowitz, D. E. 'Franz Kafka's Outside Jurisprudence' (2002) 27 *Law and Social Inquiry* 103.
Loizidou, E. 'Criminal Law and Punishment: Indexical Permission' (2004) 6(3) *Punishment and Society* 303.
Loizidou, E. 'The Body Figural and Material in the Work of Judith Butler' (2008) 28 *Australian Feminist Law Journal* 29.
Loughlin, M. *Foundations of Public Law*. Oxford: Oxford University Press, 2010.
Loughlin, M. *The Idea of Public Law*. Oxford: Oxford University Press, 2004.
Lowe, V. 'Book review of *From Apology to Utopia*' (1990) 17 *Journal of Law and Society* 384.
Lowe, V. *International Law*. Oxford: Oxford University Press, 2007.
Lyotard, J. F. *The Postmodern Condition: A Report on Knowledge*. Minnesota: Minnesota University Press, 1992.
Macey, D. *The Lives of Michel Foucault*. New York: Vintage Books, 1995.
Mackenzie, D. *An Engine Not a Camera, How Financial Models Shape Markets*. Cambridge, Mass: MIT Press, 2006.
Manderson, D. *Proximity, Levinas and the Soul of Law*. London: McGill-Queen's University Press, 2006.
Marks, S. '*False Contingency*' (2009) 62 *Current Legal Problems* 1.
Marks, S. 'Human Rights and Root Causes' (2011) 74 *Modern Law Review* 57.
Marks, S. 'Human Rights and the Bottom Billion' (2009) *European Human Rights Law Review* 37.
Marks, S. 'International Judicial Activism and the Commodity-Form Theory of International Law' (2007) 18 *European Journal of International Law* 199.
Marshall, P. *Demanding the Impossible: A History of Anarchism*. London: Fontana, 1993.
Martel, J. R. *Divine Violence: Walter Benjamin and the Eschatology of Sovereignty*. Abingdon: Routledge, 2012.
Marx, K. *Capital Volume I*. London: Penguin, 1990.
Marx, K. *The Eighteenth Brumaire of Louis Bonaparte*. Wildside Press, 1963.
Marzouki, N. 'From People to Citizens in Tunisia.' *Middle East Research and Information Project*, no 259, available at http://www.merip.org/mer/mer259/people-citizens-tunisia#_3_ (accessed 30 November 2011).
Mattei, U. and L. Nader, eds. *Plunder: When the Rule of Law is Illegal*. Oxford: Blackwell, 2008.
Matustik, M. B. *Radical Evil and the Scarcity of Hope*. Indiana: Indiana University Press, 2008.
Mbembe, A. *On the Postcolony*. Berkeley: University of California Press, 2003.

Mbembe, A. 'Provincialising France?' (2011) 23(1) *Public Culture* 85.
Merrifield, A. *Magical Marxism*. London: Pluto Press, 2011.
Mezzadra, S. 'Bringing Capital Back In: A Materialist Turn in Post-Colonial Studies?' (2011) 12(1) *Inter-Asia Cultural Studies* 154.
Mezzadra, S. 'How Many Histories of Labour? Towards a Theory of Post-Colonial Capitalism' (2011) 14(2) *Postcolonial Studies* 1.
Mieville, C. 'Multilateralism as Terror: International Law, Haiti and Imperialism' (2009) 18 *Finnish Yearbook of International Law* 63.
Mignolo, W. *The Darker Side of the Renaissance. Literacy, Territory and Colonization*. Ann Arbor: The University of Michigan Press, 1995.
Mill, J. S. *On Liberty, and Other Essays*. Oxford: Oxford University Press, 2008.
Minkkinen, P. 'Right Things: On the Question of Being and Law' (1996) 7(1) *Law and Critique* 65.
Mison, R. B. 'Homophobia in Manslaughter: The Homosexual Advance Defence as Insufficient Provocation' (1992) 80(1) *Columbia Law Review* 133.
Moran, L. J. 'Gothic Law' (2001) 10 *Griffith Law Review* 75.
Morgan, J. 'Provocation Law and Facts: Dead Women Tell no Tales, Tales Are Told About Them' (1997) 21(1) *Melbourne University Law Review* 237.
Moten, F. *In the Break: The Aesthetics of the Black Radical Tradition*. Minneapolis: University of Minnesota Press, 2003.
Mouffe, C. *On the Political*. Abingdon: Routledge, 2005.
Murphy, J. *Retribution Reconsidered: More Essays in the Philosophy of Law*. London: Kluwer, 1992.
Nancy, J.-L. *A Finite Thinking*. Edited by S. Sparks. Stanford: Stanford University Press, 2003.
Nancy, J.-L. *Being Singular Plural*. Stanford: Stanford University Press, 2000.
Nancy, J.-L. 'The Compearance: From the Existence of Communism to the Community of Existence' (1992) 20(3) *Political Theory* 371.
Nancy, J.-L. *The Creation of the World or Globalization*. Translated by F. Raffoul and D. Pettigrew. Albany: State University of New York Press, 2007.
Nancy, J.-L. *The Experience of Freedom*. Translated by B. McDonald. Stanford: Stanford University Press, 1993.
Nancy, J.-L. *The Inoperative Community*. Minneapolis: University of Minnesota Press, 1991.
Nancy, J.-L. *The Restlessness of the Negative*. Minneapolis: University of Minnesota Press, 2002.
Nancy, J.-L. *The Sense of the World*. Translated by J. S. Librett. Minneapolis: University of Minnesota Press, 1997.
Nancy, J.-L. and P. Lacoue-Labarthe. *Retreating the Political*. Edited by S. Sparks. London: Routledge, 1997.
Negarestani, R. 'Islamic Exotericism: Apocalypse in the Wake of Refractory Impossibility' (2007) 2 *Collapse. Philosophical Research & Development* 273.
Negri, A. *Insurgencies*. Translated by M. Boscagli. Minneapolis, University of Minnesota Press, 1999.
Nietzsche, F. *Beyond Good and Evil*. Translated by R. J. Hollingdale. London: Penguin Books, 2003.
Nietzsche, F. *Human, All Too Human*. Nebraska: University of Nebraska Press, 1986.
Nietzsche, F. *The Gay Science*. Translated by J. Nauckhoff. Cambridge: Cambridge University Press, 2001.
Norrie, A. *Law and the Beautiful Soul*. London: GlassHouse Press, 2005.

Nussbaum, M. 'Patriotism and Cosmopolitanism' in *For Love of Country?*, edited by J. Cohen, 2–17. Boston: Beacon Press, 2002.

Ojakangas, M. 'Impossible Dialogue on Bio-power' (2005) 2 *Foucault Studies* 5.

Orford, A. *Reading Humanitarian Intervention: Human Rights and the Use of Force in International Law.* Cambridge: Cambridge University Press, 2003.

Paras, E. *Foucault 2.0: Beyond Power and Knowledge.* New York: Other Press, 2006.

Pashukanis, E. *Law and Marxism: A General Theory.* London: Pluto Press 1989.

Patton, P. 'Agamben and Foucault on Biopower and Biopolitics' in *Giorgio Agamben: Sovereignty and Life*, edited by M. Calarco and S. DeCaroli, 201–218. Stanford: Stanford University Press, 2007.

Patton, P. 'Foucault, Critique and Rights' (2005) 6(1) *Critical Horizons* 267.

Pavlich, G. *Governing Paradoxes of Restorative Justice.* London: GlassHouse Press, 2005.

Petersen, U. *Diagonal Method and Dialectical Logic: Tools, Materials, and Groundworks for a Logical Foundation of Dialectic and Speculative Philosophy.* Tönning: Der Andere Verlag, 2002.

Pilger, J. 'Paying the Price: Killing the Children of Iraq' available at http://johnpilger.com/videos/paying-the-price-killing-the-children-of-iraq (accessed 28 November 2011).

Pillay, N. *The Tunis Imperative: Human Rights in Development Cooperation in the Wake of the Arab Spring. Statement by Ms. Navanethem Pillay, United Nations High Commissioner for Human Rights to the United Nations Chief Executives Board*, Fall Session, 2011, New York, 28 October 2011, available at http://rconline.undg.org/wp-content/uploads/2011/11/HC_Statement_to_the_CEB_Final_Format_1.pdf

Pinkard, T. *Hegel's Phenomenology: The Sociality of Reason.* Cambridge: Cambridge University Press, 1994.

Pippin, R. *Hegel's Idealism: The Satisfactions of Self-Consciousness.* Cambridge: Cambridge University Press, 1989.

Pogge, T. 'Recognized and Violated by International Law: The Human Rights of the Global Poor' (2005) 18(4) *Leiden Journal of International Law* 717.

Pogge, T. *World Poverty and Human Rights.* Cambridge: Polity, 2008.

Polanyi, K. *The Great Transformation.* Boston: Beacon Press, 1944.

Posner, R. A. 'Remarks on Law and Literature' (1991–92) 23 *Loyola University of Chicago Law Journal* 181.

Pottage, A. 'Fiction Science and Proprietary Effect' in *Living Properties: Making Knowledge and Controlling Ownership in the History of Biology*, edited by J.-P. Gaudillière, D. J. Kelves and H.-J. Rheinberger, 225–39. Berlin: Max Planck Institute for the History of Science, 2009.

Pottage, A. 'The Socio-Legal Implications of the New Biotechnologies' (2007) 3(3) *Annual Review of Law and Social Science* 3.3.1.

Pottage, A. and B. Sherman. *Figures of Invention A History of Modern Patent Law.* Oxford: Oxford University Press, 2010.

Potter, J. 'Does the "Homosexual Advance Defence" Erode Equality Before the Law in Criminal Cases?' (2001) 3(1) *e-valuate* available at http://www.law.ecel.uwa.edu.au/ejournal/Volume%203/Articles%20Vol_3/potter.pdf (accessed on 16 August 2002).

Poulantzas, N. *State, Power, Socialism.* Translated by P. Camiller. London: Verso, 2000.

Povinelli, E. *The Empire of Love: Toward a Theory of Intimacy, Genealogy, and Carnality.* Durham: Duke University Press, 2006.

Powel, B. and L. Sadiki. *Europe and Tunisia: Democratization via Association.* London: Routledge, 2010.

Pratt, J. *Governing the Dangerous.* Sydney: Federation Press, 1997.

Raban, O. 'Dworkin's "Best Light" Requirement and the Proper Methodology of Legal Theory' (2003) 23(2) *Oxford Journal of Legal Studies* 243.
Rabinow, P. *Essays on the Anthropology of Reason*. Princeton: Princeton University Press, 1996.
Rancière, J. *Disagreement: Politics and Philosophy*. Minneapolis: University of Minnesota Press, 1999.
Rasch, W. *Sovereignty and Its Discontents*. London: Birkbeck Law Press, 2004.
Rawls, J. *The Law of Peoples*. London: Harvard University Press, 1999.
Reinhart, C. and K. Rogoff. *This Time is Different*. Princeton: Princeton University Press, 2010.
Rieff, D. *A Bed for the Night: Humanitarianism in Crisis*. London: Vintage, 2002.
Rogers, J. 'Beyond the Script of Law' (2009) 18(2) *Griffith Law Review* 269.
Rose, G. *Dialectic of Nihilism: Post-Structuralism and Law*. Oxford: Blackwell, 1984.
Rose, G. *Hegel Contra Sociology*. London: Athlone, 1981.
Rose, G. *Mourning Becomes the Law: Philosophy and Representation*. Cambridge: Cambridge University Press, 1996.
Rose, G. 'Performing Inoperative Community: The Space and the Resistance of Some Community Arts Projects' in *Geographies of Resistance*, edited by S. Pile and M. Keith, 184–202. London: Routledge, 1997.
Rose, G. *The Broken Middle: Out of Our Ancient Society*. Oxford: Blackwell, 1992.
Rubin, G. S. 'Thinking Sex: Notes for a Radical Theory of the Politics of Sexuality' in *The Lesbian and Gay Studies Reader*, edited by H. Abelove, M. Aina Barale and D. M. Halperin, 3–44. New York: Routledge, 1993.
Saavedra, J. 'Sex Between Men in the Context of HIV' The Aids 2008 Jonathan Mann Memorial Lecture in Health and Human Rights, *XVII International AIDS Conference* (3–8 August 2008), Mexico City.
Salvatore, A. 'The Elusive Subject of Revolution' available at http://blogs.ssrc.org/tif/2011/02/16/the-elusive-subject-of-revolution/ (accessed 11 November 2011).
Santner, E. *On Creaturely Life*. Chicago: University of Chicago Press, 2008.
Santner, E. *The Royal Remains*. Chicago: University of Chicago Press, 2011.
Scammell, D. 'Law Reform Saves Lives: The Impact of Decriminalisation in Australia's Effective Response to HIV Among Gay Men' Unpublished conference paper.
Schaap, A. ed. *Law and Agonistic Politics*. Farnham: Ashgate, 2009.
Schlag, P. '*Le hors de texte, c'est moi*: on the Politics of Deconstruction' (1990) 11 *Cardozo Law Review* 1631.
Schofield, M. *The Stoic Idea of the City*. Cambridge: Cambridge University Press, 1991.
Scobbie, I. 'Towards the Elimination of International Law: Some Radical Scepticism About Sceptical Radicalism' (1990) 61 *British Yearbook of International Law* 339.
Sen, A. *The Idea of Justice*. London: Allen Lane, 2009.
Seshadri, K. J. 'Other/Alterity: Lacan and Agamben on Ethics, the Subject and Desubjectification' (2009) 14 *Psychoanalysis, Culture & Society* 1.
Seymour, R. *The Liberal Defence of Murder*. London: Verso, 2009.
Shah, I. *The Exploits of the Incomparable Mulla Nasrudin*. London: The Octagon Press, 1983.
Sieyès, E. J. *Political Writings*. Edited by M. Sonenscher. Indianapolis: Hackett Publishing Co, 2003.
Simpson, G. *War, Law and Crime: War Crimes Trials and Reinvention of International Law*. Cambridge: Polity, 2007.
Sontag, S. *Against Interpretation*. London: Penguin, 2009.

Sorel, G. *Reflections on Violence.* London: George Allen & Unwin, 1916.

Spivak, G. *A Critique of Post-Colonial Reason: Towards a History of the Vanishing Present.* Cambridge: Harvard University Press, 1999.

Lord Steyn. 'Guantanamo Bay: The Legal Black Hole' (2004) 53 *International and Comparative Law Quarterly* 1.

Stoler, A. L. *Race and the Education of Desire: Foucault's* History of Sexuality *and the Colonial Order of Things.* Durham: Duke University Press, 1995.

Stone, M. 'Levinas and Political Subjectivity in an Age of Global Biopower' (2010) 6(1) *Law, Culture and the Humanities* 105.

Strathern, M. 'Cutting the Network' (1996) 2(3) *The Journal of the Royal Anthropological Institute* 517.

Strathern, M. *Kinship, Law and the Unexpected: Relatives are Always a Surprise.* Cambridge: Cambridge University Press, 2005.

Suffredini, K. S. 'Pride and Prejudice: The Homosexual Panic Defense' (2001) 21 *Boston College Third World Law Journal* 279.

Supiot, A. 'A Legal Perspective on the Financial Crisis of 2008' (2010) 149(2) *International Labour Review* 151.

Taithe, B. 'Reinventing (French) Universalism: Religion, Humanitarianism and the "French Doctors"' (2004) 12(2) *Modern and Contemporary France* 150.

Tamanaha, B. 'Conceptual Analysis, Continental Social Theory, and CLS' (2000) 32 *Rutgers Law Journal* 271.

Tesón, F. 'The Liberal Case for Humanitarian Intervention' in *Humanitarian Intervention: Ethical, Legal, and Political Dilemmas,* edited by J. L. Holzgrefe and R. O. Keohane, 93–129. Cambridge: Cambridge University Press, 2003.

Teubner, G. *Juridification of Social Spheres.* New York: de Gruyter, 1987.

Thomas, K. 'Beyond the Privacy Principle' (1992) 92 *Columbia Law Review* 92 1431.

Todorov, T. *The Conquest of America: The Question of the Other.* New York: Harper & Row, 1984.

Tomsen, S. "He Had to be a Poofter or Something': Violence, Male Honour and Heterosexual Panic' (1998) 3(2) *Journal of Interdisciplinary Gender Studies* 44.

Traub, J. 'A Statesman Without Borders.' *The New York Times* (3 February 2008) available at http://www.nytimes.com/2008/02/03/magazine/03kouchner-t.html?_r=1&pagewanted=1 (accessed 19 January 2012).

Unger, R. *False Necessity: Anti-necessitarian Social Theory in the Service of Radical Democracy.* London: Verso, 2004.

Unger, R. *Law in Modern Society.* New York: The Free Press, 1976.

Usher, G. 'That Other Tunisia' *The Nation* (12 September 2011).

Valverde, M. 'Beyond Discipline and Punish: Foucault's Challenge to Criminology' (2008) 4 *The Carceral Notebooks* 201.

Valverde, M. 'Social Facticity and the Law: a Social Expert's Eyewitness Account of Law' (1996) 5(2) *Social & Legal Studies* 201.

van Houtum, H. 'Waiting Before the Law: Kafka on the Border' (2010) 19(3) *Social & Legal Studies* 285.

Veitch, S. *Law and Irresponsibility: On the Legitimation of Human Suffering.* Abingdon: Routledge-Cavendish, 2007.

Virgilio, S. and G. Agamben. *La Natura Delle Cose.* Firenze: Maschietto Editore, 2008.

Vukovich, D. 'China in Theory: The Orientalist Production of Knowledge in the Global Economy' (2010) 76 *Cultural Critique* 148.

Wald, P. 'What's in a Cell? John Moore's Spleen and the Language of Bioslavery' (2005) 36(2) *New Literary History* 205.

Waldby, C. and R. Mitchell. *Tissue Economies: Blood, Organs, and Cell Lines in Late Capitalism.* London: Duke University Press, 2006.

Wall, I.R. *Human Rights and Constituent Power.* Abingdon: Routledge, 2012.

Ward, I. 'From Literature to Ethics: The Strategies and Ambitions of Law and Literature' (1994) 14(3) *Oxford Journal of Legal Studies* 389.

Weber, M. *The Protestant Ethic and the Spirit of Capitalism.* London: George Allen & Unwin, 1930.

Weston, C. H. 'Orenthal James Simpson and Gender, Class, and Race: In That Order' (1995) 6 *Hastings Women's Law Journal* 223.

Whyte, J. 'Particular Rights and Absolute Wrongs: Giorgio Agamben on Life and Politics' (2009) 20 *Law and Critique* 20 147.

Whyte, J. '"Is Revolution Desirable?" Michel Foucault on Revolution, Neoliberalism and Rights' in *Foucaultian Legalities*, edited by Ben Golder. Abingdon: Routledge, 2012 forthcoming.

Wilby, P. 'The Awful Truth: Education Won't Stop the West Getting Poorer' *Guardian* (28 February 2011) available at http://www.guardian.co.uk/commentisfree/2011/feb/28/education-jobs-middle-class-decline (accessed 28 November 2011).

Williams, R. R. *Hegel's Ethics of Recognition.* Berkeley: University of California Press, 1997.

Wolcher, L. 'Review of *Thinking About Law in Silence With Heidegger*' (2009) 72(6) *Modern Law Review* 1035.

Wolin, R. 'Foucault the Neohumanist?' *The Chronicle Review* (1 September 2006) available at http://chronicle.com/article/Foucault-the-Neohumanist-/23118/ (accessed 19 January 2012).

Zizek, S. 'Neighbors and Other Monsters: A Plea for Ethical Violence' in *The Neighbor: Three Inquiries in Political Theology*, edited by S. Zizek, E. L. Santer and K. Reinhard, 134–90. London: University of Chicago Press, 2005.

Zizek, S. *The Sublime Object of Ideology.* London: Verso, 1989.

Cases cited

Bowers v Hardwick (1986) 478 US 186
Chhay (1992) 72 A Crim R 1
Diamond v Chakrabarty (1980) 447 US 303
Green v The Queen (1997) 191 CLR 334
Moore v Regents (1990) 51 Cal.3d 120
R v Campbell [1997] 1 NZLR 16
Smith [2000] UKHL 49

Index

Note: reference 142n41 refers to footnote 41 on page 142.

Kolibri 360 GmbH
Ferdinand-Jühlke-Straße 7
99095 Erfurt, Deutschland
produktsicherheit@kolibri360.de